E
X

THE COLLECTED
WORKS OF
JEREMY BENTHAM

General Editor

J. H. Burns

Principles of Legislation

An
INTRODUCTION
to the
PRINCIPLES OF
MORALS
and
LEGISLATION

edited by

J. H. BURNS

and

H. L. A. HART

UNIVERSITY OF LONDON
THE ATHLONE PRESS
1970

Published by
THE ATHLONE PRESS
UNIVERSITY OF LONDON
at 2 Gower Street, London wc1
Distributed by Tiptree Book Services Ltd
Tiptree, Essex

Australia and New Zealand
Melbourne University Press

U.S.A.
Oxford University Press Inc
New York

Printed in Great Britain by
WILLIAM CLOWES AND SONS, LIMITED
LONDON AND BECCLES

GENERAL PREFACE

Jeremy Bentham (1748–1832), leader of the Utilitarian reformers who became known as the Philosophical Radicals, was a major figure in the history of ideas, of law, and of social policy in the nineteenth century. Even today his influence survives in many fields. Yet there has been no modern critical edition of his works. This situation—in striking contrast with the editorial treatment of writers like Jefferson, Ricardo, and Coleridge—is in part explained by the very nature of Bentham's work. He wrote so voluminously on so many subjects that no single editor, no group of editors from any single field of scholarship, could undertake to present his work as a whole in acceptable critical form. The huge mass of manuscript material left by Bentham at his death reflected his dwindling concern, as his long life advanced, for the eventual published form of what he wrote. The task of reducing to order the uncoordinated statements and restatements of his thought he left to his 'disciples and editors'. And in fact the French redactions by Etienne Dumont which first made Bentham's ideas widely known, and the version of Utilitariansim developed by John Stuart Mill largely took the place of Bentham's own writings for most readers. The consequence has been an impoverished and at times a false picture of Bentham's thought.

For those seeking Bentham's own writings the principal resource has inevitably been the collected edition completed in 1843 under the supervision of his executor, John Bowring. This was for long out of print[1]; and even when accessible its eleven volumes of small type in daunting double columns (two volumes comprising what Leslie Stephen called 'one of the worst biographies in the language' —Bowring's *Memoirs of Bentham*) are defective in content as well as discouraging in form. Bowring excluded Bentham's anti-clerical writings, and for many works the texts in his edition derive at least as much from Dumont's French versions as from Bentham's own manuscripts. For half a century after 1843 these manuscripts lay neglected; and even now, despite the valuable work during the present century of such scholars as Elie Halévy, C. W. Everett, C. K. Ogden, and W. Stark, relatively little has been done to remedy these defects. When Bentham is known at all today at first hand,

[1] Until its reissue in 1962 by Messrs. Russell and Russell, Inc. of New York.

v

he is known largely from reprints of his *Fragment on Government* and *Introduction to the Principles of Morals and Legislation*—both dating from the first decade of an active career of over sixty years.

The present edition is an attempt to present definitive versions of Bentham's writings based, wherever possible, on the original manuscripts. The greatest single collection of Bentham papers is of course that which has been in the custody of University College London since the middle of the nineteenth century. Second only to this in importance is the large group of manuscripts—including a large part of Bentham's correspondence—acquired by the British Museum in 1889. A third source of great importance lies in the collection of the papers of Etienne Dumont now in the Bibliothèque Publique et Universitaire at Geneva. Other papers and letters, together with the various editions of Bentham's writings, will also form part of the foundation upon which the edition is built.

The edition is intended to be comprehensive in scope as well as definitive in text. All the works included by Bowring and his associate editors will be included here (though not always in the same form). Works omitted or overlooked by Bowring, but published either during Bentham's lifetime or since his death, will also be included. To these will be added any work, large or small, which exists in reasonably complete and coherent form in the manuscripts, together with any fragments judged by the editors to be of particular interest and importance. The straightforward policy of printing everything Bentham wrote is ruled out by Bentham's own method of working, his constant rehandling of the same themes and reshaping of earlier materials. But much of what he wrote, both in familiar and in unfamiliar or unknown works, will now for the first time be made available in Bentham's authentic words.

An important—indeed a fundamental—part of the edition will comprise the first comprehensive presentation of Bentham's extensive correspondence. If knowledge of Bentham's thought has been limited by the factors indicated above, understanding of his life and personality has at times been distorted by lack of access to the essential biographical data contained in his letters. Reflecting as they do the evolution of a man and his world over a period of three-quarters of a century, the volumes of Bentham's correspondence may well be among the most important, as they can hardly fail to be among the most readable, parts of the edition.

The edition is sponsored by a National Committee set up in 1959 on the initiative of University College London, and since 1961 the detailed planning and supervision of the work has been in the hands of Professor J. H. Burns as General Editor. Cooperative scholarship on a large scale over many years will undoubtedly be required before the edition is completed, each volume or group of volumes being entrusted to a scholar in the appropriate field. Editorial problems must vary widely in character from volume to volume; but in every case the introduction will indicate the basis of the texts presented, their historical context, and their mutual relationships.

The whole project will, it is estimated, require some thirty-eight volumes for its completion, though further exploration of the materials may naturally impose some revision of this estimate. The structure of the edition has been based on an attempt to classify Bentham's writings, so far as possible, according to subject matter. The working plan outlined below does not seek to be comprehensive but merely to list some of the main items within each section heading.

i. Correspondence

ii. Principles of Legislation

Introduction to the Principles of Morals and Legislation; Of Laws in General; Essay on the Influence of Time and Place in Matters of Legislation; Essay on Indirect Legislation; General view of a Complete Code of Laws; Pannomial Fragments; Codification Proposal; Nomography; Comment on the Commentaries; Fragment on Government.

iii. Penology and Criminal Law

Principles of Penal Law; Penal Code; Letters to Count Toreno; View of the Hard Labour Bill; Theory of Punishment; Panopticon.

iv. Civil Law

Principles of the Civil Code; Letters on Law Reform.

v. Constitutional Law

Constitutional Code; Three Tracts relating to Spanish and Portuguese Affairs; On the Liberty of the Press and Public Discussion; Securities against Misrule; Jeremy Bentham to his Fellow Citizens of France; Jeremy Bentham to the Belgic Nation.

VI. POLITICAL WRITINGS

Essay on Political Tactics; Anarchical Fallacies; Book of Fallacies; Parliamentary Reform; Defence of the People against Lord Erskine; Radicalism not Dangerous; Principles of International Law; Letters of Anti-Machiavel; Junctiana Proposal.

VII. JUDICIAL PROCEDURE

Principles of Judicial Procedure; Draught of a Code for Judicial Establishment in France; Scotch Reform; Equity Dispatch Court Proposal; Jury Analysed; Elements of the Art of Packing; 'Swear not at all'; Lord Brougham Displayed; Rationale of Judicial Evidence.

VIII. ECONOMICS AND SOCIETY

Defence of Usury; Institute of Political Economy; The True Alarm; Defence of a Maximum; Manual of a Political Economy; Rationale of Reward; Emancipate your Colonies!; Rid Yourselves of Ultramaria; Pauper Management Improved; Observations on the Poor Bill.

IX. PHILOSOPHY AND EDUCATION

Essays on Language, Logic, Universal Grammar, and Ontology; Deontology; Table of the Springs of Action; Chrestomathia.

X. RELIGION AND THE CHURCH

Church Establishments; Not Paul but Jesus; The Usefulness of Religion in the Present Life Examined.

PREFACE

The thanks of the Bentham Committee are due to the following bodies for financial assistance towards the cost of editorial work on this volume: The Rockefeller Foundation; The British Academy; The Pilgrim Trust; University College London. The Committee also wishes to thank the Librarian of University College and his staff for access to Mss. and for other assistance.

Professor Hart wishes to express his gratitude to the Nuffield Foundation for the award of a research fellowship enabling him to devote part of his time to this edition of Bentham's works.

Both the editors are indebted to the following for invaluable work as research assistants at various stages in the preparation of the volume: Mr G. L. Williams; Mrs Sandra Hole; Mrs Deborah Paton; Miss Helen Nowell; Mr Jan Phillips. They wish also to thank Mr Hardy Wieting, Mr Norman Pilling, Mr R. J. Bradshaw and Mr M. H. James for additional help in preparing the indices; and Mrs Valerie Bottomley for secretarial assistance.

J. H. B.
H. L. A. H.

ix

CONTENTS

INTRODUCTION   xxxvii

PREFACE   1

I OF THE PRINCIPLE OF UTILITY   11
  1. Mankind governed by pain and pleasure   11
  2. Principle of utility, what   11
     A principle, what, 11 n.
  3. Utility, what   12
4–5. Interest of the community, what   12
  6. An action conformable to the principle of utility, what   12
  7. A measure of government conformable to the principle of utility, what   13
  8. Laws or dictates of utility, what   13
  9. A partisan of the principle of utility, who   13
 10. Ought, ought not, right and wrong, &c. how to be understood   13
 11. To prove the rectitude of this principle is at once unnecessary and impossible   13
 12. It has seldom, however, as yet, been consistently pursued   13
 13. It can never be consistently combated   14
 14. Course to be taken for surmounting prejudices that may have been entertained against it   15

II OF PRINCIPLES ADVERSE TO THAT OF UTILITY   17
  1. All other principles than that of utility must be wrong   17
  2. Ways in which a principle may be wrong   17
     Asceticism, origin of the word, 17 n.; Principles of the Monks, 17 n.

xi

CONTENTS

3. Principle of asceticism, what   17

4. A partisan of the principle of asceticism, who   18

5. This principle has had in some a philosophical, in
   others a religious origin   18

6. It has been carried farther by the religious party than
   by the philosophical   18

7. The philosophical branch of it has had most influence
   among persons of education, the religious among the
   vulgar   19

8. The principle of asceticism has never been steadily
   applied by either party to the business of government   19

9. The principle of asceticism, in its origin, was but that
   of utility misapplied   21

10. It can never be consistently pursued   21

11. The principle of sympathy and antipathy, what   21

12. This is rather the negation of all principle, than any-
    thing positive   25

13. Sentiments of a partisan of the principle of antipathy   25

14. The systems that have been formed concerning the
    standard of right and wrong, are all reducible to this
    principle   25

    Various phrases, that have served as the characteristic marks
    of so many pretended systems:
    1. Moral Sense, 26 n.; 2. Common Sense, 26 n.; 3. Understanding,
    26 n.; 4. Rule of Right, 26 n.; 5. Fitness of Things, 27 n.; 6. Law
    of Nature, 27 n.; 7. Law of Reason, Right Reason, Natural
    Justice, Natural Equity, Good Order, 27 n.; 8. Truth, 27 n.;
    9. Doctrine of Election, 27 n.; 10. Repugnancy to Nature, 27n.;
    Mischief they produce, 28 n.; Whether utility is actually the sole
    ground of all the approbation we ever bestow, is a different
    consideration, 28 n.

15. This principle will frequently coincide with that of
    utility   29

16. This principle is most apt to err on the side of severity   29

17. But errs, in some instances, on the side of lenity   31

18. The theological principle, what—not a separate prin-
    ciple   31

    The principle of theology how reducible to one or another of the
    other three principles, 31 n.

xii

19. Antipathy, let the actions it dictates be ever so right, is never of itself a right ground of action   32

III   OF THE FOUR SANCTIONS OR SOURCES OF PAIN AND PLEASURE   34

1. Connexion of this chapter with the preceding   34
2. Four sanctions or sources of pleasure and pain   34
3. The physical sanction   35
4. The political   35
5. The moral or popular   35
6. The religious   35
7. The pleasures and pains which belong to the religious sanction, may regard either the present life or a future   35
8. Those which regard the present life, from which soever source they flow, differ only in the circumstances of their production   35
9. Example   36
10. Those which regard a future life are not specifically known   36
11. The physical sanction included in each of the other three   37
12. Use of this chapter   37

IV   VALUE OF A LOT OF PLEASURE OR PAIN, HOW TO BE MEASURED   38

1. Use of this chapter   38
2. Circumstances to be taken into the account in estimating the value of a pleasure or pain considered with reference to a single person, and by itself   38
3. —considered as connected with other pleasures or pains   38
4. —considered with reference to a number of persons   39
5. Process for estimating the tendency of any act or event   39
6. Use of the foregoing process   40
7. The same process applicable to good and evil, profit and mischief, and all other modifications of pleasure and pain   40
8. Conformity of men's practice to this theory   40

CONTENTS

V PLEASURE AND PAINS, THEIR KINDS   42

1. Pleasures and pains are either, (1) Simple: or (2) Complex   42
2. The simple pleasures enumerated   42
3. The simple pains enumerated   42
   Analytical view, why none given, 42 n.
4. Pleasures of sense enumerated   43
5. Pleasures of wealth, which are either of acquisition, or of possession   43
   Pleasures of skill   43
6. Pleasures of amity   43
7. Pleasures of a good name   44
8. Pleasures of power   44
9. Pleasures of piety   44
10. Pleasures of benevolence or good-will   44
11. Pleasures of malevolence or ill-will   44
12. Pleasures of the memory   45
13. Pleasures of the imagination   45
14. Pleasures of expectation   45
15. Pleasures of depending on association   45
16. Pleasures of relief   45
17. Pains of privation   46
18. These include, (1) Pains of desire   46
19. (2) Pains of disappointment   46
20. (3) Pains of regret   46
21. Pains of the senses   46
    No positive pains correspond to the pleasure of the sexual sense, 47 n.
22. Pains of awkwardness   47
    No positive pains correspond to the pleasure of novelty, 47 n., nor to those of wealth, 47 n.; Is this a distinct positive pain, or only a pain of privation? 47 n.
23. Pains of enmity   47
24. Pains of an ill-name   47
    The positive pains of an ill-name, and the pains of privation, opposed to the pleasures of a good name, run into one another. 46 n.

25. Pains of piety   48

No positive pains correspond to the pleasures of power, 48 n.; The positive pains of piety, and the pains of privation, opposed to the pleasures of piety, run into one another 48 n.

26. Pains of benevolence   48

27. Pains of malevolence   48

28. Pains of the memory   48

29. Pains of the imagination   48

30. Pains of expectation   48

31. Pains of association   49

32. Pleasures and pains are either self-regarding or extra-regarding   49

Pleasures and pains of amity and enmity distinguished from those of benevolence and malevolence, 49n.

33. In what ways the law is concerned with the above pains and pleasures   49

Complex pleasures and pains omitted, why, 49 n. Specimen.— Pleasures of a country prospect, 49 n.

VI OF CIRCUMSTANCES INFLUENCING SENSIBILITY   51

1. Pain and pleasure not uniformly proportioned to their causes   51

2. Degree or quantum of sensibility, what   51

3. Bias or quality of sensibility, what   51

4. Exciting causes pleasurable and dolorific   51

5. Circumstances influencing sensibility, what   52

6. Circumstances influencing sensibility enumerated   52

Extent and intricacy of this subject, 52 n.

7. Health   53

8. Strength   53

Measure of strength, the weight a man can lift, 54 n.; Weakness, what, 54 n.

9. Hardiness   54

Difference between strength and hardiness   54

10. Bodily imperfection   55

11. Quantity and quality of knowledge   55

12. Strength of intellectual powers   55

13. Firmness of mind   56

14. Steadiness   56

15. Bent of inclinations   56

16. Moral sensibility   57

17. Moral biases   57

18. Religious sensibility   57

19. Religious biases   57

20. Sympathetic sensibility   57

21. Sympathetic biases   57

22. Antipathetic sensibility and biases   58

23. Insanity   58

24. Habitual occupations   58

25. Pecuniary circumstances   58

26. Connexions in the way of sympathy   60

27. Connexions in the way of antipathy   61

28. Radical frame of body   61

29. Radical frame of mind   62
     Idiosyncrasy, what, 62 n.

30. This distinct from the circumstance of frame of body   62
     Whether the soul be material or immaterial makes no difference, 62 n.

31. —and from all others   62

32. Yet the result of them is not separately discernible   63

33. Frame of body indicates, but not certainly, that of mind   63

34. Secondary influencing circumstances   64

35. Sex   64

36. Age   65

37. Rank   65

38. Education   66

39. Climate   67

40. Lineage   67

41. Government   67

42. Religious profession   68

43. Use of the preceding observations   69

44. How far the circumstances in question can be taken into account   69

45. To what exciting causes there is most occasion to apply them   70

46. Analytical view of the circumstances influencing sensibility   72

Analytical view of the constituent articles in a man's pecuniary circumstances, 72 n.

VII   OF HUMAN ACTIONS IN GENERAL   74

1. The demand for punishment depends in part upon the tendency of the act   74

2. Tendency of an act determined by its consequences   74

3. Material consequences only are to be regarded   74

4. These depend in part upon the intention   74

5. The intention depends as well upon the understanding as the will   75

6. In an action are to be considered (1) the act; (2) the circumstances; (3) the intentionality; (4) the consciousness   75

7. (5) the motives; (6) the disposition   75

8. Acts positive and negative   75

Acts of omission are still acts, 75 n.

9. Negative acts may be so relatively or absolutely   76

10. Negative acts may be expressed positively; and vice versa   76

11. Acts external and internal   76

12. Acts of discourse, what   76

13. External acts may be transitive or intransitive   76

Distinction between transitive acts and intransitive, recognised by grammarians, 77 n.

14. A transitive act, its commencement, termination, and intermediate progress   77

15. An intransitive act, its commencement, and termination   77

16. Acts transient and continued   78

17. Difference between a continued act and a repetition of acts   78

CONTENTS

18. Difference between a repetition of acts and a habit   78

19. Acts are indivisible, or divisible, as well with regard to matter as to motion   78

20. Caution respecting the ambiguity of language   79

21. Circumstances are to be considered   79

22. Circumstances, what   79

    Circumstance, archetypation of the word, 79 n.

23. Circumstances material and immaterial

24. A circumstance may be related to an event in point of causality, in four ways, viz.   80

    (1) Production. (2) Derivation. (3) Collateral connexion. (4) Conjunct influence, 80

25. Example. Assassination of Buckingham   80

26. It is not every event that has circumstances related to it in all those ways   81

27. Use of this chapter   82

VIII OF INTENTIONALITY   84

1. Recapitulation   84

2. The intention may regard, (1) the act: or (2) the consequences   84

    Ambiguity of the words voluntary and involuntary, 84 n.

3. It may regard the act without any of the consequences   84

4. —or the consequences without regarding the act in all its stages   84

5. —but not without regarding the first stage   85

    An act unintentional in its first stage, may be so with respect to (1) Quantity of matter moved: (2) Direction: (3) Velocity, 85 n.

6. A consequence, when intentional, may be directly so, or obliquely   86

7. When directly, ultimately so, or mediately   86

8. When directly intentional, it may be exclusively so, or inexclusively   86

9. When inexclusively, it may be conjunctively, disjunctively, or indiscriminately so   86

10. When disjunctively, it may be with or without preference   87

Difference between an incident's being unintentional, and disjunctively intentional, when the election is in favour of the other, 87 n.

11. Example   87

12. Intentionality of the act with respect to its different stages, how far material   88

13. Goodness and badness of intention dismissed   88

IX   OF CONSCIOUSNESS   90

1. Connexion of this chapter with the foregoing   90

2. Acts advised and unadvised: consciousness, what   90

3. Unadvisedness may regard either existence, or materiality   90

4. The circumstance may have been present, past, or future   90

5. An unadvised act may be heedless, or not heedless   90

6. A misadvised act, what.—a missupposal   90

7. The supposed circumstance might have been material in the way either of prevention or of compensation   91

8. It may have been supposed present, past, or future   91

9. Example, continued from the last chapter   91

10. In what case consciousness extends the intentionality from the act to the consequences   92

11. Example continued   92

12. A misadvised act may be rash or not rash   92

13. The intention may be good or bad in itself, independently of the motive as well as the eventual consequences   92

14. It is better, when the intention is meant to be spoken of as being good or bad, not to say, the motive   93

15. Example   93

16. Intention, in what cases it may be innocent   94

17. Intentionality and consciousness, how spoken of in the Roman law   94

18. Use of this and the preceding chapter   95

CONTENTS

X OF MOTIVES   96

§ i. *Different senses of the word motive*

1. Motives, why considered   96
2. Purely speculative motives have nothing to do here   96
3. Motives to the will   96
4. Figurative and unfigurative senses of the word   97
5. Motives interior and exterior   97
6. Motive in *prospect*—motive in *esse*   98
7. Motives immediate and remote   98
8. Motives to the understanding how they may influence the will   99

§ ii. *No motives either constantly good or constantly bad*

9. Nothing can act of itself as a motive, but the ideas of pleasure or pain   100
10. No sort of motive is in itself a bad one   100
11. Inaccuracy of expressions in which good or bad are applied to motives   100
12. Any sort of motive may give birth to any sort of act   100
13. Difficulties which stand in the way of an analysis of this sort   101

§ iii. *Catalogue of motives corresponding to that of Pleasures and Pains*

14. Physical desire corresponding to pleasures of sense in general   103
15. The motive corresponding to the pleasures of the palate   103
16. Sexual desire corresponding to the pleasures of the sexual sense   104
17. Curiosity, &c. corresponding to the pleasures of curiosity   104
18. None to the other pleasures of sense   104
19. Pecuniary interest to the pleasures of wealth   105
20. None to the pleasures of skill   105

21. To the pleasures of amity, the desire of ingratiating one's self   105

22. To the pleasures of a good name, the love of reputation   105

23. To the pleasures of power, the love of power   108

24. The motive belonging to the religious sanction   108

25. Good-will, &c. to the pleasures of sympathy   109

26. Ill-will, &c. to the pleasures of antipathy   111

27. Self-preservation, to the several kinds of pains   112

28. To the pains of exertion, the love of ease   113

29. Motives can only be bad with reference to the most frequent complexion of their effects   114

30. How it is that motives, such as lust, avarice, &c are constantly bad   114

31. Under the above restrictions, motives may be distinguished into good, bad, and indifferent or neutral   115

32. Inconveniences of this distribution   115

33. It is only in individual instances that motives can be good or bad   116

34. Motives distinguished into social, dissocial, and self-regarding   116

35. —social, into purely-social, and semi-social   116

§ iv. *Order of pre-eminence among motives*

36. The dictates of good-will are the surest of coinciding with those of utility   116

    Laws and dictates conceived as issuing from motives, 116–17 n.

37. Yet do not in all cases   117

38. Next to them come those of the love of reputation   118

39. Next those of the desire of amity   119

40. Difficulty of placing those of religion   119

41. Tendency they have to improve   121

42. Afterwards come the self-regarding motives: and lastly that of displeasure   121

§ v. *Conflict among motives*

43. Motives impelling and restraining, what   122

CONTENTS

44. What are the motives most frequently at variance   122

45. Example to illustrate a struggle among contending motives   122

46. Practical use of the above disquisitions relative to motives   123

XI   OF HUMAN DISPOSITIONS IN GENERAL   125

1. Disposition, what   125

2. How far it belongs to the present subject   125

3. A mischievous disposition; a meritorious disposition; what   126

4. What a man's disposition is, can only be matter of presumption   126

5. It depends upon what the act appears to be to him   126

6. Which position is grounded on two facts: (1) The correspondence between intentions and consequences   126

7. (2) Between the intentions of the same person at different times   127

    A disposition, from which proceeds a habit of doing mischief, cannot be a good one, 127 n.

8. The disposition is to be inferred, (1) From the apparent tendency of the act: (2) from the nature of the motive   127

9. Case 1. Tendency, good—motive, self-regarding   127

10. Case 2. Tendency, bad—motive, self-regarding   127

11. Case 3. Tendency, good—motive, good-will   128

12. Case 4. Tendency, bad—motive, good-will   128

13. This case not an impossible one   128

14. Example I   128

15. Example II   129

16. Example III   129

17. Case 5. Tendency, good—motive, love of reputation   129

    The bulk of mankind apt to depreciate this motive, 129 n.

18. Case 6. Tendency, bad—motive, honour   130

19. Example I   130

20. Example II   130

21. Case 7. Tendency, good—motive, piety   131

CONTENTS

22. Case 8. Tendency, bad—motive, religion   131

23. The disposition may be bad in this case   131

24. Case 9. Tendency, good—motive, malevolence   133
    Example   133

25. Case 10. Tendency, bad—motive, malevolence   133
    Example   134

26. Problem—to measure the depravity in a man's dis-
    position   134

27. A man's disposition is constituted by the sum of his
    intentions   134

28. —which owe their birth to motives   134

29. A seducing or corrupting motive, what—a tutelary or
    preservatory motive   134

30. Tutelary motives are either standing or occasional   134

31. Standing tutelary motives are, Good-will   135

32.   The love of reputation   135

33.   The desire of amity   136

34.   The motive of religion   136

35. Occasional tutelary motives may be any whatsoever   137

36. Motives that are particularly apt to act in this charac-
    ter are, (1) Love of ease. (2) Self-preservation   137

37. Dangers to which self-preservation is most apt in this
    case to have respect, are, (1) Dangers purely physical.
    (2) Dangers depending on detection   137

38. Danger depending on detection may result from, (1)
    Opposition on the spot: (2) Subsequent punishment   138

39. The force of the two standing tutelary motives of love
    of reputation, and desire of amity, depends upon detec-
    tion   138

40. Strength of a temptation, what is meant by it   138

41. Indications afforded by this and other circumstances
    respecting the depravity of an offender's disposition   139

42. Rules for measuring the depravity of disposition indi-
    cated by an offence   140

43. Use of this chapter   141

xxiii

XII OF THE CONSEQUENCES OF
A MISCHIEVOUS ACT   143

§ i. *Shapes in which the mischief of an act may
show itself*

1. Recapitulation   143
2. Mischief of an act, the aggregate of its mischievous
consequences   143
3. The mischief of an act, primary or secondary   143
4. Primary—original or derivative   143
5. The secondary—(1) Alarm: or, (2) Danger   144
6. Example   144
7. The danger whence it arises—a past offence affords no
direct motive to a future   145
8. But it suggests feasibility, and weakens the force of
restraining motives   145
9. viz. (1) Those issuing from the political sanction   146
10.   (2) Those issuing from the moral   146
11. It is said to operate by the influence of example   147
12. The alarm and the danger, though connected, are distinguishable   147
13. Both may have respect to the same person, or to others 147
14. The primary consequences of an act may be mischievous and the secondary, beneficial   147
15. Analysis of the different shapes in which the mischief of
an act may show itself   147
—applied to the preceding cases   149
16. —to examples of other cases where the mischief is less
conspicuous   149
Example I. An act of self-intoxication   149
17. Example II. Non-payment of a tax   149
18. No alarm, when no assignable person is the object   151

§ ii. *How intentionality, &c. may influence the
mischief of an act*

19. Secondary mischief influenced by the state of the
agent's mind   152

20. Case. 1. Involuntariness 153

21. Case 2. Unintentionality with heedlessness 153

22. Case. 3. Missupposal of a complete justification, without rashness 153

23. Case 4. Missupposal of a partial justification, without rashness 153

24. Case 5. Missupposal, with rashness 153

25. Case. 6. Consequences completely intentional, and free from missupposal 154

26. The nature of a motive takes not away the mischief of the secondary consequences 154

27. Nor the beneficialness 154

28. But it may aggravate the mischievousness, where they are mischievous 155

29. But not the most in the case of the worst motives 155

30. It does the more, the more considerable the tendency of the motive to produce such acts 155

31. —which is as its strength and constancy 155

32. General efficacy of a species of motive, how measured 155

33. A mischievous act is more so, when issuing from a self-regarding than when from a dissocial motive 155

34. —so even when issuing from the motive of religion 156

35. How the secondary mischief is influenced by disposition 156

36. Connexion of this with the succeeding chapter 156

XIII CASES UNMEET FOR PUNISHMENT

156

§ i. *General view of cases unmeet for punishment*

1. The end of law is, to augment happiness 158

2. But punishment is an evil 158

    What concerns the end, and several other topics, relative to punishment, dismissed to another work, 158 n.; Concise view of the ends of punishment, 158 n.

3. Therefore ought not to be admitted 159

    Where groundless; Inefficacious; Unprofitable; Or needless, 159

CONTENTS

§ ii. *Cases in which punishment is groundless*

4. Where there has never been any mischief: as in the case of consent 159

5. Where the mischief was outweighed: as in precaution against calamity, and the exercise of powers 159

6. —or will, for a certainty, be cured by compensation 160

Hence the favours shown to the offences of responsible offenders: such as simple mercantile frauds, 160 n.

§ iii. *Cases in which punishment must be inefficacious*

7. Where the penal provision comes too late: as in (1) An ex-post-facto law—(2) an ultra-legal sentence 160

8. Or is not made known: as in a law not sufficiently promulgated 160

9. Where the will cannot be deterred from any act, as in 161

(1) infancy, (2) insanity, (3) intoxication, 161

In infancy and intoxication the case can hardly be proved to come under the rule, 161 n.; the reason for not punishing in these three cases is commonly put upon a wrong footing, 161 n.

10. Or not from the individual act in question, as in 161

(1) unintentionality, (2) unconsciousness, (3) missupposal, 161

11. Or is acted on by an opposite superior force: as by 162

(1) physical danger. (2) threatened mischief, 162

Why the influence of the moral and religious sanctions is not mentioned in the same view, 162 n.

12. —or the bodily organs cannot follow its determination: as under physical compulsion or restraint 162

§ iv. *Cases where punishment is unprofitable*

13. 1. Where, in the sort of case in question, the punishment would produce more evil than the offence would 163

14. Evil producible by a punishment—its four branches— 163

viz. (1) Restraint (2) Apprehension (3) Sufferance (4) Derivative evils, 163

15. (The evil of the offence, being different according to the nature of the offence, cannot be represented here) 163

16. 2. Or, in the individual case in question by reason of 163

(1) the multitude of delinquents, (2) The value of a delinquent's service, (3) The displeasure of the people, (4) The displeasure of foreign powers, 164

CONTENTS

§ v. *Cases where punishment is needless*

17. Where the mischief is to be prevented at a cheaper rate: as by instruction   164

XIV OF THE PROPORTION BETWEEN PUNISHMENTS AND OFFENCES   165

1. Recapitulation   165
2. Four objects of punishment   165
3. 1st Object—to prevent all offences   165
4. 2d Object—to prevent the worst   165
5. 3d Object—to keep down the mischief   165
6. 4th Object—to act at the least expense   165
7. Rules of proportion between punishments and offences   165
The same rules applicable to motives in general, 165 n.
8. Rule 1.—Outweigh the profit of the offence   166
Profit may be of any other kind, as well as pecuniary, 166 n.; Impropriety of the notion that the punishment ought not to increase with the temptation, 166 n.
9. The propriety of taking the strength of the temptation for a ground of abatement, no objection to this rule   167
10. Rule 2.—Venture more against a great offence than a small one   168
Example.—Incendiarism and coining, 168 n.
11. Rule 3.—Cause the least of two offences to be preferred   168
12. Rule 4.—Punish for each particle of the mischief   168
Example.—In blows given, and money stolen, 168 n.
13. Rule 5.—Punish in no degree without special reason   169
14. Rule 6.—Attend to circumstances influencing sensibility   169
15. Comparative view of the above rules   169
16. Into the account of the value of a punishment, must be taken its deficiency in point of certainty and proximity   169
17. Also, into the account of the mischief, and profit of the offence, the mischief and profit of other offences of the same habit   170
18. Rule 7.—Want of certainty must be made up in magnitude   170

19. Rule 8.—So also want of proximity   170

20. Rule 9.—For acts indicative of a habit, punish as for the habit   170

21. The remaining rules are of less importance   170

22. Rule 10.—For the sake of quality, increase in quantity   171

23. Rule 11.—Particularly for a moral lesson   171

    A punishment applied by way of moral lesson, what, 171 n.; Example.—In simple corporal injuries, 171 n.; Example.—In military laws, 171 n.

24. Rule 12.—Attend to circumstances which may render punishment unprofitable   171

25. Rule 13.—For simplicity's sake, small disproportions may be neglected   171

    Proportionality carried very far in the present work—why, 172 n.

26. Auxiliary force of the physical, moral, and religious sanctions, not here allowed for—why   172

27. Recapitulation   172

28. The nicety here observed vindicated from the charge of inutility   173

XV   OF THE PROPERTIES TO BE GIVEN TO A LOT OF PUNISHMENT   175

1. Properties are to be governed by proportion   175

2. Property 1. Variability   175

3. Property 2. Equability   175

4. Punishments which are apt to be deficient in this respect   176

5. Property 3. Commensurability to other punishments   177

6. How two lots of punishment may be rendered perfectly commensurable   177

7. Property 4. Characteristicalness   177

8. The mode of punishment the most eminently characteristic, is that of retaliation   178

9. Property 5.—Exemplarity   178

10. The most effectual way of rendering a punishment exemplary is by means of analogy   179

CONTENTS

11. Property 6. Frugality   179
12. Frugality belongs in perfection to pecuniary punish-
    ment   179
13. Exemplarity and frugality in what they differ and
    agree   180
14. Other properties of inferior importance   180
15. Property 7. Subserviency to reformation   180
16. —applied to offences originating in ill-will   181
17. —to offences originating in indolence joined to pecu-
    niary interest   181
18. Property 8. Efficacy with respect to disablement   181
19. —is most conspicuous in capital punishment   181
20. Other punishments in which it is to be found   182
21. Property 9. Subserviency to compensation   182
22. Property 10. Popularity   183
    Characteristicalness renders a punishment, (1) memorable (2)
    exemplary (3) popular, 183 n.
23. Mischiefs resulting from the unpopularity of a punish-
    ment—discontent among the people, and weakness in
    the law   183
24. This property supposes a prejudice which the legisla-
    ture ought to cure   183
25. Property II. Remissibility   184
26. To obtain all these properties, punishments must be
    mixed   185
27. The foregoing properties recapitulated   185
28. Connexion of this with the ensuing chapter   186

XVI DIVISION OF OFFENCES   187

    § i. *Classes of offences*
 1. Distinction between what are offences and what ought
    to be   187
    Method pursued in the following divisions, 187 n.
 2. No act ought to be an offence but what is detrimental
    to the community   188

CONTENTS

3. To be so, it must be detrimental to some one or more of its members   188

4. These may be assignable or not   188

Persons assignable, how, 188 n.

5. If assignable, the offender himself, or others   188
6. Class 1. Private offences   188
7. Class 2. Semi-public offences   189

Limits between private, semi-public, and public offences, are, strictly speaking, undistinguishable, 189 n.

8. Class 3. Self-regarding offences   189

9. Class 4. Public offences   189

10. Class 5. Multiform offences, viz.   190

(1) Offences by falsehood, (2) Offences against trust, 190

The imperfections of language an obstacle to arrangement, 190 n.; Irregularity of this class, 190 n.; —which could not be avoided on any other plan, 190 n.

§ ii. *Divisions and sub-divisions*

11. Divisions of Class 1   191

(1) Offences against person (2) Property (3) Reputation (4) Condition (5) Person and reputation (6) Person and property, 191

In what manner pleasure and pain depend upon the relation a man bears to exterior objects, 191 n.

12. Divisions of Class 2 (1) Offences through calamity   194

13. Sub-divisions of offences through calamity, dismissed   194

14. (2) Offences of mere delinquency, how they correspond with the divisions of private offences   195

15. Divisions of Class 3 coincide with those of Class 1   195

16. Divisions of Class 4   196

Exhaustive method departed from, 196 n.

17. Connection of the nine first divisions one with another   196

18. Connection of offences against religion with the foregoing ones   201

19. Connection of offences against the national interest in general with the rest   202

CONTENTS

20. Sub-divisions of Class 5 enumerated
Divisions of offences by falsehood   203

21. Offences by falsehood, in what they agree with one
another   203

22. —in what they differ   203

23. Sub-divisions of offences by falsehood are determined
by the divisions of the preceding classes   204

24. Offences of this class, in some instances, change their
names; in others, not   204

25. A trust, what   205
Power and right, why no complete definition is here given of
them, 205 n.

26. Offences against trust, condition, and property, why
ranked under separate divisions   208

27. Offences against trust—their connexion with each
other   214

28. Prodigality in trustees dismissed to Class 3   221

29. The sub-divisions of offences against trust are also
determined by the divisions of the preceding classes   221

30. Connexion between offences by falsehood and offences
against trust   221

§ iii. *Genera of class I*

31. Analysis into genera pursued no further than Class 1.   222

32. Offences against an individual may be simple in their
effects or complex   222

33. Offences against person—their genera   222

34. Offences against reputation   225

35. Offences against property   226
Payment, what, 227 n.

36. Offences against person and reputation   232

37. Offences against person and property   233

38. Offences against condition.—Conditions domestic or
civil   234

39. Domestic conditions grounded on natural relationships   234
Relations—two result from every two objects, 235 n.

40. Domestic relations which are purely of legal institution   236

41. Offences touching the condition of a master   239

42. Various modes of servitude   241

43. Offences touching the condition of a servant   241

44. Guardianship, what—Necessity of the institution   244

45. Duration to be given to it   246

46. Powers that may, and duties that ought to be, annexed to it   246

47. Offences touching the condition of a guardian   247

48. Offences touching the condition of a ward   249

49. Offences touching the condition of a parent   250

50. Offences touching the filial condition   252

51. Condition of a husband.—Powers, duties, and rights, that may be annexed to it   254

52. Offences touching the condition of a husband   255

53. Offences touching the condition of a wife   257

54. [Uncontiguous domestic relations]   257

55. Civil conditions   264

§ iv. *Advantages of the present method*

56. General idea of the method here pursued   270

57. Its advantages—It is convenient for the apprehension and the memory   272

58. —It gives room for general propositions   273

59. —It points out the reason of the law   273

60. —It is alike applicable to the laws of all nations   274

§ v. *Characters of the five classes*

61. Characters of the classes, how deducible from the above method   274

62. Characters of class 1   275

63. Characters of class 2   276

64. Characters of class 3   277

65. Characters of class 4   278

66. Characters of class 5   279

CONTENTS

XVII OF THE LIMITS OF THE PENAL
      BRANCH OF JURISPRUDENCE   281

§ i. *Limits between private ethics and the art
    of legislation*

1. Use of this chapter   281

2. Ethics in general, what   282

3. Private ethics   282

4. The art of government: that is, of legislation and
   administration   282

    Interests of the inferior animals improperly neglected in legis-
    lation, 282 n.

5. Art of education   283

6. Ethics exhibit the rules of,   283

    (1) Prudence. (2) Probity. (3) Beneficence, 283

7. Probity and beneficence how they connect with prudence   284

8. Every act which is a proper object of ethics is not of
   legislation   285

9. The limits between the provinces of private ethics and
   legislation, marked out by the cases unmeet for
   punishment   285

10. Neither ought to apply where punishment is ground-
    less   286

11. How far private ethics can apply in the cases where
    punishment would be inefficacious   286

12. How far, where it would be unprofitable   287

13. Which is may be, (1) Although confined to the guilty 287

14. (2) By enveloping the innocent   288

15. Legislation how far necessary for the enforcement of
    the dictates of prudence   289

16. —Apt to go too far in this respect   290

17. —Particularly in matters of religion   291

18. —How far necessary for the enforcement of the dic-
    tates of probity   292

19. —of the dictates of beneficence   292

20. Difference between private ethics and the art of
    legislation recapitulated   293

§ ii. *Jurisprudence, its branches*

21. Jurisprudence, expository—censorial   293

22. Expository jurisprudence, authoritative—unauthoritative   294

23. Sources of the distinctions yet remaining   294

24. Jurisprudence, local—universal   294

25. —internal and international   296

26. Internal jurisprudence, national and provincial, local or particular   297

27. Jurisprudence, ancient—living   297

28. Jurisprudence, statutory—customary   298

29. Jurisprudence, civil—penal—criminal   298
    Question, concerning the distinction between the civil branch and the penal, stated   299

CONCLUDING NOTE   301

1. Occasion and purpose of this concluding note   301

2. By a law here is not meant a statute   301

3. Every law is either a command, or a revocation of one   302

4. A declaratory law is not, properly speaking, a law   302

5. Every coercive law creates an offence   302

6. A law creating an offence, and one appointing punishment are distinct laws   302

7. A discoercive law can have no punitory one appertaining to it but through the intervention of a coercive one   302

8. But a punitory law involves the simply imperative one it belongs to   303

9. The simply imperative one might therefore be spared, but for its expository matter   303

10. Nature of such expository matter   303

11. The vastness of its comparative bulk is not peculiar to legislative commands   303

12. The same mass of expository matter may serve in common for many laws   304

13. The imperative character essential to law, is apt to be concealed in and by expository matter   304

CONTENTS

14. The concealment is favoured by the multitude of indirect forms in which imperative matter is capable of being couched — 305

15. Number and nature of the laws in a code, how determined — 305

16. General idea of the limits between a civil and a penal code — 305

17. Contents of a civil code — 306

18. Contents of a penal code — 306

19. In the Code Frederic the imperative character is almost lost in the expository matter — 306

20. So in the Roman law — 307

21. In the barbarian codes it stands conspicuous — 307

22. Constitutional code, its connexion with the two others — 307

23. Thus the matter of one law may be divided among all three codes — 308

24. Expository matter a great quantity of it exists everywhere, in no other form than that of common or judiciary law — 308

25. Hence the deplorable state of the science of legislation, considered in respect of its form — 308

26. Occasions affording an exemplification of the difficulty as well as importance of this branch of science;— attempts to limit the powers of supreme representative legislatures — 308

27. Example: American declarations of rights — 309

INDEX OF SUBJECTS — 313

INDEX OF NAMES — 341

ABBREVIATIONS

Apart from standard abbreviations, the following should be noted:

Bowring: *The Works of Jeremy Bentham*, published under the super-intendence of ... John Bowring (11 vols.), Edinburgh, 1838–43.

CW: *The Collected Works of Jeremy Bentham*, London, 1968–

Harrison: *A Fragment on Government and an Introduction to the Principles of Morals and Legislation*, by Jeremy Bentham, ed. W. Harrison (Blackwell's Political Texts), Oxford, 1948.

U.C.: Bentham papers in the Library of University College London (Roman numerals refer to boxes, Arabic to leaves).

INTRODUCTION

HISTORY OF THE WORK

Bentham himself in the preface he wrote for the first edition of *An Introduction to the Principles of Morals and Legislation*[1] outlines the essentials of its history.[2] Printed, though not completed, in 1780, it had been written with 'no other destination than that of serving as an introduction to a plan of a penal code *in terminis* designed to follow ... in the same volume'.[3] Bentham then, while attempting to remove 'some flaws' in the work, 'found himself unexpectedly entangled in an unsuspected corner of the metaphysical maze'; and his attempted disentanglement led to what is published in the present edition under the title *Of Laws in General*. Until at least 1783 it is clear from Bentham's correspondence that the possibility of publishing the present work in one form or another remained alive.[4] Thereafter 'the idea of completing the present work slid insensibly aside' until, following his return from Russia in 1788, Bentham was persuaded that, imperfect though the work seemed to him, its publication as a general introduction to the comprehensive system of legislation which he now envisaged would have at least the advantage of reducing the extent to which in future works he would have to trespass on his readers' patience with 'analytical discussions'.

Some expansion of this outline history may help to elucidate the nature of the text thus belatedly published in 1789. Bentham's first

[1] That edition (*An Introduction to the Principles of Morals and Legislation*. Printed in the year 1780, and now first published. By Jeremy Bentham, of Lincoln's Inn, Esquire. London: Printed for T. Payne, and Son, at the Mews Gate. M,DCC,LXXXIX.) was a quarto volume, pp. 9 + cccxxxv together with three preliminary leaves and 32 unnumbered pages of corrigenda, addenda, contents, and advertisements at the end. The printer was Henry Hughes of Great Turnstile, Lincoln's Inn Fields (cf. *Correspondence*, in *CW*, ii, 409 and n. 20).

[2] Below, 1–5.

[3] The fact that the pages of the first edition bear lower case Roman numerals underlines their original preliminary character.

[4] The relevant letters will be published in Vol. iii of Bentham's *Correspondence*, ed. I. R. Christie, in the present edition. Special interest attaches to Bentham's contacts with Jacques Pierre Brissot de Warville, who in December 1782, in the first number of his periodical publication the *Correspondance Universelle*, announced the forthcoming publication by Bentham of a work entitled *Principes de législation sur les lois pénales*. It is to be remarked also that Bentham had a sheet of corrections and additions to the present work printed in or about the year 1783.

major project as a writer was conceived originally as a treatise on the *Elements of Critical Jurisprudence* or the *Principles of Legal Polity*, and in its earliest form, much of what we now know as *An Introduction to the Principles of Morals and Legislation* was drafted to introduce that treatise. Even the *Plan of a Penal Code*, for which the *Introduction* as we have it was written, was a relatively late development of this major project. Bentham's work on the *Elements of Critical Jurisprudence*, probably begun in 1770, was interrupted between the autumn of 1774 and the spring of 1776 by his critique of Blackstone, issuing in *A Fragment on Government* and the *Comment on the Commentaries*. By the latter part of 1776 when Bentham had returned from this digression the general treatise was beginning to bifurcate. One of its branches became the work on the *Theory of Punishment* which absorbed most of Bentham's energy in 1777, and of which the manuscripts were later used by Etienne Dumont for the first volume of his *Théorie des Peines et des Récompenses* (London, 1811). The other branch developed more slowly. Conceived at first as a treatise on offences to match that on punishments, it was from the outset intended to 'comprize the text of a Code of Criminal Law'.[1] In the summer of 1778 Bentham at last decided to enter the competition announced by the Oeconomical Society of Berne in the autumn of 1777 for a 'Plan of Legislation on Criminal Matters'. From then on the work on his Penal Code advanced steadily, part of the product being *An Introduction to the Principles*; and a letter written by Bentham to the secretary of the Berne society at the end of March 1779 shows that the *Introduction* had already taken very largely the shape in which we know it.[2]

At the same time, the detailed *Plan of a Penal Code* which the *Introduction* was intended to introduce had proceeded a good deal further than might be supposed from what Bentham's later editors published or from what Bentham himself says in his 1789 preface. He is there concerned to explain the cryptic references in such forms as 'B.I. tit. (Irrep. Corp. Injuries)' which occur so frequently in the footnotes to the *Introduction*. But when he dismisses them as references to what 'has not as yet any existence',[3] it must not be thought that the *Plan of a Penal Code* was a mere project and no

---

[1] Bentham to the Rev. John Forster, April/May 1778: *Correspondence*, in *CW*, ii, 100.

[2] Bentham to Franz Ludwig Tribolet, 30 March 1779: ibid., 250. The writing of the *Introduction* and still more its passage through the press between April 1780 and the end of that year can be followed in some detail in Bentham's correspondence.

[3] Below, 7.

more. Most if not all of these references can be located in surviving manuscripts. This is notably true of the references to 'B.I.'—i.e. to Book I of the *Code*, which was to deal with the various classes of offences. If, as may well be the case, it proves possible to include this early *Penal Code* material in a subsequent volume of the present edition, a frame of reference which was essential to Bentham's original conception of the *Introduction* will be provided.

The publication in 1789 of *An Introduction to the Principles of Morals and Legislation* without the *Plan of a Penal Code* was precipitated by pressure brought to bear upon Bentham by his old friend George Wilson. Wilson feared that the publication of William Paley's *Principles of Moral and Political Philosophy* (1785) might otherwise rob Bentham of his claim to originality.[1] But the possibility of publishing the *Introduction* without the *Code* had occurred to Bentham himself at a very early stage. Writing to his brother Samuel on 1 April 1780, when printing was just about to begin, he says:

The Introduction to Code . . . will make a little bit of a work by itself: and who knows? probably it might be advisable to present that first; [2] and ten days later he is referring to 'the uncertainty there is whether any more . . . will be published than the introduction'.[3]

The Text

An Introduction to the Principles of Morals and Legislation presents few textual problems to an editor. It was published both in 1789 and again in 1823 with the author's full approval and co-operation. To the 1789 edition of the text which had been printed in 1780 Bentham appended a considerable number of corrigenda, addenda and supplementary notes.[4] Some of these were simply corrections of printer's errors; others were the result of second thoughts incorporated in a supplementary sheet printed off 'about the year 1783'; others again—including the most substantial in point of length— were printed for the first time in January 1789. Most, though not quite all of these were inserted in their proper places in the edition

[1] Cf. George Wilson to Bentham, 30 November 1788: Bowring, x, 194–5.

[2] Bentham to Samuel Bentham, 30 March–4 April 1780: *Correspondence*, in *CW*, ii, 411.

[3] Bentham to Samuel Bentham, 10 April 1780: ibid., 417. Even when the plan of the *Introduction* had been extended to comprise the material published in this edition as *Of Laws in General*, Bentham still thought of publishing 'what is printed of the Introduction by itself': see his letter to Lord Ashburton of 3 June 1782, *Of Laws in General*, in *CW*, Appendix E, 309.

[4] Sigs. Xx, Xx 2, Yy, following p. cccxxxv.

of 1823.[1] In that edition too, apart from the alteration of what were by then old-fashioned spellings,[2] some systematic verbal changes were made: thus the adjective 'venereal', used in the 1789 text, was replaced throughout by 'sexual'. That this and certain other changes had Bentham's positive authority is known from his manuscript notes and instructions on a copy of the 1789 edition now in the British Museum.[3] Not all these manuscript indications however were in fact followed in the 1823 edition. The omissions were partly remedied in the text of *An Introduction to the Principles* published in the first volume of the Bowring edition of Bentham's *Works* (Edinburgh, 1838). That version of the text, possibly the work of John Bowring himself, but perhaps more probably prepared by Richard Smith,[4] also picked up some corrigenda and addenda of 1789 which had been overlooked in 1823. Its other distinctive feature was the gratuitous insertion of a number of passages taken from Dumont's *Traités de Législation Civile et Pénale* (Paris, 1802). The principal insertions were made in the form of two additional chapters between Bentham's twelfth and thirteenth chapters, so that Chs. XIII–XVII appear in the Bowring edition as XV–XIX. These interpolations are, of course, omitted from the present edition. There can be no warrant for thus interfering with a text which Bentham had himself republished without any such insertions at a

[1] *An Introduction to the Principles of Morals and Legislation.* By Jeremy Bentham, Esq. Bencher of Lincoln's Inn; and late of Queen's College, Oxford, M.A. In Two Volumes. A new edition, corrected by the author. London: Printed for E. Wilson, Royal Exchange; and W. Pickering, Lincoln's-Inn Fields. 1823. Vol. i (pp. xxix, 281) comprises Chs. I–XII; vol. ii (pp. ix, 279) Chs. XIII–XVII. Two printers are named: B. Bensley, Bolt Court, Fleet Street (*verso* of title-page, both vols.); and T. White & Co., 14 Bear Alley (vol. ii, p. 279).

There is little evidence as to the preparation of this second edition. Francis Place and John Bowring seem both to have had a hand in it (cf. U.C. clxxiii. 81–2). One additional note (vol. ii, p. 68n.: cf. 194 below) is ascribed to 'the Editor', and the index of the Bowring edition of Bentham's *Works* (xi, p. cccxlviii) identifies the author of that note as Richard Smith (cf. n. 4 below). Smith may thus have superintended the preparation of the 1823 edition.

[2] This was not done consistently: e.g. both 'style' and 'stile' occur. One spelling change has had some lexicographical significance. The word 'anarchical' on 16 below was replaced in 1823 by 'anarchial'. The editors of the *O.E.D.* cited the use of the rare spelling 'anarchial' but wrongly dated it 1789. The change in 1823 may well have been a mere unnoticed printer's error.

[3] Shelfmark C.61.e.4.

[4] 'Mr. Richard Smith, of the Stamps and Taxes' prepared a fair number of the texts published in the Bowring edition (cf. x, 548), including several which relied heavily on Dumont material. He had in fact published two of these in Bentham's lifetime: *The Rationale of Reward* (1825) and *The Rationale of Punishment* (1830). Thus the insertion, noted below, of Dumont material into the Bowring edition of *An Introduction to the Principles* suggests the likelihood of its being the work of Smith, who may already, as noted above, have edited it for Bentham in 1823.

time when the Dumont material, had he wished to use it, was fully at his disposal.

It may none the less be appropriate to comment briefly at this point on Dumont's own use of *An Introduction to the Principles*. In effect he used its first six chapters as the basis for much of the opening section of the *Traités de Législation* which he published in 1802.[1] The importance of this is that, since the 1789 edition of the *Introduction* had a very restricted circulation[2] and attracted little attention when it was published,[3] these chapters of Dumont were the form in which Bentham's basic principles first obtained wide currency. Nor was that currency restricted to the areas of Europe and Latin America where Dumont's *Traités*, in their original French or in translation, made Bentham's name and ideas familiar. Not only were Dumont's original recensions themselves read and discussed in England[4]; they were in due course retranslated into English, and the chapters of the *Introduction* used by Dumont were almost certainly read more widely in this form both in Britain and in America than the book from which they were originally derived. The English translation of Dumont's *Traités* published in 1840 and 1864 by Richard Hildreth,[5] C. M. Atkinson's two-volume edition of 1914,[6] and the republication of the Hildreth translation by C. K. Ogden in 1931[7] all perpetuated the influence of a text which,

[1] *Traités de législation civile et pénale . . . par M. Jérémie Bentham, jurisconsulte anglois.* Publiés en François par Et. Dumont, de Genève, d'après les Manuscrits confiés par l'Auteur. Paris (3 vols.), 1802: t. I, pp. 1–79. Dumont also used Ch. XVII of *An Introduction to the Principles* as the basis for his twelfth chapter (ibid., 98–107); while a condensation of Ch. XVI forms part of the *Vue générale d'un corps complet de législation* which forms the second of the two parts into which his first volume is divided: cf. pp. 172–214.

[2] 'The edition was very small, and half of that devoured by the rats' (Bentham to Lord Wycombe, 1 March 1789: Bowring, x, 197).

[3] The 1789 edition seems to have received little or no notice in periodical publications at the time.

[4] See, for instance, the article by Francis Jeffrey in the *Edinburgh Review* for April 1804 (Vol. iv, pp. 1–26).

[5] *Theory of Legislation, by Jeremy Bentham.* Translated from the French of Etienne Dumont by R. Hildreth. Boston (Weeks, Jordan, Co.), 1840. The 1864 edition was published in London by Kegan Paul. Hildreth's was not in fact the first American translation of Dumont's work. John Neal, who had spent a prolonged period with Bentham in 1826–7, published in 1830 *Principles of Legislation: from the manuscript of Jeremy Bentham. . . . By M. Dumont.* Translated . . . by John Neal. Boston (Wells & Lilly); New York (G. & C. H. Carvill). This was effectively superseded, however, by Hildreth's work.

[6] *Bentham's Theory of Legislation, being Principes de législation and Traités de législation civile et pénale,* translated and edited from the French of Etienne Dumont by Charles Milner Atkinson. London (Oxford University Press), 2 vols., 1914.

[7] *The Theory of Legislation,* by Jeremy Bentham, edited with an introduction and notes by C. K. Ogden. London (Kegan Paul, Trench, Trübner and Co.); New York (Harcourt Brace and Co.), 1931.

however close to Bentham's mind, was not Bentham's own. *An Introduction to the Principles of Morals and Legislation* is the only part of the major work of Bentham's early years as a writer which was published in his lifetime in the form he gave it.

The text of the present edition is essentially that of 1823, as approved by Bentham, substantial variants from the 1789 text being indicated in the editorial footnotes. All Bentham's printed addenda and corrigenda have been inserted, together with such of his manuscript suggestions in the British Museum copy mentioned above as were not followed either in 1823 or in the Bowring edition.

With one exception no attempt has been made to supplement this established Bentham text with material from unpublished manuscripts. As is commonly the case with works whose publication Bentham had himself superintended, the main body of manuscript for *An Introduction to the Principles* is not extant, and the considerable body of related manuscript clearly calls for separate treatment.[1] The exception is the note (n. b2 to Ch. XVII) which appears on p. 299 below. This has been inserted only because the manuscript (U.C. lxxxviii (b). 344–6) bears such clear indications that it was intended for incorporation in the present work that its omission from the 1789 list of addenda must be supposed to be an oversight. Each page is headed *Limits*—Bentham's usual abbreviated title for Ch. XVII—and bears the following further description: 'Note to p. cccxxvii'. This, together with the fact that the note opened with a suprascript 'r', leaves no doubt that the material was intended as a footnote to par. 29 of Ch. XVII, where it has accordingly been placed below.

In accordance with the general policy of the present edition spelling has been systematically modernised. In matters of punctuation and, more especially, italicisation, Bentham's usage has been substantially followed, subject to some minor variations in the interests of clarity and ease of reading. Brackets occurring in Bentham's text and notes have throughout been printed as round brackets, square brackets being reserved for the rare instances of editorially inserted words.[2] Bentham's footnotes are indicated by suprascript letters running in sequence throughout each chapter;

---

[1] A place may be found elsewhere in the present edition for the numerous but largely fragmentary manuscripts in which Bentham explores more fully the themes summarised in the early chapters of *An Introduction to the Principles*.

[2] Bentham's own use of various forms of bracket in his manuscript work lacks any evident system. The 1789 and 1823 editions of the present work used square brackets round the abbreviated chapter-titles which occur so frequently in Bentham's footnotes.

footnotes to these notes (usually references) are indicated by asterisks, etc.[1] In a number of instances Bentham's rather frequent, and not always very clear or helpful, cross-references within the text of the 1789 edition were removed in 1823. Some editorial discretion has been exercised in deciding whether or not to restore these references. Editorial footnotes are indicated by suprascript numerals, with a separate numerical sequence for each page of the text.

One further point in connection with the lay-out of the text may be noted. In this edition, as in some other modern editions of *An Introduction to the Principles*, the Roman numerals for each paragraph, set in the middle of the page in both the 1789 and 1823 editions, are replaced by Arabic numerals set at the side of each paragraph. This change does in fact have Bentham's authority, though his instructions to this effect were not followed in 1823. In a note headed 'Dicenda to Bowring' and dated 9 July 1822 he indicates 'Arabic numerals for Roman, and by the side instead of the middle'.[2]

[1] Where Bentham has more than twenty-six footnotes in a chapter, a second series, a2, b2 . . . etc., has been used, followed, when required, by a third series, a3, b3 . . ., and so on.

[2] U.C. clxxiii.81 v. This note also repeats the instruction to substitute 'sexual' for 'venereal'.

PREFACE

The following sheets were, as the title-page expresses, printed so long ago as the year 1780.[1] The design, in pursuance of which they were written, was not so extensive as that announced by the present title. They had at that time no other destination than that of serving as an introduction to a plan of a penal code *in terminis*, designed to follow them, in the same volume.

The body of the work had received its completion according to the then present extent of the author's views, when, in the investigation of some flaws he had discovered, he found himself unexpectedly entangled in an unsuspected corner of the metaphysical maze.[2] A suspension, at first not apprehended to be more than a temporary one, necessarily ensued: suspension brought on coolness, and coolness, aided by other concurrent causes, ripened into disgust.

Imperfections pervading the whole mass had already been pointed out by the sincerity of severe and discerning friends; and conscience had certified the justness of their censure. The inordinate length of some of the chapters, the apparent inutility of others, and the dry and metaphysical turn of the whole, suggested an apprehension, that, if published in its present form, the work would contend under great disadvantages for any chance, it might on other accounts possess, of being read, and consequently of being of use.

But, though in this manner the idea of completing the present work slid insensibly aside, that was not by any means the case with the considerations which had led him to engage in it. Every opening, which promised to afford the lights he stood in need of, was still pursued: as occasion arose, the several departments connected with that in which he had at first engaged, were successively explored; insomuch that, in one branch or other of the pursuit, his researches have nearly embraced the whole field of legislation.

Several causes have conspired at present to bring to light, under this new title, a work which under its original one had been imperceptibly, but as it had seemed irrevocably, doomed to oblivion. In the course of eight years, materials for various works, corres-

---

[1] This of course refers to the title-page of the original 1789 edition. In 1823 the reference to 1780 was transferred to the verso of the title-page. Bentham's correspondence shows that the work of printing was begun in April and continued until November 1780.

[2] Cf. Introduction to *Of Laws in General* (in *CW*, xxxi ff.).

1

ponding to the different branches of the subject of legislation, had been produced, and some nearly reduced to shape: and, in every one of those works, the principles exhibited in the present publication had been found so necessary, that, either to transcribe them piecemeal, or to exhibit them somewhere where they could be referred to in the lump, was found unavoidable. The former course would have occasioned repetitions too bulky to be employed without necessity in the execution of a plan unavoidably so voluminous: the latter was therefore indisputably the preferable one.

To publish the materials in the form in which they were already printed, or to work them up into a new one, was therefore the only alternative: the latter had all along been his wish, and, had time and the requisite degree of alacrity been at command, it would as certainly have been realised. Cogent considerations, however, concur, with the irksomeness of the task, in placing the accomplishment of it at present at an unfathomable distance.

Another consideration is, that the suppression of the present work, had it been ever so decidedly wished, is no longer altogether in his power. In the course of so long an interval, various incidents have introduced copies into various hands, from some of which they have been transferred, by deaths and other accidents, into others that are unknown to him. Detached, but considerable extracts, have even been published, without any dishonourable views, (for the name of the author was very honestly subjoined to them) but without his privity, and in publications undertaken without his knowledge.[1]

It may perhaps be necessary to add, to complete his excuse for offering to the public a work pervaded by blemishes, which have not escaped even the author's partial eye, that the censure, so justly bestowed upon the form, did not extend itself to the matter.

In sending it thus abroad into the world with all its imperfections upon its head, he thinks it may be of assistance to the few readers he can expect, to receive a short intimation of the chief particulars, in respect of which it fails of corresponding with his

---

[1] The only publication of this kind which has been traced took place in 1786, when Bentham's friend Francois-Xavier Schwediauer published in four volumes his *Philosophical Dictionary; or, the Opinions of modern philosophers on metaphysical, moral, and political subjects*. This compilation included ten brief extracts from the present work, drawn chiefly from its early chapters, together with six extracts from *A Fragment on Government*. But it seems doubtful whether this publication took place without Bentham's 'privity': certainly Schwediauer told him that his name was to be 'most honourably mentioned' in the *Dictionary* (Schwediauer to Bentham, 12 November 1784, to be published in *Correspondence*, iii in *CW*, Letter 519; and cf. n. 5 to that letter, where the extracts from Bentham's works will be identified).

maturer views. It will thence be observed how in some respects it fails of quadrating with the design announced by its original title, as in others it does with that announced by the one it bears at present.

An introduction to a work which takes for its subject the totality of any science, ought to contain all such matters, and such matters only, as belong in common to every particular branch of that science, or at least to more branches of it than one. Compared with its present title, the present work fails in both ways of being conformable to that rule.

As an introduction to the principles of *morals*, in addition to the analysis it contains of the extensive ideas signified by the terms *pleasure, pain, motive,* and *disposition,* it ought to have given a similar analysis of the not less extensive, though much less determinate, ideas annexed to the terms *emotion, passion, appetite, virtue, vice,* and some others, including the names of the particular *virtues* and *vices.* But as the true, and, if he conceives right, the only true ground-work for the development of the latter set of terms, has been laid by the explanation of the former, the completion of such a dictionary, so to style it, would, in comparison of the commencement, be little more than a mechanical operation.

Again, as an introduction to the principles of *legislation in general,* it ought rather to have included matters belonging exclusively to the *civil* branch, than matters more particularly applicable to the *penal*: the latter being but a means of compassing the ends proposed by the former. In preference therefore, or at least in priority, to the several chapters which will be found relative to *punishment,* it ought to have exhibited a set of propositions which have since presented themselves to him as affording a standard for the operations performed by government, in the creation and distribution of proprietary and other civil rights. He means certain axioms of what may be termed *mental pathology,* expressive of the connexion betwixt the feelings of the parties concerned, and the several classes of incidents, which either call for, or are produced by, operations of the nature above mentioned.[a]

[a] For example.—*It is worse to lose than simply not to gain.*—*A loss falls the lighter by being divided.*—*The suffering, of a person hurt in gratification of enmity, is greater than the gratification produced by the same cause.* These, and a few others which he will have occasion to exhibit at the head of another publication, have the same claim to the appellation of axioms, as those given by mathematicians under that name; since, referring to universal experience as their immediate basis, they are incapable of demonstration, and require only to be developed and illustrated, in order to be recognised as incontestable.

The consideration of the division of offences, and every thing else that belongs to offences, ought, besides, to have preceded the consideration of punishment: for the idea of *punishment* presupposes the idea of *offence*: punishment, as such, not being inflicted but in consideration of offence.

Lastly, the analytical discussions relative to the classification of offences would, according to his present views, be transferred to a separate treatise, in which the system of legislation is considered solely in respect of its form: in other words, in respect of its *method* and *terminology*.

In these respects the performance fails of coming up to the author's own ideas of what should have been exhibited in a work, bearing the title he has now given it, viz. that of an *Introduction to the Principles of Morals and Legislation*. He knows however of no other that would be less unsuitable: nor in particular would so adequate an intimation of its actual contents have been given, by a title corresponding to the more limited design, with which it was written: viz. that of serving as an *introduction to a penal code*.

Yet more. Dry and tedious as a great part of the discussions it contains must unavoidably be found by the bulk of readers, he knows not how to regret the having written them, nor even the having made them public. Under every head, the practical uses, to which the discussions contained under that head appeared applicable, are indicated: nor is there, he believes, a single proposition that he has not found occasion to build upon in the penning of some article or other of those provisions of detail, of which a body of law, authoritative or unauthoritative, must be composed. He will venture to specify particularly, in this view, the several chapters shortly characterised by the words *Sensibility, Actions, Intentionality, Consciousness, Motives, Dispositions, Consequences*. Even in the enormous chapter on the division of offences, which, notwithstanding the forced compression the plan has undergone in several of its parts, in manner there mentioned, occupies no fewer than one hundred and four closely printed quarto pages,[1] the ten concluding ones are employed in a statement of the practical advantages that may be reaped from the plan of classification which it exhibits. Those in whose sight the Defence of Usury has been fortunate enough to find favour,[2] may reckon as one instance of those advantages the discovery of the principles developed in that little treatise.

---

[1] Of the 1789 edition.

[2] Bentham's *Defence of Usury*, written in Russia in the spring of 1787, was published towards the end of that year and well received.

In the preface to an anonymous tract published so long ago as in 1776,[b] he had hinted at the utility of a natural classification of offences, in the character of a test for distinguishing genuine from spurious ones. The case of usury is one among a number of instances of the truth of that observation. A note at the end of Sect. 35 Ch. XVI of the present publication,[1] may serve to show how the opinions, developed in that tract, owed their origin to the difficulty experienced in the attempt to find a place in his system for that imaginary offence. To some readers, as a means of helping them to support the fatigue of wading through an analysis of such enormous length, he would almost recommend the beginning with those ten concluding pages.

One good at least may result from the present publication; viz. that the more he has trespassed on the patience of the reader on this occasion, the less need he will have so to do on future ones: so that this may do to those, the office which is done, by books of pure mathematics, to books of mixed mathematics and natural philosophy. The narrower the circle of readers is, within which the present work may be condemned to confine itself, the less limited may be the number of those to whom the fruits of his succeeding labours may be found accessible. He may therefore in this respect find himself in the condition of those philosophers of antiquity, who are represented as having held two bodies of doctrine, a popular and an occult one: but, with this difference, that in his instance the occult and the popular will, he hopes, be found as consistent as in those they were contradictory; and that in his production whatever there is of occultness has been the pure result of sad necessity, and in no respect of choice.

Having, in the course of this advertisement, had such frequent occasion to allude to different arrangements, as having been suggested by more extensive and maturer views, it may perhaps contribute to the satisfaction of the reader, to receive a short intimation of their nature: the rather, as, without such explanation, references, made here and there to unpublished works, might be productive of perplexity and mistake. The following then are the titles of the works by the publication of which his present designs would be completed. They are exhibited in the order which seemed to him best fitted for apprehension, and in which they would

[b] A Fragment on Government, etc. reprinted 1822.[2]

[1] P. 231, n. 13 below.

[2] Bentham's reference is to paras. 58 ff. of the Preface to *A Fragment on Government* (Bowring, i, 237–8).

stand disposed, were the whole assemblage ready to come out at once: but the order, in which they will eventually appear, may probably enough be influenced in some degree by collateral and temporary considerations.

Part the 1st. Principles of legislation in matters of *civil*, more distinctively termed *private distributive*, or for shortness, *distributive*, *law*.

Part the 2d. Principles of legislation in matters of *penal law*.

Part the 3d. Principles of legislation in matters of *procedure*: uniting in one view the *criminal* and *civil* branches, between which no line can be drawn, but a very indistinct one, and that continually liable to variation.

Part the 4th. Principles of legislation in matters of *reward*.

Part the 5th. Principles of legislation in matters of *public distributive*, more concisely as well as familiarly termed *constitutional*, law.

Part the 6th. Principles of legislation in matters of *political tactics*: or of the art of maintaining *order* in the proceedings of political assemblies, so as to direct them to the end of their institution: viz. by a system of rules, which are to the constitutional branch, in some respects, what the law of procedure is to the civil and the penal.

Part the 7th. Principles of legislation in matters betwixt nation and nation, or, to use a new though not inexpressive appellation, in matters of *international* law.

Part the 8th. Principles of legislation in matters of *finance*.

Part the 9th. Principles of legislation in matters of *political economy*.

Part the 10th. Plan of a body of law, complete in all its branches, considered in respect of its *form*; in other words, in respect of its method and terminology; including a view of the origination and connexion of the ideas expressed by the short list of terms, the exposition of which contains all that can be said with propriety to belong to the head of *universal jurisprudence*.[c]

The use of the principles laid down under the above several heads is to prepare the way for the body of law itself exhibited *in terminis*; and which to be complete, with reference to any political state, must consequently be calculated for the meridian, and adapted to the circumstances, of some one such state in particular.

Had he an unlimited power of drawing upon *time*, and every

[c] Such as obligation, right, power, possession, title, exemption, immunity, franchise, privilege, nullity, validity, and the like.

6

other condition necessary, it would be his wish to postpone the publication of each part to the completion of the whole. In particular, the use of the ten parts, which exhibit what appear to him the dictates of utility in every line, being no other than to furnish reasons for the several corresponding provisions contained in the body of law itself, the exact truth of the former can never be precisely ascertained, till the provisions, to which they are destined to apply, are themselves ascertained, and that *in terminis*. But as the infirmity of human nature renders all plans precarious in the execution, in proportion as they are extensive in the design, and as he has already made considerable advances in several branches of the theory, without having made correspondent advances in the practical applications, he deems it more than probable, that the eventual order of publication will not correspond exactly with that which, had it been equally practicable, would have appeared most eligible. Of this irregularity the unavoidable result will be, a multitude of imperfections, which, if the execution of the body of law *in terminis* had kept pace with the development of the principles, so that each part had been adjusted and corrected by the other, might have been avoided. His conduct however will be the less swayed by this inconvenience, from his suspecting it to be of the number of those in which the personal vanity of the author is much more concerned, than the instruction of the public: since whatever amendments may be suggested in the detail of the principles, by the literal fixation of the provisions to which they are relative, may easily be made in a corrected edition of the former, succeeding upon the publication of the latter.

In the course of the ensuing pages, references will be found, as already intimated, some to the plan of a penal code to which this work was meant as an introduction, some to other branches of the above-mentioned general plan, under titles somewhat different from those, by which they have been mentioned here. The giving this warning is all which it is in the author's power to do, to save the reader from the perplexity of looking out for what has not as yet any existence. The recollection of the change of plan will in like manner account for several similar incongruities not worth particularizing.[1]

Allusion was made, at the outset of this advertisement, to some unspecified difficulties, as the causes of the original suspension, and

---

[1] The references mentioned in this paragraph take for the most part such forms as 'See B. I. tit. (Irrep. corp. injuries)', i.e. *Plan of a Penal Code*, Book I, title *Irreparable corporal injuries*. See above, Introduction, xxxviii–xxxix.

unfinished complexion, of the present work. Ashamed of his defeat, and unable to dissemble it, he knows not how to refuse himself the benefit of such an apology as a slight sketch of the nature of those difficulties may afford.

The discovery of them was produced by the attempt to solve the questions that will be found at the conclusion of the volume: *Wherein consisted the identity and* completeness *of a law? What the distinction, and where the separation, between* a penal *and a civil law? What the distinction, and where the separation, between the* penal *and* other branches *of* the law*?*

To give a complete and correct answer to these questions, it is but too evident that the relations and dependencies of every part of the legislative system, with respect to every other, must have been comprehended and ascertained. But it is only upon a view of these parts themselves, that such an operation could have been performed. To the accuracy of such a survey one necessary condition would therefore be, the complete existence of the fabric to be surveyed. Of the performance of this condition no example is as yet to be met with any where. *Common* law, as it styles itself in England, *judiciary* law, as it might more aptly be styled every where, that fictitious composition which has no known person for its author, no known assemblage of words for its substance, forms every where the main body of the legal fabric: like that fancied ether, which, in default of sensible matter, fills up the measure of the universe. Shreds and scraps of real law, stuck on upon that imaginary ground, compose the furniture of every national code. What follows?—that he who, for the purpose just mentioned or for any other, wants an example of a complete body of law to refer to, must begin with making one.

There is, or rather there ought to be, a *logic* of the *will*, as well as of the *understanding*: the operations of the former faculty, are neither less susceptible, nor less worthy, than those of the latter, of being delineated by rules. Of these two branches of that recondite art, Aristotle saw only the latter: succeeding logicians, treading in the steps of their great founder, have concurred in seeing with no other eyes. Yet so far as a difference can be assigned between branches so intimately connected, whatever difference there is, in point of importance, is in favour of the logic of the will. Since it is only by their capacity of directing the operations of this faculty, that the operations of the understanding are of any consequence.

Of this logic of the will, the science of *law*, considered in respect of its *form*, is the most considerable branch,—the most important application. It is, to the art of legislation, what the science of anatomy is to the art of medicine: with this difference, that the subject of it is what the artist has to work *with*, instead of being what he has to operate *upon*. Nor is the body politic less in danger from a want of acquaintance with the one science, than the body natural from ignorance in the other. One example, amongst a thousand that might be adduced in proof of this assertion, may be seen in the note which terminates this volume.

Such then were the difficulties: such the preliminaries:—an unexampled work to achieve, and then a new science to create: a new branch to add to one of the most abstruse of sciences.

Yet more: a body of proposed law, how complete soever, would be comparatively useless and uninstructive, unless explained and justified, and that in every tittle, by a continued accompaniment, a perpetual commentary of *reasons*[d]: which reasons, that the comparative value of such as point in opposite directions may be estimated, and the conjunct force, of such as point in the same direction, may be felt, must be marshalled, and put under subordination to such extensive and leading ones as are termed *principles*. There must be therefore, not one system only, but two parallel and connected systems, running on together, the one of legislative provisions, the other of political reasons, each affording to the other correction and support.

Are enterprises like these achievable? He knows not. This only he knows, that they have been undertaken, proceeded in, and that some progress has been made in all of them. He will venture to add, if at all achievable, never at least by one, to whom the fatigue of attending to discussions, as arid as those which occupy the ensuing pages, would either appear useless, or feel intolerable. He will repeat it boldly (for it has been said before him,) truths that form the basis of political and moral science, are not to be discovered but by investigations as severe as mathematical ones, and beyond all comparison more intricate and extensive. The familiarity of the terms is a presumption, but it is a most fallacious one, of the facility of the matter. Truths in general have been called stubborn things: the truths just mentioned are so in their own way. They are not to be forced into detached and general propositions, unencumbered with explanations and exceptions. They will not compress

---

[d] To the aggregate of them a common denomination has since been allotted —*the rationale.*[1]

[1] Note added in the 1823 edition.

themselves into epigrams. They recoil from the tongue and the pen of the declaimer. They flourish not in the same soil with sentiment. They grow among thorns; and are not to be plucked, like daisies, by infants as they run. Labour, the inevitable lot of humanity, is in no track more inevitable than here. In vain would an Alexander bespeak a peculiar road for royal vanity, or a Ptolemy, a smoother one, for royal indolence. There is no *King's Road*, no *Stadtholder's Gate*, to legislative, any more than to mathematic science.

CHAPTER I

OF THE PRINCIPLE OF UTILITY

1. Nature has placed mankind under the governance of two sovereign masters, *pain* and *pleasure*. It is for them alone to point out what we ought to do, as well as to determine what we shall do. On the one hand the standard of right and wrong, on the other the chain of causes and effects, are fastened to their throne. They govern us in all we do, in all we say, in all we think: every effort we can make to throw off our subjection, will serve but to demonstrate and confirm it. In words a man may pretend to abjure their empire: but in reality he will remain subject to it all the while. The *principle of utility*[a] recognises this subjection, and assumes it for the foundation of that system, the object of which is to rear the fabric of felicity by the hands of reason and of law. Systems which attempt to question it, deal in sounds instead of sense, in caprice instead of reason, in darkness instead of light.

But enough of metaphor and declamation: it is not by such means that moral science is to be improved.

2. The principle of utility is the foundation of the present work: it will be proper therefore at the outset to give an explicit and determinate account of what is meant by it. By the principle[b] of utility

Mankind governed by pain and pleasure

Principle of utility, what

---

[a] Note by the Author, July 1822.

To this denomination has of late been added, or substituted, the *greatest happiness* or *greatest felicity* principle: this for shortness, instead of saying at length *that principle* which states the greatest happiness of all those whose interest is in question, as being the right and proper, and only right and proper and universally desirable, end of human action: of human action in every situation, and in particular in that of a functionary or set of functionaries exercising the powers of Government. The word *utility* does not so clearly point to the ideas of *pleasure* and *pain* as the words *happiness* and *felicity* do: nor does it lead us to the consideration of the *number*, of the interests affected; to the *number*, as being the circumstance, which contributes, in the largest proportion, to the formation of the standard here in question; the *standard of right and wrong*, by which alone the propriety of human conduct, in every situation, can with propriety be tried. This want of a sufficiently manifest connexion between the ideas of *happiness* and *pleasure* on the one hand, and the idea of *utility* on the other, I have every now and then found operating, and with but too much efficiency, as a bar to the acceptance, that might otherwise have been given, to this principle.

[b] (Principle) The word principle is derived from the Latin *principium*: which seems to be compounded of the two words *primus*, first, or chief, and *cipium*, a

A principle, what

is meant that principle which approves or disapproves of every action whatsoever, according to the tendency which it appears to have to augment or diminish the happiness of the party whose interest is in question: or, what is the same thing in other words, to promote or to oppose that happiness. I say of every action whatsoever; and therefore not only of every action of a private individual, but of every measure of government.

Utility, what　　**3.** By utility is meant that property in any object, whereby it tends to produce benefit, advantage, pleasure, good, or happiness, (all this in the present case comes to the same thing) or (what comes again to the same thing) to prevent the happening of mischief, pain, evil, or unhappiness to the party whose interest is considered: if that party be the community in general, then the happiness of the community: if a particular individual, then the happiness of that individual.

Interest of the community, what　　**4.** The interest of the community is one of the most general expressions that can occur in the phraseology of morals: no wonder that the meaning of it is often lost. When it has a meaning, it is this. The community is a fictitious *body*, composed of the individual persons who are considered as constituting as it were its *members*. The interest of the community then is, what?—the sum of the interests of the several members who compose it.

5. It is in vain to talk of the interest of the community, without understanding what is the interest of the individual.[c] A thing is said to promote the interest, or to be *for* the interest, of an individual, when it tends to add to the sum total of his pleasures: or, what comes to the same thing, to diminish the sum total of his pains.

An action conformable to the principle of utility. what　　**6.** An action then may be said to be conformable to the principle of utility, or, for shortness sake, to utility, (meaning with respect to the community at large) when the tendency it has to augment

termination which seems to be derived from *capio*, to take, as in *mancipium, municipium*; to which are analogous *auceps, forceps*, and others. It is a term of very vague and very extensive signification: it is applied to any thing which is conceived to serve as a foundation or beginning to any series of operations: in some cases, of physical operations; but of mental operations in the present case.

The principle here in question may be taken for an act of the mind; a sentiment; a sentiment of approbation; a sentiment which, when applied to an action, approves of its utility, as that quality of it by which the measure of approbation or disapprobation bestowed upon it ought to be governed.

[c] (Interest, &c.) Interest is one of those words, which not having any superior *genus*, cannot in the ordinary way be defined.

the happiness of the community is greater than any it has to diminish it.

7. A measure of government (which is but a particular kind of action, performed by a particular person or persons) may be said to be conformable to or dictated by the principle of utility, when in like manner the tendency which it has to augment the happiness of the community is greater than any which it has to diminish it.

A measure of government conformable to the principle of utility, what

8. When an action, or in particular a measure of government, is supposed by a man to be conformable to the principle of utility, it may be convenient, for the purposes of discourse, to imagine a kind of law or dictate, called a law or dictate of utility: and to speak of the action in question, as being conformable to such law or dictate.

Laws or dictates of utility, what

9. A man may be said to be a partisan of the principle of utility, when the approbation or disapprobation he annexes to any action, or to any measure, is determined by, and proportioned to the tendency which he conceives it to have to augment or to diminish the happiness of the community: or in other words, to its conformity or unconformity to the laws or dictates of utility.

A partisan of the principle of utility, who

10. Of an action that is conformable to the principle of utility, one may always say either that it is one that ought to be done, or at least that it is not one that ought not to be done. One may say also, that it is right it should be done; at least that it is not wrong it should be done: that it is a right action; at least that it is not a wrong action. When thus interpreted, the words *ought*, and *right* and *wrong*, and others of that stamp, have a meaning: when otherwise, they have none.

Ought, ought not, right and wrong, &c. how to be understood

11. Has the rectitude of this principle been ever formally contested? It should seem that it had, by those who have not known what they have been meaning. Is it susceptible of any direct proof? it should seem not: for that which is used to prove every thing else, cannot itself be proved: a chain of proofs must have their commencement somewhere. To give such proof is as impossible as it is needless.

To prove the rectitude of this principle is at once unnecessary and impossible

12. Not that there is or ever has been that human creature breathing, however stupid or perverse, who has not on many, perhaps on most occasions of his life, deferred to it. By the natural constitution of the human frame, on most occasions of their lives men in general embrace this principle, without thinking of it: if not for the ordering of their own actions, yet for the trying of their own actions, as well as of those of other men. There have been, at the same time, not many, perhaps, even of the most intelligent, who have been disposed to embrace it purely and without reserve.

It has seldom, however, as yet, been consistently pursued

There are even few who have not taken some occasion or other to quarrel with it, either on account of their not understanding always how to apply it, or on account of some prejudice or other which they were afraid to examine into, or could not bear to part with. For such is the stuff that man is made of: in principle and in practice, in a right track and in a wrong one, the rarest of all human qualities is consistency.

It can never be consistently combated

13. When a man attempts to combat the principle of utility, it is with reasons drawn, without his being aware of it, from that very principle itself.[d] His arguments, if they prove any thing,

[d] 'The principle of utility, (I have heard it said) is a dangerous principle: it is dangerous on certain occasions to consult it.' This is as much as to say, what? that it is not consonant to utility, to consult utility: in short, that it is *not* consulting it, to consult it.

Addition by the author, July 1822.

Not long after the publication of the Fragment on Government, anno 1776, in which, in the character of an all-comprehensive and all-commanding principle, the principle of *utility* was brought to view, one person by whom observation to the above effect was made was *Alexander Wedderburn*, at that time Attorney or Solicitor General, afterwards successively Chief Justice of the Common Pleas, and Chancellor of England, under the successive titles of Lord Loughborough and Earl of Rosslyn.[1] It was made—not indeed in my hearing, but in the hearing of a person by whom it was almost immediately communicated to me. So far from being self-contradictory, it was a shrewd and perfectly true one. By that distinguished functionary, the state of the Government was thoroughly understood: by the obscure individual, at that time not so much as supposed to be so: his disquisitions had not been as yet applied, with any thing like a comprehensive view, to the field of Constitutional Law, nor therefore to those features of the English Government, by which the greatest happiness of the ruling *one* with or without that of a favoured few, are now so plainly seen to be the only ends to which the course of it has at any time been directed. The *principle of utility* was an appellative, at that time employed—employed by me, as it had been by others, to designate that which, in a more perspicuous and instructive manner, may, as above, be designated by the name of the *greatest happiness principle*. 'This principle (said Wedderburn) is a dangerous one.' Saying so, he said that which, to a certain extent, is strictly true: a principle, which lays down, as the only *right* and justifiable end of Government, the greatest happiness of the greatest number—how can it be denied to be a dangerous one? dangerous it unquestionably is, to every government which has for its *actual* end or object, the

[1] Alexander Wedderburn (1733–1805), Baron Loughborough 1780, Earl of Rosslyn 1801; Solicitor-General 1771–78, Attorney-General 1778–80, Lord Chief Justice of the Common Pleas 1780–93, Lord Chancellor 1793–1801. Bentham met Wedderburn at the house of his friend John Lind in February 1777 (*Correspondence*, in *CW*, ii, 18) and it was almost certainly Lind who told Bentham of Wedderburn's remark. See also Bentham's account of the matter in the 'Historical Preface' (1828) to the *Fragment on Government*, para. v (Bowring, i, 245–6).

prove not that the principle is *wrong*, but that, according to the applications he supposes to be made of it, it is *misapplied*. Is it possible for a man to move the earth? Yes; but he must first find out another earth to stand upon.

14. To disprove the propriety of it by arguments is impossible; but, from the causes that have been mentioned, or from some confused or partial view of it, a man may happen to be disposed not to relish it. Where this is the case, if he thinks the settling of his opinions on such a subject worth the trouble, let him take the following steps, and at length, perhaps, he may come to reconcile himself to it.

Course to be taken for surmounting prejudices that may have been entertained against it

(1) Let him settle with himself, whether he would wish to discard this principle altogether; if so, let him consider what it is that all his reasonings (in matters of politics especially) can amount to?

(2) If he would, let him settle with himself, whether he would judge and act without any principle, or whether there is any other he would judge and act by?

(3) If there be, let him examine and satisfy himself whether the principle he thinks he has found is really any separate intelligible principle; or whether it be not a mere principle in words, a kind of phrase, which at bottom expresses neither more nor less than the mere averment of his own unfounded sentiments; that is, what in another person he might be apt to call *caprice*?[1]

(4) If he is inclined to think that his own approbation or disapprobation, annexed to the idea of an act, without any regard to its consequences, is a sufficient foundation for him to judge and act upon, let him ask himself whether his sentiment is to be a standard of right and wrong, with respect to every other man, or

greatest happiness of a certain *one*, with or without the addition of some comparatively small number of others, whom it is matter of pleasure or accommodation to him to admit, each of them, to a share in the concern, on the footing of so many junior partners. *Dangerous* it therefore really was, to the interest—the sinister interest—of all those functionaries, himself included, whose interest it was, to maximize delay, vexation, and expense, in judicial and other modes of procedure, for the sake of the profit, extractable out of the expense. In a Government which had for its end in view the greatest happiness of the greatest number, Alexander Wedderburn might have been Attorney General and then Chancellor: but he would not have been Attorney General with £15,000 a year, nor Chancellor, with a peerage, with a veto upon all justice, with £25,000 a year, and with 500 sinecures at his disposal, under the name of Ecclesiastical Benefices, besides *et ceteras*.

[1] The emphasis on the word *caprice*, was suggested by Bentham in an Ms. entry in his copy of the 1789 edition, now in the British Museum (see above, Introduction, xl). The suggestion was not followed in 1823.

whether every man's sentiment has the same privilege of being a standard to itself?

(5) In the first case, let him ask himself whether his principle is not despotical, and hostile to all the rest of human race?

(6) In the second case, whether it is not anarchical,[1] and whether at this rate there are not as many different standards of right and wrong as there are men? and whether even to the same man, the same thing, which is right today, may not (without the least change in its nature) be wrong to-morrow? and whether the same thing is not right and wrong in the same place at the same time? and in either case, whether all argument is not at an end? and whether, when two men have said, 'I like this', and 'I don't like it', they can (upon such a principle) have any thing more to say?

(7) If he should have said to himself, No: for that the sentiment which he proposes as a standard must be grounded on reflection, let him say on what particulars the reflection is to turn? if on particulars having relation to the utility of the act, then let him say whether this is not deserting his own principle, and borrowing assistance from that very one in opposition to which he sets it up: or if not on those particulars, on what other particulars?

(8) If he should be for compounding the matter, and adopting his own principle in part, and the principle of utility in part, let him say how far he will adopt it?

(9) When he has settled with himself where he will stop, then let him ask himself how he justifies to himself the adopting it so far? and why he will not adopt it any farther?

(10) Admitting any other principle than the principle of utility to be a right principle, a principle that it is right for a man to pursue; admitting (what is not true) that the word *right* can have a meaning without reference to utility, let him say whether there is any such thing as a *motive* that a man can have to pursue the dictates of it: if there is, let him say what that motive is, and how it is to be distinguished from those which enforce the dictates of utility: if not, then lastly let him say what it is this other principle can be good for?

[1] Thus 1789 edn.; 1823 edn. has 'anarchial': see above, Introduction, xl n. 2.

CHAPTER II

OF PRINCIPLES ADVERSE
TO THAT OF UTILITY

1. If the principle of utility be a right principle to be governed by, and that in all cases, it follows from what has been just observed, that whatever principle differs from it in any case must necessarily be a wrong one. To prove any other principle, therefore, to be a wrong one, there needs no more than just to show it to be what it is, a principle of which the dictates are in some point or other different from those of the principle of utility: to state it is to confute it.

All other principles than that of utility must be wrong

2. A principle may be different from that of utility in two ways: 1. By being constantly opposed to it: this is the case with a principle which may be termed the principle of *asceticism.*[a] 2. By being sometimes opposed to it, and sometimes not, as it may happen: this is the case with another, which may be termed the principle of *sympathy* and *antipathy*.

Ways in which a principle may be wrong

3. By the principle of asceticism I mean that principle, which, like the principle of utility, approves or disapproves of any action, according to the tendency which it appears to have to augment or diminish the happiness of the party whose interest is in question; but in an inverse manner: approving of actions in as far as they tend

Principle of asceticism, what

---

[a] (Asceticism) Ascetic is a term that has been sometimes applied to Monks. It comes from a Greek word which signifies *exercise*. The practices by which Monks sought to distinguish themselves from other men were called their Exercises. These exercises consisted in so many contrivances they had for tormenting themselves. By this they thought to ingratiate themselves with the Deity. For the Deity, said they, is a Being of infinite benevolence: now a Being of the most ordinary benevolence is pleased to see others make themselves as happy as they can: therefore to make ourselves as unhappy as we can is the way to please the Deity. If any body asked them, what motive they could find for doing all this? Oh! said they, you are not to imagine that we are punishing ourselves for nothing: we know very well what we are about. You are to know, that for every grain of pain it costs us now, we are to have a hundred grains of pleasure by and by. The case is, that God loves to see us torment ourselves at present: indeed he has as good as told us so. But this is done only to try us, in order just to see how we should behave: which it is plain he could not know, without making the experiment. Now then, from the satisfaction it gives him to see us make ourselves as unhappy as we can make ourselves in this present life, we have a sure proof of the satisfaction it will give him to see us as happy as he can make us in a life to come.

Asceticism, origin of the word

Principles of the Monks

17

to diminish his happiness; disapproving of them in as far as they tend to augment it.

A partisan of the principle of asceticism, who
4. It is evident that any one who reprobates any the least particle of pleasure, as such, from whatever source derived, is *pro tanto* a partisan of the principle of asceticism. It is only upon that principle, and not from the principle of utility, that the most abominable pleasure which the vilest of malefactors ever reaped from his crime would be to be reprobated, if it stood alone. The case is, that it never does stand alone; but is necessarily followed by such a quantity of pain (or, what comes to the same thing, such a chance for a certain quantity of pain) that the pleasure in comparison of it, is as nothing: and this is the true and sole, but perfectly sufficient, reason for making it a ground for punishment.

This principle has had in some a philosophical, in others a religious origin
5. There are two classes of men of very different complexions, by whom the principle of asceticism appears to have been embraced; the one a set of moralists, the other a set of religionists. Different accordingly have been the motives which appear to have recommended it to the notice of these different parties. Hope, that is the prospect of pleasure, seems to have animated the former: hope, the aliment of philosophic pride: the hope of honour and reputation at the hands of men. Fear, that is the prospect of pain, the latter: fear, the offspring of superstitious fancy: the fear of future punishment at the hands of a splenetic and revengeful Deity. I say in this case fear: for of the invisible future, fear is more powerful than hope. These circumstances characterize the two different parties among the partisans of the principle of asceticism; the parties and their motives different, the principle the same.

It has been carried farther by the religious party than by the philosophical
6. The religious party, however, appear to have carried it farther than the philosophical: they have acted more consistently and less wisely. The philosophical party have scarcely gone farther than to reprobate pleasure: the religious party have frequently gone so far as to make it a matter of merit and of duty to court pain. The philosophical party have hardly gone farther than the making pain a matter of indifference. It is no evil, they have said: they have not said, it is a good. They have not so much as reprobated all pleasure in the lump. They have discarded only what they have called the gross; that is, such as are organical, or of which the origin is easily traced up to such as are organical: they have even cherished and magnified the refined. Yet this, however, not under the name of pleasure: to cleanse itself from the sordes of its impure original, it was necessary it should change its name: the honourable, the

18

glorious, the reputable, the becoming, the *honestum*, the *decorum*, it was to be called: in short, any thing but pleasure.

7. From these two sources have flowed the doctrines from which the sentiments of the bulk of mankind have all along received a tincture of this principle; some from the philosophical, some from the religious, some from both. Men of education more frequently from the philosophical, as more suited to the elevation of their sentiments: the vulgar more frequently from the superstitious, as more suited to the narrowness of their intellect, undilated by knowledge: and to the abjectness of their condition, continually open to the attacks of fear. The tinctures, however, derived from the two sources, would naturally intermingle, insomuch that a man would not always know by which of them he was most influenced: and they would often serve to corroborate and enliven one another. It was this conformity that made a kind of alliance between parties of a complexion otherwise so dissimilar: and disposed them to unite upon various occasions against the common enemy, the partisan of the principle of utility, whom they joined in branding with the odious name of Epicurean.

The philosophical branch of it has had most influence among persons of education, the religious among the vulgar

8. The principle of asceticism, however, with whatever warmth it may have been embraced by its partisans as a rule of private conduct, seems not to have been carried to any considerable length, when applied to the business of government. In a few instances it has been carried a little way by the philosophical party: witness the Spartan regimen. Though then, perhaps, it may be considered as having been a measure of security: and an application, though a precipitate and perverse application, of the principle of utility. Scarcely in any instances, to any considerable length, by the religious: for the various monastic orders, and the societies of the Quakers, Dumplers,[1] Moravians, and other religionists, have been free societies, whose regimen no man has been astricted to without the intervention of his own consent. Whatever merit a man may have thought there would be in making himself miserable, no such notion seems ever to have occurred to any of them, that it may be a merit, much less a duty, to make others miserable: although it should seem, that if a certain quantity of misery were a thing so

The principle of asceticism has never been steadily applied by either party to the Business of Government

---

[1] *O.E.D.* does not list separately this name for the Church of the Brethren, or Dunkers, a German Baptist sect who, like the Quakers and Moravian Brethren with whom Bentham groups them, had settled in Pennsylvania. The Chicago *Dictionary of American English* cites for the term *Dumplers* a travel journal of 1778 not published until 1790 and a geographical work published in 1789, the year when Bentham's *Introduction* was first published. *O.E.D.*, s. v. *Dunker*, cites the second of these passages including the word *Dumpler*, but dates it 1796, from a later edition.

19

desirable, it would not matter much whether it were brought by each man upon himself, or by one man upon another. It is true, that from the same source from whence, among the religionists, the attachment to the principle of asceticism took its rise, flowed other doctrines and practices, from which misery in abundance was produced in one man by the instrumentality of another: witness the holy wars, and the persecutions for religion. But the passion for producing misery in these cases proceeded upon some special ground: the exercise of it was confined to persons of particular descriptions: they were tormented, not as men, but as heretics and infidels. To have inflicted the same miseries on their fellow-believers and fellow-sectaries, would have been as blameable in the eyes even of these religionists, as in those of a partisan of the principle of utility. For a man to give himself a certain number of stripes was indeed meritorious: but to give the same number of stripes to another man, not consenting, would have been a sin. We read of saints, who for the good of their souls, and the mortification of their bodies, have voluntarily yielded themselves a prey to vermin: but though many persons of this class have wielded the reins of empire, we read of none who have set themselves to work, and made laws on purpose, with a view of stocking the body politic with the breed of highwaymen, housebreakers, or incendiaries. If at any time they have suffered the nation to be preyed upon by swarms of idle pensioners, or useless placemen, it has rather been from negligence and imbecility, than from any settled plan for oppressing and plundering of the people.[b] If at any time they have sapped the sources of national wealth, by cramping commerce, and driving the inhabitants into emigration, it has been with other views, and in pursuit of other ends. If they have declaimed against the pursuit of pleasure, and the use of wealth, they have commonly stopped at declamation: they have not, like Lycurgus, made express ordinances for the purpose of banishing the precious metals.[1] If they have established idleness by a law, it has been not because idleness, the mother of vice and misery, is itself a virtue, but because idleness (say they) is the road to holiness. If under the notion of fasting, they have joined in the plan of confining their subjects to a diet, thought by some to be of the most nourishing and prolific nature,

[b] So thought A⁰ 1780 and 1789; not so A⁰ 1814.[2]

[1] Like most statements about Lycurgus this is quite legendary.
[2] This Ms. note was inserted by Bentham in his copy of the 1789 edition now in the British Museum (see above, Introduction, xl). It was overlooked in 1823, but was inserted in the Bowring edition (i, 5 n.).

it has been not for the sake of making them tributaries to the nations by whom that diet was to be supplied, but for the sake of manifesting their own power, and exercising the obedience of the people. If they have established, or suffered to be established, punishments for the breach of celibacy, they have done no more than comply with the petitions of those deluded rigorists, who, dupes to the ambitious and deep-laid policy of their rulers, first laid themselves under that idle obligation by a vow.

9. The principle of asceticism seems originally to have been the reverie of certain hasty speculators, who having perceived, or fancied, that certain pleasures, when reaped in certain circumstances, have, at the long run, been attended with pains more than equivalent to them, took occasion to quarrel with every thing that offered itself under the name of pleasure. Having then got thus far, and having forgot the point which they set out from, they pushed on, and went so much further as to think it meritorious to fall in love with pain. Even this, we see, is at bottom but the principle of utility misapplied. *The principle of asceticism, in its origin, was but that of utility misapplied*

10. The principle of utility is capable of being consistently pursued; and it is but tautology to say, that the more consistently it is pursued, the better it must ever be for human-kind. The principle of asceticism never was, nor ever can be, consistently pursued by any living creature. Let but one tenth part of the inhabitants of this earth pursue it consistently, and in a day's time they will have turned it into a hell. *It can never be consistently pursued*

11. Among principles adverse to that of utility, that which at this day seems to have most influence in matters of government, is what may be called the principle of sympathy and antipathy.[c] By *The principle of sympathy and antipathy, what*

[c] The following Note was first printed in January 1789.
It ought rather to have been styled, more extensively, the principle of *caprice*. Where it applies to the choice of actions to be marked out for injunction or prohibition, for reward or punishment, (to stand, in a word, as subjects for *obligations* to be imposed), it may indeed with propriety be termed, as in the text, the principle of *sympathy* and *antipathy*. But this appellative does not so well apply to it, when occupied in the choice of the *events* which are to serve as sources of *title* with respect to *rights*: where the actions prohibited and allowed the obligations and rights, being already fixed, the only question is, under what circumstances a man is to be invested with the one or subjected to the other? from what incidents occasion is to be taken to invest a man, or to refuse to invest him, with the one, or to subject him to the other? In this latter case it may more appositely be characterized by the name of the *phantastic principle*. Sympathy and antipathy are affections of the *sensible* faculty. But the choice of *titles* with respect to *rights*, especially with respect to pro-

^c cont.

prietary rights, upon grounds unconnected with utility, has been in many instances the work, not of the affections but of the imagination.

When, in justification of an article of English Common Law, calling uncles to succeed in certain cases in preference to fathers, Lord Coke produced a sort of ponderosity he had discovered in rights, disqualifying them from ascending in a straight line,[1] it was not that he *loved* uncles particularly, or *hated* fathers, but because the analogy, such as it was, was what his imagination presented him with, instead of a reason, and because, to a judgment unobservant of the standard of utility, or unacquainted with the art of consulting it, where affection is out of the way, imagination is the only guide.

When I know not what ingenious grammarian invented the proposition *Delegatus non potest delegare*, to serve as a rule of law, it was not surely that he had any antipathy to delegates of the second order, or that it was any pleasure to him to think of the ruin which, for want of a manager at home, may befal the affairs of a traveller, whom an unforeseen accident has deprived of the object of his choice: it was, that the incongruity, of giving the same law to objects so contrasted as *active* and *passive* are, was not to be surmounted, and that *-atus* chimes, as well as it contrasts, with *-are*.

When that inexorable maxim (of which the dominion is no more to be defined, than the date of its birth, or the name of its father, is to be found) was imported from England for the government of Bengal, and the whole fabric of judicature was crushed by the thunders of *ex post facto* justice, it was not surely that the prospect of a blameless magistracy perishing in prison afforded any enjoyment to the unoffended authors of their misery; but that the music of the maxim, absorbing the whole imagination, had drowned the cries of humanity along with the dictates of common sense.* *Fiat Justitia, ruat cœlum*, says another maxim, as full of extravagance as it is of harmony: Go heaven to wreck—so justice be but done:—and what is the ruin of kingdoms, in comparison of the wreck of heaven?

* Additional Note by the Author, July 1822.

Add, and that the bad system, of Mahometan and other native law was to be put down at all events, to make way for the inapplicable and still more mischievous system of English Judge-made law, and, by the hand of his accomplice Hastings, was to be put into the pocket of Impey—Importer of this instrument of subversion, £8,000 a-year contrary to law, in addition to the £8,000 a-year lavished upon him, with the customary profusion, by the hand of law.—See the Account of this transaction in *Mill's British India.*[2]

To this Governor a statue is erecting by a vote of East India Directors and Proprietors: on it should be inscribed—*Let it but put money into our pockets, no tyranny too flagitious to be worshipped by us.* [Add. Note continues p. 23]

[1] *Coke upon Littleton*, 11a; part of Ch. I 'Fee Simple', sect. 3 (p): 'It is a maxim in law that inheritance may literally descend, but not ascend . . . if the son purchase land in fee simple, and die without issue, living his father, the uncle shall have the land as heir to the son and not the father, yet the father is nearer of blood . . .'

[2] Warren Hastings (1732–1818), Governor of Bengal 1772–4, Governor-General under the Regulating Act 1774–85, was recalled to face impeachment in 1788 and partially acquitted in 1795. Sir Elijah Impey (1732–1809) was Chief Justice of the Supreme Court at Calcutta from 1773 until 1783, when he was recalled to face charges made in the House of Commons that he had contravened the terms of his appointment by enlarging the court's jurisdiction. Cf. James Mill, *History of British India* (1818), ii, 585 ff.

^ccont.

So again, when the Prussian chancellor, inspired with the wisdom of I know not what Roman sage, proclaimed in good Latin, for the edification of German ears, *Servitus servitutis non datur*, (Cod. Fred. tom. ii. par. 2 liv. 2. tit. x. § 6. p. 308.)[1] it was not that he had conceived any aversion to the lifeholder who, during the continuance of his term, should wish to gratify a neighbour with a right of way or water, or to the neighbour who should wish to accept of the indulgence; but that, to a jurisprudential ear, *-tus -tutis* sound little less melodious than *-atus -are*. Whether the melody of the maxim was the real reason of the rule, is not left open to dispute: for it is ushered in by the conjunction *quia*, reason's appointed harbinger: *quia servitus servitutis non datur*.

Neither would equal melody have been produced, nor indeed could similar melody have been called for, in either of these instances, by the opposite provision: it is only when they are opposed to general rules, and not when by their conformity they are absorbed in them, that more specific ones can obtain a separate existence. *Delegatus potest delegare*, and *Servitus servitutis datur*, provisions already included under the general adoption of contracts, would have been as unnecessary to the apprehension and the memory, as, in comparison of their energetic negatives, they are insipid to the ear.

Were the inquiry diligently made, it would be found that the goddess of harmony has exercised more influence, however latent, over the dispensations of Themis, than her most diligent historiographers, or even her most passionate panegyrists, seem to have been aware of. Every one knows, how, by the ministry of Orpheus, it was she who first collected the sons of men beneath the shadow of the sceptre: yet, in the midst of continual experience, men seem yet to learn, with what successful diligence she has laboured to guide it in its course. Every one knows, that measured numbers were the language of the infancy of law: none seem to have observed, with what imperious sway they have governed her maturer age. In English jurisprudence in particular, the

---

*To this statue of the Arch-malefactor should be added, for a companion, that of the long robed accomplice: the one lodging the bribe in the hand of the other. The hundred millions of plundered and oppressed Hindoos and Mahometans pay for the one: a Westminster Hall subscription might pay for the other.

What they have done for Ireland with her seven millions of souls, the authorised deniers and perverters of justice have done for Hindostan with her hundred millions. In this there is nothing wonderful. The wonder is—that, under such institutions, men, though in ever such small numbers, should be found, whom the view of the injustices which, by *English Judge-made law*, they are compelled to commit, and the miseries they are thus compelled to produce, deprive of health and rest. Witness the Letter of an English Hindostan Judge, Sept. 1, 1819, which lies before me. I will not make so cruel a requital for his honesty, as to put his name in print: indeed the House of Commons' Documents already published leave little need of it.

[1] Bentham is evidently referring to the work published at Halle in two volumes in 1749 and 1751 and compiled by the jurist Samuel von Cocceji (1679–1755). This provided much of the basis for the preparation by Johann von Carmer, Frederick the Great's Chancellor from 1781, of what was eventually enacted, after Frederick's death, as the *Allgemeines Preussisches Landrecht*. A number of references in Bentham's papers reflect his interest in this major piece of codification. For a later reference in the present work see below 306.

^ccont.

connexion betwixt law and music, however less perceived than in Spartan legislation, is not perhaps less real nor less close. The music of the Office, though not of the same kind, is not less musical in its kind, than the music of the Theatre; that which hardens the heart, than that which softens it:— sostenutos as long, cadences as sonorous; and those governed by rules, though not yet promulgated, not less determinate. Search indictments, pleadings, proceedings in chancery, conveyances: whatever trespasses you may find against truth or common sense, you will find none against the laws of harmony. The English Liturgy, justly as this quality has been extolled in that sacred office, possesses not a greater measure of it, than is commonly to be found in an English Act of Parliament. Dignity, simplicity, brevity, precision, intelligibility, possibility of being retained or so much as apprehended, every thing yields to Harmony. Volumes might be filled, shelves loaded, with the sacrifices that are made to this insatiate power. Expletives, her ministers in Grecian poetry, are not less busy, though in different shape and bulk, in English legislation: in the former, they are monosyllables*: in the latter, they are whole lines.†

To return to the *principle of sympathy and antipathy*: a term preferred at first, on account of its impartiality, to the *principle of caprice*. The choice of an appellative, in the above respects too narrow, was owing to my not having, at that time, extended my views over the civil branch of law, any otherwise than as I had found it inseparably involved in the penal. But when we come to the former branch, we shall see the *phantastic* principle making at least as great a figure there, as the principle of *sympathy and antipathy* in the latter.

In the days of Lord Coke, the light of utility can scarcely be said to have as yet shone upon the face of Common Law. If a faint ray of it, under the name of the *argumentum ab inconvenienti*, is to be found in a list of about twenty topics exhibited by that great lawyer as the co-ordinate leaders of that all-perfect system, the admission, so circumstanced, is as sure a proof of neglect, as, to the statues of Brutus and Cassius, exclusion was a cause of notice. It stands, neither in the front, nor in the rear, nor in any post of honour; but huddled in towards the middle, without the smallest mark of preference. (Coke Littleton. 11. a.)[1] Nor is this Latin *inconvenience* by any means the same thing with the English one. It stands distinguished from *mischief*: and because by the vulgar it is taken for something less bad, it is given by the learned as something worse. *The law prefers a mischief to an inconvenience*, says an admired maxim, and the more admired, because as nothing is expressed by it, the more is supposed to be understood.

Not that there is any avowed, much less a constant opposition, between the prescriptions of utility and the operations of the common law: such constancy we have seen to be too much even for ascetic fervour. (Supra, par. 10) From time to time instinct would unavoidably betray them into the paths of reason: instinct which, however it may be cramped, can never be killed by education. The cobwebs spun out of the materials brought together by 'the competition

* Μεν, τοι, γε, νυν, &c.—

† And be it further enacted by the authority aforesaid, that—Provided always, and it is hereby further enacted and declared that—&c. &c.

[1] Cf. 22 n. 1 above. In this passage from *Coke upon Littleton* the tenth of twenty arguments cited is the argument 'ab inconvenienti, from that which is inconvenient'.

the principle of sympathy and antipathy, I mean that principle which approves or disapproves of certain actions, not on account of their tending to augment the happiness, nor yet on account of their tending to diminish the happiness of the party whose interest is in question, but merely because a man finds himself disposed to approve or disapprove of them: holding up that approbation or disapprobation as a sufficient reason for itself, and disclaiming the necessity of looking out for any extrinsic ground. Thus far in the general department of morals: and in the particular department of politics, measuring out the quantum (as well as determining the ground) of punishment, by the degree of the disapprobation.

12. It is manifest, that this is rather a principle in name than in reality: it is not a positive principle of itself, so much as a term employed to signify the negation of all principle. What one expects to find in a principle is something that points out some external consideration, as a means of warranting and guiding the internal sentiments of approbation and disapprobation: this expectation is but ill fulfilled by a proposition, which does neither more nor less than hold up each of those sentiments as a ground and standard for itself. *This is rather the negation of all principle, than any thing positive*

13. In looking over the catalogue of human actions (says a partisan of this principle) in order to determine which of them are to be marked with the seal of disapprobation, you need but to take counsel of your own feelings: whatever you find in yourself a propensity to condemn, is wrong for that very reason. For the same reason it is also meet for punishment: in what proportion it is adverse to utility, or whether it be adverse to utility at all, is a matter that makes no difference. In that same *proportion* also is it meet for punishment: if you hate much, punish much: if you hate little, punish little: punish as you hate. If you hate not at all, punish not at all: the fine feelings of the soul are not to be overborne and tyrannized by the harsh and rugged dictates of political utility. *Sentiments of a partisan of the principle of antipathy*

14. The various systems that have been formed concerning the standard of right and wrong, may all be reduced to the principle of sympathy and antipathy. One account may serve for all of them. They consist all of them in so many contrivances for avoiding the obligation of appealing to any external standard, and for prevailing upon the reader to accept of the author's sentiment or opinion as a *The systems that have been formed concerning the standard of right and wrong, are all reducible to this principle*

ᶜcont.

of opposite analogies', can never have ceased being warped by the silent attraction of the rational principle: though it should have been, as the needle is by the magnet, without the privity of conscience.

reason and that a sufficient one[1] for itself. The phrases different, but the principle the same.[d]

Various phrases that have served as the charac- teristic marks of so many pretended systems

1. Moral Sense

[d] It is curious enough to observe the variety of inventions men have hit upon, and the variety of phrases they have brought forward, in order to con- ceal from the world, and, if possible, from themselves, this very general and therefore very pardonable self-sufficiency.[2]

1. One man (Lord Shaftesbury, Hutchinson, Hume, etc.)[3] says, he has a thing made on purpose to tell him what is right and what is wrong; and that it is called a *moral sense*: and then he goes to work at his ease, and says, such a thing is right, and such a thing is wrong—why? 'because my moral sense tells me it is'.

2. Common Sense

2. Another man (Dr Beattie)[4] comes and alters the phrase: leaving out *moral*, and putting in *common*, in the room of it. He then tells you, that his common sense teaches him what is right and wrong, as surely as the other's moral sense did: meaning by common sense, a sense of some kind or other, which, he says, is possessed by all mankind: the sense of those, whose sense is not the same as the author's, being struck out of the account as not worth taking. This contrivance does better than the other; for a moral sense, being a new thing, a man may feel about him a good while without being able to find it out: but common sense is as old as the creation; and there is no man but would be ashamed to be thought not to have as much of it as his neighbours. It has another great advantage: by appearing to share power, it lessens envy: for when a man gets up upon this ground, in order to anathematize those who differ from him, it is not by a *sic volo sic jubeo*, but by a *velitis jubeatis*.

3. Under- standing

3. Another man (Dr Price)[5] comes, and says, that as to a moral sense indeed, he cannot find that he has any such thing: that however he has an *understanding*, which will do quite as well. This understanding, he says, is the standard of right and wrong: it tells him so and so. All good and wise men understand as he does: if other men's understandings differ in any point from his, so much the worse for them: it is a sure sign they are either defective or corrupt.

4. Rule of Right

4. Another man says, that there is an eternal and immutable Rule of Right: that that rule of right dictates so and so: and then he begins giving you his

[1] The words 'and that a sufficient one' are an addition indicated in a list first printed in 1783, appended to the 1789 edition, but not followed in this instance by the 1823 edition. The insertion was duly made in the Bowring edition (i, 8).

[2] The notes identifying the philosophers referred to in paragraphs 1, 2, 3, 5 and 8 below, were inserted in Ms. by Bentham in the copy of the 1789 edition now in the British Museum. Written in 1819, the notes were first printed in the Bowring edition (1838). The misspellings of Hutcheson, Clarke, and Wollaston are Bentham's.

[3] Anthony Ashley Cooper (1671–1713), 3rd Earl of Shaftesbury, used the phrase 'Moral Sense' in his *Inquiry concerning Virtue* (1699). Francis Hutcheson (1694– 1746) was a disciple of Shaftesbury, whose principles he expounded in his *Inquiry into the Original of our Ideas of Beauty and Virtue* (1720); he also wrote an *Essay on the Nature and Conduct of the Passions* (1728) and the posthumously published *System of Moral Philosophy* (1755). David Hume (1711–76) expounded his ethical theory principally in his *Enquiry concerning the Principles of Morals* (1751).

[4] James Beattie (1735–1803) attacked Hume in his *Essay on the Nature and Im- mutability of Truth* (1770) and published *Elements of Moral Science* in 1790–3.

[5] Richard Price (1723–91) first established his reputation by his *Review of the Principal Questions in Morals* (1758).

^dcont.

sentiments upon any thing that comes uppermost: and these sentiments (you are to take for granted) are so many branches of the eternal rule of right.

5. Another man (Dr Clark)[1], or perhaps the same man (it's no matter) says, that there are certain practices conformable, and others repugnant, to the Fitness of Things; and then he tells you, at his leisure, what practices are conformable and what repugnant: just as he happens to like a practice or dislike it.

5. Fitness of Things

6. A great multitude of people are continually talking of the Law of Nature; and then they go on giving you their sentiments about what is right and what is wrong: and these sentiments, you are to understand, are so many chapters and sections of the Law of Nature.

6. Law of Nature

7. Instead of the phrase, Law of Nature, you have sometimes, Law of Reason, Right Reason, Natural Justice, Natural Equity, Good Order. Any of them will do equally well. This latter is most used in politics. The three last are much more tolerable than the others, because they do not very explicitly claim to be any thing more than phrases: they insist but feebly upon the being looked upon as so many positive standards of themselves, and seem content to be taken, upon occasion, for phrases expressive of the conformity of the thing in question to the proper standard, whatever that may be. On most occasions, however, it will be better to say *utility*: *utility* is clearer, as referring more explicitly to pain and pleasure.

7. Law of Reason, Right Reason, Natural Justice, Natural Equity, Good Order

8. We have one philosopher (Woolaston),[2] who says, there is no harm in any thing in the world but in telling a lie: and that if, for example, you were to murder your own father, this would only be a particular way of saying, he was not your father. Of course, when this philosopher sees any thing that he does not like, he says, it is a particular way of telling a lie. It is saying, that the act ought to be done, or may be done, when, *in truth*, it ought not to be done.

8. Truth

9. The fairest and openest of them all is that sort of man who speaks out, and says, I am of the number of the Elect: now God himself takes care to inform the Elect what is right: and that with so good effect, that let them strive ever so, they cannot help not only knowing it but practising it. If therefore a man wants to know what is right and what is wrong, he has nothing to do but to come to me.

9. Doctrine of Election

It is upon the principle of antipathy that such and such acts are often reprobated on the score of their being *unnatural*: the practice of exposing children, established among the Greeks and Romans, was an unnatural practice. Unnatural, when it means any thing, means unfrequent: and there it means something; although nothing to the present purpose. But here it means no such thing: for the frequency of such acts is perhaps the great complaint. It therefore means nothing; nothing, I mean, which there is in the act itself. All it can serve to express is, the disposition of the person who is talking of it: the disposition he is in to be angry at the thoughts of it. Does it merit his anger? Very likely it may: but whether it does or no is a question, which, to be answered rightly, can only be answered upon the principle of utility.

Repugnancy to Nature

Unnatural, is as good a word as moral sense, or common sense; and would

---

[1] Samuel Clarke (1675–1729), whose most celebrated work was his *Discourse concerning the Being and Attributes of God*.

[2] i.e. William Wollaston (1660–1724), whose principal work, *The Religion of Nature Delineated*, was privately printed in 1722 and published in 1724.

ᵈcont.

be as good a foundation for a system. Such an act is unnatural; that is, repugnant to nature: for I do not like to practise it; and, consequently, do not practise it. It is therefore repugnant to what ought to be the nature of every body else.

Mischief they produce

The mischief common to all these ways of thinking and arguing (which, in truth, as we have seen, are but one and the same method, couched in different forms of words) is their serving as a cloak, and pretence, and aliment, to despotism: if not a despotism in practice, a despotism however in disposition: which is but too apt, when pretence and power offer, to show itself in practice. The consequence is, that with intentions very commonly of the purest kind, a man becomes a torment either to himself or his fellow-creatures. If he be of the melancholy cast (Dr Price),[1] he sits in silent grief, bewailing their blindness and depravity: if of the irascible (Dr Beattie),[1] he declaims with fury and virulence against all who differ from him; blowing up the coals of fanaticism, and branding with the charge of corruption and insincerity, every man who does not think, or profess to think, as he does.

If such a man happens to possess the advantages of style, his book may do a considerable deal of mischief before the nothingness of it is understood.

These principles, if such they can be called, it is more frequent to see applied to morals than to politics: but their influence extends itself to both. In politics, as well as morals, a man will be at least equally glad of a pretence for deciding any question in the manner that best pleases him, without the trouble of inquiry. If a man is an infallible judge of what is right and wrong in the actions of private individuals, why not in the measures to be observed by public men in the direction of such actions?[2] accordingly (not to mention other chimeras) I have more than once known the pretended law of nature set up in legislative debates, in opposition to arguments derived from the principle of utility.

Whether utility is actually the sole ground of all the approbation we ever bestow, is a different consideration

'But is it never, then, from any other considerations than those of utility, that we derive our notions of right and wrong?' I do not know: I do not care. Whether a moral sentiment can be originally conceived from any other source than a view of utility, is one question: whether upon examination and reflection it can, in point of fact, be actually persisted in and justified on any other ground, by a person reflecting within himself, is another: whether in point of right it can properly be justified on any other ground, by a person addressing himself to the community, is a third. The two first are questions of speculation: it matters not, comparatively speaking, how they are decided. The last is a question of practice: the decision of it is of as much importance as that of any can be.

'I feel in myself', (say you) 'a disposition to approve of such or such an action in a moral view: but this is not owing to any notions I have of its being a useful one to the community. I do not pretend to know whether it be an useful one or not: it may be, for aught I know, a mischievous one.' 'But is it then', (say I) 'a mischievous one? examine; and if you can make yourself sensible that it is so, then, if duty means any thing, that is, moral duty, it is your *duty* at least to abstain from it: and more than that, if it is what lies in

[1] These insertions have the same origin as those explained in 26 n. 2 above.

[2] The text as printed in 1780 reads 'of such actions of those individuals'. In the list of errata appended to the 1789 edition the deletion of the last three words is indicated; but the 1823 edition (i, 33n.) followed by the Bowring edition (i, 9n.), mistakenly reads 'of those actions'.

15. It is manifest, that the dictates of this principle will fre- *This prin-*
quently coincide with those of utility, though perhaps without *ciple will*
frequently
intending any such thing. Probably more frequently than not: and *coincide with*
that of utility
hence it is that the business of penal justice is carried on upon that
tolerable sort of footing upon which we see it carried on in common
at this day. For what more natural or more general ground of
hatred to a practice can there be, than the mischievousness of such
practice? What all men are exposed to suffer by, all men will be
disposed to hate. It is far yet, however, from being a constant
ground: for when a man suffers, it is not always that he knows what
it is he suffers by. A man may suffer grievously, for instance, by a
new tax, without being able to trace up the cause of his sufferings
to the injustice of some neighbour, who has eluded the payment of
an old one.

16. The principle of sympathy and antipathy is most apt to err *This prin-*
on the side of severity. It is for applying punishment in many *ciple is most*
apt to err on
cases which deserve none: in many cases which deserve some, it is *the side of*
severity
for applying more than they deserve. There is no incident imaginable, be it ever so trivial, and so remote from mischief, from which
this principle may not extract a ground of punishment. Any difference in taste: any difference in opinion: upon one subject as well
as upon another. No disagreement so trifling which perseverance
and altercation will not render serious. Each becomes in the other's
^dcont.

your power, and can be done without too great a sacrifice, to endeavour to
prevent it. It is not your cherishing the notion of it in your bosom, and giving
it the name of virtue, that will excuse you.'

'I feel in myself', (say you again) 'a disposition to detest such or such an
action in a moral view; but this is not owing to any notions I have of its being
a mischievous one to the community. I do not pretend to know whether it be
a mischievous one or not: it may be not a mischievous one: it may be, for aught
I know, an useful one.'—'May it indeed?' (say I) 'an useful one? but let me
tell you then, that unless duty, and right and wrong, be just what you please
to make them, if it really be not a mischievous one, and any body has a mind
to do it, it is no duty of yours, but, on the contrary, it would be very wrong
in you, to take upon you to prevent him: detest it within yourself as much
as you please; that may be a very good reason (unless it be also a useful one)
for your not doing it yourself: but if you go about, by word or deed, to do any
thing to hinder him, or make him suffer for it, it is you, and not he, that have
done wrong: it is not your setting yourself to blame his conduct, or branding
it with the name of vice, that will make him culpable, or you blameless. Therefore, if you can make yourself content that he shall be of one mind, and you of
another, about that matter, and so continue, it is well: but if nothing will serve
you, but that you and he must needs be of the same mind, I'll tell you what
you have to do: it is for you to get the better of your antipathy, not for him to
truckle to it.'

eyes an enemy, and, if laws permit, a criminal.[e] This is one of the

[e] King James the First of England had conceived a violent antipathy against Arians: two of whom he burnt.[*1] This gratification he procured himself without much difficulty: the notions of the times were favourable to it. He wrote a furious book against Vorstius, for being what was called an Arminian: for Vorstius was at a distance.[2] He also wrote a furious book, called 'A Counterblast to Tobacco', against the use of that drug, which Sir Walter Raleigh had then lately introduced.[3] Had the notions of the times co-operated with him, he would have burnt the Anabaptist and the smoker of tobacco in the same fire. However he had the satisfaction of putting Raleigh to death afterwards, though for another crime.

Disputes concerning the comparative excellence of French and Italian music have occasioned very serious bickerings at Paris. One of the parties would not have been sorry (says Mr D'Alembert[†])[4] to have brought government into the quarrel. Pretences were sought after and urged. Long before that, a dispute of like nature, and of at least equal warmth, had been kindled at London upon the comparative merits of two composers at London; where riots between the approvers and disapprovers of a new play are, at this day, not unfrequent. The ground of quarrel between the Big-endians and the Little-endians in the fable,[5] was not more frivolous than many an one which has laid empires desolate. In Russia, it is said, there was a time when some thousands of persons lost their lives in a quarrel, in which the government had taken part, about the number of fingers to be used in making the sign of the cross. This was in days of yore: the ministers of Catherine II[‡] are better *instructed*[6] than to

* Hume's Hist. vol. 6.
† Melanges Essai sur la Liberté de la Musique.
‡ Instruct. art. 474, 475, 476.

[1] Cf. David Hume, *History of Great Britain*, 1773 edn., v, 163: 'Stowe says, that these Arians were offered their pardon at the stake, if they would merit it by a recantation.' The executions took place in 1612.

[2] Conrad Vorst (1569–1622) was accused of Arminianism after publishing in 1610 his *Tractatus Theologicus de Deo*. James I had the book burnt in England and in 1612 published *A Declaration concerning the Proceedings with the States Generall, of the United Provinces of the Low Countreys, in the Cause of D. Conradus Vorstius.*

[3] James I's *A Counterblaste to Tobacco* was published in 1604.

[4] Cf. *Oeuvres Philosophiques, Historiques et Littéraires de d'Alembert*, 1805, iii, 337–409.   [5] i.e. Swift's *Gulliver's Travels.*

[6] Bentham had long been interested in Catherine the Great's *Instructions to the Commissioners for composing a New Code of Laws* (1767; English translation, 1768): cf. *Correspondence*, in *CW*, ii, 99 and n. 4. The articles he refers to here read as follows:—

'474. A Roman Governor wrote Word to an Emperor, that a Process was preparing against a Judge for High-treason, who had pronounced a Sentence contrary to the Ordinances of that Emperor; the Emperor replied, that, in his reign the Crimes of indirect High-treason were not to be admitted in the Courts of Judicature.

'475. There was a Law among the Romans, which ordained, that whoever should throw anything, though by Accident, against the Images of the Emperors, should be punished as guilty of High-treason.

'476. There was a Law in England, which declared all those guilty of High-treason who should foretell the Death of the King. In the last illness of that King, no Physician dared to inform him of the Danger he was in: We may presume, that they acted in the same Manner with respect to the cure.'

Cf. W. F. Reddaway, *Documents of Catherine the Great* (1931), 286.

circumstances by which the human race is distinguished (not much indeed to its advantage) from the brute creation.

17. It is not, however, by any means unexampled for this principle to err on the side of lenity. A near and perceptible mischief moves antipathy. A remote and imperceptible mischief, though not less real, has no effect. Instances in proof of this will occur in numbers in the course of the work.[f] It would be breaking in upon the order of it to give them here.

But errs, in some instances, on the side of lenity

18. It may be wondered, perhaps, that in all this while no mention has been made of the *theological* principle; meaning that principle which professes to recur for the standard of right and wrong to the will of God. But the case is, this is not in fact a distinct principle. It is never any thing more or less than one or other of the three before-mentioned principles presenting itself under another shape. The *will* of God here meant cannot be his revealed will, as contained in the sacred writings: for that is a system which nobody ever thinks of recurring to at this time of day, for the details of political administration: and even before it can be applied to the details of private conduct, it is universally allowed, by the most eminent divines of all persuasions, to stand in need of pretty ample interpretations; else to what use are the works of those divines? And for the guidance of these interpretations, it is also allowed, that some other standard must be assumed. The will then which is meant on this occasion, is that which may be called the *presumptive* will: that is to say, that which is presumed to be his will on account of the conformity of its dictates to those of some other principle. What then may be this other principle? it must be one or other of the three mentioned above: for there cannot, as we have seen, be any more. It is plain, therefore, that, setting revelation out of the question, no light can ever be thrown upon the standard of right and wrong, by any thing that can be said upon the question, what is God's will. We may be perfectly sure, indeed, that whatever is right is conformable to the will of God: but so far is that from answering the purpose of showing us what is right, that it is necessary to know first whether a thing is right, in order to know from thence whether it be conformable to the will of God.[g]

The theological principle, what— not a separate principle

take any other part in such disputes, than that of preventing the parties concerned from doing one another a mischief.

[f] See Ch. XVI (Division) par. 42, 44.

[g] The principle of theology refers every thing to God's pleasure. But what is God's pleasure? God does not, he confessedly does not now, either speak or write to us. How then are we to know what is his pleasure? By observing

The principle of theology reducible to one or another of the other three principles

Antipathy, let the actions it dictates be ever so right, is never of itself a right ground of action

19. There are two things which are very apt to be confounded, but which it imports us carefully to distinguish:—the motive or cause, which, by operating on the mind of an individual,[1] is productive of any act: and the ground or reason which warrants a legislator, or other by-stander, in regarding that act with an eye of approbation. When the act happens, in the particular instance in question, to be productive of effects which we approve of, much more if we happen to observe that the same motive may frequently be productive, in other instances, of the like effects, we are apt to transfer our approbation to the motive itself, and to assume, as the just ground for the approbation we bestow on the act, the circumstance of its originating from that motive. It is in this way that the sentiment of antipathy has often been considered as a just ground of action. Antipathy, for instance, in such or such a case, is the cause of an action which is attended with good effects: but this does not make it a right ground of action in that case, any more than in any other. Still farther. Not only the effects are good, but the agent sees beforehand that they will be so. This may make the action indeed a perfectly right action: but it does not make antipathy a right ground of action. For the same sentiment of antipathy, if implicitly deferred to, may be, and very frequently is, productive of the very worst effects. Antipathy, therefore, can never be a right ground of action. No more, therefore, can resentment, which, as will be seen more particularly hereafter, is but a modification of antipathy. The only right ground of action, that can possibly subsist, is, after all, the consideration of utility, which, if it is a right principle of action, and of approbation, in any one case, is so in every other. Other principles in abundance, that is, other motives, may be the reasons why such and such an act *has* been done: that is, the reasons or

what is our own pleasure, and pronouncing it to be his. Accordingly, what is called the pleasure of God, is and must necessarily be (revelation apart) neither more nor less than the good pleasure of the person, whoever he be, who is pronouncing what he believes, or pretends, to be God's pleasure. How know you it to be God's pleasure that such or such an act should be abstained from? whence come you even to suppose as much? 'Because the engaging in it would, I imagine, be prejudicial upon the whole to the happiness of mankind'; says the partisan of the principle of utility: 'Because the commission of it is attended with a gross and sensual, or at least with a trifling and transient satisfaction'; says the partisan of the principle of asceticism: 'Because I detest the thoughts of it; and I cannot, neither ought I to be called upon to tell why'; says he who proceeds upon the principle of antipathy. In the words of one or other of these must that person necessarily answer (revelation apart) who professes to take for his standard the will of God.

[1] The 1789 edition here reads 'by operating in a man's mind'.

32

causes of its being done: but it is this alone that can be the reason why it might or ought to have been done. Antipathy or resentment requires always to be regulated, to prevent its doing mischief: to be regulated by what? always by the principle of utility. The principle of utility neither requires nor admits of any other regulator than itself.

CHAPTER III

OF THE FOUR SANCTIONS OR SOURCES OF PAIN AND PLEASURE

Connexion of this chapter with the preceding

1. It has been shown that the happiness of the individuals, of whom a community is composed, that is their pleasures and their security, is the end and the sole end which the legislator ought to have in view: the sole standard, in conformity to which each individual ought, as far as depends upon the legislator, to be *made* to fashion his behaviour. But whether it be this or any thing else that is to be *done*, there is nothing by which a man can ultimately be *made* to do it, but either pain or pleasure. Having taken a general view of these two grand objects (viz. pleasure, and what comes to the same thing, immunity from pain) in the character of *final* causes; it will be necessary to take a view of pleasure and pain itself, in the character of *efficient* causes or means.

Four sanctions or sources of pleasure and pain

2. There are four distinguishable sources from which pleasure and pain are in use to flow: considered separately, they may be termed the *physical*, the *political*, the *moral*, and the *religious*: and inasmuch as the pleasures and pains belonging to each of them are capable of giving a binding force to any law or rule of conduct, they may all of them be termed *sanctions*.[a]

[a] *Sanctio*, in Latin, was used to signify the *act of binding*, and, by a common grammatical transition, *any thing which serves to bind a man*: to wit, to the observance of such or such a mode of conduct. According to a Latin grammarian,* the import of the word is derived by rather a far-fetched process (such as those commonly are, and in a great measure indeed must be, by which intellectual ideas are derived from sensible ones) from the word *sanguis*, blood: because, among the Romans, with a view to inculcate into the people a persuasion that such or such a mode of conduct would be rendered obligatory upon a man by the force of what I call the religious sanction (that is, that he would be made to suffer by the extraordinary interposition of some superior being, if he failed to observe the mode of conduct in question) certain ceremonies were contrived by the priests: in the course of which ceremonies the blood of victims was made use of.

A sanction then is a source of obligatory powers or *motives*: that is, of *pains*

* Servius. See Ainsworth's Dict. ad verbum *Sanctio*.[1]

[1] Robert Ainsworth (1660–1743) published his Latin dictionary between 1714 and 1736: it went through many later editions. The derivation of *sancio* is given as: 'à sanguis, quod fuso sanguine hostiae aliquid sanciretur—Servius'. Bentham's reference to the noun *sanctio* is perhaps a slip or misprint for the verbal form.

3. If it be in the present life, and from the ordinary course of *1. The physical sanction* nature, not purposely modified by the interposition of the will of any human being, nor by any extraordinary interposition of any superior invisible being, that the pleasure or the pain takes place or is expected, it may be said to issue from or to belong to the *physical sanction.*

4. If at the hands of a *particular* person or set of persons in the *2. The political[1]* community, who under names correspondent to that of *judge*, are chosen for the particular purpose of dispensing it, according to the will of the sovereign or supreme ruling power in the state, it may be said to issue from the *political sanction.*

5. If at the hands of such *chance* persons in the community, as *3. The moral or popular* the party in question may happen in the course of his life to have concerns with, according to each man's spontaneous disposition, and not according to any settled or concerted rule, it may be said to issue from the *moral* or *popular sanction.*[b]

6. If from the immediate hand of a superior invisible being, *4. The religious* either in the present life, or in a future, it may be said to issue from the *religious sanction.*

7. Pleasures or pains which may be expected to issue from the *physical*, *political*, or *moral* sanctions, must all of them be expected to be experienced, if ever, in the *present* life: those which may be expected to issue from the *religious* sanction, may be expected to be experienced either in the *present* life or in a *future*.

The pleasures and pains which belong to the religious sanction, may regard either the present life or a future

8. Those which can be experienced in the present life, can of course be no others than such as human nature in the course of the present life is susceptible of: and from each of these sources may flow

Those which regard the present life, from which soever source they flow, differ only in the circumstances of their production

and *pleasures*; which, according as they are connected with such or such modes of conduct, operate, and are indeed the only things which can operate, as *motives*. See Ch. x (Motives).

[b] (Moral Sanction).[2] Better termed *popular*, as more directly indicative of its constituent cause; as likewise of its relation to the more common phrase *public opinion*, in French *opinion publique*, the name there given to that tutelary power, of which of late so much is said, and by which so much is done. The latter appellation is however unhappy and inexpressive; since if *opinion* is material, it is only in virtue of the influence it exercises over action, through the medium of the affections and the will.

[1] 1823 *'politic'*.

[2] This footnote was an addition made in January 1789. When it was inserted in the 1823 edition (i, 43n.) the bracketed words 'Moral Sanction' (indicating, in accordance with Bentham's common practice, the subject of the note) were omitted, presumably because the text at the end of para. 5 (and the corresponding marginal heading) had been emended by inserting the words 'or popular' after 'moral'.

all the pleasures or pains of which, in the course of the present life, human nature is susceptible. With regard to these then (with which alone we have in this place any concern) those of them which belong to any one of those sanctions, differ not ultimately in kind from those which belong to any one of the other three: the only difference there is among them lies in the circumstances that accompany their production. A suffering which befalls a man in the natural and spontaneous course of things, shall be styled, for instance, a *calamity*; in which case, if it be supposed to befall him through any imprudence of his, it may be styled a punishment issuing from the *physical* sanction. Now this same suffering, if inflicted by the law, will be what is commonly called a *punishment*; if incurred for want of any friendly assistance, which the misconduct, or supposed misconduct, of the sufferer has occasioned to be withholden, a punishment issuing from the *moral* sanction; if through the immediate interposition of a particular providence, a punishment issuing from the *religious* sanction.

Example

9. A man's goods, or his person, are consumed by fire. If this happened to him by what is called an accident, it was a *calamity*: if by reason of his own imprudence (for instance, from his neglecting to put his candle out) it may be styled a punishment of the *physical* sanction: if it happened to him by the sentence of the political magistrate, a punishment belonging to the *political* sanction; that is, what is commonly called a *punishment*: if for want of any assistance which his *neighbour* withheld from him out of some dislike to his *moral* character, a punishment of the *moral* sanction: if by an immediate act of *God's* displeasure, manifested on account of some *sin* committed by him, or through any distraction of mind, occasioned by the dread of such displeasure, a punishment of the *religious* sanction.[c]

Those which regard a future life are not specifically known

10. As to such of the pleasures and pains belonging to the religious sanction, as regard a future life, of what kind these may be we cannot know. These lie not open to our observation. During the present life they are matter only of expectation: and, whether that expectation be derived from natural or revealed religion, the particular kind of pleasure or pain, if it be different from all those which lie open to our observation, is what we can have no idea of. The best ideas we can obtain of such pains and pleasures are altogether

---

[c] A suffering conceived to befall a man by the immediate act of God, as above, is often, for shortness sake, called a *judgment*: instead of saying, a suffering inflicted on him in consequence of a special judgment formed, and resolution thereupon taken, by the Deity.

unliquidated in point of quality. In what other respects our ideas of them *may* be liquidated will be considered in another place.[d]

11. Of these four sanctions the physical is altogether, we may observe, the ground-work of the political and the moral: so is it also of the religious, in as far as the latter bears relation to the present life. It is included in each of those other three. This may operate in any case, (that is, any of the pains or pleasures belonging to it may operate) independently of *them*: none of *them* can operate but by means of this. In a word, the powers of nature may operate of themselves; but neither the magistrate, nor men at large, *can* operate, nor is God in the case in question *supposed* to operate, but through the powers of nature.

The physical sanction included in each of the other three

12. For these four objects, which in their nature have so much in common, it seemed of use to find a common name. It seemed of use, in the first place, for the convenience of giving a name to certain pleasures and pains, for which a name equally characteristic could hardly otherwise have been found: in the second place, for the sake of holding up the efficacy of certain moral forces, the influence of which is apt not to be sufficiently attended to. Does the political sanction exert an influence over the conduct of mankind? The moral, the religious sanctions do so too. In every inch of his career are the operations of the political magistrate liable to be aided or impeded by these two foreign powers: who, one or other of them, or both, are sure to be either his rivals or his allies. Does it happen to him to leave them out in his calculations? he will be sure almost to find himself mistaken in the result. Of all this we shall find abundant proofs in the sequel of this work. It behoves him, therefore, to have them continually before his eyes; and that under such a name as exhibits the relation they bear to his own purposes and designs.

Use of this chapter

[d] See Ch. XIII (Cases unmeet) par. 2. Note.

CHAPTER IV

VALUE OF A LOT OF PLEASURE OR PAIN, HOW TO BE MEASURED

Use of this chapter

1. Pleasures then, and the avoidance of pains, are the *ends* which the legislator has in view: it behoves him therefore to understand their *value*. Pleasures and pains are the *instruments* he has to work with: it behoves him therefore to understand their force, which is again, in another point of view,[1] their value.

Circumstances to be taken into the account in estimating the value of a pleasure or pain considered with reference to a single person, and by itself

2. To a person considered *by himself*, the value of a pleasure or pain considered *by itself*, will be greater or less, according to the four following circumstances[a]:

1. Its *intensity*.
2. Its *duration*.
3. Its *certainty* or *uncertainty*.
4. Its *propinquity* or *remoteness*.

—considered as connected with other pleasures or pains

3. These are the circumstances which are to be considered in estimating a pleasure or a pain considered each of them by itself. But when the value of any pleasure or pain is considered for the

[a] These circumstances have since been denominated *elements* or *dimensions* of *value* in a pleasure or a pain.

Not long after the publication of the first edition, the following memoriter verses were framed, in the view of lodging more effectually, in the memory, these points, on which the whole fabric of morals and legislation may be seen to rest.

> *Intense, long, certain, speedy, fruitful, pure—*
> Such marks in *pleasures* and in *pains* endure.
> Such pleasures seek, if *private* be thy end:
> If it be *public*, wide let them *extend*.
> Such *pains* avoid, whichever be thy view:
> If pains *must* come, let them *extend* to few.[2]

[1] The words 'in another point of view' were substituted for 'in other words' in the sheet of corrections and additions printed in 1783 and appended to the 1789 edition, but were overlooked on this occasion in 1823 (i, 49). The correction was made in the Bowring edition (i, 16).

[2] Note added in the 1823 edition. The mnemonic verses, headed 'Memoriter Verses, expressive of the Elements or Dimensions of Value in Pleasures and Pains' were written by Bentham at the end of his copy of the 1789 edition, now in the British Museum (see above, Introduction, xl). They are there dated 'A° 1780', so that Bentham's reference in the present note to their composition 'not long after the *publication* of the first edition' is probably a slip for 'printing'.

purpose of estimating the tendency of any *act* by which it is produced, there are two other circumstances to be taken into the account; these are,

5. Its *fecundity*, or the chance it has of being followed by sensations of the *same* kind: that is, pleasures, if it be a pleasure: pains, if it be a pain.

6. Its *purity*, or the chance it has of *not* being followed by sensations of the *opposite* kind: that is, pains, if it be a pleasure: pleasures, if it be a pain.

These two last, however, are in strictness scarcely to be deemed properties of the pleasure or the pain itself; they are not, therefore, in strictness to be taken into the account of the value of that pleasure or that pain. They are in strictness to be deemed properties only of the act, or other event, by which such pleasure or pain has been produced; and accordingly are only to be taken into the account of the tendency of such act or such event.

4. To a *number* of persons, with reference to each of whom the value of a pleasure or a pain is considered, it will be greater or less, according to seven circumstances: to wit, the six preceding ones; viz. *—considered with reference to a number of persons*

1. Its *intensity*.
2. Its *duration*.
3. Its *certainty* or *uncertainty*.
4. Its *propinquity* or *remoteness*.
5. Its *fecundity*.
6. Its *purity*.

And one other; to wit:

7. Its *extent*; that is, the number of persons to whom it *extends*; or (in other words) who are affected by it.

5. To take an exact account then of the general tendency of any act, by which the interests of a community are affected, proceed as follows. Begin with any one person of those whose interests seem most immediately to be affected by it: and take an account, *Process for estimating the tendency of any act or event*

1. Of the value of each distinguishable *pleasure* which appears to be produced by it in the *first* instance.

2. Of the value of each *pain* which appears to be produced by it in the *first* instance.

3. Of the value of each pleasure which appears to be produced by it *after* the first. This constitutes the *fecundity* of the first *pleasure* and the *impurity* of the first *pain*.

4. Of the value of each *pain* which appears to be produced by it

after the first. This constitutes the *fecundity* of the first *pain*, and the *impurity* of the first pleasure.

5. Sum up all the values of all the *pleasures* on the one side, and those of all the *pains* on the other. The balance, if it be on the side of pleasure, will give the *good* tendency of the act upon the whole, with respect to the interests of that *individual* person; if on the side of pain, the *bad* tendency of it upon the whole.

6. Take an account of the *number* of persons whose interests appear to be concerned; and repeat the above process with respect to each. *Sum up* the numbers expressive of the degrees of *good* tendency, which the act has, with respect to each individual, in regard to whom the tendency of it is *good* upon the whole: do this again with respect to each individual, in regard to whom the tendency of it is *good* upon the whole: do this again with respect to each individual, in regard to whom the tendency of it is *bad* upon the whole. Take the *balance*; which, if on the side of *pleasure*, will give the general *good tendency* of the act, with respect to the total number or community of individuals concerned; if on the side of pain, the general *evil tendency*, with respect to the same community.

Use of the foregoing process

6. It is not to be expected that this process should be strictly pursued previously to every moral judgment, or to every legislative or judicial operation. It may, however, be always kept in view: and as near as the process actually pursued on these occasions approaches to it, so near will such process approach to the character of an exact one.

The same process applicable to good and evil, profit and mischief, and all other modifications of pleasure and pain

7. The same process is alike applicable to pleasure and pain, in whatever shape they appear: and by whatever denomination they are distinguished: to pleasure, whether it be called *good* (which is properly the cause or instrument of pleasure) or *profit* (which is distant pleasure, or the cause or instrument of distant pleasure,) or *convenience*, or *advantage, benefit, emolument, happiness*, and so forth: to pain, whether it be called *evil*, (which corresponds to *good*) or *mischief*, or *inconvenience*, or *disadvantage*, or *loss*, or *unhappiness*, and so forth.

Conformity of men's practice to this theory

8. Nor is this a novel and unwarranted, any more than it is a useless theory. In all this there is nothing but what the practice of mankind, wheresoever they have a clear view of their own interest, is perfectly conformable to. An article of property, an estate in land, for instance, is valuable, on what account? On account of the pleasures of all kinds which it enables a man to produce, and what comes to the same thing the pains of all kinds which it enables him to avert. But the value of such an article of property is universally

understood to rise or fall according to the length or shortness of the time which a man has in it: the certainty or uncertainty of its coming into possession: and the nearness or remoteness of the time at which, if at all, it is to come into possession. As to the *intensity* of the pleasures which a man may derive from it, this is never thought of, because it depends upon the use which each particular person may come to make of it; which cannot be estimated till the particular pleasures he may come to derive from it, or the particular pains he may come to exclude by means of it, are brought to view. For the same reason, neither does he think of the *fecundity* or *purity* of those pleasures.

Thus much for pleasure and pain, happiness and unhappiness, in *general*. We come now to consider the several particular kinds of pain and pleasure.

CHAPTER V

PLEASURES AND PAINS,
THEIR KINDS

Pleasures and pains are either, 1. Simple: or, 2. Complex

1. Having represented what belongs to all sorts of pleasures and pains alike, we come now to exhibit, each by itself, the several sorts of pains and pleasures. Pains and pleasures may be called by one general word, interesting perceptions. Interesting perceptions are either simple or complex. The simple ones are those which cannot any one of them be resolved into more: complex are those which are resolvable into divers simple ones. A complex interesting perception may accordingly be composed either, 1. Of pleasures alone: 2. Of pains alone: or, 3. Of a pleasure or pleasures, and a pain or pains together. What determines a lot of pleasure, for example, to be regarded as one complex pleasure, rather than as divers simple ones, is the nature of the exciting cause. Whatever pleasures are excited all at once by the action of the same cause, are apt to be looked upon as constituting all together but one pleasure.

The simple pleasures enumerated

2. The several simple pleasures of which human nature is susceptible, seem to be as follows: 1. The pleasures of sense. 2. The pleasures of wealth. 3. The pleasures of skill. 4. The pleasures of amity. 5. The pleasures of a good name. 6. The pleasures of power. 7. The pleasures of piety. 8. The pleasures of benevolence. 9. The pleasures of malevolence. 10. The pleasures of memory. 11. The pleasures of imagination. 12. The pleasures of expectation. 13. The pleasures dependent on association. 14. The pleasures of relief.

The simple pains enu-merated

3. The several simple pains seem to be as follows: 1. The pains of privation. 2. The pains of the senses. 3. The pains of awkwardness. 4. The pains of enmity. 5. The pains of an ill name. 6. The pains of piety. 7. The pains of benevolence. 8. The pains of malevolence. 9. The pains of the memory. 10. The pains of the imagination. 11. The pains of expectation. 12. The pains dependent on associa-tion.[a][1]

Analytical view, why none given

[a] The catalogue here given, is what seemed to be a complete list of the several simple pleasures and pains of which human nature is susceptible: insomuch, that if, upon any occasion whatsoever, a man feels pleasure or pain, it is either referable at once to some one or other of these kinds, or resolvable into such as are. It might perhaps have been a satisfaction to the reader, to have seen

[1] The last item in this list is an addition made in the 1823 edition.

4. (1) The pleasures of sense seem to be as follows: 1. The plea- *Pleasures of* sures of the taste or palate; including whatever pleasures are exper- *sense enu-* ienced in satisfying the appetites of hunger and thirst. 2. The *merated* pleasure of intoxication.[1] 3. The pleasures of the organ of smelling. 4. The pleasures of the touch. 5. The simple pleasures of the ear; independent of association. 6. The simple pleasures of the eye; independent of association. 7. The pleasure of the sexual[2] sense. 8. The pleasure of health: or, the internal pleasurable feeling or flow of spirits (as it is called,) which accompanies a state of full health and vigour; especially at times of moderate bodily exertion. 9. The pleasures of novelty: or, the pleasures derived from the gratification of the appetite of curiosity, by the application of new objects to any of the senses.[b]

5. (2) By the pleasures of wealth may be meant those pleasures *Pleasures of* which a man is apt to derive from the consciousness of possessing *wealth, which* any article or articles which stand in the list of instruments of enjoy- *are either of* ment or security, and more particularly at the time of his first ac- *acquisition* quiring them; at which time the pleasure may be styled a pleasure *or of posses-* of gain or a pleasure of acquisition: at other times a pleasure of *sion* possession.

(3) The pleasures of skill, as exercised upon particular objects, *3. Pleasures* are those which accompany the application of such particular *of skill* instruments of enjoyment to their uses, as cannot be so applied without a greater or less share of difficulty or exertion.[c]

6. (4) The pleasures of amity, or self-recommendation, are the *4. Pleasures* pleasures that may accompany the persuasion of a man's being *of amity*

an analytical view of the subject, taken upon an exhaustive plan, for the pur- pose of demonstrating the catalogue to be what it purports to be, a complete one. The catalogue is in fact the result of such an analysis; which, however, I thought it better to discard at present, as being of too metaphysical a cast, and not strictly within the limits of this design. See Ch. XIII (Cases unmeet) Par. 2. Note.

[b] There are also pleasures of novelty, excited by the appearance of new ideas: these are pleasures of the imagination. See infra 13.[3]

[c] For instance, the pleasure of being able to gratify the sense of hearing, by singing, or performing upon any musical instrument. The pleasure thus obtained, is a thing super-added to, and perfectly distinguishable from, that which a man enjoys from hearing another person perform in the same manner.

[1] This item was an insertion proposed in the 1783 sheet of corrections and addi- tions, and made in 1823, the numbering of subsequent items being altered according- ly.

[2] Here and in all subsequent instances, with one exception, the 1789 text reads 'venereal' for 1823 'sexual'.

[3] Note added in 1783.

in the acquisition or the possession of the good-will of such or such assignable person or persons in particular: or, as the phrase is, of being upon good terms with him or them: and as a fruit of it, of his being in a way to have the benefit of their spontaneous and gratuitous services.

5. Pleasures of a good name

7. (5) The pleasures of a good name are the pleasures that accompany the persuasion of a man's being in the acquisition or the possession of the good-will of the world about him; that is, of such members of society as he is likely to have concerns with; and as a means of it, either their love or their esteem, or both: and as a fruit of it, of his being in the way to have the benefit of their spontaneous and gratuitous services. These may likewise be called the pleasures of good repute, the pleasures of honour, or the pleasures of the moral sanction.[d]

6. Pleasures of power

8. (6) The pleasures of power are the pleasures that accompany the persuasion of a man's being in a condition to dispose people, by means of their hopes and fears, to give him the benefit of their services: that is, by the hope of some service, or by the fear of some disservice, that he may be in the way to render them.

7. Pleasures of piety

9. (7) The pleasures of piety are the pleasures that accompany the belief of a man's being in the acquisition or in possession of the good-will or favour of the Supreme Being: and as a fruit of it, of his being in a way of enjoying pleasures to be received by God's special appointment, either in this life, or in a life to come. These may also be called the pleasures of religion, the pleasures of a religious disposition, or the pleasures of the religious sanction.[e]

8. Pleasures of benevolence or good-will

10. (8) The pleasures of benevolence are the pleasures resulting from the view of any pleasures supposed to be possessed by the beings who may be the objects of benevolence; to wit, the sensitive beings we are acquainted with; under which are commonly included, 1. The Supreme Being. 2. Human beings. 3. Other animals. These may also be called the pleasures of good-will, the pleasures of sympathy, or the pleasures of the benevolent or social affections.

9. Pleasures of malevolence or ill-will

11. (9) The pleasures of malevolence are the pleasures resulting from the view of any pain supposed to be suffered by the beings who may become the objects of malevolence: to wit, 1. Human beings. 2. Other animals. These may also be styled the pleasures of ill-will, the pleasures of the irascible appetite, the pleasures of antipathy, or the pleasures of the malevolent or dissocial affections.

[d] See Ch. III (Sanctions).
[e] See Ch. III (Sanctions).

12. (10) The pleasures of the memory are the pleasures which, after having enjoyed such and such pleasures, or even in some case after having suffered such and such pains, a man will now and then experience, at recollecting them exactly in the order and in the circumstances in which they were actually enjoyed or suffered. These derivative pleasures may of course be distinguished into as many species as there are of original perceptions, from whence they may be copied. They may also be styled pleasures of simple recollection.

10. Pleasures of the memory

13. (11) The pleasures of the imagination are the pleasures which may be derived from the contemplation of any such pleasures as may happen to be suggested by the memory, but in a different order, and accompanied by different groups of circumstances. These may accordingly be referred to any one of the three cardinal points of time, present, past, or future. It is evident they may admit of as many distinctions as those of the former class.

11. Pleasures of the imagination

14. (12) The pleasures of expectation are the pleasures that result from the contemplation of any sort of pleasure, referred to time *future*, and accompanied with the sentiment of *belief*. These also may admit of the same distinctions.[f]

12. Pleasures of expectation

15. (13) The pleasures of association are the pleasures which certain objects or incidents may happen to afford, not of themselves, but merely in virtue of some association they have contracted in the mind with certain objects or incidents which are in themselves pleasurable. Such is the case, for instance, with the pleasure of skill, when afforded by such a set of incidents as compose a game of chess. This derives its pleasurable quality from its association partly with the pleasures of skill, as exercised in the production of incidents pleasurable of themselves: partly from its association with the pleasures of power. Such is the case also with the pleasure of good luck, when afforded by such incidents as compose the game of hazard, or any other game of chance, when played at for nothing. This derives its pleasurable quality from its association with one of the pleasures of wealth; to wit, with the pleasure of acquiring it.

13. Pleasures depending on association

16. (14) Farther on we shall see pains grounded upon pleasures; in like manner may we now see pleasures grounded upon pains. To the catalogue of pleasures may accordingly be added the pleasures

14. Pleasures of relief

[f] In contradistinction to these, all other pleasures may be termed pleasures of *enjoyment*.[1]

[1] Note added in 1783.

of *relief*: or, the pleasures which a man experiences when, after he has been enduring a pain of any kind for a certain time, it comes to cease, or to abate. These may of course be distinguished into as many species as there are of pains: and may give rise to so many pleasures of memory, of imagination, and of expectation.

1. Pains of privation

17. (1) Pains of privation are the pains that may result from the thought of not possessing in the time present any of the several kinds of pleasures. Pains of privation may accordingly be resolved into as many kinds as there are of pleasures to which they may correspond, and from the absence whereof they may be derived.

These include, (1) Pains of desire

18. There are three sorts of pains which are only so many modifications of the several pains of privation. When the enjoyment of any particular pleasure happens to be particularly desired, but without any expectation approaching to assurance, the pain of privation which thereupon results takes a particular name, and is called the pain of *desire*, or of unsatisfied desire.

(2) Pains of disappointment

19. Where the enjoyment happens to have been looked for with a degree of expectation approaching to assurance, and that expectation is made suddenly to cease, it is called a pain of disappointment.

(3) Pains of regret

20. A pain of privation takes the name of a pain of regret in two cases: 1. Where it is grounded on the memory of a pleasure, which having been once enjoyed, appears not likely to be enjoyed again: 2. Where it is grounded on the idea of a pleasure, which was never actually enjoyed, nor perhaps so much as expected, but which might have been enjoyed (it is supposed,) had such or such a contingency happened, which, in fact, did not happen.

2. Pains of the senses

21. (2) The several pains of the senses seem to be as follows: 1. The pains of hunger and thirst: or the disagreeable sensations produced by the want of suitable substances which need at times to be applied to the alimentary canal. 2. The pains of the taste: or the disagreeable sensations produced by the application of various substances to the palate, and other superior parts of the same canal. 3. The pains of the organ of smell: or the disagreeable sensations produced by the effluvia of various substances when applied to that organ. 4. The pains of the touch: or the disagreeable sensations produced by the application of various substances to the skin. 5. The simple pains of the hearing: or the disagreeable sensations excited in the organ of that sense by various kinds of sounds: independently (as before,) of association. 6. The simple pains of the sight: or the disagreeable sensations if any such there be, that may be excited in the organ of that sense by visible images, independent of the principle of association. 7.[g] The pains resulting from excessive heat or cold, unless these be referable to the touch. 8. The pains of disease: or the acute and uneasy sensations resulting from the several diseases and indispositions to which human nature is liable. 9. The pain of exertion, whether bodily or mental: or the uneasy sensation which is apt to accompany any intense effort, whether of mind or body.

22. (3)[h] The pains of awkwardness are the pains which sometimes result from the unsuccessful endeavour to apply any particular instruments of enjoyment or security to their uses, or from the difficulty a man experiences in applying them.[i]

3. Pains of awkwardness

23. (4) The pains of enmity are the pains that may accompany the persuasion of a man's being obnoxious to the ill-will of such or such an assignable person or persons in particular: or, as the phrase is, of being upon ill terms with him or them: and, in consequence, of being obnoxious to certain pains of some sort or other, of which he may be the cause.

4. Pains of enmity

24. (5) The pains of an ill-name, are the pains that accompany the persuasion of a man's being obnoxious, or in a way to be obnoxious to the ill-will of the world about him. These may likewise be called the pains of ill-repute, the pains of dishonour, or the pains of the moral sanction.[j]

5. Pains of an ill name

[g] The pleasure of the sexual sense seems to have no positive pain to correspond to it: it has only a pain of privation, or pain of the mental class, the pain of unsatisfied desire. If any positive pain of body result from the want of such indulgence, it belongs to the head of pains of disease.

No positive pains correspond to the pleasure of the sexual sense

[h] The pleasures of novelty have no positive pains corresponding to them. The pain which a man experiences when he is in the condition of not knowing what to do with himself, that pain, which in French is expressed by a single word *ennui*, is a pain of privation: a pain resulting from the absence, not only of all the pleasures of novelty, but of all kinds of pleasure whatsoever.

No positive pains correspond to the pleasure of novelty

The pleasures of wealth have also no positive pains corresponding to them: the only pains opposed to them are pains of privation. If any positive pains result from the want of wealth, they are referable to some other class of positive pains; principally to those of the senses. From the want of food, for instance, result the pains of hunger; from the want of clothing, the pains of cold; and so forth.

–nor to those of wealth

[i] It may be a question, perhaps, whether this be a positive pain of itself, or whether it be nothing more than a pain of privation, resulting from the consciousness of a want of skill. It is, however, but a question of words, nor does it matter which way it be determined.

Is this a distinct positive pain, or only a pain of privation?

[j] In as far as a man's fellow-creatures are supposed to be determined by any event not to regard him with any degree of esteem or *good* will, or to regard him with a less degree of esteem or *good* will than they would otherwise; not to do him any sorts of *good* offices, or not to do him so many *good* offices as they would otherwise; the pain resulting from such consideration may be

The positive pains of an ill name, and the pains of privation, opposed to the pleasures of a good name, run into one another

6. Pains of piety

25. (6)[k] The pains of piety are the pains that accompany the belief of a man's being obnoxious to the displeasure of the Supreme Being: and in consequence to certain pains to be inflicted by his especial appointment, either in this life or in a life to come. These may also be called the pains of religion; the pains of a religious disposition; or the pains of the religious sanction. When the belief is looked upon as well-grounded, these pains are commonly called religious terrors; when looked upon as ill-grounded, superstitious terrors.[1]

7. Pains of benevolence

26. (7) The pains of benevolence are the pains resulting from the view of any pains supposed to be endured by other beings. These may also be called the pains of good-will, of sympathy, or the pains of the benevolent or social affections.

8. Pains of malevolence

27. (8) The pains of malevolence are the pains resulting from the view of any pleasures supposed to be enjoyed by any beings who happen to be the objects of a man's displeasure. These may also be styled the pains of ill-will, of antipathy, or the pains of the malevolent or dissocial affections.

9. Pains of the memory

28. (9) The pains of the memory may be grounded on every one of the above kinds, as well of pains of privation as of positive pains. These correspond exactly to the pleasures of the memory.

10. Pains of the imagina-tion

29. (10) The pains of the imagination may also be grounded on any one of the above kinds, as well of pains of privation as of positive pains: in other respects they correspond exactly to the pleasures of the imagination.

11. Pains of expectation

30. (11) The pains of expectation may be grounded on each one

reckoned a pain of privation: as far as they are supposed to regard him with such a degree of aversion or disesteem as to be disposed to do him positive *ill* offices, it may be reckoned a positive pain. The pain of privation, and the positive pain, in this case run one into another indistinguishably.

No positive pains corres-pond to the pleasures of power

[k] There seem to be no positive pains to correspond to the pleasures of power. The pains that a man may feel from the want or the loss of power, in as far as power is distinguished from all other sources of pleasure, seem to be nothing more than pains of privation.

The positive pains of piety, and the pains of pri-vation, op-posed to the pleasures of piety, run into one an-other

[1] The positive pains of piety, and the pains of privation, opposed to the pleasures of piety, run one into another in the same manner as the positive pains of enmity, or of an ill name, do with respect to the pains of privation, opposed to the pleasures of amity, and those of a good name. If what is apprehended at the hands of God is barely the not receiving pleasure, the pain is of the privative class: if, moreover, actual pain be apprehended, it is of the class of positive pains.

of the above kinds, as well of pains of privation as of positive pains. These may be also termed pains of apprehension.[m]

31. (12) The pains of association correspond exactly to the pleasures of association.

32. Of the above list there are certain pleasures and pains which suppose the existence of some pleasure or pain of some other person, to which the pleasure or pain of the person in question has regard: such pleasures and pains may be termed *extra-regarding*. Others do not suppose any such thing: these may be termed *self-regarding*.[n] The only pleasures and pains of the extra-regarding class are those of benevolence, and those of malevolence: all the rest are self-regarding.[o]

33. Of all these several sorts of pleasures and pains, there is scarce any one which is not liable, on more accounts than one, to come under the consideration of the law. Is an offence committed? it is the tendency which it has to destroy, in such or such persons, some of these pleasures, or to produce some of these pains, that constitutes the mischief of it, and the ground for punishing it. It is the prospect of some of these pleasures, or of security from some of these pains, that constitutes the motive or temptation, it is the attainment of them that constitutes the profit of the offence. Is the offender to be punished? It can be only by the production of one or more of these pains, that the punishment can be inflicted.[p]

[m] In contradistinction to these, all other pains may be termed pains of *sufferance*.[1]

[n] See Ch. x (Motives).

[o] By this means the pleasures and pains of amity may be the more clearly distinguished from those of benevolence: and on the other hand, those of enmity from those of malevolence. The pleasures and pains of amity and enmity are of the self-regarding cast: those of benevolence and malevolence of the extra-regarding.

[p] It would be a matter not only of curiosity, but of some use, to exhibit a catalogue of the several complex pleasures and pains, analyzing them at the same time into the several simple ones, of which they are respectively composed. But such a disquisition would take up too much room to be admitted here. A short specimen, however, for the purpose of illustration, can hardly be dispensed with.

The pleasures taken in at the eye and ear are generally very complex. The pleasures of a country scene, for instance, consist commonly, amongst others, of the following pleasures:

I. Pleasures of the senses

1. The simple pleasures of sight, excited by the perception of agreeable colours and figures, green fields, waving foliage, glistening water, and the like.

[1] Note added in 1783.

2. The simple pleasures of the ear, excited by the perceptions of the chirping of birds, the murmuring of waters, the rustling of the wind among the trees.

3. The pleasures of the smell, excited by the perceptions of the fragrance of flowers, of new-mown hay, or other vegetable substances, in the first stages of fermentation.

4. The agreeable inward sensation, produced by a brisk circulation of the blood, and the ventilation of it in the lungs by a pure air, such as that in the country frequently is in comparison of that which is breathed in towns.

II. Pleasures of the imagination produced by association

1. The idea of the plenty, resulting from the possession of the objects that are in view, and of the happiness arising from it.

2. The idea of the innocence and happiness of the birds, sheep, cattle, dogs, and other gentle or domestic animals.

3. The idea of the constant flow of health, supposed to be enjoyed by all these creatures: a notion which is apt to result from the occasional flow of health enjoyed by the supposed spectator.

4. The idea of gratitude, excited by the contemplation of the all-powerful and beneficent Being, who is looked up to as the author of these blessings.

These four last are all of them, in some measure at least, pleasures of sympathy.

The depriving a man of this group of pleasures is one of the evils apt to result from imprisonment; whether produced by illegal violence, or in the way of punishment, by appointment of the laws.

dolorific.

CHAPTER VI

OF CIRCUMSTANCES INFLUENCING SENSIBILITY

1. Pain and pleasure are produced in men's minds by the action of certain causes. But the quantity of pleasure and pain runs not uniformly in proportion to the cause; in other words, to the quantity of force exerted by such cause. The truth of this observation rests not upon any metaphysical nicety in the import given to the terms *cause*, *quantity*, and *force*: it will be equally true in whatsoever manner such force be measured. *Pain and pleasure not uniformly proportioned to their causes*

2. The disposition which any one has to feel such or such a quantity of pleasure or pain, upon the application of a cause of given force, is what we term the degree or *quantum* of his sensibility. This may be either *general*, referring to the sum of the causes that act upon him during a given period: or *particular*, referring to the action of any one particular cause, or sort of cause. *Degree or quantum of sensibility, what*

3. But in the same mind such and such causes of pain or pleasure will produce more pain or pleasure than such or such other causes of pain or pleasure: and this proportion will in different minds be different. The disposition which any one has to have the proportion in which he is affected by two such causes, different from that in which another man is affected by the same two causes, may be termed the quality or *bias* of his sensibility. One man, for instance, may be most affected by the pleasures of the taste; another by those of the ear. So also, if there be a difference in the nature or proportion of two pains or pleasures which they respectively experience from the same cause; a case not so frequent as the former. From the same injury, for instance, one man may feel the same quantity of grief and resentment together as another man: but one of them shall feel a greater share of grief than of resentment: the other, a greater share of resentment than of grief. *Bias or quality of sensibility, what*

4. Any incident which serves as a cause, either of pleasure or of pain, may be termed an *exciting* cause: if of pleasure, a pleasurable cause: if of pain, a painful, afflictive, or dolorific cause.[a] *Exciting causes pleasurable and dolorific*

---

[a] The exciting cause, the pleasure or pain produced by it, and the intention produced by such pleasure or pain in the character of a motive, are objects so intimately connected, that, in what follows, I fear I have not, on every occasion, been able to keep them sufficiently distinct. I thought it necessary to give

*Circum-
stances in-
fluencing
sensibility,
what*

5. Now the quantity of pleasure, or of pain, which a man is liable to experience upon the application of an exciting cause, since they will not depend altogether upon that cause, will depend in some measure upon some other circumstance or circumstances: these circumstances, whatsoever they be, may be termed *circumstances influencing sensibility*.[b]

*Circum-
stances in-
fluencing
sensibility
enumerated*

6. These circumstances will apply differently to different exciting causes; insomuch that to a certain exciting cause, a certain circumstance shall not apply at all, which shall apply with great force to another exciting cause. But without entering for the present into these distinctions, it may be of use to sum up all the circumstances which can be found to influence the effect of *any* exciting cause. These, as on a former occasion, it may be as well first to sum up together in the concisest manner possible, and afterwards to allot a few words to the separate explanation of each article. They seem to be as follows:[1] 1. Health. 2. Strength. 3. Hardiness. 4. Bodily imperfection. 5. Quantity and quality of knowledge. 6. Strength of intellectual powers. 7. Firmness of mind. 8. Steadiness of mind. 9. Bent of inclination. 10. Moral sensibility. 11. Moral biases. 12. Religious sensibility. 13. Religious biases. 14. Sympathetic sensibility. 15. Sympathetic biases. 16. Antipathetic sensibility. 17. Antipathetic biases. 18. Insanity. 19. Habitual occupations. 20. Pecuniary circumstances. 21. Connexions in the way of sympathy. 22. Connexions in the way of antipathy. 23. Radical frame of body. 24. Radical frame of mind. 25. Sex. 26. Age. 27. Rank. 28. Education. 29. Climate. 30. Lineage. 31. Government. 32. Religious profession.[c]

the reader this warning; after which, should there be found any such mistakes, it is to be hoped they will not be productive of much confusion.

[b] Thus, in physical bodies, the momentum of a ball put in motion by impulse, will be influenced by the circumstance of gravity: being in some directions increased, in others diminished by it. So in a ship, put in motion by the wind, the momentum and direction will be influenced not only by the attraction of gravity, but by the motion and resistance of the water, and several other circumstances.

*Extent and
intricacy of
this subject*

[c] An analytical view of all these circumstances will be given at the conclusion of the chapter: to which place it was necessary to refer it, as it could not well have been understood, till some of them had been previously explained.

To search out the vast variety of exciting or moderating causes, by which the

[1] In the margin of this list in his copy of the 1789 edition now in the British Museum Bentham wrote the following: 'Antipathy before sympathy? Habitual occupation before Insanity?' But the tentatively suggested change in the orders of items 14, 15, 16 and 17, 18 and 19, and 21 and 22, was not taken up either in 1823 or in the Bowring edition.

7. (1) Health is the absence of disease, and consequently of all *1. Health* those kinds of pain which are among the symptoms of disease. A man may be said to be in a state of health, when he is not conscious of any uneasy sensations, the primary seat of which can be perceived to be any where in his body.[d] In point of general sensibility, a man who is under the pressure of any bodily indisposition, or, as the phrase is, is in an ill state of health, is less sensible to the influence of any pleasurable cause, and more so to that of any afflictive one, than if he were *well*.

8. (2) The circumstance of strength, though in point of causality *2. Strength* closely connected with that of health, is perfectly distinguishable from it. The same man will indeed generally be stronger in a good state of health than in a bad one. But one man, even in a bad state of health, may be stronger than another even in a good one. Weakness is a common concomitant of disease: but in consequence of his

degree or bias of a man's sensibility may be influenced, to define the boundaries of each, to extricate them from the entanglements in which they are involved, to lay the effect of each article distinctly before the reader's eye, is, perhaps, if not absolutely the most difficult task, at least one of the most difficult tasks, within the compass of moral physiology. Disquisitions on this head can never be completely satisfactory without examples. To provide a sufficient collection of such examples, would be a work of great labour as well as nicety: history and biography would need to be ransacked: a vast course of reading would need to be travelled through on purpose. By such a process the present work would doubtless have been rendered more amusing; but in point of bulk, so enormous, that this single chapter would have been swelled into a considerable volume. Feigned cases, although they may upon occasion serve to render the general matter tolerably intelligible, can never be sufficient to render it palatable. On this therefore, as on so many other occasions, I must confine myself to dry and general instruction: discarding illustration, although sensible that without it instruction cannot manifest half its efficacy. The subject, however, is so difficult, and so new, that I shall think I have not ill succeeded, if, without pretending to exhaust it, I shall have been able to mark out the principal points of view, and to put the matter in such a method as may facilitate the researches of happier inquirers.

The great difficulty lies in the nature of the words; which are not, like pain and pleasure, names of homogeneous real entities, but names of various fictitious entities, for which no common genus is to be found: and which therefore, without a vast and roundabout chain of investigation, can never be brought under any exhaustive plan of arrangement, but must be picked up here and there as they happen to occur.

[d] It may be thought, that in a certain degree of health, this negative account of the matter hardly comes up to the case. In a certain degree of health, there is often such a kind of feeling diffused over the whole frame, such a comfortable feel, or flow of spirits, as it is called, as may with propriety come under the head of positive pleasure. But without experiencing any such pleasurable

radical frame of body, a man may be weak all his life long, without experiencing any disease. Health, as we have observed, is principally a negative circumstance: strength a positive one. The degree of a man's strength can be measured with tolerable accuracy.[e]

3. Hardiness   9. (3) Hardiness is a circumstance which, though closely connected with that of strength, is distinguishable from it. Hardiness is the absence of irritability. Irritability respects either pain, resulting from the action of mechanical causes; or disease, resulting from the action of causes purely physiological. Irritability, in the former sense, is the disposition to undergo a greater or less degree of pain upon the application of a mechanical cause; such as are most of those applications by which simple afflictive punishments are inflicted, as whipping, beating, and the like. In the latter sense, it is the disposition to contract disease with greater or less facility, upon the application of any instrument acting on the body by its physiological properties; as in the case of fevers, or of colds, or other inflammatory diseases, produced by the application of damp air: or to experience immediate uneasiness, as in the case of relaxation or chilliness produced by an over or under proportion of the matter of heat.

Difference between strength and hardiness   Hardiness, even in the sense in which it is opposed to the action of mechanical causes, is distinguishable from strength. The external indications of strength are the abundance and firmness of the muscular fibres: those of hardiness, in this sense, are the firmness of the muscular fibres, and the callosity of the skin. Strength is more peculiarly the gift of nature: hardiness, of education. Of two persons who have had, the one the education of a gentleman, the other,

feeling, if a man experience no painful one, he may be well enough said to be in health.

Measure of strength, the weight a man can lift   [e] The most accurate measure that can be given of a man's strength, seems to be that which is taken from the weight or number of pounds and ounces he can lift with his hands in a given attitude. This indeed relates immediately only to his arms: but these are the organs of strength which are most employed; of which the strength corresponds with most exactness to the general state of the body with regard to strength; and in which the quantum of strength is easiest measured. Strength may accordingly be distinguished into *general* and *particular*.

Weakness, what   Weakness is a negative term, and imports the absence of strength. It is, besides, a relative term, and accordingly imports the absence of such a quantity of strength as makes the share, possessed by the person in question, less than that of some person he is compared to. Weakness, when it is at such a degree as to make it painful for a man to perform the motions necessary to the going through the ordinary functions of life, such as to get up, to walk, to dress one's self, and so forth, brings the circumstance of health into question, and puts a man into that sort of condition in which he is said to be in ill health.

that of a common sailor, the first may be the stronger, at the same time that the other is the hardier.

10. (4) By bodily imperfection may be understood that condition *4. Bodily imperfection* which a person is in, who either stands distinguished by any remarkable deformity, or wants any of those parts or faculties, which the ordinary run of persons of the same sex and age are furnished with: who, for instance, has a hare-lip, is deaf, or has lost a hand. This circumstance, like that of ill-health, tends in general to diminish more or less the effect of any pleasurable circumstance, and to increase that of any afflictive one. The effect of this circumstance, however, admits of great variety: inasmuch as there are a great variety of ways in which a man may suffer in his personal appearance, and in his bodily organs and faculties: all which differences will be taken notice of in their proper places.[f]

11. (5) So much for circumstances belonging to the condition of *5. Quantity and quality of knowledge* the body: we come now to those which concern the condition of the mind: the use of mentioning these will be seen hereafter. In the first place may be reckoned the quantity and quality of the knowledge the person in question happens to possess: that is, of the ideas which he has actually in store, ready upon occasion to call to mind: meaning such ideas as are in some way or other of an interesting nature: that is, of a nature in some way or other to influence his happiness, or that of other men. When these ideas are many, and of importance, a man is said to be a man of knowledge; when few, or not of importance, *ignorant.*

12. (6) By strength of intellectual powers may be understood the *6. Strength of intellectual powers* degree of facility which a man experiences in his endeavours to call to mind as well such ideas as have been already aggregated to his stock of knowledge, as any others, which, upon any occasion that may happen, he may conceive a desire to place there. It seems to be on some such occasion as this that the words *parts* and *talents* are commonly employed. To this head may be referred the several qualities of readiness of apprehension, accuracy and tenacity of memory, strength of attention, clearness of discernment, amplitude of comprehension, vividity and rapidity of imagination. Strength of intellectual powers, in general, seems to correspond pretty exactly to general strength of body: as any of these qualities in particular does to particular strength.

[f] See B. I. Tit. (Irrep. corp. Injuries).[1]

[1] For this and similar subsequent references to Bentham's *Plan of a Penal Code* see above, Introduction, xxxviii-xxxix.

7. Firmness of mind

13. (7) Firmness of mind on the one hand, and irritability on the other, regard the proportion between the degrees of efficacy with which a man is acted upon by an exciting cause, of which the value lies chiefly in magnitude, and one of which the value lies chiefly in propinquity.[g] A man may be said to be of a firm mind, when small pleasures or pains, which are present or near, do not affect him, in a greater proportion to their value, than greater pleasures or pains, which are uncertain or remote[h]; of an irritable mind, when the contrary is the case.

8. Steadiness

14. (8) Steadiness regards the time during which a given exciting cause of a given value continues to affect a man in nearly the same manner and degree as at first, no assignable external event or change of circumstances intervening to make an alteration in its force.[i]

9. Bent of inclinations

15. (9) By the bent of a man's inclinations may be understood the propensity he has to expect pleasure or pain from certain objects, rather than from others. A man's inclinations may be said to have such or such a bent, when, amongst the several sorts of objects which afford pleasure in some degree to all men, he is apt to expect more pleasure from one particular sort, than from another particular sort, or more from any given particular sort, than another man would expect from that sort; or when, amongst the several sorts of objects, which to one man afford pleasure, whilst to another they afford none, he is apt to expect, or not to expect, pleasure from an object of such or such a sort: so also with regard to pains. This circumstance, though intimately connected with that of the bias of a man's sensibility, is not undistinguishable from it. The quantity of pleasure or pain, which on any given occasion a man may experience from an application of any sort, may be greatly influenced by the expectations he has been used to entertain of pleasure or pain from that quarter; but it will not be

---

[g] See Ch. IV (Value).

[h] When, for instance, having been determined, by the prospect of some inconvenience, not to disclose a fact, although he should be put to the rack, he perseveres in such resolution after the rack is brought into his presence, and even applied to him.

[i] The facility with which children grow tired of their play-things, and throw them away, is an instance of unsteadiness: the perseverance with which a merchant applies himself to his traffic, or an author to his book, may be taken for an instance of the contrary. It is difficult to judge of the quantity of pleasure or pain in these cases, but from the effects which it produces in the character of a motive: and even then it is difficult to pronounce, whether the change of conduct happens by the extinction of the old pleasure or pain, or by the intervention of a new one.

absolutely determined by them: for pleasure or pain may come upon him from a quarter from which he was not accustomed to expect it.

16. (10) The circumstances of *moral, religious, sympathetic*, and *antipathetic sensibility*, when closely considered, will appear to be included in some sort under that of *bent of inclination*. On account of their particular importance they may, however, be worth mentioning apart. A man's moral sensibility may be said to be strong, when the pains and pleasures of the moral sanction[j] show greater in his eyes, in comparison with other pleasures and pains (and consequently exert a stronger influence) than in the eyes of the persons he is compared with; in other words, when he is acted on with more than ordinary efficacy by the sense of honour: it may be said to be weak, when the contrary is the case. *10. Moral sensibility*

17. (11) Moral sensibility seems to regard the average effect or influence of the pains and pleasures of the moral sanction, upon all sorts of occasions to which it is applicable, or happens to be applied. It regards the average force or *quantity* of the impulses the mind receives from that source during a given period. Moral *bias* regards the particular acts on which, upon so many particular occasions, the force of that sanction is looked upon as attaching. It regards the *quality* or direction of those impulses. It admits of as many varieties, therefore, as there are dictates which the moral sanction may be conceived to issue forth. A man may be said to have such or such a *moral bias*, or to have a moral bias in favour of such or such an action, when he looks upon it as being of the number of those of which the performance is dictated by the moral sanction. *11. Moral biases*

18. (12) What has been said with regard to moral sensibility, may be applied, *mutatis mutandis*, to religious. *12. Religious sensibility*

19. (13) What has been said with regard to moral biases, may also be applied, *mutatis mutandis*, to religious biases. *13. Religious biases*

20. (14) By sympathetic sensibility is to be understood the propensity that a man has to derive pleasure from the happiness, and pain from the unhappiness, of other sensitive beings. It is the stronger, the greater the ratio of the pleasure or pain he feels on their account is to that of the pleasure or pain which (according to what appears to him) they feel for themselves. *14. Sympathetic sensibility*

21. (15) Sympathetic bias regards the description of the parties who are the objects of a man's sympathy: and of the acts or other circumstances of or belonging to those persons, by which the sympathy is excited. These parties may be, 1. Certain individuals. 2. Any subordinate class of individuals. 3. The whole nation. 4. *15. Sympathetic biases*

---

[j] See Ch. v (Pleasures and Pains).

Human kind in general. 5. The whole sensitive creation. According as these objects of sympathy are more numerous, the *affection*, by which the man is biased, may be said to be the more *enlarged*.

16, 17. Anti-pathetic sen-sibility, and biases

22. (16, 17) Antipathetic sensibility and antipathetic biases are just the reverse of sympathetic sensibility and sympathetic biases. By antipathetic sensibility is to be understood the propensity that a man has to derive pain from the happiness, and pleasure from the unhappiness, of other sensitive beings.

18. Insanity

23. (18) The circumstance of insanity of mind corresponds to that of bodily imperfection. It admits, however, of much less variety, inasmuch as the soul is (for aught we can perceive) one indivisible thing, not distinguishable, like the body, into parts. What lesser degrees of imperfection the mind may be susceptible of, seem to be comprisable under the already-mentioned heads of ignorance, weakness of mind, irritability, or unsteadiness; or under such others as are reducible to them. Those which are here in view are those extraordinary species and degrees of mental imperfection, which, wherever they take place, are as conspicuous and as unquestionable as lameness or blindness in the body: operating partly, it should seem, by inducing an extraordinary degree of the imperfections above mentioned, partly by giving an extraordinary and preposterous bent to the inclinations.

19. Habitual occupations

24. (19) Under the head of a man's habitual occupations, are to be understood, on this occasion, as well those which he pursues for the sake of profit, as those which he pursues for the sake of present pleasure. The consideration of the profit itself belongs to the head of a man's pecuniary circumstances. It is evident, that if by any means a punishment, or any other exciting cause, has the effect of putting it out of his power to continue in the pursuit of any such occupation, it must on that account be so much the more distressing. A man's habitual occupations, though intimately connected in point of causality with the bent of his inclinations, are not to be looked upon as precisely the same circumstance. An amusement, or channel of profit, may be the object of a man's *inclinations*, which has never been the subject of his *habitual occupations*: for it may be, that though he wished to betake himself to it, he never did, it not being in his power: a circumstance which may make a good deal of difference in the effect of any incident by which he happens to be debarred from it.

20. Pecu-niary circum-stances

25. (20) Under the head of pecuniary circumstances, I mean to bring to view the proportion which a man's *means* bear to his *wants*: the sum total of his means of every kind, to the sum total of his

wants of every kind. A man's means depend upon three circumstances: 1. His property. 2. The profit of his labour. 3. His connexions in the way of support. His wants seem to depend upon four
circumstances. 1. His habits of expense. 2. His connexions in the
way of burthen. 3. Any present casual demand he may have.
4. The strength of his expectation. By a man's property is to be
understood, whatever he has in store independent of his labour.
By the profit of his labour is to be understood the growing profit.
As to labour, it may be either of the body principally, or of the mind
principally, or of both indifferently: nor does it matter in what
manner, nor on what subject, it be applied, so it produce a profit.
By a man's connexions in the way of support, are to be understood
the pecuniary assistances, of whatever kind, which he is in a way of
receiving from any persons who, on whatever account, and in whatever proportion, he has reason to expect should contribute *gratis* to
his maintenance: such as his parents, patrons, and relations. It
seems manifest, that a man can have no other means than these.
What he uses, he must have either of his own, or from other people:
if from other people, either *gratis* or for a price. As to habits of
expense, it is well known, that a man's desires are governed in a
great degree by his habits. Many are the cases in which desire (and
consequently the pain of privation connected with it[k]) would not
even subsist at all, but for previous enjoyment. By a man's connexions in the way of burthen, are to be understood whatever
expense he has reason to look upon himself as bound to be at in the
support of those who by law, or the customs of the world, are
warranted in looking up to him for assistance; such as children,
poor relations, superannuated servants, and any other dependents
whatsoever. As to present casual demand, it is manifest, that there
are occasions on which a given sum will be worth infinitely more
to a man than the same sum would at another time: where, for
example, in a case of extremity, a man stands in need of extraordinary medical assistance: or wants money to carry on a law-suit,
on which his all depends: or has got a livelihood waiting for him in a
distant country, and wants money for the charges of conveyance.
In such cases, any piece of good or ill fortune, in the pecuniary way,
might have a very different effect from what it would have at any
other time. With regard to strength of expectation; when one
man expects to gain or to keep a thing which another does not, it is
plain the circumstance of not having it will affect the former very

[k] See Ch. v (Pleasures and Pains).

differently from the latter; who, indeed, commonly will not be affected by it at all.

21. Con-
nexions in
the way of
sympathy

26. (21) Under the head of a man's connexions in the way of sympathy, I would bring to view the number and description of the persons in whose welfare he takes such a concern, as that the idea of their happiness should be productive of pleasure, and that of their unhappiness of pain to him: for instance, a man's wife, his children, his parents, his near relations, and intimate friends. This class of persons, it is obvious, will for the most part include the two classes by which his pecuniary circumstances are affected: those, to wit, from whose means he may expect support, and those whose wants operate on him as a burthen. But it is obvious, that besides these, it may very well include others, with whom he has no such pecuniary connexion: and even with regard to these, it is evident that the pecuniary dependence, and the union of affections, are circumstances perfectly distinguishable. Accordingly, the connexions here in question, independently of any influence they may have on a man's pecuniary circumstances, have an influence on the effect of any exciting causes whatsoever. The tendency of them is to increase a man's general sensibility; to increase, on the one hand, the pleasure produced by all pleasurable causes; on the other, the pain produced by all afflictive ones. When any pleasurable incident happens to a man, he naturally, in the first moment, thinks of the pleasure it will afford immediately to himself: presently afterwards, however (except in a few cases, which is not worth while here to insist on) he begins to think of the pleasure which his friends will feel upon their coming to know of it: and this secondary pleasure is commonly no mean addition to the primary one. First comes the self-regarding pleasure: then comes the idea of the pleasure of sympathy, which you suppose that pleasure of yours will give birth to in the bosom of your friend: and this idea excites again in your's a new pleasure of sympathy, grounded upon his. The first pleasure issuing from your own bosom, as it were from a radiant point, illuminates the bosom of your friend: reverberated from thence, it is reflected with augmented warmth to the point from whence it first proceeded: and so it is with pains.[1]

Nor does this effect depend wholly upon affection. Among near

[1] This is one reason why legislators in general like better to have married people to deal with than single; and people that have children than such as are childless. It is manifest that the stronger and more numerous a man's connexions in the way of sympathy are, the stronger is the hold which the law has upon him. A wife and children are so many pledges a man gives to the world for his good behaviour.

relations, although there should be no kindness, the pleasures and pains of the moral sanction are quickly propagated by a peculiar kind of sympathy: no article, either of honour or disgrace, can well fall upon a man, without extending to a certain distance within the circle of his family. What reflects honour upon the father, reflects honour upon the son: what reflects disgrace, disgrace. The *cause* of this singular and seemingly unreasonable circumstance (that is, its analogy to the rest of the phenomena of the human mind) belongs not to the present purpose. It is sufficient if the effect be beyond dispute.

27. (22) Of a man's connexions in the way of antipathy, there needs not any thing very particular to be observed. Happily there is no primeval and constant source of antipathy in human nature, as there is of sympathy. There are no permanent sets of persons who are naturally and of course the objects of antipathy to a man, as there are who are the objects of the contrary affection. Sources, however, but too many, of antipathy, are apt to spring up upon various occasions during the course of a man's life: and whenever they do, this circumstance may have a very considerable influence on the effects of various exciting causes. As on the one hand a punishment, for instance, which tends to separate a man from those with whom he is connected in the way of sympathy, so on the other hand, one which tends to force him into the company of those with whom he is connected in the way of antipathy, will, on that account, be so much the more distressing. It is to be observed, that sympathy itself multiplies the sources of antipathy. Sympathy for your friend gives birth to antipathy on *your* part against all those who are objects of antipathy, as well as to sympathy for those who are objects of sympathy to *him*. In the same manner does antipathy multiply the sources of sympathy; though commonly perhaps with rather a less degree of efficacy. Antipathy against your enemy is apt to give birth to sympathy on *your* part towards those who are objects of antipathy, as well as to antipathy against those who are objects of sympathy, to *him*. *22. Connexions in the way of antipathy*

28. (23) Thus much for the circumstances by which the effect of any exciting cause may be influenced, when applied upon any given occasion, at any given period. But besides these supervening incidents, there are other circumstances relative to a man, that may have their influence, and which are coeval to his birth. In the first place, it seems to be universally agreed, that in the original frame or texture of every man's body, there is a something which, independently of all subsequently intervening circumstances, renders *23. Radical frame of body*

61

him liable to be affected by causes producing bodily pleasure or pain, in a manner different from that in which another man would be affected by the same causes. To the catalogue of circumstances influencing a man's sensibility, we may therefore add his original or radical frame, texture, constitution, or temperament of body.

24. Radical frame of mind

29. (24) In the next place, it seems to be pretty well agreed, that there is something also in the original frame or texture of every man's mind, which, independently of all exterior and subsequently intervening circumstances, and even of his radical frame of body, makes him liable to be differently affected by the same exciting causes, from what another man would be. To the catalogue of circumstances influencing a man's sensibility, we may therefore further add his original or radical frame, texture, constitution or temperament of mind.[m]

This distinct from the circumstance of frame of body;

30. It seems pretty certain, all this while, that a man's sensibility to causes producing pleasure or pain, even of mind, may depend in a considerable degree upon his original and acquired frame of body. But we have no reason to think that it can depend altogether upon that frame: since, on the one hand, we see persons whose frame of body is as much alike as can be conceived, differing very considerably in respect of their mental frame: and, on the other hand, persons whose frame of mind is as much alike as can be conceived, differing very conspicuously in regard to their bodily frame.[n]

—and from all others

31. It seems indisputable also, that the different sets of external occurrences that may befall a man in the course of his life, will make great differences in the subsequent texture of his mind at any given period: yet still those differences are not solely to be attributed to such occurrences. Equally far from the truth seems that opinion

Idiosyncrasy, what

[m] The characteristic circumstances whereby one man's frame of body or mind, considered at any given period, stands distinguished from that of another, have been comprised by metaphysicians and physiologists under the name *idiosyncrasy*, from ιδιος, peculiar, and συνκρασις, composition.

Whether the soul be material or immaterial makes no difference

[n] Those who maintain, that the mind and the body are one substance, may here object, that upon that supposition the distinction between frame of mind and frame of body is but nominal, and that accordingly there is no such thing as a frame of mind distinct from the frame of body. But granting, for argument-sake, the antecedent, we may dispute the consequence. For if the mind be but a part of the body, it is at any rate of a nature very different from the other parts of the body.

A man's frame of body cannot in any part of it undergo any considerable alteration without its being immediately indicated by phænomena discernible by the senses. A man's frame of mind may undergo very considerable alterations, his frame of body remaining the same to all appearance; that is, for any thing that is indicated to the contrary by phænomena cognizable to the senses: meaning those of other men.

to be (if any such be maintained) which attributes all to nature, and that which attributes all to education. The two circumstances will therefore still remain distinct, as well from one another, as from all others.

32. Distinct however as they are, it is manifest, that at no period in the active part of a man's life can they either of them make their appearance by themselves. All they do is to constitute the latent ground-work which the other supervening circumstances have to work upon: and whatever influence those original principles may have, is so changed and modified, and covered over, as it were, by those other circumstances, as never to be separately discernible. The effects of the one influence are indistinguishably blended with those of the other. *Yet the result of them is not separately discernible*

33. The emotions of the body are received, and with reason, as probable indications of the temperature of the mind. But they are far enough from conclusive. A man may exhibit, for instance, the exterior appearances of grief, without really grieving at all, or at least in any thing near the proportion in which he appears to grieve. Oliver Cromwell, whose conduct indicated a heart more than ordinarily callous, was as remarkably profuse in tears.° Many men can command the external appearances of sensibility with very little real feeling.ᵖ The female sex commonly with greater facility than the male: hence the proverbial expression of a woman's tears. *Frame of body indicates, but not certainly, that of mind*

° Hume's Hist.[1]

ᵖ The quantity of the sort of pain, which is called grief, is indeed hardly to be measured by any external indications. It is neither to be measured, for instance, by the quantity of the tears, nor by the number of moments spent in crying. Indications rather less equivocal may, perhaps, be afforded by the pulse. A man has not the motions of his heart at command as he has those of the muscles of his face. But the particular significancy of these indications is still very uncertain. All they can express is, that the man is affected; they cannot express in what manner, nor from what cause. To an affection resulting in reality from such or such a cause, he may give an artificial colouring, and attribute it to such or such another cause. To an affection directed in reality to such or such a person as its object, he may give an artificial bias, and represent it as if directed to such or such another object. Tears of rage he may attribute to contrition. The concern he feels at the thoughts of a punishment that awaits him, he may impute to a sympathetic concern for the mischief produced by his offence.

A very tolerable judgment, however, may commonly be formed by a discerning mind, upon laying all the external indications exhibited by a man together, and at the same time comparing them with his actions.   ᵖ[cont.]

[1] After giving an account of Cromwell's reactions to the opening of Barebone's Parliament on 4 July 1653, Hume says: 'I suppose at this passage he cried: For he was very much given to weeping, and could at any time shed abundance of tears.' (*History of Great Britain.* 1773, vii, 228n.).

To have this kind of command over one's self, was the characteristic excellence of the orator of ancient times, and is still that of the player in our own.

34. The remaining circumstances may, with reference to those already mentioned, be termed *secondary* influencing circumstances. These have an influence, it is true, on the quantum or bias of a man's sensibility, but it is only by means of the other primary ones. The manner in which these two sets of circumstances are concerned, is such that the primary ones do the business, while the secondary ones lie most open to observation. The secondary ones, therefore, are those which are most heard of; on which account it will be necessary to take notice of them: at the same time that it is only by means of the primary ones that their influence can be explained: whereas the influence of the primary ones will be apparent enough, without any mention of the secondary ones.

35. (25) Among such of the primitive modifications of the corporeal frame as may appear to influence the quantum and bias of sensibility, the most obvious and conspicuous are those which constitute the *sex*. In point of quantity, the sensibility of the female sex appears in general to be greater than that of the male. The health of the female is more delicate than that of the male: in point of strength and hardiness of body, in point of quantity and quality of knowledge, in point of strength of intellectual powers, and firmness of mind, she is commonly inferior: moral, religious, sympathetic, and antipathetic sensibility are commonly stronger in her than in the male. The quality of her knowledge, and the bent of her inclinations, are commonly in many respects different. Her moral biases are also, in certain respects, remarkably different: chastity, modesty, and delicacy, for instance, are prized more than courage in a woman: courage, more than any of those qualities, in a man. The religious biases in the two sexes are not apt to be remarkably different; except that the female is rather more inclined than the male to superstition; that is, to observances not dictated by the principle of utility; a difference that may be pretty well accounted for by some of the before-mentioned circumstances. Her sympathetic biases are in many respects different: for her own offspring all their lives long, and for children in general while young, her

ᴾcont.

A remarkable instance of the power of the will, over the external indications of sensibility, is to be found in Tacitus's story of the Roman soldier, who raised a mutiny in the camp, pretending to have lost a brother by the lawless cruelty of the General. The truth was, he never had had a brother.[1]

[1] *Annals*, ɪ.xxii–xxiii. The soldier was Vibulenus, the general Blaesus, and the mutiny took place in Pannonia.

affection is commonly stronger than that of the male. Her affections are apt to be less enlarged: seldom expanding themselves so much as to take in the welfare of her country in general, much less that of mankind, or the whole sensitive creation: seldom embracing any extensive class or division, even of her own countrymen, unless it be in virtue of her sympathy for some particular individuals that belong to it. In general, her antipathetic, as well as sympathetic biases, are apt to be less conformable to the principle of utility than those of the male; owing chiefly to some deficiency in point of knowledge, discernment, and comprehension. Her habitual occupations of the amusing kind are apt to be in many respects different from those of the male. With regard to her connexions in the way of sympathy, there can be no difference. In point of pecuniary circumstances, according to the customs of perhaps all countries, she is in general less independent.

36. (26) Age is of course divided into divers periods, of which *26. Age* the number and limits are by no means uniformly ascertained. One might distinguish it, for the present purpose, into, 1. Infancy. 2. Adolescence. 3. Youth. 4. Maturity. 5. Decline. 6. Decrepitude. It were lost time to stop on the present occasion to examine it at each period, and to observe the indications it gives, with respect to the several primary circumstances just reviewed. Infancy and decrepitude are commonly inferior to the other periods, in point of health, strength, hardiness, and so forth. In infancy, on the part of the female, the imperfections of that sex are enhanced: on the part of the male, imperfections take place mostly similar in quality, but greater in quantity, to those attending the states of adolescence, youth, and maturity in the female. In the stage of decrepitude both sexes relapse into many of the imperfections of infancy. The generality of these observations may easily be corrected upon a particular review.

37. (27) Station, or rank in life, is a circumstance, that, among *27. Rank* a civilized people, will commonly undergo a multiplicity of variations. *Cæteris paribus*, the quantum of sensibility appears to be greater in the higher ranks of men than in the lower. The primary circumstances in respect of which this secondary circumstance is apt to induce or indicate a difference, seem principally to be as follows: 1. Quantity and quality of knowledge. 2. Strength of mind. 3. Bent of inclination. 4. Moral sensibility. 5. Moral biases. 6. Religious sensibility. 7. Religious biases. 8. Sympathetic sensibility. 9. Sympathetic biases. 10. Antipathetic sensibility. 11. Antipathetic biases. 12. Habitual occupations. 13. Nature and productiveness of a man's means of livelihood. 14. Connexions importing profit. 15. Habit of expense. 16. Connexions importing burthen. A man of a certain rank will frequently have a number of dependents besides those whose dependency is the result of natural relationship. As to health, strength, and hardiness, if rank has any influence on these circumstances, it is but in a remote way, chiefly by the influence it may have on his habitual occupations.

28. Education

38. (28) The influence of education is still more extensive. Education stands upon a footing somewhat different from that of the circumstances of age, sex, and rank. These words, though the influence of the circumstances they respectively denote exerts itself principally, if not entirely, through the medium of certain of the primary circumstances before mentioned, present, however, each of them a circumstance which has a separate existence of itself. This is not the case with the word education: which means nothing any farther than as it serves to call up to view some one or more of those primary circumstances. Education may be distinguished into physical and mental; the education of the body and that of the mind: mental, again, into intellectual and moral; the culture of the understanding, and the culture of the affections. The education a man receives, is given to him partly by others, partly by himself. By education then nothing more can be expressed than the condition a man is in in respect of those primary circumstances, as resulting partly from the management and contrivance of others, principally of those who in the early periods of his life have had dominion over him, partly from his own. To the physical part of his education, belong the circumstances of health, strength, and hardiness: sometimes, by accident, that of bodily imperfection; as where by intemperance or negligence an irreparable mischief happens to his person. To the intellectual part, those of quantity and quality of knowledge, and in some measure perhaps those of firmness of mind and steadiness. To the moral part, the bent of his inclinations, the quantity and quality of his moral, religious, sympathetic, and antipathetic sensibility: to all three branches indiscriminately, but under the superior control of external occurrences, his habitual recreations, his property, his means of livelihood, his connexions in the way of profit and of burthen, and his habits of expense. With respect indeed to all these points, the influence of education is modified, in a manner more or less apparent, by that of exterior occurrences; and in a manner scarcely at all apparent, and altogether out of the reach of calculation, by the original texture and constitution as well of his body as of his mind.

39. (29) Among the external circumstances by which the in- *29. Climate*
fluence of education is modified, the principal are those which come
under the head of *climate*. This circumstance places itself in front,
and demands a separate denomination, not merely on account of
the magnitude of its influence, but also on account of its being conspicuous to every body, and of its applying indiscriminately to
great numbers at a time. This circumstance depends for its *essence*
upon the situation of that part of the earth which is in question,
with respect to the course taken by the whole planet in its revolu-
tion round the sun: but for its *influence* it depends upon the condition of the bodies which compose the earth's surface at that part,
principally upon the quantities of sensible heat at different periods,
and upon the density, and purity, and dryness or moisture of the
circumambient air. Of the so often mentioned primary circumstances, there are few of which the production is not influenced by
this secondary one; partly by its manifest effects upon the body;
partly by its less perceptible effects upon the mind. In hot climates
men's health is apt to be more precarious than in cold: their strength
and hardiness less: their vigour, firmness, and steadiness of mind
less: and thence indirectly their quantity of knowledge: the bent
of their inclinations different: most remarkably so in respect of their
superior propensity to sexual enjoyments, and in respect of the
earliness of the period at which that propensity begins to manifest
itself: their sensibilities of all kinds more intense: their habitual
occupations savouring more of sloth than of activity: their radical
frame of body less strong, probably, and less hardy: their radical
frame of mind less vigorous, less firm, less steady.

40. (30) Another article in the catalogue of secondary circum- *30. Lineage*
stances, is that of *race* or *lineage*: the national race or lineage a man
issues from. This circumstance, independently of that of climate,
will commonly make some difference in point of radical frame of
mind and body. A man of negro race, born in France or England,
is a very different being, in many respects, from a man of French
or English race. A man of Spanish race, born in Mexico or Peru, is
at the hour of his birth a different sort of being, in many respects,
from a man of the original Mexican or Peruvian race. This circumstance, as far as it is distinct from climate, rank, and education,
and from the two just mentioned, operates chiefly through the
medium of moral, religious, sympathetic, and antipathetic biases.

41. (31) The last circumstance but one, is that of government: *31. Govern-*
the government a man lives under at the time in question; or rather *ment*
that under which he has been accustomed most to live. This circum-

stance operates principally through the medium of education: the magistrate operating in the character of a tutor upon all the members of the state, by the direction he gives to their hopes and to their fears. Indeed under a solicitous and attentive government, the ordinary preceptor, nay even the parent himself, is but a deputy, as it were, to the magistrate: whose controlling influence, different in this respect from that of the ordinary preceptor, dwells with a man to his life's end. The effects of the peculiar power of the magistrate are seen more particularly in the influence it exerts over the quantum and bias of men's moral, religious, sympathetic, and antipathetic sensibilities. Under a well-constituted, or even under a well-administered though ill-constituted government, men's moral sensibility is commonly stronger, and their moral biases more conformable to the dictates of utility: their religious sensibility frequently weaker, but their religious biases less unconformable to the dictates of utility: their sympathetic affections more enlarged, directed to the magistrate more than to small parties or to individuals, and more to the whole community than to either: their antipathetic sensibilities less violent, as being more obsequious to the influence of well-directed moral biases, and less apt to be excited by that of ill-directed religious ones: their antipathetic biases more conformable to well-directed moral ones, more apt (in proportion) to be grounded on enlarged and sympathetic than on narrow and self-regarding affections, and accordingly, upon the whole, more conformable to the dictates of utility.

32. Religious profession

42. (32) The last circumstance is that of religious profession: the religious profession a man is of: the religious fraternity of which he is a member. This circumstance operates principally through the medium of religious sensibility and religious biases. It operates, however, as an indication more or less conclusive, with respect to several other circumstances. With respect to some, scarcely but through the medium of the two just mentioned: this is the case with regard to the quantum and bias of a man's moral, sympathetic, and antipathetic sensibility: perhaps in some cases with regard to quantity and quality of knowledge, strength of intellectual powers, and bent of inclination. With respect to others, it may operate immediately of itself: this seems to be the case with regard to man's habitual occupations, pecuniary circumstances, and connexions in the way of sympathy and antipathy. A man who pays very little inward regard to the dictates of the religion which he finds it necessary to profess, may find it difficult to avoid joining in the ceremonies of it, and bearing a part in the pecuniary burthens it imposes.q By the force of habit and example he may even be led to entertain a partiality for persons of the same profession, and a proportionable antipathy against those of a rival one. In particular, the antipathy against persons of different persuasions is one of the last points of religion which men part with. Lastly, it is obvious, that the religious profession a man is of cannot but have a considerable influence on his education. But, considering the import of the term education, to say this is perhaps no more than saying in other words what has been said already.

43. These circumstances, all or many of them, will need to be attended to as often as upon any occasion any account is taken of any quantity of pain or pleasure, as resulting from any cause. Has any person sustained an injury? they will need to be considered in estimating the mischief of the offence. Is satisfaction to be made to him? they will need to be attended to in adjusting the *quantum* of that satisfaction. Is the injurer to be punished? they will need to be attended to in estimating the force of the impression that will be made on him by any given punishment. *Use of the preceding observations*

44. It is to be observed, that though they seem all of them, on some account or other, to merit a place in the catalogue, they are not all of equal use in practice. Different articles among them are applicable to different exciting causes. Of those that may influence the effect of the same exciting cause, some apply indiscriminately to whole classes of persons together; being applicable to all, without any remarkable difference in degree: these may be directly and pretty fully provided for by the legislator. This is the case, for instance, with the primary circumstances of bodily imperfection, and insanity: with the secondary circumstance of sex: perhaps with that of age: at any rate with those of rank, of climate, of lineage, and of religious profession. Others, however they may apply to whole classes of persons, yet in their application to different individuals are susceptible of perhaps an indefinite variety of degrees. These cannot be fully provided for by the legislator; but, as the existence of them, in every sort of case, is capable of being ascertained, and the degree in which they take place is capable of being measured, provision may be made for them by the judge, or other *How far the circumstances in question can be taken into account*

q The ways in which a religion may lessen a man's means, or augment his wants, are various. Sometimes it will prevent him from making a profit of his money: sometimes from setting his hand to labour. Sometimes it will oblige him to buy dearer food instead of cheaper: sometimes to purchase useless labour: sometimes to pay men for not labouring: sometimes to purchase trinkets, on which imagination alone has set a value: sometimes to purchase exemptions from punishment, or titles to felicity in the world to come.

executive magistrate, to whom the several individuals that happen to be concerned may be made known. This is the case, 1. With the circumstance of health. 2. In some sort with that of strength. 3. Scarcely with that of hardiness: still less with those of quantity and quality of knowledge, strength of intellectual powers, firmness or steadiness of mind; except in as far as a man's condition, in respect of those circumstances, may be indicated by the secondary circumstances of sex, age, or rank: hardly with that of bent of inclination, except in as far as that latent circumstance is indicated by the more manifest one of habitual occupations: hardly with that of a man's moral sensibility or biases, except in as far as they may be indicated by his sex, age, rank, and education: not at all with his religious sensibility and religious biases, except in as far as they may be indicated by the religious profession he belongs to: not at all with the quantity or quality of his sympathetic or antipathetic sensibilities, except in as far as they may be presumed from his sex, age, rank, education, lineage, or religious profession. It is the case, however, with his habitual occupations, with his pecuniary circumstances, and with his connexions in the way of sympathy. Of others, again, either the existence cannot be ascertained, or the degree cannot be measured. These, therefore, cannot be taken into account, either by the legislator or the executive magistrate. Accordingly, they would have no claim to be taken notice of, were it not for those secondary circumstances by which they are indicated, and whose influence could not well be understood without them. What these are has been already mentioned.

To what exciting causes there is most occasion to apply them

45. It has already been observed, that different articles in this list of circumstances apply to different exciting causes: the circumstance of bodily strength, for instance, has scarcely any influence of itself (whatever it may have in a roundabout way, and by accident) on the effect of an incident which should increase or diminish the quantum of a man's property. It remains to be considered, what the exciting causes are with which the legislator has to do. These may, by some accident or other, be any whatsoever: but those with which he has principally to do, are those of the painful or afflictive kind. With pleasurable ones he has little to do, except now and then by accident: the reasons of which may be easily enough perceived, at the same time that it would take up too much room to unfold them here. The exciting causes with which he has principally to do, are, on the one hand, the mischievous acts, which it his business to prevent; on the other hand, the punishments, by the terror of which it is his endeavour to prevent them. Now of these two sets of exciting causes, the latter only is of his production: being produced partly by his own special appointment, partly in conformity to his general appointment, by the special appointment of the judge. For the legislator, therefore, as well as for the judge, it is necessary (if they would know what it is they are doing when they are appointing punishment) to have an eye to all these circumstances. For the legislator, lest, meaning to apply a certain quantity of punishment to all persons who shall put themselves in a given predicament, he should unawares apply to some of those persons much more or much less than he himself intended: for the judge, lest, in applying to a particular person a particular measure of punishment, he should apply much more or much less than was intended, perhaps by himself, and at any rate by the legislator. They ought each of them, therefore, to have before him, on the one hand, a list of the several circumstances by which sensibility may be influenced; on the other hand, a list of the several species and degrees of punishment which they purpose to make use of: and then, by making a comparison between the two, to form a detailed estimate of the influence of each of the circumstances in question, upon the effect of each species and degree of punishment.

There are two plans or orders of distribution, either of which might be pursued in the drawing up this estimate. The one is to make the name of the circumstance take the lead, and under it to represent the different influences it exerts over the effects of the several modes of punishment: the other is to make the name of the punishment take the lead, and under it to represent the different influences which are exerted over the effects of it by the several circumstances above mentioned. Now of these two sorts of objects, the punishment is that to which the intention of the legislator is directed in the first instance. This is of his own creation, and will be whatsoever he thinks fit to make it: the influencing circumstance exists independently of him, and is what it is whether he will or no. What he has occasion to do is to establish a certain species and degree of punishment: and it is only with reference to that punishment that he has occasion to make any inquiry concerning any of the circumstances here in question. The latter of the two plans therefore is that which appears by far the most useful and commodious. But neither upon the one nor the other plan can any such estimate be delivered here.[r]

---

[r] This is far from being a visionary proposal, not reducible to practice. I speak from experience, having actually drawn up such an estimate, though upon the least commodious of the two plans, and before the several circum-

Analytical view of the circumstances influencing sensibility

46. Of the several circumstances contained in this catalogue, it may be of use to give some sort of analytic view; in order that it may be the more easily discovered if any which ought to have been inserted are omitted; and that, with regard to those which are inserted, it may be seen how they differ and agree.

In the first place, they may be distinguished into *primary* and *secondary*: those may be termed primary, which operate immediately of themselves: those secondary, which operate not but by the medium of the former. To this latter head belong the circumstances of sex, age, station in life, education, climate, lineage, government, and religious profession: the rest are primary. These again are either *connate* or *adventitious*: those which are connate, are radical frame of body and radical frame of mind. Those which are adventitious, are either *personal*, or *exterior*. The personal, again, concern either a man's *dispositions*, or his *actions*. Those which concern his dispositions, concern either his *body* or his *mind*. Those which concern his body are health, strength, hardiness, and bodily imperfection. Those which concern his mind, again, concern either his *understanding* or his *affections*. To the former head belong the circumstances of quantity and quality of knowledge, strength of understanding, and insanity. To the latter belong the circumstances of firmness of mind, steadiness, bent of inclination, moral sensibility, moral biases, religious sensibility, religious biases, sympathetic sensibility, sympathetic biases, antipathetic sensibility, and antipathetic biases. Those which regard his actions, are his habitual occupations. Those which are exterior to him, regard either the *things* or the *persons* which he is concerned with; under the former head come his pecuniary circumstances[s]; under the latter, his connexions in the way of sympathy and antipathy.

stances in question had been reduced to the precise number and order in which they are here enumerated. This is a part of the matter destined for another work. See Ch. XIII (Cases unmeet) par 2. Note. There are some of these circumstances that bestow particular denominations on the persons they relate to: thus, from the circumstance of bodily imperfections, persons are denominated deaf, dumb, blind, and so forth: from the circumstance of insanity, idiots, and maniacs: from the circumstance of age, infants: for all which classes of persons particular provision is made in the Code. See B. I. tit. (Exemptions). Persons thus distinguished will form so many articles in the *catalogus personarum*

Analytical view of the constituent articles in a man's pecuniary circumstances

privilegiatarum. See Appendix. tit. (Composition).[1]

[s] As to a man's pecuniary circumstances, the causes on which those circumstances depend, do not come all of them under the same class. The absolute quantum of a man's property does indeed come under the same class with his

[1] This refers to what would have been one section in an appendix to the *Plan of a Penal Code* dealing generally with the text as opposed to the substance of the code.

pecuniary circumstances in general: so does the profit he makes from the occupation which furnishes him with the means of livelihood. But the occupation itself concerns his own person, and comes under the same head as his habitual amusements: as likewise his habits of expense: his connexions in the ways of profit and of burthen, under the same head as his connexions in the way of sympathy: and the circumstances of his present demand for money, and strength of expectation, come under the head of those circumstances relative to his person which regard his affections.

CHAPTER VII

OF HUMAN ACTIONS IN GENERAL

The demand for punishment depends in part upon the tendency of the act

1. The business of government is to promote the happiness of the society, by punishing and rewarding. That part of its business which consists in punishing, is more particularly the subject of penal law. In proportion as an act tends to disturb that happiness, in proportion as the tendency of it is pernicious, will be the demand it creates for punishment. What happiness consists of we have already seen: enjoyment of pleasures, security from pains.

Tendency of an act determined by its consequences

2. The general tendency of an act is more or less pernicious, according to the sum total of its consequences: that is, according to the difference between the sum of such as are good, and the sum of such as are evil.

Material consequences only are to be regarded

3. It is to be observed, that here, as well as henceforward, wherever consequences are spoken of, such only are meant as are *material*. Of the consequences of any act, the multitude and variety must needs be infinite: but such of them only as are material are worth regarding. Now among the consequences of an act, be they what they may, such only, by one who views them in the capacity of a legislator, can be said to be material,[a] as either consist of pain or pleasure, or have an influence in the production of pain or pleasure.[b]

These depend in part upon the intention

4. It is also to be observed, that into the account of the consequences of the act, are to be taken not such only as might have ensued, were intention out of the question, but such also as depend upon the connexion there may be between these first-mentioned consequences and the intention. The connexion there is between the intention and certain consequences is, as we shall see hereafter,[c]

[a] Or *of importance.*

[b] In certain cases the consequences of an act may be material by serving as evidences indicating the existence of some other material fact, which is even *antecedent* to the act of which they are the consequences: but even here, they are material only because, in virtue of such their evidentiary quality, they have an influence, at a subsequent period of time, in the production of pain and pleasure: for example, by serving as grounds for conviction, and thence for punishment. See tit. (Simple Falsehoods) *verbo* (material.)[1]

[c] See B. I. tit. (Exemptions) and tit. (Extenuations).

[1] This is probably intended to refer to the *Plan of a Penal Code*, as does note *c* below. But the subject is also discussed in Ch. xvi below, paras. 20 ff.

a means of producing other consequences. In this lies the difference between rational agency and irrational.

5. Now the intention, with regard to the consequences of an act, will depend upon two things: 1. The state of the will or intention, with respect to the act itself. And, 2. The state of the understanding, or perceptive faculties, with regard to the circumstances which it is, or may appear to be, accompanied with. Now with respect to these circumstances, the perceptive faculty is susceptible of three states: consciousness, unconsciousness, and false consciousness. Consciousness, when the party believes precisely those circumstances, and no others, to subsist, which really do subsist: unconsciousness, when he fails of perceiving certain circumstances to subsist, which, however, do subsist: false consciousness, when he believes or imagines certain circumstances to subsist, which in truth do not subsist. *The intention depends as well upon the understanding as the will*

6. In every transaction, therefore, which is examined with a view to punishment, there are four articles to be considered: 1. The *act* itself, which is done. 2. The *circumstances* in which it is done. 3. The *intentionality* that may have accompanied it. 4. The *consciousness*, unconsciousness, or false consciousness, that may have accompanied it. *In an action are to be considered, 1. The act. 2. The circumstances. 3. The intentionality. 4. The consciousness*

What regards the act and the circumstances will be the subject of the present chapter: what regards intention and consciousness, that of the two succeeding.

7. There are also two other articles on which the general tendency of an act depends: and on that, as well as on other accounts, the demand which it creates for punishment. These are, 1. The particular *motive* or motives which gave birth to it. 2. The general *disposition* which it indicates. These articles will be the subject of two other chapters. *5. The motives. 6. The disposition*

8. Acts may be distinguished in several ways, for several purposes. *Acts positive and negative*

They may be distinguished, in the first place, into *positive* and *negative*. By positive are meant such as consist in motion or exertion: by negative, such as consist in keeping at rest; that is, in forbearing to move or exert one's self in such and such circumstances. Thus, to strike is a positive act: not to strike on a certain occasion, a negative one. Positive acts are styled also acts of commission; negative, acts of omission or forbearance.[d]

[d] The distinction between positive and negative acts runs through the whole system of offences, and sometimes makes a material difference with regard to their consequences. To reconcile us the better to the extensive, and, as it *Acts of omission are still acts*

Negative acts may be so relatively or absolutely

9. Such acts, again, as are negative, may either be *absolutely* so, or *relatively*: absolutely, when they import the negation of all positive agency whatsoever; for instance, not to strike at all: relatively, when they import the negation of such or such a particular mode of agency; for instance, not to strike such a person or such a thing, or in such a direction.

Negative acts may be expressed positively; and vice versa

10. It is to be observed, that the nature of the act, whether positive or negative, is not to be determined immediately by the form of the discourse made use of to express it. An act which is positive in its nature may be characterized by a negative expression: thus, not to be at rest, is as much as to say to move. So also an act, which is negative in its nature, may be characterized by a positive expression: thus, to forbear or omit to bring food to a person in certain circumstances, is signified by the single and positive term *to starve*.

Acts external and internal

11. In the second place, acts may be distinguished into *external* and *internal*. By external, are meant corporal acts; acts of the body: by internal, mental acts; acts of the mind. Thus, to strike is an external or exterior[e] act: to intend to strike, an internal or interior one.

Acts of discourse, what

12. Acts of *discourse* are a sort of mixture of the two: external acts, which are no ways material, nor attended with any consequences, any farther than as they serve to express the existence of internal ones. To speak to another to strike, to write to him to strike, to make signs to him to strike, are all so many acts of discourse.

External acts may be transitive or intransitive

13. Third,[1] acts that are external may be distinguished into *transitive* and *intransitive*. Acts may be called transitive, when the

may appear on some occasions, the inconsistent signification here given to the word *act*, it may be considered, 1. That in many cases, where no exterior or overt act is exercised, the state which the mind is in at the time when the supposed act is said to happen, is as truly and directly the result of the will, as any exterior act, how plain and conspicuous soever. The not revealing a conspiracy, for instance, may be as perfectly the act of the will, as the joining in it. In the next place, that even though the mind should never have had the incident in question in contemplation (insomuch that the event of its not happening should not have been so much as obliquely intentional) still the state the person's mind was in at the time when, if he *had* so willed, the incident might have happened, is in many cases productive of as material consequences, and not only as likely, but as fit to call for the interposition of other agents, as the opposite one. Thus, when a tax is imposed, your not paying it is an act which at any rate must be punished in a certain manner, whether you happened to think of paying it or not.

[e] (Exterior.) An exterior act is also called by lawyers *overt*.

[1] Here and in a number of later instances the 1823 edition reads 'Third' for 1789 'Thirdly' and so on.

motion is communicated from the person of the agent to some foreign body: that is, to such a foreign body on which the effects of it are considered as being *material*; as where a man runs against you, or throws water in your face. Acts may be called intransitive, when the motion is communicated to no other body, on which the effects of it are regarded as material, than some part of the same person in whom it originated: as where a man runs, or washes himself.[f]

14. An act of the transitive kind may be said to be in its *commencement*, or in the *first* stage of its progress, while the motion is confined to the person of the agent, and has not yet been communicated to any foreign body, on which the effects of it can be material. It may be said to be in its *termination*, or to be in the last stage of its progress, as soon as the motion or impulse has been communicated to some such foreign body. It may be said to be in the *middle* or intermediate stage or stages of its progress, while the motion, having passed from the person of the agent, has not yet been communicated to any such foreign body. Thus, as soon as a man has lifted up his hand to strike, the act he performs in striking you is in its commencement: as soon as his hand has reached you, it is in its termination. If the act be the motion of a body which is separated from the person of the agent before it reaches the object, it may be said, during that interval, to be in its intermediate progress,[g] or *in gradu mediativo*: as in the case where a man throws a stone or fires a bullet at you.

A transitive act, its commencement, termination, and intermediate progress

15. An act of the *in*transitive kind may be said to be in its commencement, when the motion or impulse is as yet confined to the member or organ in which it originated; and has not yet been communicated to any member or organ that is distinguishable from the former. It may be said to be in its termination, as soon as it has been applied to any other part of the same person. Thus, where a man

An intransitive act, its commencement, and termination

---

[f] The distinction is well known to the latter grammarians: it is with them indeed that it took its rise: though by them it has been applied rather to the names than to the things themselves. To verbs, signifying transitive acts, as here described, they have given the name of transitive verbs: those significative of intransitive acts they have termed intransitive. These last are still more frequently called *neuter*; that is, *neither* active nor passive. The appellation seems improper: since, instead of their being *neither*, they are both in one.

Distinction between transitive acts and intransitive, recognized by grammarians

To the class of acts that are here termed intransitive, belong those which constitute the 3d class in the system of offences. See Ch. (Division.)[1] and B. I. tit. (Self-regarding Offences).

[g] Or *in its migration*, or *in transitu*.

[1] i.e. Ch. xvi below, paras. 8, 15, 64.

poisons himself, while he is lifting up the poison to his mouth, the act is in its commencement: as soon as it has reached his lips, it is in its termination.[h]

Acts transient and continued

16. In the third place, acts may be distinguished into *transient* and *continued*. Thus, to strike is a transient act: to lean, a continued one. To buy, a transient act: to keep in one's possession, a continued one.

Difference between a continued act and a repetition of acts

17. In strictness of speech there is a difference between a *continued* act and a *repetition* of acts. It is a repetition of acts, when there are intervals filled up by acts of different natures: a continued act, when there are no such intervals. Thus, to lean, is one continued act: to keep striking, a repetition of acts.

Difference between a repetition of acts and a habit

18. There is a difference, again, between a *repetition* of acts, and a *habit* or *practice*. The term repetition of acts may be employed, let the acts in question be separated by ever such short intervals, and let the sum total of them occupy ever so short a space of time. The term habit is not employed but when the acts in question are supposed to be separated by long-continued intervals, and the sum total of them to occupy a considerable space of time. It is not (for instance) the drinking ever so many times, nor ever so much at a time, in the course of the same sitting, that will constitute a habit of drunkenness: it is necessary that such sittings themselves be frequently repeated. Every habit is a repetition of acts; or, to speak more strictly, when a man has frequently repeated such and such acts after considerable intervals, he is said to have persevered in or contracted a habit: but every repetition of acts is not a habit.[i]

Acts are indivisible, or divisible, and divisible, as well with regard to matter as to motion

19. Fourth, acts may be distinguished into *indivisible* and *divisible*. Indivisible acts are merely imaginary: they may be easily conceived, but can never be known to be exemplified. Such as are divisible may be so, with regard either to matter or to motion. An act indivisible with regard to matter, is the motion or rest of one single atom of matter. An act indivisible with regard to motion, is the motion of any body, from one single atom of space to the next to it.

Fifth, acts may be distinguished into *simple* and *complex*: simple, such as the act of striking, the act of leaning, or the act of drinking, above instanced: complex, consisting each of a multitude

[h] These distinctions will be referred to in the next chapter: Ch. VIII (Intentionality): and applied to practice in B. I. tit. (Extenuations).

[i] (Habit.) A habit, it should seem, can hardly in strictness be termed an aggregate of acts: acts being a sort of real archetypal entities, and habits a kind of fictitious entities or imaginary beings, supposed to be constituted by, or to result as it were out of, the former.

of simple acts, which, though numerous and heterogeneous, derive a sort of unity from the relation they bear to some common design or end; such as the act of giving a dinner, the act of maintaining a child, the act of exhibiting a triumph, the act of bearing arms, the act of holding a court, and so forth.[1]

20. It has been every now and then made a question, what it is in such a case that constitutes *one* act: where one act has ended, and another act has begun: whether what has happened has been one act or many.[j] These questions, it is now evident, may frequently be answered, with equal propriety, in opposite ways: and if there be any occasions on which they can be answered only in one way, the answer will depend upon the nature of the occasion, and the purpose for which the question is proposed. A man is wounded in two fingers at one stroke—Is it one wound or several? A man is beaten at 12 o'clock, and again at 8 minutes after 12—Is it one beating or several? You beat one man, and instantly in the same breath you beat another—Is this one beating or several? In any of these cases it may be *one*, perhaps, as to some purposes, and *several* as to others. These examples are given, that men may be aware of the ambiguity of language: and neither harass themselves with unsolvable doubts, nor one another with interminable disputes.

Caution respecting the ambiguity of language

21. So much with regard to acts considered in themselves: we come now to speak of the *circumstances* with which they may have been accompanied. These must necessarily be taken into the account before any thing can be determined relative to the consequences. What the consequences of an act may be upon the whole can never otherwise be ascertained: it can never be known whether it is beneficial, or indifferent, or mischievous. In some circumstances even to kill a man may be a beneficial act: in others, to set food before him may be a pernicious one.

Circumstances are to be considered

22. Now the circumstances of an act, are, what? Any objects[k] whatsoever. Take any act whatsoever, there is nothing in the nature of things that excludes any imaginable object from being a circumstance to it. Any given object may be a circumstance to any other.[l]

Circumstances, what

---

[j] Distinctions like these come frequently in question in the course of Procedure.

[k] Or entities. See B. II. tit. (Evidence). § (Facts).

[l] The etymology of the word *circumstance* is perfectly characteristic of its import: *circum stantia*, things standing round: objects standing round a given object. I forget what mathematician it was that defined God to be a circle, of

Circumstance, archetypation of the word

[1] This paragraph is an addition of 1783, inserted in the 1823 edition (where 'Fifth', as in other cases, is substituted for the earlier reading 'Fifthly').

*Circum-
stances
material and
immaterial*

23. We have already had occasion to make mention for a moment of the *consequences* of an act: these were distinguished into material and immaterial. In like manner may the circumstances of it be distinguished. Now *materiality* is a relative term: applied to the consequences of an act, it bore relation to pain and pleasure: applied to the circumstances, it bears relation to the consequences. A circumstance may be said to be material, when it bears a visible relation in point of causality to the consequences: immaterial, when it bears no such visible relation.

*A circum-
stance may
be related to
an event in
point of cau-
sality, in four
ways, viz. 1.
Production.
2. Deriva-
tion. 3. Col-
lateral con-
nexion. 4.
Conjunct
influence*

24. The consequences of an act are events.[m] A circumstance may be related to an event in point of causality in any one of four ways: 1. In the way of causation or production. 2. In the way of derivation. 3. In the way of collateral connexion. 4. In the way of conjunct influence. It may be said to be related to the event in the way of causation, when it is of the number of those that contribute to the production of such event: in the way of derivation, when it is of the number of the events to the production of which that in question has been contributory: in the way of collateral connexion, where the circumstance in question, and the event in question, without being either of them instrumental in the production of the other, are related, each of them, to some common object, which has been concerned in the production of them both: in the way of conjunct influence, when, whether related in any other way or not, they have both of them concurred in the production of some common consequence.

*Example,
Assassina-
tion of Buck-
ingham*

25. An example may be of use. In the year 1628, Villiers, Duke of Buckingham, favourite and minister of Charles I of England, received a wound and died. The man who gave it him was one Felton, who, exasperated at the maladministration of which that minister was accused, went down from London to Portsmouth, where Buckingham happened then to be, made his way into his ante-chamber, and finding him busily engaged in conversation with a number of people round him, got close to him, drew a knife and stabbed him. In the effort, the assassin's hat fell off, which was

which the centre is every where, but the circumference no where.[1] In like manner the field of circumstances, belonging to any act, may be defined a circle, of which the circumference is no where, but of which the act in question is the centre. Now then, as any act may, for the purpose of discourse, be considered as a centre, any other act or object whatsoever may be considered as of the number of those that are standing round it.

[m] See B. II. tit. (Evidence). § (Facts).

[1] Evidence for the origin of this idea is inconclusive: in the *Oxford Dictionary of Quotations* it is attributed to Empedocles.

found soon after, and, upon searching him, the bloody knife. In
the crown of the hat were found scraps of paper, with sentences
expressive of the purpose he was come upon.[1] Here then, suppose
the event in question is the wound received by Buckingham: Felton's drawing out his knife, his making his way into the chamber,
his going down to Portsmouth, his conceiving an indignation at the
idea of Buckingham's administration, that administration itself,
Charles's appointing such a minister, and so on, higher and higher
without end, are so many circumstances, related to the event of
Buckingham's receiving the wound, in the way of causation or
production: the bloodiness of the knife, a circumstance related to
the same event in the way of derivation: the finding of the hat upon
the ground, the finding the sentences in the hat, and the writing
them, so many circumstances related to it in the way of collateral
connexion: and the situation and conversations of the people about
Buckingham, were circumstances related to the circumstances of
Felton's making his way into the room, going down to Portsmouth,
and so forth, in the way of conjunct influence; inasmuch as they
contributed in common to the event of Buckingham's receiving
the wound, by preventing him from putting himself upon his guard
upon the first appearance of the intruder.[n]

26. These several relations do not all of them attach upon an
event with equal certainty. In the first place, it is plain, indeed,
that every event must have some circumstance or other, and in
truth, an indefinite multitude of circumstances, related to it in the
way of production: it must of course have a still greater multitude
of circumstances related to it in the way of collateral connexion.
But it does not appear necessary that every event should have

*It is not
every event
that has cir-
cumstances
related to it
in all those
ways*

[n] The division may be farther illustrated and confirmed by the more simple
and particular case of animal generation. To production corresponds paternity: to derivation, filiation: to collateral connexion, collateral consanguinity:
to conjunct influence, marriage and copulation.

If necessary, it might be again illustrated by the material image of a chain,
such as that which, according to the ingenious fiction of the ancients, is attached to the throne of Jupiter. A section of this chain should then be exhibited
by way of specimen, in the manner of the *diagram* of a pedigree. Such a figure
I should accordingly have exhibited, had it not been for the apprehension that
an exhibition of this sort, while it made the subject a small matter clearer
to one man out of a hundred, might, like the mathematical formularies we see
sometimes employed for the like purpose, make it more obscure and formidable
for the other ninety-nine.

[1] George Villiers (1592–1628), 1st Duke of Buckingham, was assassinated on 23
August 1628 by John Felton (1595?–1628), a lieutenant in the army to whom he had
refused promotion. Felton was hanged at Tyburn on 28 November 1628.

circumstances related to it in the way of derivation: nor therefore that it should have any related to it in the way of conjunct influence. But of the circumstances of all kinds which actually do attach upon an event, it is only a very small number that can be discovered by the utmost exertion of the human faculties: it is a still smaller number that ever actually do attract our notice: when occasion happens, more or fewer of them will be discovered by a man in proportion to the strength, partly of his intellectual powers, partly of his inclination.° It appears therefore that the multitude and description of such of the circumstances belonging to an act, as may appear to be material, will be determined by two considerations: 1. By the nature of things themselves. 2. By the strength or weakness of the faculties of those who happen to consider them.

Use of this chapter

27. Thus much it seemed necessary to premise in general concerning acts, and their circumstances, previously to the consideration of the particular sorts of acts with their particular circumstances, with which we shall have to do in the body of the work. An act of some sort or other is necessarily included in the notion of every offence. Together with this act, under the notion of the same offence, are included certain circumstances: which circumstances enter into the essence of the offence, contribute by their conjunct influence to the production of its consequences, and in conjunction with the act are brought into view by the name by which it stands distinguished. These we shall have occasion to distinguish hereafter

° The more remote a connexion of this sort is, of course the more obscure. It will often happen that a connexion, the idea of which would at first sight appear extravagant and absurd, shall be rendered highly probable, and indeed indisputable, merely by the suggestion of a few intermediate circumstances.

At Rome, 390 years before the Christian era, a goose sets up a cackling: two thousand years afterwards a king of France is murdered. To consider these two events, and nothing more, what can appear more extravagant than the notion that the former of them should have had any influence on the production of the latter? Fill up the gap, bring to mind a few intermediate circumstances, and nothing can appear more probable. It was the cackling of a parcel of geese, at the time the Gauls had surprised the Capitol, that saved the Roman commonwealth: had it not been for the ascendancy that commonwealth acquired afterwards over most of the nations of Europe, amongst others over France, the Christian religion, humanly speaking, could not have established itself in the manner it did in that country. Grant then, that such a man as Henry IV would have existed, no man, however, would have had those motives, by which Ravaillac, misled by a mischievous notion concerning the dictates of that religion, was prompted to assassinate him.[1]

[1] Henry of Navarre (1553–1610), Henry IV of France from 1589, was assassinated in 1610, when about to make war on Spain and the Empire, by François Ravaillac (1578–1610), a Catholic fanatic.

by the name of *criminative* circumstances.[p] Other circumstances again entering into combination with the act and the former set of circumstances, are productive of still farther consequences. These additional consequences, if they are of the beneficial kind, bestow, according to the value they bear in that capacity, upon the circumstances to which they owe their birth, the appellation of *exculpative*[q] or *extenuative* circumstances:[r] if of the mischievous kind, they bestow on them the appellation of *aggravative* circumstances.[s] Of all these different sets of circumstances, the criminative are connected with the consequences of the original offence, in the way of production; with the act, and with one another, in the way of conjunct influence: the consequences of the original offence with them, and with the act respectively, in the way of derivation: the consequences of the modified offence, with the criminative, exculpative, and extenuative circumstances respectively, in the way also of derivation: these different sets of circumstances, with the consequences of the modified act or offence, in the way of production: and with one another (in respect of the consequences of the modified act or offence) in the way of conjunct influence. Lastly, whatever circumstances can be seen to be connected with the consequences of the offence, whether directly in the way of derivation, or obliquely in the way of collateral affinity (to wit, in virtue of its being connected, in the way of derivation, with some of the circumstances with which they stand connected in the same manner) bear a *material* relation to the offence in the way of evidence, they may accordingly by styled *evidentiary* circumstances, and may become of use, by being held forth upon occasion as so many proofs, indications, or evidences of its having been committed.[t][u]

[p] See B. I. tit. (Crim. circumstances).
[q] See B. I. tit. (Justifications).
[r] See B. I. tit. (Extenuations).
[s] See B. I. tit. (Aggravations).
[t] See B. I. tit. (Accessory Offences) and B. II. tit. (Evidence).
[u] It is evident that this analysis is equally applicable to incidents of a purely physical nature, as to those in which moral agency is concerned. If therefore it be just and useful here, it might be found not impossible, perhaps, to find some use for it in natural philosophy.

CHAPTER VIII

OF INTENTIONALITY

*Recapitula-
tion*

1. So much with regard to the two first of the articles upon which the evil tendency of an action may depend: viz. the act itself, and the general assemblage of the circumstances with which it may have been accompanied. We come now to consider the ways in which the particular circumstance of *intention* may be concerned in it.

*The inten-
tion may re-
gard, 1. The
act: or, 2.
The conse-
quences*

2. First, then, the intention or will may regard either of two objects: 1. The act itself: or, 2. Its consequences. Of these objects, that which the intention regards may be styled *intentional*. If it regards the act, then the act may be said to be intentional[a]: if the consequences, so also then may the consequences. If it regards both the act and consequences, the whole *action* may be said to be intentional. Whichever of those articles is not the object of the intention, may of course be said to be *unintentional*.

*It may re-
gard the act
without any
of the conse-
quences*

3. The act may very easily be intentional without the consequences; and often is so. Thus, you may intend to touch a man, without intending to hurt him: and yet, as the consequences turn out, you may chance to hurt him.

*–or the con-
sequences
without re-
garding the
act in all its
stages*

4. The consequences of an act may also be intentional, without the act's being intentional throughout; that is, without its being intentional in every stage of it: but this is not so frequent a case as the former. You intend to hurt a man, suppose, by running against him, and pushing him down: and you run towards him

*Ambiguity of
the words
voluntary
and involun-
tary*

[a] On this occasion the words *voluntary* and *involuntary* are commonly employed. These, however, I purposely abstain from, on account of the extreme ambiguity of their signification. By a voluntary act is meant sometimes, any act, in the performance of which the will has had any concern at all; in this sense it is synonymous to *intentional*: sometimes such acts only, in the production of which the will has been determined by motives not of a painful nature; in this sense it is synonymous to unconstrained, or *uncoerced*: sometimes such acts only, in the production of which the will has been determined by motives, which, whether of the pleasurable or painful kind, occurred to a man himself, without being suggested by any body else; in this sense it is synonymous to *spontaneous*. The sense of the word involuntary does not correspond completely to that of the word voluntary. Involuntary is used in opposition to intentional; and to unconstrained: but not to spontaneous. It might be of use to confine the signification of the words voluntary and involuntary to one single and very narrow case, which will be mentioned in the next note.

accordingly: but a second man coming in on a sudden between you and the first man, before you can stop yourself, you run against the second man, and by him push down the first.

5. But the consequences of an act cannot be intentional, without the act's being itself intentional in at least the first stage. If the act be not intentional in the first stage, it is no act of yours: there is accordingly no intention on your part to produce the consequences: that is to say, the individual consequences. All there can have been on your part is a distant intention to produce other consequences, of the same nature, by some act of yours, at a future time: or else, without any intention, a bare *wish* to see such event take place. The second man, suppose, runs of his own accord against the first, and pushes him down. You had intentions of doing a thing of the same nature: viz. To run against him, and push him down yourself; but you had done nothing in pursuance of those intentions: the individual consequences therefore of the act, which the second man performed in pushing down the first, cannot be said to have been on your part intentional.[b]

—but not without regarding the first stage

[b] To render the analysis here given of the possible states of the mind in point of intentionality absolutely complete, it must be pushed to such a farther degree of minuteness, as to some eyes will be apt to appear trifling. On this account it seemed advisable to discard what follows, from the text to a place where any one who thinks proper may pass by it. An act of the body, when of the positive kind, is a motion: now in motion there are always three articles to be considered: 1. The quantity of matter that moves: 2. The direction in which it moves: and, 3. The velocity with which it moves. Correspondent to these three articles, are so many modes of intentionality, with regard to an act, considered as being only in its first stage. To be completely unintentional, it must be unintentional with respect to every one of these three particulars. This is the case with those acts which alone are properly termed *involuntary*: acts, in the performance of which the will has no sort of share: such as the contraction of the heart and arteries.

An act unintentional in its first stage, may be so with respect to, 1. Quantity of matter moved: 2. Direction: 3. Velocity

Upon this principle, acts that are unintentional in their first stage, may be distinguished into such as are completely unintentional, and such as are incompletely unintentional: and these again may be unintentional, either in point of quantity of matter alone, in point of direction alone, in point of velocity alone, or in any two of these points together.

The example given further on may easily be extended to this part of the analysis, by any one who thinks it worth the while.

There seem to be occasions in which even these disquisitions, minute as they may appear, may not be without their use in practice. In the case of homicide, for example, and other corporal injuries, all the distinctions here specified may occur, and in the course of trial may, for some purpose or other, require to be brought to mind, and made the subject of discourse. What may contribute to render the mention of them pardonable, is the use that might possibly be made of them in natural philosophy. In the hands of an expert

6. Second. A consequence, when it is intentional, may either be *directly* so, or only *obliquely*. It may be said to be directly or lineally intentional, when the prospect of producing it constituted one of the links in the chain of causes by which the person was determined to do the act. It may be said to be obliquely or collaterally intentional, when, although the consequence was in contemplation, and appeared likely to ensue in case of the act's being performed, yet the prospect of producing such consequence did not constitute a link in the aforesaid chain.

A consequence, when intentional, may be directly so, or obliquely

7. Third. An incident, which is directly intentional, may either be *ultimately* so, or only *mediately*. It may be said to be ultimately intentional, when it stands last of all exterior events in the aforesaid chain of motives; insomuch that the prospect of the production of such incident, could there be a certainty of its taking place, would be sufficient to determine the will, without the prospect of its producing any other. It may be said to be mediately intentional, and no more, when there is some other incident, the prospect of producing which forms a subsequent link in the same chain: insomuch that the prospect of producing the former would not have operated as a motive, but for the tendency which it seemed to have towards the production of the latter.

When directly, ultimately so, or mediately

8. Fourth. When an incident is directly intentional, it may either be *exclusively* so, or *inexclusively*. It may be said to be exclusively intentional, when no other but that very individual incident would have answered the purpose, insomuch that no other incident had any share in determining the will to the act in question. It may be said to have been inexclusively[c] intentional, when there was some other incident, the prospect of which was acting upon the will at the same time.

When directly intentional, it may be exclusively so, or inexclusively

9. Fifth. When an incident is inexclusively intentional, it may be either *conjunctively* so, *disjunctively*, or *indiscriminately*. It may be said to be conjunctively intentional with regard to such other incident, when the intention is to produce both: disjunctively, when the intention is to produce either the one or the other indifferently, but not both: indiscriminately, when the intention is indifferently to produce either the one or the other, or both, as it may happen.

When inexclusively, it may be conjunctively, disjunctively, or indiscriminately so

metaphysician, these, together with the foregoing chapter on human actions, and the section on facts in general, in title Evidence of the Book of Procedure,[1] might, perhaps, be made to contribute something towards an exhaustive analysis of the possible varieties of mechanical inventions.

    c Or concurrently.

    [1] i.e. Book II of the *Plan of a Penal Code.*

10. Sixth. When two incidents are disjunctively intentional, they may be so with or without *preference*. They may be said to be so with preference, when the intention is, that one of them in particular should happen rather than the other: without preference, when the intention is equally fulfilled, whichever of them happens.[d]

When disjunctively, it may be with or without preference

11. One example will make all this clear. William II king of England, being out a stag-hunting, received from Sir Walter Tyrrel a wound, of which he died.[e] Let us take this case, and diversify it with a variety of suppositions, correspondent to the distinctions just laid down.

Example

1. First then, Tyrrel did not so much as entertain a thought of the king's death; or, if he did, looked upon it as an event of which there was no danger. In either of these cases the incident of his killing the king was altogether unintentional.

2. He saw a stag running that way, and he saw the king riding that way at the same time: what he aimed at was to kill the stag: he did not wish to kill the king: at the same time he saw, that if he shot, it was as likely he should kill the king as the stag: yet for all that he shot, and killed the king accordingly. In this case the incident of his killing the king was intentional, but obliquely so.

3. He killed the king on account of the hatred he bore him, and for no other reason than the pleasure of destroying him. In this case the incident of the king's death was not only directly but ultimately intentional.

4. He killed the king, intending fully so to do; not for any hatred he bore him, but for the sake of plundering him when dead. In this case the incident of the king's death was directly intentional, but not ultimately: it was mediately intentional.

[d] There is a difference between the case where an incident is altogether unintentional, and that in which, it being disjunctively intentional with reference to another, the preference is in favour of that other. In the first case, it is not the intention of the party that the incident in question should happen at all: in the latter case, the intention is rather that the other should happen: but if that cannot be, then that this in question should happen rather than that neither should, and that both, at any rate, should not happen.

Difference between an incident's being unintentional, and disjunctively intentional, when the election is in favour of the other

All these are distinctions to be attended to in the use of the particle *or*: a particle of very ambiguous import, and of great importance in legislation. See Append. tit. (Composition).[1]

[e] Hume's Hist.[2]

[1] See above 72 n. 1.
[2] Cf. Hume, *History of Great Britain*, 1773, i, 306–7: 'Walter Tyrrel, a French gentleman, remarkable for his address in archery, attended him [William II] in this recreation, of which the new forest was the scene . . . let fly an arrow at a stag . . . The arrow, glancing from a tree, struck the king in the breast, and instantly slew him.'

5. He intended neither more nor less than to kill the king. He had no other aim nor wish. In this case it was exclusively as well as directly intentional: exclusively, to wit, with regard to every other material incident.

6. Sir Walter shot the king in the right leg, as he was plucking a thorn out of it with his left hand. His intention was, by shooting the arrow into his leg through his hand, to cripple him in both those limbs at the same time. In this case the incident of the king's being shot in the leg was intentional: and that conjunctively with another which did not happen; viz. his being shot in the hand.

7. The intention of Tyrrel was to shoot the king either in the hand or in the leg, but not in both; and rather in the hand than in the leg. In this case the intention of shooting in the hand[1] was disjunctively concurrent, with regard to the other incident, and that with pre-ference.

8. His intention was to shoot the king either in the leg or the hand, whichever might happen; but not in both. In this case the intention was inexclusive, but disjunctively so: yet that, however, without preference.

9. His intention was to shoot the king either in the leg or the hand, or in both, as it might happen. In this case the intention was indiscriminately concurrent, with respect to the two incidents.

Intention-ality of the act with res-pect to its different stages, how far material

12. It is to be observed, that an act may be unintentional in any stage or stages of it, though intentional in the preceding: and, on the other hand, it may be intentional in any stage or stages of it, and yet unintentional in the succeeding.[f] But whether it be intentional or no in any preceding stage, is immaterial, with respect to the con-sequences, so it be unintentional in the last. The only point, with respect to which it is material, is the proof. The more stages the act is unintentional in, the more apparent it will commonly be, that it was unintentional with respect to the last. If a man, intending to strike you on the cheek, strikes you in the eye, and puts it out, it will probably be difficult for him to prove that it was not his intention to strike you in the eye. It will probably be easier, if his intention was really not to strike you, or even not to strike at all.

Goodness and badness of intention dis-missed

13. It is frequent to hear men speak of a good intention, of a bad intention; of the goodness and badness of a man's intention: a circumstance on which great stress is generally laid. It is indeed of no small importance, when properly understood: but the import of it is to the last degree ambiguous and obscure. Strictly speaking,

[f] See Ch. VII (Actions) par. 14.

[1] 1789 edn. mistakenly reads 'leg': correction made in 1789 list of errata.

nothing can be said to be good or bad, but either in itself; which is the case only with pain or pleasure: or on account of its effects; which is the case only with things that are the causes or preventives of pain and pleasure. But in a figurative and less proper way of speech, a thing may also be styled good or bad, in consideration of its cause. Now the effects of an intention to do such or such an act, are the same objects which we have been speaking of under the appellation of its *consequences*: and the causes of intention are called *motives*. A man's intention then on any occasion may be styled good or bad, with reference either to the consequences of the act, or with reference to his motives. If it be deemed good or bad in any sense, it must be either because it is deemed to be productive of good or of bad consequences, or because it is deemed to originate from a good or from a bad motive. But the goodness or badness of the consequences depend upon the circumstances. Now the circumstances are no objects of the intention. A man intends the act: and by his intention produces the act: but as to the circumstances, he does not intend *them*: he does not, inasmuch as they are circumstances of it, produce them. If by accident there be a few which he has been instrumental in producing, it has been by former intentions, directed to former acts, productive of those circumstances as the consequences: at the time in question he takes them as he finds them. Acts, with their consequences, are objects of the will as well as of the understanding: circumstances, as such, are objects of the understanding only. All he can do with these, as such, is to know or not to know them: in other words, to be conscious of them, or not conscious. To the title of Consciousness belongs what is to be said of the goodness or badness of a man's intention, as resulting from the consequences of the act: and to the head of Motives, what is to be said of his intention, as resulting from the motive.

CHAPTER IX

OF CONSCIOUSNESS

Connexion
of this
chapter with
the foregoing

1. So far with regard to the ways in which the will or intention may be concerned in the production of any incident: we come now to consider the part which the understanding or perceptive faculty may have borne, with relation to such incident.

Acts advised
and unad-
vised: con-
sciousness,
what

2. A certain act has been done, and that intentionally: that act was attended with certain circumstances: upon these circumstances depended certain of its consequences; and amongst the rest, all those which were of a nature purely physical. Now then, take any one of these circumstances, it is plain, that a man, at the time of doing the act from whence such consequences ensued, may have been either conscious, with respect to this circumstance, or unconscious. In other words, he may either have been aware of the circumstance, or not aware: it may either have been present to his mind, or not present. In the first case, the act may be said to have been an *advised* act, with respect to that circumstance: in the other case, an *unadvised* one.

Unadvised-
ness may
regard either
existence, or
materiality

3. There are two points, with regard to which an act may have been advised or unadvised: 1. The *existence* of the circumstance itself. 2. The *materiality* of it.[a]

The circum-
stance may
have been
present, past,
or future

4. It is manifest, that with reference to the time of the act, such circumstance may have been either *present, past,* or *future*.

An unad-
vised act may
be heedless,
or not heed-
less

5. An act which is unadvised, is either *heedless*, or not heedless. It is termed heedless, when the case is thought to be such, that a person of ordinary prudence,[b] if prompted by an ordinary share of benevolence, would have been likely to have bestowed such and so much attention and reflection upon the material circumstances, as would have effectually disposed him to prevent the mischievous incident from taking place: not heedless, when the case is not thought to be such as above mentioned.[c]

A mis-
advised act,
what.—A
mis-supposal

6. Again. Whether a man did or did not suppose the existence or materiality of a given circumstance, it may be that he *did* suppose the existence and materiality of some circumstance, which either did not exist, or which, though existing, was not material. In such

[a] See Ch. vii (Actions) par. 3.
[b] See Ch. vi (Sensibility) par. 12.
[c] See B. I. tit. (Extenuations).

case the act may be said to be *mis-advised*, with respect to such imagined circumstance: and it may be said, that there has been an erroneous supposition, or a *mis-supposal* in the case.

7. Now a circumstance, the existence of which is thus erroneously supposed, may be material either, 1. In the way of prevention: or, 2. In that of compensation. It may be said to be material in the way of prevention, when its effect or tendency, had it existed, would have been to prevent the obnoxious consequences: in the way of compensation, when that effect or tendency would have been to produce other consequences, the beneficialness of which would have out-weighed the mischievousness of the others. *The supposed circumstance might have been material in the way either of prevention or of compensation*

8. It is manifest that, with reference to the time of the act, such imaginary circumstance may in either case have been supposed either to be *present, past,* or *future*. *It may have been supposed present, past, or future*

9. To return to the example exhibited in the preceding chapter. *Example, continued from the last chapter*

10. Tyrrel intended to shoot in the direction in which he shot; but he did not know that the king was riding so near that way. In this case the act he performed in shooting, the act of shooting, was unadvised, with respect to the *existence* of the circumstance of the king's being so near riding that way.

11. He knew that the king was riding that way: but at the distance at which the king was, he knew not of the probability there was that the arrow would reach him. In this case the act was unadvised, with respect to the *materiality* of the circumstance.

12. Somebody had dipped the arrow in poison, without Tyrrel's knowing of it. In this case the act was unadvised, with respect to the existence of a *past* circumstance.

13. At the very instant that Tyrrel drew the bow, the king, being screened from his view by the foliage of some bushes, was riding furiously, in such manner as to meet the arrow in a direct line: which circumstance was also more than Tyrrel knew of. In this case the act was unadvised, with respect to the existence of a *present* circumstance.

14. The king being at a distance from court, could get nobody to dress his wound till the next day; of which circumstance Tyrrel was not aware. In this case the act was unadvised, with respect to what was then a *future* circumstance.

15. Tyrrel knew of the king's being riding that way, of his being so near, and so forth; but being deceived by the foliage of the bushes, he thought he saw a bank between the spot from which he shot, and that to which the king was riding. In this case the act was *mis-*

advised, proceeding on the *mis-supposal* of a *preventive* circumstance.

16. Tyrrel knew that every thing was as above, nor was he deceived by the supposition of any preventive circumstance. But he believed the king to be an usurper: and supposed he was coming up to attack a person whom Tyrrel believed to be the rightful king, and who was riding by Tyrrel's side. In this case the act was also mis-advised, but proceeded on the mis-supposal of a *compensative* circumstance.

In what case consciousness extends the intentionality from the act to the consequences

10. Let us observe the connexion there is between intentionality and consciousness. When the act itself is intentional, and with respect to the existence of all the circumstances *advised*, as also with respect to the materiality of those circumstances, in relation to a given consequence, and there is no mis-supposal with regard to any preventive circumstance, that consequence must also be intentional: in other words; advisedness, with respect to the circumstances, if clear from the mis-supposal of any preventive circumstance, extends the intentionality from the act to the consequences. Those consequences may be either directly intentional, or only obliquely so: but at any rate they cannot but be intentional.

Example continued

11. To go on with the example. If Tyrrel intended to shoot in the direction in which the king was riding up, and knew that the king was coming to meet the arrow, and knew the probability there was of his being shot in that same part in which he was shot, or in another as dangerous, and with that same degree of force, and so forth, and was not misled by the erroneous supposition of a circumstance by which the shot would have been prevented from taking place, or any such other preventive circumstance, it is plain he could not but have intended the king's death. Perhaps he did not positively wish it; but for all that, in a certain sense he intended it.

A misadvised act may be rash or not rash

12. What heedlessness is in the case of an unadvised act, rashness is in the case of a misadvised one. A misadvised act then may be either rash or not rash. It may be termed rash, when the case is thought to be such, that a person of ordinary prudence, if prompted by an ordinary share of benevolence, would have employed such and so much attention and reflection to the imagined circumstance, as, by discovering to him the non-existence, improbability, or immateriality of it, would have effectually disposed him to prevent the mischievous incident from taking place.

The intention may be good or bad in itself, independently of the motive as well as the eventual consequences

13. In ordinary discourse, when a man does an act of which the consequences prove mischievous, it is a common thing to speak of him as having acted with a good intention or with a bad intention,

of his intention's being a good one or a bad one. The epithets good and bad are all this while applied, we see, to the intention: but the application of them is most commonly governed by a supposition formed with regard to the nature of the motive. The act, though eventually it prove mischievous, is said to be done with a good intention, when it is supposed to issue from a motive which is looked upon as a good motive: with a bad intention, when it is supposed to be the result of a motive which is looked upon as a bad motive. But the nature of the consequences intended, and the nature of the motive which gave birth to the intention, are objects which, though intimately connected, are perfectly distinguishable. The intention might therefore with perfect propriety be styled a good one, whatever were the motive. It might be styled a good one, when not only the consequences of the act *prove* mischievous, but the motive which gave birth to it *was* what is called a bad one. To warrant the speaking of the intention as being a good one, it is sufficient if the consequences of the act, had they proved what to the agent they seemed likely to be, *would* have been of a beneficial nature. And in the same manner the intention may be bad, when not only the consequences of the act prove beneficial, but the motive which gave birth to it was a good one.

14. Now, when a man has a mind to speak of your *intention* as being good or bad, with reference to the consequences, if he speaks of it at all he must use the word intention, for there is no other. But if a man means to speak of the *motive* from which your intention originated, as being a good or a bad one, he is certainly not obliged to use the word intention: it is at least as well to use the word motive. By the supposition he means the motive; and very likely he may *not* mean the intention. For what is true of the one is very often not true of the other. The motive may be good when the intention is bad: the intention may be good when the motive is bad: whether they are both good or both bad, or the one good and the other bad, makes, as we shall see hereafter, a very essential difference with regard to the consequences.[d] It is therefore much better, when motive is meant, never to say intention.

It is better when the intention is meant to be spoken of as being good or bad, not to say, the motive

15. An example will make this clear. Out of malice a man prosecutes you for a crime of which he believes you to be guilty, but of which in fact you are not guilty. Here the *consequences* of his conduct are mischievous: for they are mischievous to you at any rate, in virtue of the shame and anxiety which you are made to suffer while the prosecution is depending: to which is to be added, in case

Example

d See Ch. XII (Consequences).

of your being convicted, the evil of the punishment. To you therefore they are mischievous; nor is there any one to whom they are
beneficial. The man's *motive* was also what is called a bad one: for
malice will be allowed by every body to be a bad motive. However,
the *consequences* of his conduct, had they proved such as he believed them likely to be, would have been good: for in them would
have been included the punishment of a criminal, which is a benefit to all who are exposed to suffer by a crime of the like nature.
The *intention* therefore, in this case, though not in a common way
of speaking the motive, might be styled a *good* one. But of motives
more particularly in the next chapter.

Intention, in what cases it may be inno-cent

16. In the same sense the intention, whether it be positively good
or no, so long as it is not bad, may be termed innocent. Accordingly,
let the consequences have proved mischievous, and let the motive
have been what it will, the intention may be termed innocent in
either of two cases: 1. In the case of *un*-advisedness with respect to
any of the circumstances on which the mischievousness of the consequences depended: 2. In the case of *mis*-advisedness with respect to any circumstance, which, had it been what it appeared to
be, would have served either to prevent or to outweigh the mischief.

Intention-ality and consciousness, how spoken of in the Roman law

17. A few words for the purpose of applying what has been said
to the Roman law. Unintentionality, and innocence of intention,
seem both to be included in the case of *infortunium*, where there is
neither *dolus* nor *culpa*. Unadvisedness coupled with heedlessness,
and mis-advisedness coupled with rashness, correspond to the *culpa
sine dolo*. Direct intentionality corresponds to *dolus*. Oblique intentionality seems hardly to have been distinguished from direct; were
it to occur, it would probably be deemed also to correspond to *dolus*.
The division into *culpa, lata, levis*, and *levissima*, is such as nothing
certain can correspond to. What is it that it expresses? A distinction, not in the case itself, but only in the sentiments which any
person (a judge, for instance) may find himself disposed to entertain
with relation to it: supposing it already distinguished into three
subordinate cases by other means.

The word *dolus* seems ill enough contrived: the word *culpa* as
indifferently. *Dolus*, upon any other occasion, would be understood
to imply deceit, concealment,[e] clandestinity:[f] but here it is extended

---

[e] See B. I. tit. (Theft) *verbo* (amenable).

[f] Dolus, an virtus quis in hoste requirit?   VIRGIL.[1]
    — δολῳ ηε και αμφαδον.   HOMER.[2]

[1] *Aeneid*, II.390. The last word should read *requirat*.
[2] *Odyssey*, IV.435.

94

to open force. *Culpa*, upon any other occasion, would be understood to extend to blame of every kind. It would therefore include *dolus*.[g]

18. The above-mentioned definitions and distinctions are far from being mere matters of speculation. They are capable of the most extensive and constant application, as well to moral discourse as to legislative practice. Upon the degree and bias of a man's intention, upon the absence or presence of consciousness or mis-supposal, depend a great part of the good and bad, more especially of the bad consequences of an act; and on this, as well as other grounds, a great part of the demand for punishment.[h] The presence of intention with regard to such or such a consequence, and of consciousness with regard to such or such a circumstance, of the act, will form so many criminative circumstances,[i] or essential ingredients in the composition of this or that offence: applied to other circumstances, consciousness will form a ground of aggravation, annexable to the like offence.[j] In almost all cases, the absence of intention with regard to certain consequences, and the absence of consciousness, or the presence of mis-supposal, with regard to certain circumstances, will constitute so many grounds of extenuation.[k]

Use of this and the preceding chapter

[g] I pretend not here to give any determinate explanation of a set of words, of which the great misfortune is, that the import of them is confused and indeterminate. I speak only by approximation. To attempt to determine the precise import that has been given them by a hundredth part of the authors that have used them, would be an endless task. Would any one talk intelligibly on this subject in Latin? let him throw out *dolus* altogether: let him keep *culpa*, for the purpose of expressing not the case itself, but the sentiment that is entertained concerning a case described by other means. For intentionality, let him coin a word boldly, and say *intentionalitas*: for unintentionality, *non-intentionalitas*. For unadvisedness, he has already the word *inscitia*; though the words *imprudentia, inobservantia*, were it not for the other senses they are used in, would do better: for unadvisedness coupled with heedlessness, let him say *inscitia culpabilis*: for unadvisedness without heedlessness, *inscitia inculpabilis*: for mis-advisedness coupled with rashness, *error culpabilis, error temerarius*, or *error cum temeritate*: for mis-advisedness without rashness, *error inculpabilis, error non-temerarius*, or *error sine temeritate*.

It is not unfrequent likewise to meet with the phrase, *malo animo*: a phrase still more indeterminate, if possible, than any of the former. It seems to have reference either to intentionality, or to consciousness, or to the motive, or to the disposition, or to any two or more of these taken together; nobody can tell which: these being objects which seem to have never hitherto been properly distinguished and defined.

[h] See Ch. XIII (Cases unmeet).
[i] See B. I. tit. (Circumstances influencing).
[j] See B. I. tit. (Aggravations).
[k] See B. I. tit. (Extenuations).

CHAPTER X

OF MOTIVES

§ i. *Different senses of the word motive*[a]

Motives, why considered

1. It is an acknowledged truth, that every kind of act whatever, and consequently every kind of offence, is apt to assume a different character, and be attended with different effects, according to the nature of the *motive* which gives birth to it. This makes it requisite to take a view of the several motives by which human conduct is liable to be influenced.

Purely speculative motives have nothing to do here

2. By a motive, in the most extensive sense in which the word is ever used with reference to a thinking being, is meant any thing that can contribute to give birth to, or even to prevent, any kind of action. Now the action of a thinking being is the act either of the body, or only of the mind: and an act of the mind is an act either of the intellectual faculty, or of the will. Acts of the intellectual faculty will sometimes rest in the understanding merely, without exerting any influence in the production of any acts of the will. Motives, which are not of a nature to influence any other acts than those, may be styled purely *speculative* motives, or motives resting in speculation. But as to these acts, neither do they exercise any influence over external acts, or over their consequences, nor consequently over any pain or any pleasure that may be in the number of such consequences. Now it is only on account of their tendency to produce either pain or pleasure, that any acts can be material. With acts, therefore, that rest purely in the understanding, we have not here any concern: nor therefore with any object, if any such there be, which, in the character of a motive, can have no influence on any other acts than those.

Motives to the will

3. The motives with which alone we have any concern, are such

[a] Note by the author, July 1822.

For a tabular simultaneous view of the whole list of MOTIVES, in conjunction with the correspondent *pleasures* and *pains*, *interests* and *desires*, see, by the same author, *Table of the Springs of Action*, &c. with Explanatory Notes and Observations. London 1817, Hunter, St Paul's Church Yard, 8vo. pp. 32.[1]

The word *inducement* has of late presented itself, as being in its signification more comprehensive than the word *motive*, and on some occasions more apposite.

[1] Cf. Bowring, i, 195–219, esp. 215–19.

as are of a nature to act upon the will. By a motive then, in this sense of the word, is to be understood any thing whatsoever, which by influencing the will of a sensitive being, is supposed to serve as a means of determining him to act, or voluntarily to forbear to act,[b] upon any occasion. Motives of this sort, in contradistinction to the former, may be styled *practical* motives, or motives applying to practice.

4. Owing to the poverty and unsettled state of language, the word *motive* is employed indiscriminately to denote two kinds of objects, which, for the better understanding of the subject, it is necessary should be distinguished. On some occasions it is employed to denote any of those really existing incidents from whence the act in question is supposed to take its rise. The sense it bears on these occasions may be styled its literal or *unfigurative* sense. On other occasions it is employed to denote a certain fictitious entity, a passion, an affection of the mind, an ideal being which upon the happening of any such incident is considered as operating upon the mind, and prompting it to take that course, towards which it is impelled by the influence of such incident. Motives of this class are Avarice, Indolence, Benevolence, and so forth; as we shall see more particularly farther on. This latter may be styled the *figurative* sense of the term *motive*.

Figurative and unfigurative senses of the word

5. As to the real incidents to which the name of motive is also given, these too are of two very different kinds. They may be either, 1. The *internal* perception of any individual lot of pleasure or pain, the expectation of which is looked upon as calculated to determine you to act in such or such a manner; as the pleasure of acquiring such a sum of money, the pain of exerting yourself on such an occasion, and so forth: Or, 2. Any *external* event, the happening whereof is regarded as having a tendency to bring about the perception of such pleasure or such pain: for instance, the coming up of a lottery ticket, by which the possession of the money devolves to you; or the breaking out of a fire in the house you are in, which

Motives interior and exterior

[b] When the effect or tendency of a motive is to determine a man to forbear to act, it may seem improper to make use of the term *motive*: since motive, properly speaking, means that which disposes an object to *move*. We must however use that improper term, or a term which, though proper enough, is scarce in use, the word *determinative*. By way of justification, or at least apology, for the popular usage in this behalf, it may be observed, that even forbearance to act, or the negation of motion (that is, of bodily motion) supposes an act done, when such forbearance is voluntary. It supposes, to wit, an act of the will, which is as much a positive act, as much a motion, as any other act of the thinking substance.

makes it necessary for you to quit it. The former kind of motives may be termed interior, or internal: the latter exterior, or external.

Motive in prospect— motive in esse

6. Two other senses of the term *motive* need also to be distinguished. Motive refers necessarily to action. It is a pleasure, pain, or other event, that prompts to action. Motive then, in one sense of the word, must be previous to such event. But, for a man to be governed by any motive, he must in every case look beyond that event which is called his action; he must look to the consequences of it: and it is only in this way that the idea of pleasure, of pain, or of any other event, can give birth to it. He must look, therefore, in every case, to some event posterior to the act in contemplation: an event which as yet exists not, but stands only in prospect. Now, as it is in all cases difficult, and in most cases unnecessary, to distinguish between objects so intimately connected, as the posterior possible object which is thus looked forward to, and the present existing object or event which takes place upon a man's looking forward to the other, they are both of them spoken of under the same appellation, *motive*. To distinguish them, the one first mentioned may be termed a motive in *prospect*, the other a motive in *esse*: and under each of these denominations will come as well exterior as internal motives. A fire breaks out in your neighbour's house: you are under apprehension of its extending to your own: you are apprehensive, that if you stay in it, you will be burnt: you accordingly run out of it. This then is the act: the others are all motives to it. The event of the fire's breaking out in your neighbour's house is an external motive, and that in *esse*: the idea or belief of the probability of the fire's extending to your own house, that of your being burnt if you continue, and the pain you feel at the thought of such a catastrophe, are all so many internal events, but still in *esse*: the event of the fire's actually extending to your own house, and that of your being actually burnt by it, external motives in prospect: the pain you would feel at seeing your house a burning, and the pain you would feel while your yourself were burning, internal motives in prospect: which events, according as the matter turns out, may come to be in *esse*: but then of course they will cease to act as motives.

Motives immediate and remote

7. Of all these motives, that which stands nearest to the act, to the production of which they all contribute, is that internal motive in *esse* which consists in the expectation of the internal motive in prospect:[1] the pain or uneasiness you feel at the thoughts of being

---

[1] The 1789 text has been restored here in place of the meaningless reading in 1823 and later editions: 'Of all these motives, which stand nearest to the act . . .' etc.

burnt.[c] All other motives are more or less remote: the motives in
prospect, in proportion as the period at which they are expected
to happen is more distant from the period at which the act takes
place, and consequently later in point of time: the motives in *esse*,
in proportion as they also are more distant from that period, and
consequently earlier in point of time.[d]

8. It has already been observed, that with motives of which the
influence terminates altogether in the understanding, we have
nothing here to do. If then, amongst objects that are spoken of as
motives with reference to the understanding, there be any which
concern us here, it is only in as far as such objects may, through the
medium of the understanding, exercise an influence over the will.
It is in this way, and in this way only, that any objects, in virtue
of any tendency they may have to influence the sentiment of belief,
may in a practical sense act in the character of motives. Any objects, by tending to induce a belief concerning the existence, actual,
or probable, of a practical motive; that is, concerning the probability of a motive in prospect, or the existence of a motive in *esse*;
may exercise an influence on the will, and rank with those other
motives that have been placed under the name of practical. The
pointing out of motives such as these, is what we frequently mean
when we talk of giving *reasons*. Your neighbour's house is on fire
as before. I observe to you, that at the lower part of your neighbour's house is some wood-work, which joins on to your's; that the
flames have caught this wood-work, and so forth; which I do in
order to dispose you to believe as I believe, that if you stay in your
house much longer you will be burnt. In doing this, then, I suggest

Motives to the under-standing, how they may influence the will

[c] Whether it be the expectation of being burnt, or the pain that accompanies
that expectation, that is the immediate internal motive spoken of, may be
difficult to determine. It may even be questioned, perhaps, whether they are
distinct entities. Both questions, however, seem to be mere questions of words,
and the solution of them altogether immaterial. Even the other kinds of
motives, though for some purposes they demand a separate consideration, are,
however, so intimately allied, that it will often be scarce practicable, and not
always material, to avoid confounding them, as they have always hitherto
been confounded.

[d] Under the term *esse* must be included as well *past* existence, with reference
to a given period, as *present*. They are equally real, in comparison with[1] what
is as yet but future. Language is materially deficient, in not enabling us to distinguish with precision between *existence* as opposed to *unreality*, and *present*
existence as opposed to past. The word existence in English, and *esse*, adopted
by lawyers from the Latin, have the inconvenience of appearing to confine the
existence in question to some single period considered as being present.

[1] 1789 'of'.

motives to your understanding; which motives, by the tendency they have to give birth to or strengthen a pain, which operates upon you in the character of an internal motive in *esse*, join their force, and act as motives upon the will.

§ ii. *No motives either constantly good, or constantly bad*

Nothing can act of itself as a motive but the ideas of pleasure or pain

9. In all this chain of motives, the principal or original link seems to be the last internal motive in prospect; it is to this that all the other motives in prospect owe their materiality: and the immediately acting motive its existence. This motive in prospect, we see, is always some pleasure, or some pain; some pleasure, which the act in question is expected to be a means of continuing or producing: some pain which it is expected to be a means of discontinuing or preventing. A motive is substantially nothing more than pleasure or pain, operating in a certain manner.

No sort of motive is in itself a bad one

10. Now, pleasure is in *itself* a good: nay, even setting aside immunity from pain, the only good: pain is in itself an evil; and, indeed, without exception, the only evil; or else the words good and evil have no meaning. And this is alike true of every sort of pain, and of every sort of pleasure. It follows, therefore, immediately and incontestibly, that *there is no such thing as any sort of motive that is in itself a bad one.*[e]

Inaccuracy of expressions in which good or bad are applied to motives

11. It is common, however, to speak of actions as proceeding from *good* or *bad* motives: in which case the motives meant are such as are internal. The expression is far from being an accurate one; and as it is apt to occur in the consideration of almost every kind of offence, it will be requisite to settle the precise meaning of it, and observe how far it quadrates with the truth of things.

Any sort of motive may give birth to any sort of act

12. With respect to goodness and badness, as it is with every thing else that is not itself either pain or pleasure, so is it with motives. If they are good or bad, it is only on account of their effects: good, on account of their tendency to produce pleasure, or avert pain: bad, on account of their tendency to produce pain, or avert pleasure. Now the case is, that from one and the same motive, and from every kind of motive, may proceed actions that are good,

[e] Let a man's motive be ill-will; call it even malice, envy, cruelty; it is still a kind of pleasure that is his motive: the pleasure he takes at the thought of the pain which he sees, or expects to see, his adversary undergo. Now even this wretched pleasure, taken by itself, is good: it may be faint; it may be short: it must at any rate be impure: yet while it lasts, and before any bad consequences arrive, it is as good as any other that is not more intense. See Ch. iv (Value).

others that are bad, and others that are indifferent. This we shall proceed to shew with respect to all the different kinds of motives, as determined by the various kinds of pleasures and pains.

13. Such an analysis, useful as it is, will be found to be a matter of no small difficulty; owing, in great measure, to a certain perversity of structure which prevails more or less throughout all languages. To speak of motives, as of any thing else, one must call them by their names. But the misfortune is, that it is rare to meet with a motive of which the name expresses that and nothing more. Commonly along with the very name of the motive, is tacitly involved a proposition imputing to it a certain quality; a quality which, in many cases, will appear to include that very goodness or badness, concerning which we are here inquiring whether, properly speaking, it be or be not imputable to motives. To use the common phrase, in most cases, the name of the motive is a word which is employed either only in a *good sense*, or else only in a *bad sense*. Now, when a word is spoken of as being used in a good sense, all that is necessarily meant is this: that in conjunction with the idea of the object it is put to signify, it conveys an idea of *approbation*: that is, of a pleasure or satisfaction, entertained by the person who employs the term at the thoughts of such object. In like manner, when a word is spoken of as being used in a bad sense, all that is necessarily meant is this: that, in conjunction with the idea of the object it is put to signify, it conveys an idea of *disapprobation*: that is, of a displeasure entertained by the person who employs the term at the thoughts of such object. Now, the circumstance on which such approbation is grounded will, as naturally as any other, be the opinion of the *goodness* of the object in question, as above explained: such, at least, it must be, upon the principle of utility: so, on the other hand, the circumstance on which any such disapprobation is grounded, will, as naturally as any other, be the opinion of the *badness* of the object: such, at least, it must be, in as far as the principle of utility is taken for the standard.

Now there are certain motives which, unless in a few particular cases, have scarcely any other name to be expressed by but such a word as is used only in a good sense. This is the case, for example, with the motives of piety and honour. The consequence of this is, that if, in speaking of such a motive, a man should have occasion to apply the epithet bad to any actions which he mentions as apt to result from it, he must appear to be guilty of a contradiction in terms. But the names of motives which have scarcely any other name to be expressed by, but such a word as is used only in a bad sense, are many more.[f] This is the case, for example, with the motives of lust and avarice. And accordingly, if in speaking of any such motive, a man should have occasion to apply the epithets good or indifferent to any actions which he mentions as apt to result from it, he must here also appear to be guilty of a similar contradiction.[g]

This perverse association of ideas cannot, it is evident, but throw great difficulties in the way of the inquiry now before us. Confining himself to the language most in use, a man can scarce avoid running, in appearance, into perpetual contradictions. His propositions will appear, on the one hand, repugnant to truth; and on the other hand, adverse to utility. As paradoxes, they will excite contempt: as mischievous paradoxes, indignation. For the truths he labours to convey, however important, and however salutary, his reader is never the better: and he himself is much the worse. To obviate this inconvenience, completely, he has but this one unpleasant remedy; to lay aside the old phraseology and invent a new one. Happy the man whose language is ductile enough to permit him this resource. To palliate the inconvenience, where that method of obviating it is impracticable, he has nothing left for it but to enter into a long discussion, to state the whole matter at large, to confess, that for the sake of promoting the purposes, he has violated the established laws of language, and to throw himself upon the mercy of his readers.[h]

[f] For the reason, see Ch. xi (Dispositions) par. 17 note.

[g] To this imperfection of language, and nothing more, are to be attributed, in great measure, the violent clamours that have from time to time been raised against those ingenious moralists, who, travelling out of the beaten tract of speculation, have found more or less difficulty in disentangling themselves from the shackles of ordinary language: such as Rochefoucault,[1] Mandeville,[2] and Helvetius.[3] To the unsoundness of their opinions, and, with still greater injustice, to the corruption of their hearts, was often imputed, what was most commonly owing either to a want of skill, in matters of language on the part of the author, or a want of discernment, possibly now and then in some instances a want of probity, on the part of the commentator.

[h] Happily, language is not always so intractable, but that by making use of two words instead of one, a man may avoid the inconvenience of fabricating words that are absolutely new. Thus instead of the word lust, by putting together two words in common use, he may frame the neutral expression, sexual desire: instead of the word avarice, by putting together two other words also

[1] François, 6th duc de la Rochefoucauld (1613–80): Bentham is presumably referring to his *Maximes*—i.e. *Réflexions, ou Sentences et Maximes morales* (1664).

[2] Bernard Mandeville (1670–1733), author of *The Fable of the Bees; or, Private Vices, Public Benefits* (1714).

[3] Claude Adrien Helvétius (1715–71), whose *De l'esprit* (1758) was one of the most important early influences on Bentham's own work.

§ iii. *Catalogue of motives corresponding to that of Pleasures and Pains*

14. From the pleasures of the senses, considered in the gross, results the motive which in a neutral sense, may be termed physical desire: in a bad sense, it is termed sensuality. Name used in a good sense it has none. Of this, nothing can be determined, till it be considered separately, with reference to the several species of pleasures to which it corresponds.

Physical desire corresponding to pleasures of sense in general

15. In particular, then, to the pleasures of the taste or palate corresponds a motive, which in a neutral sense having received no name that can serve to express it in all cases, can only be termed, by circumlocution, the love of the pleasures of the palate. In particular cases it is styled hunger: in others, thirst.[1] The love of good cheer expresses this motive, but seems to go beyond: intimating, that the pleasure is to be partaken of in company, and involving a kind of sympathy. In a bad sense, it is styled in some cases greediness, voraciousness, gluttony: in others, principally when applied to children, lickerishness.[1] It may in some cases also be represented by the word daintiness. Name used in a good sense it has none. 1. A boy, who does not want for victuals, steals a cake out of a pastrycook's shop, and eats it. In this case his motive will be universally deemed a bad one: and if it be asked what it is, it may be answered, perhaps, lickerishness.[1] 2. A boy buys a cake out of a pastrycook's shop, and eats it. In this case his motive can scarcely be looked upon as either good or bad, unless his master should be out of humour with him; and then perhaps he may call it lickerishness,[1]

The motive corresponding to the pleasures of the palate

in common use, he may frame the neutral expression, pecuniary interest. This, accordingly, is the course which I have taken. In these instances, indeed, even the combination is not novel: the only novelty there is consists in the steady adherence to the one neutral expression, rejecting altogether the terms, of which the import is infected by adventitious and unsuitable ideas.

In the catalogue of motives, corresponding to the several sorts of pains and pleasures, I have inserted such as have occurred to me. I cannot pretend to warrant it complete. To make sure of rendering it so, the only way would be, to turn over the dictionary from beginning to end: an operation which, in a view to perfection, would be necessary for more purposes than this. See B. I. tit. (Defamation) and Append. tit. (Composition).[2]

[1] Hunger and thirst, considered in the light of motives, import not so much the desire of a particular kind of pleasure, as the desire of removing a positive kind of pain. They do not extend to the desire of that kind of pleasure which depends on the choice of foods and liquors.

[1] 1789 'liquorishness'.
[2] See above 72 n. 1.

as before. In both cases, however, his motive is the same. It is neither more nor less than the motive corresponding to the pleasures of the palate.[j]

Sexual desires corresponding to the pleasure of the sexual sense

16. To the pleasures of the sexual sense corresponds the motive which, in a neutral sense, may be termed sexual desire. In a bad sense, it is spoken of under the name of lasciviousness, and a variety of other names of reprobation. Name used in a good sense, it has none.[k]

1. A man ravishes a virgin. In this case the motive is, without scruple, termed by the name of lust, lasciviousness, and so forth; and is universally looked upon as a bad one. 2. The same man, at another time exercises the rights of marriage with his wife. In this case the motive is accounted, perhaps, a good one, or at least indifferent: and here people would scruple to call it by any of those names. In both cases, however, the motive may be precisely the same. In both cases it may be neither more nor less than sexual desire.

Curiosity, &c. corresponding to the pleasures of curiosity

17. To the pleasures of curiosity corresponds the motive known by the same name: and which may be otherwise called the love of novelty, or the love of experiment; and, on particular occasions, sport, and sometimes play.

1. A boy, in order to divert himself, reads an improving book: the motive is accounted, perhaps, a good one: at any rate not a bad one. 2. He sets his top a spinning: the motive is deemed, at any rate, not a bad one. 3. He sets loose a mad ox among a crowd; his motive is now, perhaps, termed an abominable one. Yet in all three cases the motive may be the very same: it may be neither more nor less than curiosity.

None to the other pleasures of sense

18. As to the other pleasures of sense they are of too little consequence to have given any separate denominations to the corresponding motives.

[j] It will not be worth while, in every case, to give an instance in which the action may be indifferent: if good as well as bad actions may result from the same motive, it is easy to conceive, that so also may indifferent.[1]

[k] Love indeed includes sometimes this idea: but then it can never answer the purpose of exhibiting it separately: since there are three motives, at least, that may all of them be included in it, besides this: the love of beauty corresponding to the pleasures of the eye, and the motives corresponding to those of amity and benevolence. We speak of the love of children, of the love of parents, of the love of God. These pious uses protect the appellation, and preserve it from the ignominy poured forth upon its profane associates. Even sensual love would not answer the purpose; since that would include the love of beauty.

[1] The 1789 reading for the last clause has been restored, in place of the mistaken 1823 emendation to read 'that also may be indifferent'.

19. To the pleasures of wealth corresponds the sort of motive which, in a neutral sense, may be termed pecuniary interest: in a bad sense, it is termed, in some cases, avarice, covetousness, rapacity, or lucre: in other cases, niggardliness: in a good sense, but only in particular cases, economy and frugality; and in some cases the word industry may be applied to it: in a sense nearly indifferent, but rather bad than otherwise, it is styled, though only in particular cases, parsimony. *Pecuniary interest to the pleasures of wealth*

1. For money you gratify a man's hatred, by putting his adversary to death. 2. For money you plough his field for him.–In the first case your motive is termed lucre, and is accounted corrupt and abominable: and in the second, for want of a proper appellation, it is styled industry; and is looked upon as innocent at least, if not meritorious. Yet the motive is in both cases precisely the same: it is neither more nor less than pecuniary interest.

20. The pleasures of skill are neither distinct enough, nor of consequence enough, to have given any name to the corresponding motive. *None to the pleasures of skill*

21. To the pleasures of amity corresponds a motive which, in a neutral sense, may be termed the desire of ingratiating one's self. In a bad sense it is in certain cases, styled servility: in a good sense it has no name that is peculiar to it: in the cases in which it has been looked on with a favourable eye, it has seldom been distinguished from the motive of sympathy or benevolence, with which, in such cases, it is commonly associated. *To the pleasures of amity the desire of ingratiating one's self*

1. To acquire the affections of a woman before marriage, to preserve them afterwards, you do every thing, that is consistent with other duties, to make her happy: in this case your motive is looked upon as laudable, though there is no name for it. 2. For the same purpose, you poison a woman with whom she is at enmity: in this case your motive is looked upon as abominable, though still there is no name for it. 3. To acquire or preserve the favour of a man who is richer or more powerful than yourself, you make yourself subservient to his pleasures. Let them even be lawful pleasures, if people choose to attribute your behaviour to this motive, you will not get them to find any other name for it than servility. Yet in all three cases the motive is the same: it is neither more nor less than the desire of ingratiating yourself.

22. To the pleasures of the moral sanction, or, as they may otherwise be called, the pleasures of a good name, corresponds a motive which, in a neutral sense, has scarcely yet obtained any adequate appellative. It may be styled, the love of reputation. It is nearly *To the pleasures of a good name, the love of reputation* related to the motive last preceding: being neither more nor less than the desire of ingratiating one's self with, or, as in this case we should rather say, of recommending one's self to, the world at large. In a good sense, it is termed honour, or the sense of honour: or rather, the word honour is introduced somehow or other upon the occasion of its being brought to view: for in strictness the word honour is put rather to signify that imaginary object, which a man is spoken of as possessing upon the occasion of his obtaining a conspicuous share of the pleasures that are in question. In particular cases, it is styled the love of glory. In a bad sense, it is styled, in some cases, false honour; in others, pride: in others, vanity. In a sense not decidedly bad, but rather bad than otherwise, ambition. In an indifferent sense, in some cases, the love of fame: in others, the sense of shame. And, as the pleasures belonging to the moral sanction run undistinguishably into the pains derived from the same source,[1] it may also be styled, in some cases, the fear of dishonour, the fear of disgrace, the fear of infamy, the fear of ignominy, or the fear of shame.

1. You have received an affront from a man: according to the custom of the country, in order, on the one hand, to save yourself from the shame of being thought to bear it patiently[m]; on the other

[1] See Ch. vi (Pleasures and Pains) par. 24 note.

[m] A man's bearing an affront patiently, that is, without taking this method of doing what is called wiping it off, is thought to import one or other of two things: either that he does not possess that sensibility to the pleasures and pains of the moral sanction, which, in order to render himself a respectable member of society, a man ought to possess: or, that he does not possess courage enough to stake his life for the chance of gratifying that resentment which a proper sense of the value of those pleasures and those pains it is thought would not fail to inspire. True it is, that there are divers other motives, by any of which the same conduct might equally be produced: the motives corresponding to the religious sanction, and the motives that come under the head of benevolence. Piety towards God, the practice in question being generally looked upon as repugnant to the dictates of the religious sanction: sympathy for your antagonist himself, whose life would be put to hazard at the same time with your own; sympathy for his connexions; the persons who are dependent on him in the way of support, or connected with him in the way of sympathy: sympathy for your own connexions: and even sympathy for the public, in cases where the man is such that the public appears to have a material interest in his life. But in comparison with the love of life, the influence of the religious sanction is known to be in general but weak: especially among people of those classes who are here in question: a sure proof of which is the prevalence of this very custom. Where it is so strong as to preponderate, it is so rare, that, perhaps, it gives a man a place in the calendar: and, at any rate, exalts him to the rank of martyr. Moreover, the instances in which either private benevolence

hand, to obtain the reputation of courage; you challenge him to fight with mortal weapons. In this case your motive will by some people be accounted laudable, and styled honour: by others it will be accounted blameable, and these, if they call it honour, will prefix an epithet of improbation to it, and call it false honour. 2. In order to obtain a post of rank and dignity, and thereby to increase the respects paid you by the public, you bribe the electors who are to confer it, or the judge before whom the title to it is in dispute. In this case your motive is commonly accounted corrupt and abominable, and is styled, perhaps, by some such name as dishonest or corrupt ambition, as there is no single name for it. 3. In order to obtain the good-will of the public, you bestow a large sum in works of private charity or public utility. In this case people will be apt not to agree about your motive. Your enemies will put a bad colour upon it, and call it ostentation: your friends, to save you from this reproach, will choose to impute your conduct not to this motive but to some other: such as that of charity (the denomination in this case given to private sympathy) or that of public spirit. 4. A king, for the sake of gaining the admiration annexed to the name of conqueror (we will suppose power and resentment out of the question) engages his kingdom in a bloody war. His motive, by the multitude (whose sympathy for millions is easily overborne by the pleasure which their imagination finds in gaping at any novelty they observe in the conduct of a single person) is deemed an admirable one. Men of feeling and reflection, who disapprove of the dominion exercised by this motive on this occasion, without always perceiving that it is the same motive which in other instances meets with their approbation, deem it an abominable one; and because the multitude, who are the manufacturers of language, have not given them a simple name to call it by, they will call it by some such compound name as the love of false glory or false ambition.

or public spirit predominate over the love of life, will also naturally be but rare: and, owing to the general propensity to detraction, it will also be much rarer for them to be thought to do so. Now, when three or more motives, any one of them capable of producing a given mode of conduct, apply at once, that which appears to be the most powerful, is that which will of course be deemed to have actually done the *most*: and, as the bulk of mankind, on this as on other occasions, are disposed to decide peremptorily upon superficial estimates, it will generally be looked upon as having done the whole.

The consequence is, that when a man of a certain rank forbears to take this chance of revenging an affront, his conduct will, by most people, be imputed to the love of life: which, when it predominates over the love of reputation, is, by a not unsalutary association of ideas, stigmatized with the reproachful name of cowardice.

Yet in all four cases the motive is the same: it is neither more nor less than the love of reputation.

23. To the pleasures of power corresponds the motive which, in a neutral sense, may be termed the love of power. People, who are out of humour with it sometimes, call it the lust of power. In a good sense, it is scarcely provided with a name. In certain cases this motive, as well as the love of reputation, are confounded under the same name, ambition. This is not to be wondered at, considering the intimate connexion there is between the two motives in many cases: since it commonly happens, that the same object which affords the one sort of pleasure, affords the other sort at the same time: for instance, offices, which are at once posts of honour and places of trust: and since at any rate reputation is the road to power.

1. If, in order to gain a place in administration, you poison the man who occupies it. 2. If, in the same view, you propose a salutary plan for the advancement of the public welfare; your motive is in both cases the same. Yet in the first case it is accounted criminal and abominable: in the second case allowable, and even laudable.

24. To the pleasures as well as to the pains of the religious sanction corresponds a motive which has, strictly speaking, no perfectly neutral name applicable to all cases, unless the word religion be admitted in this character: though the word religion, strictly speaking, seems to mean not so much the motive itself, as a kind of fictitious personage, by whom the motive is supposed to be created, or an assemblage of acts, supposed to be dictated by that personage: nor does it seem to be completely settled into a neutral sense. In the same sense it is also, in some cases, styled religious zeal: in other cases, the fear of God. The love of God, though commonly contrasted with the fear of God, does not come strictly under this head. It coincides properly with a motive of a different denomination; viz. a kind of sympathy or good-will, which has the Deity for its object. In a good sense, it is styled devotion, piety, and pious zeal. In a bad sense, it is styled, in some cases, superstition, or superstitious zeal: in other cases, fanaticism, or fanatic zeal: in a sense not decidedly bad, because not appropriated to this motive, enthusiasm, or enthusiastic zeal.

1. In order to obtain the favour of the Supreme Being, a man assassinates his lawful sovereign. In this case the motive is now almost universally looked upon as abominable, and is termed fanaticism: formerly it was by great numbers accounted laudable, and was by them called pious zeal. 2. In the same view, a man lashes

himself with thongs. In this case, in yonder house, the motive is accounted laudable, and is called pious zeal: in the next house it is deemed contemptible, and called superstition. 3. In the same view, a man eats a piece of bread (or at least what to external appearance is a piece of bread) with certain ceremonies. In this case, in yonder house, his motive is looked upon as laudable, and is styled piety and devotion: in the next house it is deemed abominable, and styled superstition, as before: perhaps even it is absurdly styled impiety. 4. In the same view, a man holds a cow by the tail while he is dying. On the Thames the motive would in this case be deemed contemptible, and called superstition. On the Ganges it is deemed meritorious, and called piety. 5. In the same view, a man bestows a large sum in works of charity, or public utility. In this case the motive is styled laudable, by those at least to whom the works in question appear to come under this description: and by these at least it would be styled piety. Yet in all these cases the motive is precisely the same: it is neither more nor less than the motive belonging to the religious sanction.[n]

25. To the pleasures of sympathy corresponds the motive which, in a neutral sense, is termed good-will. The word sympathy may also be used on this occasion: though the sense of it seems to be rather more extensive. In a good sense, it is styled benevolence: and in certain cases, philanthropy; and, in a figurative way, brotherly love; in others, humanity; in others, charity; in others, pity and compassion; in others, mercy; in others, gratitude; in others, tenderness; in others, patriotism; in others, public spirit. Love is also employed in this as in so many other senses. In a bad sense, it has no name applicable to it in all cases: in particular cases it is styled partiality. The word *zeal*, with certain epithets prefixed to it, might also be employed sometimes on this occasion, though the sense of it be more extensive; applying sometimes to ill as well as to good will. It is thus we speak of *party* zeal, *national* zeal, and *public* zeal. The word *attachment* is also used with the like epithets: we also say *family-attachment*. The French expression, *esprit de corps*, for which as yet there seems to be scarcely any name in English, might be rendered, in some cases, though rather

Good-will, &c. to the pleasures of sympathy

---

[n] I am aware, or at least I hope, that people in general, when they see the matter thus stated, will be ready to acknowledge, that the motive in these cases, whatever be the tendency of the acts which it produces, is not a bad one: but this will not render it the less true, that hitherto, in popular discourse, it has been common for men to speak of acts, which they could not but acknowledge to have originated from this source, as proceeding from a bad motive. The same observation will apply to many of the other cases.

inadequately, by the terms corporation spirit, corporation attachment, or corporation zeal.[1]

1. A man who has set a town on fire is apprehended and committed: out of regard or compassion for him, you help him to break prison. In this case the generality of people will probably scarcely know whether to condemn your motive or to applaud it: those who condemn your conduct, will be disposed rather to impute it to some other motive: if they style it benevolence or compassion, they will be for prefixing an epithet, and calling it false benevolence or false compassion.° 2. The man is taken again, and is put upon his trial: to save him you swear falsely in his favour. People, who would not call your motive a bad one before, will perhaps call it so now. 3. A man is at law with you about an estate: he has no right to it: the judge knows this, yet, having an esteem or affection for your adversary, adjudges it to him. In this case the motive is by every body deemed abominable, and is termed injustice and partiality. 4. You detect a statesman in receiving bribes: out of regard to the public interest, you give information of it, and prosecute him. In this case, by all who acknowledge your conduct to have originated from this motive, your motive will be deemed a laudable one, and styled public spirit. But his friends and adherents will not choose to account for your conduct in any such manner: they will rather attribute it to party enmity. 5. You find a man on the point of starving: you relieve him; and save his life. In this case your motive will by every body be accounted laudable, and it will be termed compas-

° Among the Greeks, perhaps the motive, and the conduct it gave birth to, would, in such a case, have been rather approved than disapproved of. It seems to have been deemed an act of heroism on the part of Hercules, to have delivered his friend Theseus from hell: though divine justice, which held him there, should naturally have been regarded as being at least upon a footing with human justice.[2] But to divine justice, even when acknowledged under that character, the respect paid at that time of day does not seem to have been very profound, or well-settled: at present, the respect paid to it is profound and settled enough, though the name of it is but too often applied to dictates which could have had no other origin than the worst sort of human caprice.

[1] In the 1789 edition the end of this paragraph reads '. . . by the terms professional spirit, professional attachment, or professional zeal'. The change made in 1823 was in accordance with the following Ms. note by Bentham in the copy of the 1789 edition now in the British Museum: 'for professional say corporation spirit etc.; which is more extensive'. The italicising above of the words *zeal, party, national, public, attachment,* and *family-attachment* is another Ms. suggestion by Bentham, which, however, was not adopted in the 1823 or Bowring editions.

[2] The twelfth labour of Hercules was to fetch Cerberus from the underworld. One of many later additions to the story was that Hercules rescued Theseus, who was in Hades for helping Peirithous in his attempt to carry off Persephone from the underworld.

sion, pity, charity, benevolence. Yet in all these cases the motive is the same: it is neither more nor less than the motive of good-will.

26. To the pleasures of malevolence, or antipathy, corresponds the motive which, in a neutral sense, is termed antipathy or displeasure: and, in particular cases, dislike, aversion, abhorrence, and indignation: in a neutral sense, or perhaps a sense leaning a little to the bad side, ill-will: and, in particular cases, anger, wrath, and enmity. In a bad sense it is styled, in different cases, wrath, spleen, ill-humour, animosity,[1] hatred, malice, rancour, rage, fury, cruelty, tyranny, envy, jealousy, revenge, misanthropy, and by other names, which it is hardly worth while to endeavour to collect.[p] Like good-will, it is used with epithets expressive of the persons who are the objects of the affection. Hence we hear of party enmity, party rage, and so forth. In a good sense there seems to be no single name for it. In compound expressions it may be spoken of in such a sense, by epithets, such as *just* and *laudable*, prefixed to words that are used in a neutral or nearly neutral sense.

Ill-will, &c. to the pleasures of antipathy

1. You rob a man: he prosecutes you, and gets you punished: out of resentment you set upon him, and hang him with your own hands. In this case your motive will universally be deemed detestable, and will be called malice, cruelty, revenge, and so forth. 2. A man has stolen a little money from you: out of resentment you prosecute him, and get him hanged by course of law. In this case people will probably be a little divided in their opinions about your motive: your friends will deem it a laudable one, and call it a just or laudable resentment: your enemies will perhaps be disposed to deem it blameable, and call it cruelty, malice, revenge, and so forth: to obviate which, your friends will try perhaps to change the motive and call it public spirit. 3. A man has murdered your father: out of resentment you prosecute him, and get him put to death in course of law. In this case your motive will be universally deemed a laudable one, and styled, as before, a just or laudable resentment: and your friends, in order to bring forward the more amiable prin-

---

[p] Here, as elsewhere, it may be observed, that the same words which are mentioned as names of motives, are also many of them names of passions, appetites, and affections: fictitious entities, which are framed only by considering pleasures or pains in some particular point of view. Some of them are also names of moral qualities. This branch of nomenclature is remarkably entangled: to unravel it completely would take up a whole volume; not a syllable of which would belong properly to the present design.

[1] The word 'animosity' was an insertion made in Ms. by Bentham in the copy of the 1789 edition now in the British Museum: overlooked in 1823, the insertion was made in the Bowring edition (i, 53).

ciple from which the malevolent one, which was your immediate motive, took its rise, will be for keeping the latter out of sight, speaking of the former only, under some such name as filial piety. Yet in all these cases the motive is the same: it is neither more nor less than the motive of ill-will.

Self-preser-
vation, to
the several
kinds of
pains

27. To the several sorts of pains, or at least to all such of them as are conceived to subsist in an intense degree, and to death, which, as far as we can perceive, is the termination of all the pleasures, as well as all the pains we are acquainted with, corresponds the motive, which in a neutral sense is styled, in general, self-preservation: the desire of preserving one's self from the pain or evil in question. Now in many instances the desire of pleasure, and the sense of pain, run into one another undistinguishably. Self-preservation, therefore, where the degree of the pain which it corresponds to is but slight will scarcely be distinguishable, by any precise line, from the motives corresponding to the several sorts of pleasures. Thus in the case of the pains of hunger and thirst: physical want will in many cases be scarcely distinguishable from physical desire. In some cases it is styled, still in a neutral sense, self-defence. Between the pleasures and the pains of the moral and religious sanctions, and consequently of the motives that correspond to them, as likewise between the pleasures of amity, and the pains of enmity, this want of boundaries has already been taken notice of.[q] The case is the same between the pleasures of wealth, and the pains of privation corresponding to those pleasures. There are many cases, therefore, in which it will be difficult to distinguish the motive of self-preservation from pecuniary interest, from the desire of ingratiating one's self, from the love of reputation, and from religious hope: in which cases, those more specific and explicit names will naturally be preferred to this general and inexplicit one. There are also a multitude of compound names, which either are already in use, or might be devised, to distinguish the specific branches of the motive of self-preservation from those several motives of a pleasurable origin: such as the fear of poverty, the fear of losing such or such a man's regard, the fear of shame, and the fear of God. Moreover, to the evil of death corresponds, in a neutral sense, the love of life; in a bad sense, cowardice: which corresponds also to the pains of the senses, at least when considered as subsisting in an acute degree. There seems to be no name for the love of life that has a good sense; unless it be the vague and general name of prudence.

1. To save yourself from being hanged, pilloried, imprisoned, or

[q] See Ch. v (Pleasures and Pains) par. 24, 25.

fined, you poison the only person who can give evidence against you. In this case your motive will universally be styled abominable: but as the term self-preservation has no bad sense, people will not care to make this use of it: they will be apt rather to change the motive, and call it malice. 2. A woman, having been just delivered of an illegitimate child, in order to save herself from shame, destroys the child, or abandons it. In this case, also, people will call the motive a bad one, and, not caring to speak of it under a neutral name, they will be apt to change the motive, and call it by some such name as cruelty. 3. To save the expense of a halfpenny, you suffer a man, whom you could preserve at that expense, to perish with want, before your eyes. In this case your motive will be universally deemed an abominable one; and, to avoid calling it by so indulgent a name as self-preservation, people will be apt to call it avarice and niggardliness, with which indeed in this case it indistinguishably coincides: for the sake of finding a more reproachful appellation, they will be apt likewise to change the motive, and term it cruelty. 4. To put an end to the pain of hunger, you steal a loaf of bread. In this case your motive will scarcely, perhaps, be deemed a very bad one; and, in order to express more indulgence for it, people will be apt to find a stronger name for it than self-preservation, terming it *necessity*. 5. To save yourself from drowning, you beat off an innocent man who has got hold of the same plank. In this case your motive will in general be deemed neither good nor bad, and it will be termed self-preservation, or necessity, or the love of life. 6. To save your life from a gang of robbers, you kill them in the conflict. In this case the motive may, perhaps, be deemed rather laudable than otherwise, and, besides self-preservation, is styled also self-defence. 7. A soldier is sent out upon a party against a weaker party of the enemy: before he gets up with them, to save his life, he runs away. In this case the motive will universally be deemed a contemptible one, and will be called cowardice. Yet in all these various cases, the motive is still the same. It is neither more nor less than self-preservation.

28. In particular, to the pains of exertion corresponds the motive, which, in a neutral sense, may be termed the love of ease, or by a longer circumlocution, the desire of avoiding trouble. In a bad sense, it is termed indolence.[r] It seems to have no name that carries with it a good sense. *To the pains of exertion, the love of ease*

[r] It may seem odd at first sight to speak of the love of ease as giving birth to action: but exertion is as natural an effect of the love of ease as inaction is, when a smaller degree of exertion promises to exempt a man from a greater.

1. To save the trouble of taking care of it, a parent leaves his child to perish. In this case the motive will be deemed an abominable one, and, because indolence will seem too mild a name for it, the motive will, perhaps, be changed, and spoken of under some such term as cruelty. 2. To save yourself from an illegal slavery, you make your escape. In this case the motive will be deemed certainly not a bad one: and, because indolence, or even the love of ease, will be thought too unfavourable a name for it, it will, perhaps, be styled the love of liberty. 3. A mechanic, in order to save his labour, makes an improvement in his machinery. In this case, people will look upon his motive as a good one; and finding no name for it that carries a good sense, they will be disposed to keep the motive out of sight: they will speak rather of his ingenuity, than of the motive which was the means of his manifesting that quality. Yet in all these cases the motive is the same: it is neither more nor less than the love of ease.

Motives can only be bad with reference to the most frequent complexion of their effects

29. It appears then that there is no such thing as any sort of motive which is a bad one in itself: nor, consequently, any such thing as a sort of motive, which in itself is exclusively a good one. And as to their effects, it appears too that these are sometimes bad, at other times either indifferent or good: and this appears to be the case with every sort of motive. *If any sort of motive then is either good or bad on the score of its effects, this is the case only on individual occasions, and with individual motives;* and this is the case with one sort of motive as well as with another. *If any sort of motive then can, in consideration of its effects, be termed with any propriety a bad one*, it can only be with reference to the balance of all the effects it may have had of both kinds within a given period, that is, of its most usual tendency.

How it is that motives, such as lust, avarice, &c. are constantly bad

30. What then? (it will be said) are not lust, cruelty, avarice, bad motives? Is there so much as any one individual occasion, in which motives like these can be otherwise than bad? No, certainly: and yet the proposition, that there is no one *sort* of motive but what will on many occasions be a good one, is nevertheless true. The fact is, that these are names which, if properly applied, are never applied but in the cases where the motives they signify happen to be bad. The names of these motives, considered apart from their effects, are sexual desire, displeasure, and pecuniary interest. To sexual desire, when the effects of it are looked upon as bad, is given the name of lust. Now lust is always a bad motive. Why? Because if the case be such, that the effects of the motive are not bad, it does not go, or at least ought not to go, by the name of lust. The case is, then, that when I say, 'Lust is a bad motive', it is a proposition that merely concerns the import of the word lust; and which would be false if transferred to the other word used for the same motive, sexual desire. Hence we see the emptiness of all those rhapsodies of common-place morality, which consist in the taking of such names as lust, cruelty, and avarice, and branding them with marks of reprobation: applied to the *thing*, they are false; applied to the *name*, they are true indeed, but nugatory. Would you do a real service to mankind, show them the cases in which sexual desire *merits* the name of lust; displeasure, that of cruelty; and pecuniary interest, that of avarice.

31. If it were necessary to apply such denominations as good, bad, and indifferent to motives, they might be classed in the following manner, in consideration of the most frequent complexion of their effects. In the class of good motives might be placed the articles of, 1. Good-will. 2. Love of reputation. 3. Desire of amity. And, 4. Religion. In the class of bad motives, 5. Displeasure. In the class of neutral or indifferent motives, 6. Physical desire. 7. Pecuniary interest. 8. Love of power. 9. Self-preservation; as including the fear of the pains of the senses, the love of ease, and the love of life.

Under the above restrictions, motives may be distinguished into good, bad, and indifferent or neutral

32. This method of arrangement, however, cannot but be imperfect; and the nomenclature belonging to it is in danger of being fallacious. For by what method of investigation can a man be assured, that with regard to the motives ranked under the name of good, the good effects they have had, from the beginning of the world, have, in each of the four species comprised under this name, been superior to the bad? still more difficulty would a man find in assuring himself, that with regard to those which are ranked under the name of neutral or indifferent, the effects they have had have exactly balanced each other, the value of the good being neither greater nor less than that of the bad. It is to be considered, that the interests of the person himself can no more be left out of the estimate, than those of the rest of the community. For what would become of the species, if it were not for the motives of hunger and thirst, sexual desire, the fear of pain, and the love of life? Nor in the actual constitution of human nature is the motive of displeasure less necessary, perhaps, than any of the others: although a system, in which the business of life might be carried on without it, might possibly be conceived. It seems, therefore, that they could scarcely, without great danger of mistakes, be distinguished in this manner even with reference to each other.

Inconveniences of this distribution

It is only in individual instances that motives can be good or bad

33. The only way, it should seem, in which a motive can with safety and propriety be styled good or bad, is with reference to its effects in each individual instance; and principally from the intention it gives birth to: from which arise, as will be shown hereafter, the most material part of its effects. A motive is good, when the intention it gives birth to is a good one; bad, when the intention is a bad one: and an intention is good or bad, according to the material consequences that are the objects of it. So far is it from the goodness of the intention's being to be known only from the species of the motive. But from one and the same motive, as we have seen, may result intentions of every sort of complexion whatsoever. This circumstance, therefore, can afford no clue for the arrangement of the several sorts of motives.

Motives distinguished into social, dissocial, and self-regarding

34. A more commodious method, therefore, it should seem, would be to distribute them according to the influence which they appear to have on the interests of the other members of the community, laying those of the party himself out of the question: to wit, according to the tendency which they appear to have to unite, or disunite, his interests and theirs. On this plan they may be distinguished into *social*, *dissocial*, and *self-regarding*. In the social class may be reckoned, 1. Good-will. 2. Love of reputation. 3. Desire of amity. 4. Religion. In the dissocial may be placed, 5. Displeasure. In the self-regarding class, 6. Physical desire. 7. Pecuniary interest. 8. Love of power. 9. Self-preservation; as including the fear of the pains of the senses, the love of ease, and the love of life.

–social, into purely-social, and semi-social

35. With respect to the motives that have been termed social, if any farther distinction should be of use, to that of good-will alone may be applied the epithet of *purely-social*; while the love of reputation, the desire of amity, and the motive of religion, may together be comprised under the division of *semi-social*: the social tendency being much more constant and unequivocal in the former than in any of the three latter. Indeed these last, social as they may be termed, are self-regarding at the same time.[s]

§ iv. *Order of pre-eminence among motives*

The dictates of good-will are the surest of coinciding with those of utility

36. Of all these sorts of motives, good-will is that of which the dictates,[t] taken in a general view, are surest of coinciding with

[s] 'Religion', says the pious Addison, somewhere in the Spectator, 'is the highest species of self-love'.[1]

[t] When a man is supposed to be prompted by any motive to engage, or not

Laws and dictates conceived as issuing from motives

[1] These precise words do not seem to occur in any of the *Spectator* papers attributed to Addison. The sentiments they express, however, can be found in several places: cf. *Spectator*, nos. 185, 186, 213, 447, etc.

116

those of the principle of utility. For the dictates of utility are neither more nor less than the dictates of the most extensive[u] and enlightened (that is *well-advised*[v]) benevolence. The dictates of the other motives may be conformable to those of utility, or repugnant, as it may happen.

37. In this, however, it is taken for granted, that in the case in question the dictates of benevolence are not contradicted by those of a more extensive, that is enlarged, benevolence. Now when the dictates of benevolence, as respecting the interests of a certain set of persons, are repugnant to the dictates of the same motive, as respecting the more important[w] interests of another set of persons, the former dictates, it is evident, are repealed, as it were, by the latter: and a man, were he to be governed by the former, could scarcely, with propriety, be said to be governed by the dictates of benevolence. On this account, were the motives on both sides sure to be alike present to a man's mind, the case of such a repugnancy would hardly be worth distinguishing, since the partial benevolence might be considered as swallowed up in the more extensive: if the former prevailed, and governed the action, it must be considered as not owing its birth to benevolence, but to some other motive: if the latter prevailed, the former might be considered as having no effect. But the case is, that a partial benevolence may govern the action, without entering into any direct competition with the more extensive benevolence, which would forbid it; because the interests of the less numerous assemblage of persons may be present to a man's mind, at a time when those of the more numerous are either not present, or, if present, make no impression. It is in this way that the dictates of this motive may be repugnant to utility, yet still be the dictates of benevolence. What makes those of private benevolence conformable upon the whole to the principle of utility, is, that in general they stand unopposed by those of public: if they are repugnant to them, it is only by accident. What makes them the more conformable, is, that in a civilized society, in most of the cases in which they would of themselves be apt to run counter to those of public benevolence, they find themselves opposed by stron-

Yet do not in all cases

---

to engage, in such or such an action, it may be of use, for the convenience of discourse, to speak of such motive as giving birth to an imaginary kind of *law* or *dictate*, injoining him to engage, or not to engage, in it.*

[u] See Ch. iv (Value) and Ch. vi (Sensibility) 21.

[v] See Ch. ix (Consciousness).

[w] Or valuable. See Ch. iv (Value).

* See Ch. i.

ger motives of the self-regarding class, which are played on against them by the laws; and that it is only in cases where they stand unopposed by the other more salutary dictates, that they are left free. An act of injustice or cruelty, committed by a man for the sake of his father or his son, is punished, and with reason, as much as if it were committed for his own.

Next to them come those of the love of reputation

38. After good-will, the motive of which the dictates seem to have the next best chance for coinciding with those of utility, is that of the love of reputation. There is but one circumstance which prevents the dictates of this motive from coinciding in all cases with those of the former. This is, that men in their likings and dislikings, in the dispositions they manifest to annex to any mode of conduct their approbation or their disapprobation, and in consequence to the person who appears to practise it, their good or their ill will, do not govern themselves exclusively by the principle of utility. Sometimes it is the principle of asceticism they are guided by: sometimes the principle of sympathy and antipathy. There is another circumstance, which diminishes, not their conformity to the principle of utility, but only their efficacy in comparison with the dictates of the motive of benevolence. The dictates of this motive will operate as strongly in secret as in public: whether it appears likely that the conduct which they recommend will be known or not: those of the love of reputation will coincide with those of benevolence only in proportion as a man's conduct seems likely to be known. This circumstance, however, does not make so much difference as at first sight might appear. Acts, in proportion as they are material, are apt to become known[x]: and in point of reputation, the slightest suspicion often serves for proof. Besides, if an act be a disreputable one, it is not any assurance a man can have of the secrecy of the particular act in question, that will of course surmount the objections he may have against engaging in it. Though the act in question should remain secret, it will go towards forming a habit, which may give birth to other acts, that may not meet with the same good fortune. There is no human being, perhaps, who is at years of discretion, on whom considerations of this sort have not some weight: and they have the more weight upon a man, in proportion to the strength of his intellectual powers, and the firmness of his mind.[y] Add to this, the influence which habit itself, when once formed, has in restraining a man from acts towards which, from the view of the disrepute annexed to them, as well as from any other

[x] See B. II. tit. (Evidence).
[y] See Ch. vi (Sensibility) par. 12, 13.

cause, he has contracted an aversion. The influence of habit, in such cases, is a matter of fact, which, though not readily accounted for, is acknowledged and indubitable.[z]

39. After the dictates of the love of reputation come, as it should *Next those of the desire of amity* seem, those of the desire of amity. The former are disposed to coincide with those of utility, inasmuch as they are disposed to coincide with those of benevolence. Now those of the desire of amity are apt also to coincide, in a certain sort, with those of benevolence. But the sort of benevolence with the dictates of which the love of reputation coincides, is the more extensive; that with which those of the desire of amity coincide, the less extensive. Those of the love of amity have still, however, the advantage of those of the self-regarding motives. The former, at one period or other of his life, dispose a man to contribute to the happiness of a considerable number of persons: the latter, from the beginning of life to the end of it, confine themselves to the care of that single individual. The dictates of the desire of amity, it is plain, will approach nearer to a coincidence with those of the love of reputation, and thence with those of utility, in proportion, *cæteris paribus*, to the number of the persons whose amity a man has occasion to desire: and hence it is, for example, that an English member of parliament, with all his own weaknesses, and all the follies of the people whose amity he has to cultivate, is probably, in general, a better character than the secretary of a visier at Constantinople, or of a naïb[1] in Indostan.

40. The dictates of religion are, under the infinite diversity of *Difficulty of placing those of religion* religions, so extremely variable, that it is difficult to know what general account to give of them, or in what rank to place the motive they belong to. Upon the mention of religion, people's first thoughts turn naturally to the religion they themselves profess. This is a great source of miscalculation, and has a tendency to place this sort of motive in a higher rank than it deserves. The dictates of religion would coincide, in all cases, with those of utility, were the Being, who is the object of religion, universally supposed to be as

[z] Strictly speaking, habit, being but a fictitious entity, and not really any thing distinct from the acts or perceptions by which it is said to be formed, cannot be the cause of any thing. The enigma, however, may be satisfactorily solved upon the principle of association, of the nature and force of which a very satisfactory account may be seen in Dr Priestley's edition of Hartley on Man.[2]

[1] This alternative form of *nawab* or *nabob* is frequently used by James Mill in his *History of British India* (1818) to refer, as it does here, to the governor or deputy-governor of a town or district.

[2] This was an abridgement of David Hartley's *Observations on Man, his frame, his duty, and his expectations* (1749) published by Joseph Priestley in 1775 as *Hartley's Theory of the Human Mind, on the Principles of the Association of Ideas.*

benevolent as he is supposed to be wise and powerful; and were the notions entertained of his benevolence, at the same time, as correct as those which are entertained of his wisdom and his power. Unhappily, however, neither of these is the case. He is universally supposed to be all-powerful: for by the Deity, what else does any man mean than the Being, whatever he be, by whom every thing is done? And as to knowledge, by the same rule that he should know one thing he should know another. These notions seem to be as correct, for all material purposes, as they are universal. But among the votaries of religion (of which number the multifarious fraternity of Christians is but a small part) there seem to be but few (I will not say how few) who are real believers in his benevolence. They call him benevolent in words, but they do not mean that he is so in reality. They do not mean, that he is benevolent as man is conceived to be benevolent: they do not mean that he is benevolent in the only sense in which benevolence has a meaning. For if they did, they would recognise that the dictates of religion could be neither more nor less than the dictates of utility: not a tittle different: not a tittle less or more. But the case is, that on a thousand occasions they turn their backs on the principle of utility. They go astray after the strange principles its antagonists: sometimes the principle of sympathy and antipathy.[a2] Accordingly, the idea they bear in their minds, on such occasions, is but too often the idea of malevolence; to which idea, stripping it of its own proper name, they bestow the specious appellation of the social motive.[b2] The dictates of religion, in short, are no other than the dictates of that principle which has been already mentioned under the name of the theological principle.[c2] These, as has been observed, are just as it may happen, according to the biases of the person in question, copies of the dictates of one or other of the three original principles: sometimes, indeed, of the dictates of utility: but frequently of

[a2] Ch. II (Principles Adverse) 18.

[b2] Sometimes, in order the better to conceal the cheat (from their own eyes doubtless as well as from others) they set up a phantom of their own, which they call Justice: whose dictates are to modify (which being explained, means to oppose) the dictates of benevolence. But justice, in the only sense in which it has a meaning, is an imaginary personage, feigned for the convenience of discourse, whose dictates are the dictates of utility, applied to certain particular cases. Justice, then, is nothing more than an imaginary instrument, employed to forward on certain occasions, and by certain means, the purposes of benevolence. The dictates of justice are nothing more than a part of the dictates of benevolence, which, on certain occasions, are applied to certain subjects; to wit, to certain actions.

[c2] See Ch. II (Principles Adverse, &c).

those of asceticism, or those of sympathy and antipathy. In this respect they are only on a par with the dictates of the love of reputation: in another they are below it. The dictates of religion are in all places intermixed more or less with dictates unconformable to those of utility, deduced from texts, well or ill interpreted, of the writings held for sacred by each sect: unconformable, by imposing practices sometimes inconvenient to a man's self, sometimes pernicious to the rest of the community. The sufferings of uncalled martyrs, the calamities of holy wars and religious persecutions, the mischiefs of intolerant laws, (objects which can here only be glanced at, not detailed) are so many additional mischiefs over and above the number of those which were ever brought into the world by the love of reputation. On the other hand, it is manifest, that with respect to the power of operating in secret, the dictates of religion have the same advantage over those of the love of reputation, and the desire of amity, as is possessed by the dictates of benevolence.

41. Happily, the dictates of religion seem to approach nearer and nearer to a coincidence with those of utility every day. But why? Because the dictates of the moral sanction do so: and those coincide with or are influenced by these. Men of the worst religions, influenced by the voice and practice of the surrounding world, borrow continually a new and a new leaf out of the book of utility: and with these, in order not to break with their religion, they endeavour, sometimes with violence enough, to patch together and adorn the repositories of their faith. *Tendency, they have to improve*

42. As to the self-regarding and dissocial motives, the order that takes place among these, and the preceding one, in point of extraregarding influence, is too evident to need insisting on. As to the order that takes place among the motives of the self-regarding class, considered in comparison with one another, there seems to be no difference which on this occasion would be worth mentioning. With respect to the dissocial motive, it makes a difference (with regard to its extra-regarding effects) from which of two sources it originates; whether from self-regarding or from social considerations. The displeasure you conceive against a man may be founded either on some act which offends you in the first instance, or on an act which offends you no otherwise than because you look upon it as being prejudicial to some other party on whose behalf you interest yourself: which other party may be of course either a determinate individual, or any assemblage of individuals, determinate or indeterminate.[d2] It is obvious enough, that a motive, though in *Afterwards come the self-regarding motives: and, lastly, that of displeasure*

[d2] See Ch. vi (Sensibility) par. 21.

itself dissocial, may, by issuing from a social origin, possess a social tendency; and that its tendency, in this case, is likely to be the more social, the more enlarged the description is of the persons whose interests you espouse. Displeasure, venting itself against a man, on account of a mischief supposed to be done by him to the public, may be more social in its effects than any good-will, the exertions of which are confined to an individual.[e2]

§ v. *Conflict among motives*

Motives impelling and restraining, what

43. When a man has it in contemplation to engage in any action, he is frequently acted upon at the same time by the force of divers motives: one motive, or set of motives, acting in one direction; another motive, or set of motives, acting as it were in an opposite direction. The motives on one side disposing him to engage in the action: those on the other, disposing him not to engage in it. Now, any motive, the influence of which tends to dispose him to engage in the action in question, may be termed an *impelling* motive: any motive, the influence of which tends to dispose him not to engage in it, a *restraining* motive. But these appellations may of course be interchanged, according as the act is of the positive kind, or the negative.[f2]

What are the motives most frequently at variance

44. It has been shown, that there is no sort of motive but may give birth to any sort of action. It follows, therefore, that there are no two motives but may come to be opposed to one another. Where the tendency of the act is bad, the most common case is for it to have been dictated by a motive either of the self-regarding, or of the dissocial class. In such case the motive of benevolence has commonly been acting, though ineffectually, in the character of a restraining motive.

Example to illustrate a struggle among contending motives

45. An example may be of use, to show the variety of contending motives, by which a man may be acted upon at the same time. Crillon, a Catholic (at a time when it was generally thought meritorious among Catholics to extirpate Protestants) was ordered by his king, Charles IX of France, to fall privately upon Coligny, a Protestant, and assassinate him: his answer was, 'Excuse me, Sire; but I'll fight him with all my heart'.[g2][1] Here then, were all the

---

[e2] See supra, par. 37.   [f2] See Ch. VII (Actions) par. 8.

[g2] The idea of the case here supposed is taken from an anecdote in real history, but varies from it in several particulars.

[1] Louis Balbais de Berton de Crillon (1543–1615) refused to assassinate Gaspard III de Coligny (1519–72), the Huguenot leader, when asked to do by Charles IX (1560–74), though he was and remained a vigorous supporter of Catholicism and of the monarchy.

122

three forces above mentioned, including that of the political sanction, acting upon him at once. By the political sanction, or at least
so much of the force of it as such a mandate, from such a sovereign,
issued on such an occasion, might be supposed to carry with it, he
was enjoined to put Coligny to death in the way of assassination:
by the religious sanction, that is, by the dictates of religious zeal,
he was enjoined to put him to death in any way: by the moral sanction, or in other words, by the dictates of honour, that is, of the
love of reputation, he was permitted (which permission, when
coupled with the mandates of his sovereign, operated, he conceived,
as an injunction) to fight the adversary upon equal terms: by the
dictates of enlarged benevolence (supposing the mandate to be
unjustifiable) he was enjoined not to attempt his life in any way,
but to remain at peace with him: supposing the mandate to be
unjustifiable, by the dictates of private benevolence, he was enjoined not to meddle with him at any rate. Among this confusion
of repugnant dictates, Crillon, it seems, gave the preference, in the
first place, to those of honour: in the next place, to those of benevolence. He would have fought, had his offer been accepted; as it
was not, he remained at peace.

Here a multitude of questions might arise. Supposing the dictates
of the political sanction to follow the mandate of the sovereign, of
what kind were the motives which they afforded him for compliance? The answer is, of the self-regarding kind at any rate:
inasmuch as, by the supposition, it was in the power of the sovereign to punish him for non-compliance, or reward him for compliance. Did they afford him the motive of religion? (I mean independently of the circumstance of heresy above mentioned) the answer
is, Yes, if his notion was, that it was God's pleasure he should comply with them; No, if it was not. Did they afford him the motive
of the love of reputation? Yes, if it was his notion that the world
would expect and require that he should comply with them: No,
if it was not. Did they afford him that of benevolence? Yes, if it
was his notion that the community would upon the whole be the
better for his complying with them: No, if it was not. But did the
dictates of the political sanction, in the case in question, actually
follow the mandates of the sovereign: in other words, was such a
mandate legal? This we see is a mere question of local jurisprudence,
altogether foreign to the present purpose.

46. What is here said about the goodness and badness of motives, *Practical*
is far from being a mere matter of words. There will be occasion to *use of the*
make use of it hereafter for various important purposes. I shall have *above dis-*
quisitions
relative to
motives

need of it for the sake of dissipating various prejudices, which are of disservice to the community, sometimes by cherishing the flame of civil dissensions,[h2] at other times, by obstructing the course of justice. It will be shown, that in the case of many offences,[12] the consideration of the motive is a most material one: for that in the first place it makes a very material difference in the magnitude of the mischief[j2]: in the next place, that it is easy to be ascertained; and thence may be made a ground for a difference in the demand for punishment: but that in other cases it is altogether incapable of being ascertained; and that, were it capable of being ever so well ascertained, good or bad, it could make no difference in the demand for punishment: that in all cases, the motive that may happen to govern a prosecutor, is a consideration totally immaterial: whence may be seen the mischievousness of the prejudice that is so apt to be entertained against informers; and the consequence it is of that the judge, in particular, should be proof against the influence of such delusions.

Lastly, the subject of motives is one with which it is necessary to be acquainted, in order to pass a judgment on any means that may be proposed for combating offences in their source.[k2]

But before the theoretical foundation for these practical observations can be completely laid, it is necessary we should say something on the subject of *disposition*: which, accordingly, will furnish matter for the ensuing chapter.

[h2] See B. I. tit. (Rebellion).
[12] Ibid. tit. (Simp. corp. injuries). Ibid. tit. (Homicide).
[j2] See Ch. xi (Dispositions).
[k2] See Essay on Indirect Legislation.[1]

[1] This footnote originally (1780) read 'See Append. tit. (Preventive Institutions)', but a correction of 1783, overlooked in the 1823 edition, altered it to read as above. The discussion of 'indirect legislation' went through several phases as Bentham's plans evolved. At one stage it was a section in the appendix to the *Plan of a Penal Code*. It then figured for a time as Ch. xviii of the present work (cf., e.g., 220 n. q2 below). In the extended version of *An Introduction to the Principles* 'Indirect Legislation' was to be, at various stages, Ch. xxxviii or xxxix. But by the summer of 1782 Bentham had decided to deal with it in a separate essay. The Mss. for this were partly used by Dumont in *Traités de Législation Civile et Pénale* (1802): cf. Bowring, i, 533–80.

CHAPTER XI

OF HUMAN DISPOSITIONS IN GENERAL

1. In the foregoing chapter it has been shown at large, that good- *Disposition,* ness or badness cannot, with any propriety, be predicated of mo- *what* tives. Is there nothing then about a man that can properly be termed good or bad, when, on such or such an occasion, he suffers himself to be governed by such or such a motive? Yes, certainly: his *disposition*. Now disposition is a kind of fictitious entity, feigned for the convenience of discourse, in order to express what there is supposed to be *permanent* in a man's frame of mind, where, on such or such an occasion, he has been influenced by such or such a motive, to engage in an act, which, as it appeared to him, was of such or such a tendency.

2. It is with disposition as with every thing else: it will be good *–how far it* or bad according to its effects: according to the effects it has in *belongs to* augmenting or diminishing the happiness of the community. A *the present* man's disposition may accordingly be considered in two points of *subject* view: according to the influence it has, either, 1. on his own happiness: or, 2. on the happiness of others. Viewed in both these lights together, or in either of them indiscriminately, it may be termed, on the one hand, good; on the other, bad; or, in flagrant cases, depraved.[a] Viewed in the former of these lights, it has scarcely any peculiar name, which has as yet been appropriated to it. It might be termed, though but inexpressively, frail or infirm, on the one hand: sound or firm, on the other. Viewed in the other light, it might be termed beneficent, or meritorious, on the one hand: pernicious or mischievous, on the other. Now of that branch of a man's disposition, the effects of which regard in the first instance only

[a] It might also be termed virtuous, or vicious. The only objection to the use of those terms on the present occasion is, the great quantity of good and bad repute that respectively stand annexed to them. The inconvenience of this is, their being apt to annex an ill-proportioned measure of disrepute to dispositions which are ill-constituted only with respect to the party himself: involving them in such a degree of ignominy as should be appropriated to such dispositions only as are mischievous with regard to others. To exalt weaknesses to a level with crimes, is a way to diminish the abhorrence which ought to be reserved for crimes. To exalt small evils to a level with great ones, is the way to diminish the share of attention which ought to be paid to great ones.

himself, there needs not much to be said here. To reform it when bad, is the business rather of the moralist than the legislator: nor is it susceptible of those various modifications which make so material a difference in the effects of the other. Again, with respect to that part of it, the effects whereof regard others in the first instance, it is only in as far as it is of a mischievous nature that the penal branch of law has any immediate concern with it: in as far as it may be of a beneficent nature, it belongs to a hitherto but little cultivated, and as yet unnamed branch of law, which might be styled the remuneratory.

A mischievous disposition; a meritorious disposition; what

3. A man then is said to be of a mischievous disposition, when, by the influence of no matter what motives, he is *presumed* to be more apt to engage, or form intentions of engaging, in acts which are *apparently* of a pernicious tendency, than in such as are apparently of a beneficial tendency: of a meritorious or beneficent disposition in the opposite case.

What a man's disposition is, can only be matter of presumption

4. I say *presumed*: for, by the supposition, all that appears is one single action, attended with one single train of circumstances: but from that degree of consistency and uniformity which experience has shown to be observable in the different actions of the same person, the probable existence (past or future) of a number of acts of a similar nature, is naturally and justly inferred from the observation of one single one. Under such circumstances, such as the motive proves to be in one instance, such is the disposition to be presumed to be in others.

It depends upon what the act appears to be to him

5. I say *apparently* mischievous: that is, apparently with regard to him: such as to him appear to possess that tendency: for from the mere event, independent of what to him it appears beforehand likely to be, nothing can be inferred on either side. If to him it appears likely to be mischievous, in such case, though in the upshot it should prove innocent, or even beneficial, it makes no difference; there is not the less reason for presuming his disposition to be a bad one: if to him it appears likely to be beneficial or innocent, in such case, though in the upshot it should prove pernicious, there is not the more reason on that account for presuming his disposition to be a good one. And here we see the importance of the circumstances of intentionality,[b] consciousness,[c] unconsciousness,[c] and mis-supposal.[c]

Which position is grounded on two facts: 1. The correspondence

6. The truth of these positions depends upon two others, both of them sufficiently verified by experience: the one is, that in the ordinary course of things the consequences of actions commonly

[b] See Ch. VIII.   [c] See Ch. IX.

turn out conformable to intentions. A man who sets up a butcher's shop, and deals in beef, when he intends to knock down an ox, commonly does knock down an ox; though by some unlucky accident he may chance to miss his blow and knock down a man: he who sets up a grocer's shop, and deals in sugar, when he intends to sell sugar, commonly does sell sugar: though by some unlucky accident he may chance to sell arsenic in the room of it. *between intentions and consequences:*

7. The other is, that a man who entertains intentions of doing mischief at one time is apt to entertain the like intentions at another.[d] *2. Between the intentions of the same person at different times*

8. There are two circumstances upon which the nature of the disposition, as indicated by any act, is liable to depend: 1. The apparent tendency of the act: 2. The nature of the motive which gave birth to it. This dependency is subject to different rules, according to the nature of the motive. In stating them, I suppose all along the apparent tendency of the act to be, as it commonly is, the same as the real. *The disposition is to be inferred, 1. From the apparent tendency of the act:*

9. (1) Where the tendency of the act is *good*, and the motive is of the *self-regarding* kind. In this case the motive affords no inference on either side. It affords no indication of a good disposition: but neither does it afford any indication of a bad one. *2. From the nature of the motive*

A baker sells his bread to a hungry man who asks for it. This, we see, is one of those acts of which, in ordinary cases, the tendency is unquestionably good. The baker's motive is the ordinary commercial motive of pecuniary interest. It is plain, that there is nothing in the transaction, thus stated, that can afford the least ground for presuming that the baker is a better or a worse man than any of his neighbours. *Case 1. Tendency, good—motive, self-regarding*

10. (2) Where the tendency of the act is *bad*, and the motive, as before, is of the *self-regarding* kind. In this case the disposition indicated is a mischievous one. *Case 2. Tendency, bad—motive, self-regarding*

A man steals bread out of a baker's shop: this is one of those acts of which the tendency will readily be acknowledged to be bad. Why, and in what respects it is so, will be stated farther on.[e] His motive,

---

[d] To suppose a man to be of a good disposition, and at the same time likely, in virtue of that very disposition, to engage in an habitual train of mischievous actions, is a contradiction in terms: nor could such a proposition ever be advanced, but from the giving, to the thing which the word disposition is put for, a reality which does *not* belong to it. If then, for example, a man of religious disposition should, in virtue of that very disposition, be in the habit of doing mischief, for instance, by persecuting his neighbours, the case must be, either that his disposition, though good in certain respects, is not good upon the whole: or that a religious disposition is not in general a good one. *A disposition, from which proceeds a habit of doing mischief, cannot be a good one*

[e] See Ch. XII (Consequences) and Code, B. I. tit. (Theft).

we will say, is that of pecuniary interest; the desire of getting the value of the bread for nothing. His disposition, accordingly, appears to be a bad one: for every one will allow a thievish disposition to be a bad one.

Case 3. Tendency, good—motive, good-will

11. (3) Where the tendency of the act is *good*, and the motive is the purely social one of *good-will*. In this case the disposition indicated is a beneficent one.

A baker gives a poor man a loaf of bread. His motive is compassion; a name given to the motive of benevolence, in particular cases of its operation. The disposition indicated by the baker, in this case, is such as every man will be ready enough to acknowledge to be a good one.

Case 4. Tendency, bad—motive, good-will

12. (4) Where the tendency of the act is *bad*, and the motive is the purely social one of good-will. Even in this case the disposition which the motive indicates is dubious: it may be a mischievous or a meritorious one, as it happens; according as the mischievousness of the act is more or less apparent.

This case not an impossible one

13. It may be thought, that a case of this sort cannot exist; and that to suppose it, is a contradiction in terms. For the act is one, which, by the supposition, the agent knows to be a mischievous one. How then can it be, that good-will, that is, the desire of doing good, could have been the motive that led him into it? To reconcile this, we must advert to the distinction between enlarged benevolence and confined.[f] The motive that led him into it, was that of confined benevolence. Had he followed the dictates of enlarged benevolence, he would not have done what he did. Now, although he followed the dictates of that branch of benevolence, which in any single instance of its exertion is mischievous, when opposed to the other, yet, as the cases which call for the exertion of the former are, beyond comparison, more numerous than those which call for the exertion of the latter, the disposition indicated by him, in following the impulse of the former, will often be such as in a man, of the common run of men, may be allowed to be a good one upon the whole.

Example I

14. A man with a numerous family of children, on the point of starving, goes into a baker's shop, steals a loaf, divides it all among the children, reserving none of it for himself. It will be hard to infer that that man's disposition is a mischievous one upon the whole. Alter the case, give him but one child, and that hungry perhaps, but in no imminent danger of starving: and now let the man set

---

[f] See Ch. x (Motives).

fire to a house full of people, for the sake of stealing money out of it to buy the bread with. The disposition here indicated will hardly be looked upon as a good one.

15. Another case will appear more difficult to decide than either. *Example II* Ravaillac assassinated one of the best and wisest of sovereigns, at a time when a good and wise sovereign, a blessing at all times so valuable to a state, was particularly precious: and that to the inhabitants of a populous and extensive empire. He is taken, and doomed to the most excruciating tortures. His son, well persuaded of his being a sincere penitent, and that mankind, in case of his being at large, would have nothing more to fear from him, effectuates his escape[1]: Is this then a sign of a good disposition in the son, or of a bad one? Perhaps some will answer, of a bad one; for besides the interest which the nation has in the sufferings of such a criminal, on the score of the example, the future good behaviour of such a criminal is more than any one can have sufficient ground to be persuaded of.

16. Well then, let Ravaillac, the son, not facilitate his father's *Example III* escape; but content himself with conveying poison to him, that at the price of an easier death he may escape his torments. The decision will now, perhaps, be more difficult. The *act* is a wrong one, let it be allowed, and such as ought by all means to be punished: but is the *disposition* manifested by it a bad one? Because the young man breaks the laws in this one instance, is it probable, that if let alone, he would break the laws in ordinary instances, for the satisfaction of any inordinate desires of his own? The answer of most men would probably be in the negative.

17. (5) Where the tendency of the act is *good*, and the motive is a *Case 5.* semi-social one, the *love of reputation*. In this case the disposition *Tendency,* indicated is a good one. *good—motive, love of*

In a time of scarcity, a baker, for the sake of gaining the esteem *reputation* of the neighbourhood, distributes bread *gratis* among the industrious poor. Let this be taken for granted: and let it be allowed to be a matter of uncertainty, whether he had any real feeling for the sufferings of those whom he has relieved, or no. His disposition, for all that, cannot, with any pretence of reason, be termed otherwise than a good and beneficent one. It can only be in consequence of some very idle prejudice, if it receives a different name.[g]

g The bulk of mankind, ever ready to depreciate the character of their *The bulk of* neighbours, in order, indirectly, to exalt their own, will take occasion to refer *mankind apt to depreciate this* [1] For Ravaillac cf. above 82 n. 1. Bentham's reference to Ravaillac's son appears *motive* to be hypothetical.

Case 6.
Tendency,
bad—mo-
tive, honour

18. (6) Where the tendency of the act is *bad*, and the motive, as before, is a semi-social one, the love of reputation. In this case, the disposition which it indicates is more or less good or bad: in the first place, according as the tendency of the act is more or less mischievous: in the next place, according as the dictates of the moral sanction, in the society in question, approach more or less to a coincidence with those of utility. It does not seem probable, that in any nation, which is in a state of tolerable civilization, in short, in any nation in which such rules as these can come to be consulted, the dictates of the moral sanction will so far recede from a coincidence with those of utility (that is, of enlightened benevolence) that the disposition indicated in this case can be otherwise than a good one upon the whole.

Example I

19. An Indian receives an injury, real or imaginary, from an Indian of another tribe. He revenges it upon the person of his antagonist with the most excruciating torments: the case being, that cruelties inflicted on such an occasion, gain him reputation in his own tribe. The disposition manifested in such a case can never be deemed a good one, among a people ever so few degrees advanced, in point of civilization, above the Indians.

Example II

20. A nobleman (to come back to Europe) contracts a debt with a poor tradesman. The same nobleman, presently afterwards, contracts a debt, to the same amount, to another nobleman, at play.

a motive to the class of bad ones as often as they can find one still better, to which the act might have owed its birth. Conscious that his own motives are not of the best class, or persuaded that if they be, they will not be referred to that class by others; afraid of being taken for a dupe, and anxious to show the reach of his penetration; each man takes care, in the first place, to impute the conduct of every other man to the least laudable of the motives that can account for it: in the next place, when he has gone as far that way as he can, and cannot drive down the individual motive to any lower class, he changes his battery, and attacks the very class itself. To the love of reputation he will accordingly give a bad name upon every occasion, calling it ostentation, vanity, or vain-glory.

Partly to the same spirit of detraction, the natural consequence of the sensibility of men to the force of the moral sanction, partly to the influence of the principle of asceticism, may, perhaps, be imputed the great abundance of bad names of motives, in comparison of such as are good or neutral: and, in particular, the total want of neutral names for the motives of sexual desire, physical desire in general, and pecuniary interest. The superior abundance, even of good names, in comparison of neutral ones, would, if examined, be found rather to confirm than disprove the above remark. The language of a people on these points may, perhaps, serve in some measure as a key to their moral sentiments. But such speculative disquisitions are foreign to the purpose of the present work.

130

He is unable to pay both: he pays the whole debt to the companion of his amusements, and no part of it to the tradesman. The disposition manifested in this case can scarcely be termed otherwise than a bad one. It is certainly, however, not so bad as if he had paid neither. The principle of love of reputation, or (as it is called in the case of this partial application of it) honour, is here opposed to the worthier principle of benevolence, and gets the better of it. But it gets the better also of the self-regarding principle of pecuniary interest. The disposition, therefore, which it indicates, although not so good a one as that in which the principle of benevolence predominates, is better than one in which the principle of self-interest predominates. He would be the better for having more benevolence: but would he be the better for having no honour? This seems to admit of great dispute.[h]

21. (7) Where the tendency of the act is *good*, and the motive is the semi-social one of *religion*. In this case, the disposition indicated by it (considered with respect to the influence of it on the man's conduct towards others) is manifestly a beneficent and meritorious one. *Case 7. Tendency, good—motive, piety*

A baker distributes bread *gratis* among the industrious poor. It is not that he feels for their distresses: nor is it for the sake of gaining reputation among his neighbours. It is for the sake of gaining the favour of the Deity: to whom, he takes for granted, such conduct will be acceptable. The disposition manifested by such conduct is plainly what every man would call a good one.

22. (8) Where the tendency of the act is *bad*, and the motive is that of religion, as before. In this case the disposition is dubious. It is good or bad, and more or less good or bad, in the first place, as the tendency of the act is more or less mischievous; in the next place, according as the religious tenets of the person in question approach more or less to a coincidence with the dictates of utility. *Case 8. Tendency, bad—motive, religion*

23. It should seem from history, that even in nations in a tolerable state of civilization in other respects, the dictates of religion have been found so far to recede from a coincidence with those of utility; in other words, from those of enlightened benevolence; that the disposition indicated in this case may even be a bad one upon the whole. This however is no objection to the inference which it affords of a good disposition in those countries (such as perhaps are most of the countries of Europe at present) in which its dictates respecting the conduct of a man towards other men approach very nearly to a coincidence with those of utility. The dictates of religion, *The disposition may be bad in this case*

[h] See the case of Duels discussed in B. I. tit. (Homicide).

in their application to the conduct of a man in what concerns himself alone, seem in most European nations to savour a good deal of the ascetic principle: but the obedience to such mistaken dictates indicates not any such disposition as is likely to break out into acts of pernicious tendency with respect to others. Instances in which the dictates of religion lead a man into acts which are pernicious in this latter view, seem at present to be but rare: unless it be acts of persecution, or impolitic measures on the part of government, where the law itself is either the principal actor or an accomplice in the mischief. Ravaillac, instigated by no other motive than this, gave his country one of the most fatal stabs that a country ever received from a single hand: but happily the Ravaillacs are but rare. They have been more frequent, however, in France than in any other country during the same period: and it is remarkable, that in every instance it is this motive that has produced them. When they do appear, however, nobody, I suppose, but such as themselves, will be for terming a disposition, such as they manifest, a good one. It seems hardly to be denied, but that they are just so much the worse for their notions of religion; and that had they been left to the sole guidance of benevolence, and the love of reputation, without any religion at all, it would have been but so much the better for mankind. One may say nearly the same thing, perhaps, of those persons who, without any particular obligation, have taken an active part in the execution of laws made for the punishment of those who have the misfortune to differ with the magistrate in matters of religion, much more of the legislator himself, who has put it in their power. If Louis XIV had had no religion, France would not have lost 800,000 of its most valuable subjects. The same thing may be said of the authors of the wars called holy ones: whether waged against persons called Infidels, or persons branded with the still more odious name of Heretics. In Denmark, not a great many years ago, a sect is said to have arisen, who, by a strange perversion of reason, took it into their heads, that, by leading to repentance, murder, or any other horrid crime, might be made the road to heaven.[1] It should all along, however, be observed, that instances of this latter kind were always rare: and that in almost all the countries of Europe, instances of the former kind, though once abundantly frequent, have for some time ceased. In certain countries, however,

---

[1] Unlike the reference just above to Louis XIV's revocation of the Edict of Nantes the present reference is far from easy to elucidate. Bentham may have encountered a misrepresentation of the religious revival inspired by the visit to Copenhagen in 1727 of the pietist Dippel, who, however, certainly did not hold or teach the doctrine here described.

persecution at home, or (what produces a degree of restraint, which is one part of the mischiefs of persecution) I mean the *disposition* to persecute, whensoever occasion happens, is not yet at an end: insomuch that if there is no *actual* persecution, it is only because there are no heretics; and if there are no heretics, it is only because there are no thinkers.[1]

24. (9) Where the tendency of the act is *good*, and the motive (as before) is the dissocial one of ill-will. In this case the motive seems not to afford any indication on either side. It is no indication of a good disposition; but neither is it any indication of a bad one.

Case 9. Tendency, good—motive, male- volence

You have detected a baker in selling short weight: you prosecute him for the cheat. It is not for the sake of gain that you engaged in the prosecution; for there is nothing to be got by it: it is not from public spirit: it is not for the sake of reputation; for there is no reputation to be got by it: it is not in the view of pleasing the Deity: it is merely on account of a quarrel you have with the man you prosecute. From the transaction, as thus stated, there does not seem to be any thing to be said either in favour of your disposition or against it. The tendency of the act is good: but you would not have engaged in it, had it not been from a motive which there seems no particular reason to conclude will ever prompt you to engage in an act of the same kind again. Your motive is of that sort which may, with least impropriety, be termed a bad one: but the act is of that sort, which, were it engaged in ever so often, could never have any evil tendency; nor indeed any other tendency than a good one. By the supposition, the motive it happened to be dictated by was that of ill-will: but the act itself is of such a nature as to have wanted nothing but sufficient discernment on your part in order to have been dictated by the most enlarged benevolence. Now, from a man's having suffered himself to be induced to gratify his resent- ment by means of an act of which the tendency is good, it by no means follows that he would be ready on another occasion, through the influence of the same sort of motive, to engage in any act of which the tendency is a bad one. The motive that impelled you was a dissocial one: but what social motive could there have been to restrain you? None, but what might have been outweighed by a more enlarged motive of the same kind. Now, because the dissocial motive prevailed when it stood alone, it by no means follows that it would prevail when it had a social one to combat it.

Example

25. (10) Where the tendency of the act is *bad*, and the motive is

Case 10. Tendency, bad—mo- tive, male- volence

[1] See B. I. tit. (Offences against Religion).

the dissocial one of malevolence. In this case the disposition it indicates is of course a mischievous one.

Example

The man who stole the bread from the baker, as before, did it with no other view than merely to impoverish and afflict him: accordingly, when he had got the bread, he did not eat, or sell it; but destroyed it. That the disposition, evidenced by such a transaction, is a bad one, is what every body must perceive immediately.

Problem—to measure the depravity in a man's disposition

26. Thus much with respect to the circumstances from which the mischievousness or meritoriousness of a man's disposition is to be inferred in the gross: we come now to the *measure* of that mischievousness or meritoriousness, as resulting from those circumstances. Now with meritorious acts and dispositions we have no direct concern in the present work. All that penal law is concerned to do, is to measure the depravity of the disposition where the act is mischievous. To this object, therefore, we shall here confine ourselves.

A man's disposition is constituted by the sum of his intentions:

27. It is evident, that the nature of a man's disposition must depend upon the nature of the motives he is apt to be influenced by: in other words, upon the degree of his sensibility to the force of such and such motives. For his disposition is, as it were, the sum of his intentions: the disposition he is of during a certain period, the sum or result of his intentions during that period. If, of the acts he has been intending to engage in during the supposed period, those which are apparently of a mischievous tendency, bear a large proportion to those which appear to him to be of the contrary tendency, his disposition will be of the mischievous cast: if but a small proportion, of the innocent or upright.

—which owe their birth to motives

28. Now intentions, like every thing else, are produced by the things that are their causes: and the causes of intentions are motives. If, on any occasion, a man forms either a good or a bad intention, it must be by the influence of some motive.

A seducing or corrupting motive, what—a tutelary or preservatory motive

29. When the act, which a motive prompts a man to engage in, is of a mischievous nature, it may, for distinction's sake, be termed a *seducing* or corrupting motive: in which case also any motive which, in opposition to the former, acts in the character of a restraining motive, may be styled a *tutelary*, conservatory,[1] preservatory, or preserving motive.

Tutelary motives are either standing or occasional

30. Tutelary motives may again be distinguished into *standing*

[1] The word 'conservatory' is an insertion made in Ms. by Bentham in his copy of the 1789 edition now in the British Museum. It was overlooked in 1823 but duly made in the Bowring edition (i, 65).

or constant, and *occasional*. By standing tutelary motives, I mean such as act with more or less force in all, or at least in most cases, tending to restrain a man from *any* mischievous acts he may be prompted to engage in; and that with a force which depends upon the general nature of the act, rather than upon any accidental circumstance with which any individual act of that sort may happen to be accompanied. By occasional tutelary motives, I mean such motives as may chance to act in this direction or not, according to the nature of the act, and of the particular occasion on which the engaging in it is brought into contemplation.

31. Now it has been shown, that there is no sort of motive by which a man may not be prompted to engage in acts that are of a mischievous nature; that is, which may not come to act in the capacity of a seducing motive. It has been shown, on the other hand, that there are some motives which are remarkably less likely to operate in this way than others. It has also been shown, that the least likely of all is that of benevolence or good-will: the most common tendency of which, it has been shown, is to act in the character of a tutelary motive. It has also been shown, that even when by accident it acts in one way in the character of a seducing motive, still in another way it acts in the opposite character of a tutelary one. The motive of good-will, in as far as it respects the interests of one set of persons, may prompt a man to engage in acts which are productive of mischief to another and more extensive set: but this is only because his good-will is imperfect and confined: not taking into contemplation the interests of all the persons whose interests are at stake. The same motive, were the affection it issued from more enlarged, would operate effectually, in the character of a constraining motive, against that very act to which, by the supposition, it gives birth. This same sort of motive may therefore, without any real contradiction or deviation from truth, be ranked in the number of standing tutelary motives, notwithstanding the occasions in which it may act at the same time in the character of a seducing one.

Standing tutelary motives are, 1. Good-will

32. The same observation, nearly, may be applied to the semi-social motive of love of reputation. The force of this, like that of the former, is liable to be divided against itself. As in the case of good-will, the interests of some of the persons, who may be the objects of that sentiment, are liable to be at variance with those of others: so in the case of love of reputation, the sentiments of some of the persons, whose good opinion is desired, may be at variance with the sentiments of other persons of that number. Now in the case of an act, which is really of a mischievous nature, it can scarcely happen

2. The love of reputation

that there shall be no persons whatever who will look upon it with an eye of disapprobation. It can scarcely ever happen, therefore, that an act really mischievous shall not have some part at least, if not the whole, of the force of this motive to oppose it; nor, therefore, that this motive should not act with some degree of force in the character of a tutelary motive. This, therefore, may be set down as another article in the catalogue of standing tutelary motives.

3. The desire of amity

33. The same observation may be applied to the desire of amity, though not in altogether equal measure. For, notwithstanding the mischievousness of an act, it may happen, without much difficulty, that all the persons for whose amity a man entertains any particular present desire which is accompanied with expectation, may concur in regarding it with an eye rather of approbation than the contrary. This is but too apt to be the case among such fraternities as those of thieves, smugglers, and many other denominations of offenders. This, however, is not constantly, nor indeed most commonly the case: insomuch, that the desire of amity may still be regarded, upon the whole, as a tutelary motive, were it only from the closeness of its connexion with the love of reputation. And it may be ranked among standing tutelary motives, since, where it does apply, the force with which it acts, depends not upon the occasional circumstances of the act which it opposes, but upon principles as general as those upon which depend the action of the other semi-social motives.

4. The motive of religion

34. The motive of religion is not altogether in the same case with the three former. The force of it is not, like theirs, liable to be divided against itself. I mean in the civilized nations of modern times, among whom the notion of the unity of the Godhead is universal. In time of classical antiquity it was otherwise. If a man got Venus on his side, Pallas was on the other: if Æolus was for him, Neptune was against him. Æneas, with all his piety, had but a partial interest at the court of heaven. That matter stands upon a different footing now-a-days. In any given person, the force of religion, whatever it be, is now all of it on one side. It may balance, indeed, on which side it shall declare itself: and it may declare itself, as we have seen already in but too many instances, on the wrong as well as on the right. It has been, at least till lately, perhaps is still, accustomed so much to declare itself on the wrong side, and that in such material instances, that on that account it seemed not proper to place it, in point of social tendency, on a level altogether with the motive of benevolence. Where it does act, however, as it does in by far the greatest number of cases, in opposition to the ordinary seducing motives, it acts, like the motive of benevolence, in an uniform manner, not depending upon the particular circumstances that may attend the commission of the act; but tending to oppose it, merely on account of its mischievousness; and therefore, with equal force, in whatsoever circumstances it may be proposed to be committed. This, therefore, may also be added to the catalogue of standing tutelary motives.

35. As to the motives which may operate occasionally in the character of tutelary motives, these, it has been already intimated, are of various sorts, and various degrees of strength in various offences: depending not only upon the nature of the offence, but upon the accidental circumstances in which the idea of engaging in it may come in contemplation. Nor is there any sort of motive which may not come to operate in this character; as may be easily conceived. A thief, for instance, may be prevented from engaging in a projected scheme of house-breaking, by sitting too long over his bottle,[j] by a visit from his doxy, by the occasion he may have to go elsewhere, in order to receive his dividend of a former booty[k]; and so on. *Occasional tutelary motives may be any whatsoever*

36. There are some motives, however, which seem more apt to act in this character than others; especially as things are now constituted, now that the law has every where opposed to the force of the principal seducing motives, artificial tutelary motives of its own creation. Of the motives here meant it will be necessary to take a general view. They seem to be reducible to two heads; viz. **1.** The love of ease; a motive put into action by the prospect of the trouble of the attempt; that is, the trouble which it may be necessary to bestow, in overcoming the physical difficulties that may accompany it. **2.** Self-preservation, as opposed to the dangers to which a man may be exposed in the prosecution of it. *Motives that are particularly apt to act in in this character are, 1. Love of ease 2. Self-preservation*

37. These dangers may be either, 1. Of a purely physical nature: or, 2. Dangers resulting from moral agency; in other words, from the conduct of any such persons to whom the act, if known, may be expected to prove obnoxious. But moral agency supposes knowledge with respect to the circumstances that are to have the effect of external motives in giving birth to it. Now the obtaining such knowledge, with respect to the commission of any obnoxious act, on the part of any persons who may be disposed to make the agent suffer for it, is called *detection*; and the agent concerning whom such knowledge is obtained, is said to be detected. *Dangers to which self-preservation is most apt in this case to have respect, are, 1. Dangers purely physical 2. Dangers depending on detection*

[j] Love of the pleasures of the palate.
[k] Pecuniary interest.

The dangers, therefore, which may threaten an offender from this quarter, depend, whatever they may be, on the event of his detection; and may, therefore, be all of them comprised under the article of the *danger of detection*.

Danger depending on detection may result from, 7. Opposition on the spot: 2. Subsequent punishment

38. The danger depending upon detection may be divided again into two branches: 1. That which may result from any opposition that may be made to the enterprise by persons on the spot; that is, at the very time the enterprise is carrying on: 2. That which respects the legal punishment, or other suffering, that may await at a distance upon the issue of the enterprise.

The force of the two standing tutelary motives of love of reputation and desire of amity, depends upon detection

39. It may be worth calling to mind on this occasion, that among the tutelary motives, which have been styled constant ones, there are two of which the force depends (though not so entirely as the force of the occasional ones which have been just mentioned, yet in a great measure) upon the circumstance of detection. These, it may be remembered, are, the love of reputation, and the desire of amity. In proportion, therefore, as the chance of being detected appears greater, these motives will apply with the greater force: with the less force, as it appears less. This is not the case with the two other standing tutelary motives, that of benevolence, and that of religion.

Strength of a temptation, what is meant by it

40. We are now in a condition to determine, with some degree of precision, what is to be understood by the *strength of a temptation,* and what indication it may give of the degree of mischievousness in a man's disposition in the case of any offence. When a man is prompted to engage in any mischievous act, we will say, for shortness, in an offence, the strength of the temptation depends upon the ratio between the force of the seducing motives on the one hand, and such of the occasional tutelary ones, as the circumstances of the case call forth into action, on the other. The temptation, then, may be said to be strong, when the pleasure or advantage to be got from the crime is such as in the eyes of the offender must appear great in comparison of the trouble and danger that appear to him to accompany the enterprise: slight or weak, when that pleasure or advantage is such as must appear small in comparison of such trouble and such danger. It is plain the strength of the temptation depends not upon the force of the impelling (that is of the seducing) motives altogether: for let the opportunity be more favourable, that is, let the trouble, or any branch of the danger, be made less than before, it will be acknowledged, that the temptation is made so much the stronger: and on the other hand, let the opportunity become less favourable, or, in other words, let the trouble, or any branch of the danger, be made greater than before, the temptation will be so much the weaker.

Now, after taking account of such tutelary motives as have been styled occasional, the only tutelary motives that can remain are those which have been termed standing ones. But those which have been termed the standing tutelary motives, are the same that we have been styling social. It follows, therefore, that the strength of the temptation, in any case, after deducting the force of the social motives, is as the sum of the forces of the seducing, to the sum of the forces of the occasional tutelary motives.

41. It remains to be inquired, what indication concerning the mischievousness or depravity of a man's disposition is afforded by the strength of the temptation, in the case where any offence happens to have been committed. It appears, then, that the weaker the temptation is, by which a man has been overcome, the more depraved and mischievous it shows his disposition to have been. For the goodness of his disposition is measured by the degree of his sensibility to the action of the social motives[1]: in other words, by the strength of the influence which those motives have over him: now, the less considerable the force is by which their influence on him has been overcome, the more convincing is the proof that has been given of the weakness of that influence. *Indications afforded by this and other circumstances respecting the depravity of an offender's disposition*

Again, The degree of a man's sensibility to the force of the social motives being given, it is plain that the force with which those motives tend to restrain him from engaging in any mischievous enterprise, will be as the apparent mischievousness of such enterprise, that is, as the degree of mischief with which it appears to *him* likely to be attended. In other words, the less mischievous the offence appears to him to be, the less averse he will be, as far as he is guided by social considerations, to engage in it; the more mischievous, the more averse. If then the nature of the offence is such as must appear to him highly mischievous, and yet he engages in it notwithstanding, it shows, that the degree of his sensibility to the force of the social motives is but slight; and consequently that his disposition is proportionably depraved. Moreover, the less the strength of the temptation was, the more pernicious and depraved does it show his disposition to have been. For the less the strength of the temptation was, the less was the force which the influence of those motives had to overcome: the clearer therefore is the proof that has been given of the weakness of that influence.

[1] Supra, par. 27, 28.

Rules for
measuring
the depravity
of disposi-
tion indi-
cated by an
offence

42. From what has been said, it seems, that, for judging of the indication that is afforded concerning the depravity of a man's disposition by the strength of the temptation, compared with the mischievousness of the enterprise, the following rules may be laid down:

Rule 1. *The strength of the temptation being given, the mischievousness of the disposition manifested by the enterprise, is as the apparent mischievousness of the act.*

Thus, it would show a more depraved disposition, to murder a man for a reward of a guinea, or falsely to charge him with a robbery for the same reward, than to obtain the same sum from him by simple theft: the trouble he would have to take, and the risk he would have to run, being supposed to stand on the same footing in the one case as in the other.

Rule 2. *The apparent mischievousness of the act being given, a man's disposition is the more depraved, the slighter the temptation is by which he has been overcome.*

Thus, it shows a more depraved and dangerous disposition, if a man kill another out of mere sport, as the Emperor of Morocco, Muley Mahomet, is said to have done great numbers,[1] than out of revenge, as Sylla and Marius did thousands,[2] or in the view of self-preservation, as Augustus killed many, or even for lucre, as the same Emperor is said to have killed some.[3] And the effects of such a depravity, on that part of the public which is apprized of it, run in the same proportion. From Augustus, some persons only had to fear, under some particular circumstances. From Muley Mahomet, every man had to fear at all times.

Rule 3. *The apparent mischievousness of the act being given, the evidence which it affords of the depravity of a man's disposition is the less conclusive, the stronger the temptation is by which he has been overcome.*

Thus, if a poor man, who is ready to die with hunger, steal a loaf of bread, it is a less explicit sign of depravity, than if a rich man were to commit a theft to the same amount. It will be observed, that in this rule all that is said is, that the evidence of depravity is

[1] This most probably refers to Moulay Mohammed, prince of Fez, during whose reign (1613–23) there was much anarchy. But the reference may be to Moulay Ismail (1672–1727) who was well known in Europe, where he was regarded as 'a monster of cruelty', though in Morocco he was regarded as a great ruler.

[2] A reference to the extensive proscriptions and the recurrent reign of terror arising from the bitter rivalry between Lucius Cornelius Sulla (138–78 B.C.) and Gaius Marius (155–86 B.C.).

[3] 300 senators and 2000 knights died as a result of the proscriptions issued by Octavian (later Augustus) together with Mark Antony and Lepidus during the struggle for power which followed the murder of Julius Caesar.

in this case the less conclusive: it is not said that the depravity is positively the less. For in this case it is possible, for any thing that appears to the contrary, that the theft might have been committed, even had the temptation been not so strong. In this case, the alleviating circumstance is only a matter of presumption; in the former, the aggravating circumstance is a matter of certainty.

Rule 4. *Where the motive is of the dissocial kind, the apparent mischievousness of the act, and the strength of the temptation, being given the depravity is as the degree of deliberation with which it is accompanied.*

For in every man, be his disposition ever so depraved, the social motives are those which, wherever the self-regarding ones stand neuter, regulate and determine the general tenor of his life. If the dissocial motives are put in action, it is only in particular circumstances, and on particular occasions; the gentle but constant force of the social motives, being for a while subdued. The general and standing bias of every man's nature is, therefore, towards that side to which the force of the social motives would determine him to adhere. This being the case, the force of the social motives tends continually to put an end to that of the dissocial ones; as, in natural bodies, the force of friction tends to put an end to that which is generated by impulse. Time, then, which wears away the force of the dissocial motives, adds to that of the social. The longer, therefore, a man continues, on a given occasion, under the dominion of the dissocial motives, the more convincing is the proof that has been given of his insensibility to the force of the social ones.

Thus, it shows a worse disposition, where a man lays a deliberate plan for beating his antagonist, and beats him accordingly, than if he were to beat him upon the spot, in consequence of a sudden quarrel: and worse again, if, after having had him a long while together in his power, he beats him at intervals, and at his leisure.[m]

43. The depravity of disposition, indicated by an act, is a material consideration in several respects. Any mark of extraordinary depravity, by adding to the terror already inspired by the crime, and by holding up the offender as a person from whom there may be more mischief to be apprehended in future, adds in that way to the demand for punishment. By indicating a general want of sensibility on the part of the offender, it may add in another way also to the demand for punishment. The article of disposition is of the more importance, inasmuch as, in measuring out the quantum of punishment, the principle of sympathy and antipathy is apt to

Use of this chapter

[m] See B. I. tit. (Confinement).

look at nothing else. A man who punishes because he hates, and only because he hates, such a man, when he does not find any thing odious in the disposition, is not for punishing at all; and when he does, he is not for carrying the punishment further than his hatred carries him. Hence the aversion we find so frequently expressed against the maxim, that the punishment must rise with the strength of the temptation; a maxim, the contrary of which, as we shall see, would be as cruel to offenders themselves, as it would be subversive of the purposes of punishment.

CHAPTER XII

OF THE CONSEQUENCES OF A MISCHIEVOUS ACT

§ i. *Shapes in which the mischief of an act may show itself*

1. Hitherto we have been speaking of the various articles or objects on which the consequences or tendency of an act may depend: of the bare *act* itself: of the *circumstances* it may have been, or may have been supposed to be, accompanied with: of the *consciousness* a man may have had with respect to any such circumstances: of the *intentions* that may have preceded the act: of the *motives* that may have given birth to those intentions: and of the *disposition* that may have been indicated by the connexion between such intentions and such motives. We now come to speak of *consequences* or tendency: an article which forms the concluding link in all this chain of causes and effects, involving in it the materiality of the whole. Now, such part of this tendency as is of a mischievous nature, is all that we have any direct concern with; to that, therefore, we shall here confine ourselves. *Recapitulation*

2. The tendency of an act is mischievous when the consequences of it are mischievous; that is to say, either the certain consequences or the probable. The consequences, how many and whatsoever they may be, of an act, of which the tendency is mischievous, may, such of them as are mischievous, be conceived to constitute one aggregate body, which may be termed the mischief of the act. *Mischief of an act, the aggregate of its mischievous consequences*

3. This mischief may frequently be distinguished, as it were, into two shares or parcels: the one containing what may be called the primary mischief; the other, what may be called the secondary. That share may be termed the *primary*, which is sustained by an assignable individual, or a multitude of assignable individuals. That share may be termed the *secondary*, which, taking its origin from the former, extends itself either over the whole community, or over some other multitude of unassignable individuals. *The mischief of an act, primary or secondary*

4. The primary mischief of an act may again be distinguished into two branches: 1. The *original*: and, 2. The *derivative*. By the original branch, I mean that which alights upon and is confined to any person who is a sufferer in the first instance, and on his own account: the person, for instance, who is beaten, robbed, or murdered. By the derivative branch, I mean any share of mischief which *Primary—original, or derivative* may befall any other assignable persons in consequence of his being a sufferer, and no otherwise. These persons must, of course, be persons who in some way or other are connected with him. Now the ways in which one person may be connected with another, have been already seen: they may be connected in the way of *interest* (meaning self-regarding interest) or merely in the way of *sympathy*. And again, persons connected with a given person, in the way of interest may be connected with him either by affording *support* to him, or by deriving it from him.[a]

The secondary—
1. Alarm: or,
2. Danger

5. The secondary mischief, again, may frequently be seen to consist of two other shares or parcels: the first consisting of *pain*; the other of *danger*. The pain which it produces is a pain of apprehension: a pain grounded on the apprehension of suffering such mischiefs or inconveniencies, whatever they may be, as it is the nature of the primary mischief to produce. It may be styled, in one word, the *alarm*. The danger is the *chance*, whatever it may be, which the multitude it concerns may in consequence of the primary mischief, stand exposed to, of suffering such mischiefs or inconveniences. For danger is nothing but the chance of pain, or, what comes to the same thing, of loss of pleasure.

Example

6. An example may serve to make this clear. A man attacks you on the road, and robs you. You suffer a pain on the occasion of losing so much money[b]: you also suffered a pain at the thoughts of the personal ill-treatment you apprehended he might give you, in case of your not happening to satisfy his demands.[c] These together constitute the original branch of the primary mischief, resulting from the act of robbery. A creditor of yours, who expected you to pay him with part of that money, and a son of yours, who expected you to have given him another part, are in consequence disappointed. You are obliged to have recourse to the bounty of your father, to make good part of the deficiency. These mischiefs together make up the derivative branch. The report of this robbery circulates from hand to hand, and spreads itself in the neighbourhood. It finds its way into the newspapers, and is propagated over the whole country. Various people, on this occasion, call to mind the danger which they and their friends, as it appears from this example, stand exposed to in travelling; especially such as may have occasion to travel the same road. On this occasion they naturally feel a certain

[a] See Ch. vi (Sensibility).

[b] Viz. a *pain of privation*. See Ch. v (Pleasures and Pains) 17.

[c] Viz. a *pain of apprehension*, grounded on the prospect of organical pain, or whatever other mischiefs might have ensued from the ill treatment. Ibid. 30.

degree of pain: slighter or heavier, according to the degree of ill-treatment they may understand you to have received; the frequency of the occasion each person may have to travel in that same road, or its neighbourhood; the vicinity of each person to the spot; his personal courage; the quantity of money he may have occasion to carry about with him; and a variety of other circumstances. This constitutes the first part of the secondary mischief, resulting from the act of robbery; viz. the alarm. But people of one description or other, not only are disposed to conceive themselves to incur a chance of being robbed, in consequence of the robbery committed upon you, but (as will be shown presently) they do really incur such a chance. And it is this chance which constitutes the remaining part of the secondary mischief of the act of robbery; viz. the danger.

7. Let us see what this chance amounts to; and whence it comes. *The danger, whence it arises—a past offence affords no direct motive to a future* How is it, for instance, that one robbery can contribute to produce another? In the first place, it is certain that it cannot create any direct motive. A motive must be the prospect of some pleasure, or other advantage, to be enjoyed in future: but the robbery in question is past: nor would it furnish any such prospect were it to come: for it is not one robbery that will furnish pleasure to him who may be about to commit another robbery. The consideration that is to operate upon a man, as a motive or inducement to commit a robbery, must be the idea of the pleasure he expects to derive from the fruits of that very robbery: but this pleasure exists independently of any other robbery.

8. The means, then, by which one robbery tends, as it should seem, to produce another robbery, are two. 1. By suggesting to a *But it suggests feasibility, and weakens the force of restraining motives* person exposed to the temptation, the idea of committing such another robbery (accompanied, perhaps, with the belief of its facility). In this case the influence it exerts applies itself, in the first place, to the understanding. 2. By weakening the force of the tutelary motives which tend to restrain him from such an action, and thereby adding to the strength of the temptation.[d] In this case the influence applies itself to the will. These forces are, 1. The motive of benevolence, which acts as a branch of the physical sanction.[e] 2. The motive of self-preservation, as against the punishment that may stand provided by the political sanction. 3. The fear of shame:

[d] See Ch. xi (Dispositions) 40.

[e] To wit, in virtue of the pain it may give a man to be a witness to, or otherwise conscious of, the sufferings of a fellow-creature: especially when he is himself the cause of them: in a word, the pain of sympathy. See Ch. v (Pleasures and Pains) 26.

a motive belonging to the moral sanction. 4. The fear of the divine displeasure: a motive belonging to the religious sanction. On the first and last of these forces it has, perhaps, no influence worth insisting on: but it has on the other two.

viz. 1. Those issuing from the political sanction

9. The way in which a past robbery may weaken the force with which the *political* sanction tends to prevent a future robbery, may be thus conceived. The way in which this sanction tends to prevent a robbery, is by denouncing some particular kind of punishment against any who shall be guilty of it: the *real* value of which punishment will of course be diminished by the *real* uncertainty: as also, if there be any difference, the *apparent* value by the *apparent* uncertainty. Now this uncertainty is proportionably increased by every instance in which a man is known to commit the offence, without undergoing the punishment. This, of course, will be the case with every offence for a certain time; in short, until the punishment allotted to it takes place, If punishment takes place at last, this branch of the mischief of the offence is then at last, but not till then, put a stop to.

2. Those issuing from the moral

10. The way in which a past robbery may weaken the force with which the *moral* sanction tends to prevent a future robbery, may be thus conceived. The way in which the moral sanction tends to prevent a robbery, is by holding forth the indignation of mankind as ready to fall upon him who shall be guilty of it. Now this indignation will be the more formidable, according to the number of those who join in it: it will be the less so, the fewer they are who join in it. But there cannot be a stronger way of showing that a man does not join in whatever indignation may be entertained against a practice, than the engaging in it himself. It shows not only that he himself feels no indignation against it, but that it seems to him there is no sufficient reason for apprehending what indignation may be felt against it by others. Accordingly, where robberies are frequent, and unpunished, robberies are committed without shame. It was thus amongst the Grecians formerly.[f] It is thus among the Arabs still.

[f] See Hom. Odyss. L. xix 1. 395. ibid. L. iii 1, 71.[1] Plato de Rep. L. i. p. 576. edit. Ficin.[2] Thucyd. L. i.[3]—and see B. I. tit. (Offences against external security.)

[1] *Odyssey*, xix.395 refers to Autolycus '. . . who excelled all men in thievery and in oaths'; iii.71 refers to Telemachus, while in search of his father, being asked by Nestor whether he and his followers come on business or 'even as pirates'.

[2] In this passage (*Republic*, i, 334) Plato echoes the Homeric reference to Autolycus (cf. n. 1 above). Bentham refers to the Latin version by Marsiglio Ficino (1433–99), edited by Sebastian Fox Morzilius (1556).

[3] Thucydides, *History of the Peloponnesian War*, i.iv-v, vii.

11. In whichever way then a past offence tends to pave the way for the commission of a future offence, whether by suggesting the idea of committing it, or by adding to the strength of the temptation, in both cases it may be said to operate by the force or *influence of example*.

12. The two branches of the secondary mischief of an act, the alarm and the danger, must not be confounded: though intimately connected, they are perfectly distinct: either may subsist without the other. The neighbourhood may be alarmed with the report of a robbery, when, in fact, no robbery, either has been committed or is in a way to be committed: a neighbourhood may be on the point of being disturbed by robberies, without knowing any thing of the matter. Accordingly, we shall soon perceive, that some acts produce alarm without danger: others, danger without alarm.

13. As well the danger as the alarm may again be divided, each of them, into two branches: the first, consisting of so much of the alarm or danger as may be apt to result from the future behaviour of the same agent: the second, consisting of so much as may be apt to result from the behaviour of other persons: such others, to wit, as may come to engage in acts of the same sort and tendency.[g]

14. The distinction between the primary and the secondary consequences of an act, must be carefully attended to. It is so just, that the latter may often be of a directly opposite nature to the former. In some cases, where the primary consequences of the act are attended with a mischief, the secondary consequences may be beneficial, and that to such a degree, as even greatly to outweigh the mischief of the primary. This is the case, for instance, with all acts of punishment, when properly applied. Of these, the primary mischief being never intended to fall but upon such persons as may happen to have committed some act which it is expedient to prevent, the secondary mischief, that is, the alarm and the danger, extends no farther than to such persons as are under temptation to commit it: in which case, in as far as it tends to restrain them from committing such acts, it is of a beneficial nature.

15. Thus much with regard to acts that produce positive pain, and that immediately. This case, by reason of its simplicity, seemed the fittest to take the lead. But acts may produce mischief in various other ways; which, together with those already specified, may all be comprized by the following abridged analysis.

[g] To the former of these branches is opposed so much of the force of any punishment, as is said to operate in the way of *reformation*: to the latter, so much as is said to operate in the way of *example*. See Ch. XIII (Cases unmeet) 2 note.

Mischief may admit of a division in any one of three points of view. 1. According to its own *nature*. 2. According to its *cause*. 3. According to the person, or other party, who is the *object* of it.[h] With regard to its nature, it may be either *simple* or *complex*[i]: when simple, it may either be *positive* or *negative*: positive, consisting of actual pain: negative, consisting of the loss of pleasure. Whether simple or complex, and whether positive or negative, it may be either *certain* or *contingent*. When it is negative, it consists of the loss of some benefit or advantage: this benefit may be material in both or either of two ways: 1. By affording actual pleasure: or, 2. By averting pain or *danger*, which is the chance of pain: that is, by affording *security*. In so far, then, as the benefit which a mischief tends to avert, is productive of security, the tendency of such mischief is to produce *insecurity*. 2. With regard to its *cause*, mischief may be produced either by one *single* action, or not without the *concurrence* of other actions: if not without the concurrence of other actions, these others may be the actions either of the *same person*, or of *other* persons: in either case, they may be either acts of the *same kind* as that in question, or of *other* kinds. 3. Lastly, with regard to the party who is the *object* of the mischief, or, in other words, who is in a way to be affected by it, such party may be either an *assignable*[j] individual, or assemblage of individuals, or else a multitude of *unassignable* individuals. When the object is an assignable individual, this individual may either be the person *himself* who is the author of the mischief, or some *other* person. When the individuals, who are the objects of it, are an unassignable multitude, this multitude may be either the *whole* political community or state, or some *subordinate* division of it. Now when the object of the mischief is the author himself, it may be styled *self-regarding*: when any other party is the object, *extra-regarding*: when such other party is an individual, it may be styled *private*: when a subordinate branch of the community, *semi-public*: when the whole community, *public*. Here, for the present, we must stop. To pursue the subject through its inferior distinctions, will be the business of the chapter which exhibits the division of offences.[k]

[h] There may be other points of view, according to which mischief might be divided, besides these: but this does not prevent the division here given from being an exhaustive one. A line may be divided in any one of an infinity of ways, and yet without leaving in any one of those cases any remainder. See Ch. xvi (Division) 1 note.

[i] Ch. v (Pleasures and Pains) 1.

[j] See Ch. xvi (Division) 4 note.

[k] Ch. xvi.

The cases which have been already illustrated, are those in which *–applied to the preceding cases* the primary mischief is not necessarily otherwise than a simple one, and that positive: present, and therefore certain: producible by a single action, without any necessity of the concurrence of any other action, either on the part of the same agent, or of others; and having for its object an assignable individual, or, by accident, an assemblage of assignable individuals: extra-regarding therefore, and private. This primary mischief is accompanied by a secondary: the first branch of which is sometimes contingent and sometimes certain, the other never otherwise than contingent: both extra-regarding and semi-public: In other respects, pretty much upon a par with the primary mischief: except that the first branch, viz. the alarm, though inferior in magnitude to the primary, is, in point of extent, and therefore, upon the whole, in point of magnitude, much superior.

16. Two instances more will be sufficient to illustrate the most *–to examples of other cases where the mischief is less conspicuous* material of the modifications above exhibited.

A man drinks a certain quantity of liquor, and intoxicates himself. The intoxication in this particular instance does him no sort of harm: or, what comes to the same thing, none that is perceptible. *Example I. An act of self-intoxication* But it is probable, and indeed next to certain, that a given number of acts of the same kind would do him a very considerable degree of harm: more or less according to his constitution and other circumstances: for this is no more than what experience manifests every day. It is also certain, that one act of this sort, by one means or other, tends considerably to increase the disposition a man may be in to practice other acts of the same sort: for this also is verified by experience. This, therefore, is one instance where the mischief producible by the act is contingent: in other words, in which the tendency of the act is no otherwise mischievous than in virtue of its producing a *chance* of mischief. This chance depends upon the concurrence of other acts of the same kind; and those such as must be practised by the same person. The object of the mischief is that very person himself who is the author of it, and he only, unless by accident. The mischief is therefore private and self-regarding.

As to its secondary mischief, alarm, it produces none: it produces indeed a certain quantity of danger by the influence of example: but it is not often that this danger will amount to a quantity worth regarding.

17. Again. A man omits paying his share to a public tax. This *Example II. Non-payment of a tax* we see is an act of the negative kind.[1] Is this then to be placed upon

[1] See Ch. VII (Actions) 8.

the list of mischievous acts? Yes, certainly. Upon what grounds? Upon the following. To defend the community against its external as well as its internal adversaries, are tasks, not to mention others of a less indispensable nature, which cannot be fulfilled but at a considerable expense. But whence is the money for defraying this expense to come? It can be obtained in no other manner than by contributions to be collected from individuals; in a word, by taxes. The produce then of these taxes is to be looked upon as a kind of *benefit* which it is necessary the governing part of the community should receive for the use of the whole. This procedure, before it can be applied to its destination, requires that there should be certain persons commissioned to receive and to apply it. Now if these persons, had they received it, would have applied it to its proper destination, it would have been a benefit: the not putting them in a way to receive it, is then a mischief. But it is possible, that if received, it might not have been applied to its proper destination; or that the services, in consideration of which it was bestowed, might not have been performed. It is possible, that the under-officer, who collected the produce of the tax, might not have paid it over to his principal: it is possible that the principal might not have forwarded it on according to its farther destination; to the judge, for instance, who is to protect the community against its clandestine enemies from within, or the soldier, who is to protect it against its open enemies from without: it is possible that the judge, or the soldier, had they received it, would not however have been induced by it to fulfil their respective duties: it is possible, that the judge would not have sat for the punishment of criminals, and the decision of controversies: it is possible that the soldier would not have drawn his sword in the defence of the community. These, together with an infinity of other intermediate acts, which for the sake of brevity I pass over, form a connected chain of duties, the discharge of which is necessary to the preservation of the community. They must every one of them be discharged, ere the benefit to which they are contributory can be produced. If they are all discharged, in that case the benefit subsists, and any act, by tending to intercept that benefit, may produce a mischief. But if any of them are not, the benefit fails: it fails of itself: it would not have subsisted, although the act in question (the act of non-payment) had not been committed. The benefit is therefore contingent; and, accordingly, upon a certain supposition, the act which consists in the averting of it is not a mischievous one. But this supposition, in any tolerably-ordered government, will rarely indeed be verified. In the very worst-ordered government that exists, the greatest part of the duties that are levied are paid over according to their destination: and, with regard to any particular sum, that is attempted to be levied upon any particular person upon any particular occasion, it is therefore manifest, that, unless it be certain that it will not be so disposed of, the act of withholding it is a mischievous one.

The act of payment, when referable to any particular sum, especially if it be a small one, might also have failed of proving beneficial on another ground: and, consequently, the act of non-payment, of proving mischievous. It is possible that the same services, precisely, might have been rendered without the money as with it. If, then, speaking of any small limited sum, such as the greatest which any one person is called upon to pay at a time, a man were to say, that the non-payment of it would be attended with mischievous consequences; this would be far from certain: but what comes to the same thing as if it were, it is perfectly certain when applied to the whole. It is certain, that if all of a sudden the payment of all taxes was to cease, there would no longer be any thing effectual done, either for the maintenance of justice, or for the defence of the community against its foreign adversaries: that therefore the weak would presently be oppressed and injured in all manner of ways, by the strong at home, and both together overwhelmed by oppressors from abroad. Upon the whole, therefore, it is manifest, that in this case, though the mischief is remote and contingent, though in its first appearance it consists of nothing more than the interception of a *benefit*, and though the individuals, in whose favour that benefit would have been reduced into the explicit form of pleasure or security, are altogether unassignable, yet the mischievous tendency of the act is not on all these accounts the less indisputable. The mischief, in point of *intensity* and *duration*, is indeed unknown: it is *uncertain*: it is *remote*. But in point of *extent* it is immense; and in point of *fecundity*, pregnant to a degree that baffles calculation.

18. It may now be time to observe, that it is only in the case where the mischief is extra-regarding, and has an assignable person or persons for its object, that so much of the secondary branch of it as consists in *alarm* can have place. When the individuals it affects are uncertain, and altogether out of sight, no alarm can be produced: as there is nobody whose sufferings you can see, there is nobody whose sufferings you can be alarmed at. No alarm, for instance, is produced by non-payment to a tax. If at any distant and uncertain period of time such offence should chance to be productive

No alarm, when no assignable person is the object

of any kind of alarm, it would appear to proceed, as indeed immediately it would proceed, from a very different cause. It might be immediately referable, for example, to the act of a legislator, who should deem it necessary to lay on a new tax, in order to make up for the deficiency occasioned in the produce of the old one. Or it might be referable to the act of an enemy, who, under favour of a deficiency thus created in the fund allotted for defence, might invade the country, and exact from it much heavier contributions than those which had been thus withholden from the sovereign.[m]

As to any alarm which such an offence might raise among the few who might chance to regard the matter with the eyes of statesmen, it is of too slight and uncertain a nature to be worth taking into the account.

§ ii. *How intentionality, &c. may influence the mischief of an act*

Secondary mischief influenced by the state of the agent's mind

19. We have seen the nature of the secondary mischief, which is apt to be reflected, as it were, from the primary, in the cases where the individuals who are the objects of the mischief are assignable. It is now time to examine into the circumstances upon which the production of such secondary mischief depends. These circumstances are no others than the four articles which have formed the subjects of the four last preceding chapters: viz. 1. The intentionality. 2. The consciousness. 3. The motive. 4. The disposition. It is to be observed all along, that it is only the *danger* that is immediately governed by the *real* state of the mind in respect to those articles: it is by the *apparent* state of it that the *alarm* is governed. It is governed by the real only in as far as the apparent happens, as in most cases it may be expected to do, to quadrate with the real. The different influences of the articles of intentionality and consciousness may be represented in the several cases following.

[m] The investigation might, by a process rendered obvious by analogy, be extended to the consequences of an act of a beneficial nature.

In both instances a *third* order of consequences may be reckoned to have taken place, when the influence of the act, through the medium of the passive faculty of the patient, has come to affect his active faculty. In this way, 1. *Evil may flow out of evil:*—instance, the exertions of industry put a stop to by the extinction of inducement, resulting from a continued chain of acts of robbery or extortion. 2. *Good out of evil:*—instance, habits of depredation put a stop to by a steady course of punishment. 3. *Evil out of good:*—instance, habits of industry put a stop to by an excessive course of gratuitous bounty. 4. *Good out of good:*—instance, a constant and increasing course of industry, excited and kept up by the rewards afforded by a regular and increasing market for the fruits of it.

20. Case 1. Where the act is so completely unintentional, as to be altogether *involuntary.* In this case it is attended with no secondary mischief at all.

A bricklayer is at work upon a house: a passenger is walking in the street below. A fellow-workman comes and gives the bricklayer a violent push, in consequence of which he falls upon the passenger, and hurts him. It is plain there is nothing in this event that can give other people, who may happen to be in the street, the least reason to apprehend any thing in future on the part of the man who fell, whatever there may be with regard to the man who pushed him.

Case 1. In-voluntariness

21. Case 2. Where the act, though not unintentional, is *un-advised,* insomuch that the mischievous part of the consequences is unintentional, but the unadvisedness is attended with *heedlessness.* In this case the act is attended with some small degree of secondary mischief, in proportion to the degree of heedlessness.

A groom being on horseback, and riding through a frequented street, turns a corner at a full pace, and rides over a passenger, who happens to be going by. It is plain, by this behaviour of the groom, some degree of alarm may be produced, less or greater, according to the degree of heedlessness betrayed by him: according to the quickness of his pace, the fullness of the street, and so forth. He has done mischief, it may be said, by his carelessness, already: who knows but that on other occasions the like cause may produce the like effect?

Case 2. Un-intentionality with heed-lessness

22. Case 3. Where the act is *misadvised* with respect to a circumstance, which, had it existed, would *fully* have excluded or (what comes to the same thing) outweighed the primary mischief: and there is no rashness in the case. In this case the act is attended with no secondary mischief at all.

It is needless to multiply examples any farther.

Case 3. Mis-supposal of a complete justification, without rashness

23. Case 4. Where the act is misadvised with respect to a circumstance which would have excluded or counterbalanced the primary mischief *in part,* but not entirely: and still there is no rashness. In this case the act is attended with some degree of secondary mischief, in proportion to that part of the primary which remains unexcluded or uncounterbalanced.

Case 4. Mis-supposal of a partial justi-fication, without rashness

24. Case 5. Where the act is misadvised with respect to a circumstance, which, had it existed, would have excluded or counterbalanced the primary mischief entirely, or in part: and there is a degree of *rashness* in the supposal. In this case, the act is also attended with a farther degree of secondary mischief, in proportion to the degree of rashness.

Case 5. Mis-supposal, with rashness

Case 6. Con-
sequences
completely
intentional,
and free
from mis-
supposal

The nature
of a motive
takes not
away the
mischief of
the second-
ary conse-
quences

25. Case 6. Where the consequences are *completely* intentional, and there is no missupposal in the case. In this case the secondary mischief is at the highest.

26. Thus much with regard to intentionality and consciousness. We now come to consider in what manner the secondary mischief is affected by the nature of the *motive*.

Where an act is pernicious in its primary consequences, the secondary mischief is not obliterated by the *goodness* of the motive; though the motive be of the best kind. For, notwithstanding the goodness of the motive, an act of which the primary consequences are pernicious, is produced by it in the instance in question, by the supposition. It may, therefore, in other instances: although this is not so likely to happen from a good motive as from a bad one.[n]

Nor the bene-
ficialness

27. An act, which, though pernicious in its primary consequences, is rendered in other respects beneficial upon the whole, by virtue of its secondary consequences, is not changed back again, and rendered pernicious upon the whole by the *badness* of the motive: although the motive be of the worst kind.[o]

[n] An act of homicide, for instance, is not rendered innocent, much less beneficial, merely by its proceeding from a principle of religion, of honour (that is, of love of reputation) or even of benevolence. When Ravaillac assassinated Henry IV it was from a principle of religion. But this did not so much as abate from the mischief of the act. It even rendered the act still more mischievous, for a reason that we shall see presently, than if it had originated from a principle of revenge. When the conspirators against the late king of Portugal attempted to assassinate him, it is said to have been from a principle of honour.[1] But this, whether it abated or no, will certainly not be thought to have outweighed, the mischief of the act. Had a son of Ravaillac's, as in the case before supposed,* merely on the score of filial affection, and not in consequence of any participation in his crime, put him to death in order to rescue him from the severer hands of justice, the motive, although it should not be thought to afford any proof of a mischievous disposition, and should, even in case of punishment, have made such rescuer an object of pity, would hardly have made the act of rescue a beneficial one.

[o] The prosecution of offences, for instance, proceeds most commonly from one or other, or both together, of two motives, the one of which is of the self-regarding, the other of the dissocial kind: viz. pecuniary interest, and ill-will: from pecuniary interest, for instance, whenever the obtaining pecuniary amends for damage suffered is one end of the prosecution. It is common enough indeed to hear men speak of prosecutions undertaken from *public spirit*; which is a branch, as we have seen,† of the principle of benevolence. Far be it from

* Ch. XI (Disposition) 15.

† See Ch. x (Motives) 25.

[1] Joseph I of Portugal (1750–77) was wounded when an attempt was made on his life in 1758. The Marquis de Pombal, whom Joseph allowed to govern in his name, claimed that the nobility and the Jesuits were responsible for the attempt. The Jesuits were expelled in 1759.

28. But when not only the primary consequences of an act are pernicious, but, in other respects, the secondary likewise, the secondary mischief may be *aggravated* by the nature of the motive: so much of that mischief, to wit, as respects the future behaviour of the same person. *But it may aggravate the mischievousness, where they are mischievous*

29. It is not from the worst kind of motive, however, that the secondary mischief of an act receives its greatest aggravation. *But not the most in the case of the worst motives*

30. The aggravation which the secondary mischief of an act, in as far as it respects the future behaviour of the same person, receives from the nature of a motive in an individual case, is as the tendency of the motive to produce, on the part of the same person, acts of the like bad tendency with that of the act in question. *It does the more, the more considerable the tendency of the motive to produce such acts*

31. The tendency of a motive to produce acts of the like kind, on the part of any given person, is as the *strength* and *constancy* of its influence on that person, as applied to the production of such effects. *—which is as its strength and constancy*

32. The tendency of a species of motive to give birth to acts of any kind, among persons in general, is as the *strength, constancy,* and *extensiveness*[p] of its influence, as applied to the production of such effects. *General efficacy of a species of motive, how measured*

33. Now the motives, whereof the influence is at once most powerful, most constant, and most extensive, are the motives of physical desire, the love of wealth, the love of ease, the love of life, and the fear of pain: all of them self-regarding motives. The motive of displeasure, whatever it may be in point of strength and extensiveness, is not near so constant in its influence (the case of mere antipathy excepted) as any of the other three. A pernicious act, therefore, when committed through vengeance, or otherwise through displeasure, is not near so mischievous as the same pernicious act, when committed by force of any one of those other motives.[q] *A mischievous act is more so, when issuing from a self-regarding than when from a dissocial motive*

me to deny but that such a principle may very frequently be an ingredient in the sum of motives, by which men are engaged in a proceeding of this nature. But whenever such a proceeding is engaged in from the sole influence of public spirit, uncombined with the least tincture of self interest, or ill-will, it must be acknowledged to be a proceeding of the heroic kind. Now acts of heroism are, in the very essence of them, but rare: for if they were common, they would not be acts of heroism. But prosecutions for crimes are very frequent, and yet, unless in very particular circumstances indeed, they are never otherwise than beneficial.

[p] Ch. iv (Value).

[q] It is for this reason that a threat, or other personal outrage, when committed on a stranger, in pursuance of a scheme of robbery, is productive of more mischief in society, and accordingly is, perhaps, every where more

—so even when issuing from the motive of religion

34. As to the motive of religion, whatever it may sometimes prove to be in point of strength and constancy, it is not in point of extent so universal, especially in its application to acts of a mischievous nature, as any of the three preceding motives. It may, however, be as universal in a particular state, or in a particular district of a particular state. It is liable indeed to be very irregular in its operations. It is apt, however, to be frequently as powerful as the motive of vengeance, or indeed any other motive whatsoever. It will sometimes even be more powerful than any other motive. It is at any rate much more constant.[r] A pernicious act, therefore, when committed through the motive of religion, is more mischievous than when committed through the motive of ill-will.

How the secondary mischief is influenced by disposition

35. Lastly, The secondary mischief, to wit, so much of it as hath respect to the future behaviour of the same person, is aggravated or lessened by the apparent depravity or beneficence of his disposition: and that in the proportion of such apparent depravity or beneficence.

Connexion of this with the succeeding chapter

36. The consequences we have hitherto been speaking of, are the *natural* consequences, of which the act, and the other articles we have been considering, are the causes: consequences that result from the behaviour of the individual, who is the offending agent,

---

severely punished, than an outrage of the same kind offered to an acquaintance, in prosecution of a scheme of vengeance. No man is always in a rage. But, at all times, every man, more or less, loves money. Accordingly, although a man by his quarrelsomeness should for once have been engaged in a bad action, he may nevertheless remain a long while, or even his whole lifetime, without engaging in another bad action of the same kind: for he may very well remain his whole life-time without engaging in so violent a quarrel: nor at any rate will he quarrel with more than one, or a few people at a time. But if a man, by his love of money, has once been engaged in a bad action, such as a scheme of robbery, he may at any time, by the influence of the same motive, be engaged in acts of the same degree of enormity. For take men throughout, if a man loves money to a certain degree to-day, it is probable that he will love it, at least in equal degree, to-morrow. And if a man is disposed to acquire it in that way, he will find inducement to rob, wheresoever and whensoever there are people to be robbed.

[r] If a man happen to take it into his head to assassinate with his own hands, or with the sword of justice, those whom he calls heretics, that is, people who think, or perhaps only speak, differently upon a subject which neither party understands, he will be as much inclined to do this as one time as at another. Fanaticism never sleeps: it is never glutted: it is never stopped by philanthropy; for it makes a merit of trampling on philanthropy: it is never stopped by conscience; for it has pressed conscience into its service. Avarice, lust, and vengeance, have piety, benevolence, honour; fanaticism has nothing to oppose it.

without the interference of political authority. We now come to speak of *punishment*: which, in the sense in which it is here considered, is an *artificial* consequence, annexed by political authority to an offensive act, in one instance; in the view of putting a stop to the production of events similar to the obnoxious part of its natural consequences, in other instances.

CHAPTER XIII

CASES UNMEET FOR PUNISHMENT

§ i. *General view of cases unmeet for punishment*

The end of law is, to augment happiness

1. The general object which all laws have, or ought to have, in common, is to augment the total happiness of the community; and therefore, in the first place, to exclude, as far as may be, every thing that tends to subtract from that happiness: in other words, to exclude mischief.

But punishment is an evil

2. But all punishment is mischief: all punishment in itself is evil. Upon the principle of utility, if it ought at all to be admitted, it ought only to be admitted in as far as it promises to exclude some greater evil.[a]

What concerns the end, and several other topics relative to punishment, dismissed to another work

[a] What follows, relative to the subject of punishment ought regularly to be preceded by a distinct chapter on the ends of punishment. But having little to say on that particular branch of the subject, which has not been said before, it seemed better, in a work, which will at any rate be but too voluminous, to omit this title, reserving it for another hereafter to be published, intituled *The Theory of Punishment.** To the same work I must refer the analysis of the several possible modes of punishment, a particular and minute examination of the nature of each, and of its advantages and disadvantages, and various other disquisitions, which did not seem absolutely necessary to be inserted here. A very few words, however, concerning the *ends* of punishment, can scarcely be dispensed with.

Concise view of the ends of punishment

The immediate principal end of punishment is to control action. This action is either that of the offender, or of others: that of the offender it controls by its influence, either on his will, in which case it is said to operate in the way of *reformation*; or on his physical power, in which case it is said to operate by *disablement*: that of others it can influence no otherwise than by its influence over their wills; in which case it is said to operate in the way of *example*. A kind of collateral end, which it has a natural tendency to answer, is that of affording a pleasure or satisfaction to the party injured, where there is one, and, in general, to parties whose ill-will, whether on a self-regarding account,

* This is the work which, from the Author's papers, has since been published by Mr Dumont in French, in company with *The Theory of Reward* added to it, for the purpose of mutual illustration. It is in contemplation to publish them both in English, from the Author's manuscripts, with the benefit of any amendments that have been made by Mr Dumont.[1]

[1] Note added to 1823 edition. For Bentham's *Theory of Punishment* and its relationship to the present work see above, Introduction, xxxviii. The projected publication mentioned here took place in the form of Richard Smith's editions of *The Rationale of Reward* (1825) and *The Rationale of Punishment* (1830).

3. It is plain, therefore, that in the following cases punishment ought not to be inflicted.

1. Where it is *groundless*; where there is no mischief for it to prevent; the act not being mischievous upon the whole.

2. Where it must be *inefficacious*: where it cannot act so as to prevent the mischief.

3. Where it is *unprofitable*, or too *expensive*; where the mischief it would produce would be greater than what it prevented.

4. Where it is *needless*: where the mischief may be prevented, or cease of itself, without it: that is, at a cheaper rate.

§ ii. *Cases in which punishment is groundless*

These are,

4. (1) Where there has never been any mischief: where no mischief has been produced to any body by the act in question. Of this number are those in which the act was such as might, on some occasions, be mischievous or disagreeable, but the person whose interest it concerns gave his *consent* to the performance of it.[b] This consent, provided it be free, and fairly obtained,[b] is the best proof that can be produced, that, to the person who gives it, no mischief, at least no immediate mischief, upon the whole, is done. For no man can be so good a judge as the man himself, what it is gives him pleasure or displeasure.

5. (2) Where the mischief was *outweighed*: although a mischief was produced by that act, yet the same act was necessary to the production of a benefit which was of greater value[c] than the mischief. This may be the case with any thing that is done in the way of precaution against instant calamity, as also with any thing that is done in the exercise of the several sorts of powers necessary to be

or on the account of sympathy or antipathy, has been excited by the offence. This purpose, as far as it can be answered *gratis*, is a beneficial one. But no punishment ought to be allotted merely to this purpose, because (setting aside its effects in the way of control) no such pleasure is ever produced by punishment as can be equivalent to the pain. The punishment, however, which is allotted to the other purpose, ought, as far as it can be done without expence, to be accommodated to this. Satisfaction thus administered to a party injured, in the shape of a dissocial pleasure,* may be styled a vindictive satisfaction or compensation: as a compensation, administered in the shape of a self-regarding profit, or stock of pleasure, may be styled a lucrative one. See B. I. tit. VI (Compensation). Example is the most important end of all, in proportion as the *number* of the persons under temptation to offend is to *one*.

[b] See B. I. tit. (Justifications).

[c] See supra, Ch. IV (Value).

* See Ch. x (Motives).

established in every community, to wit, domestic, judicial, military, and supreme.[d]

3. –or will, for a certainty, be cured by compensation

6. (3) Where there is a certainty of an adequate compensation: and that in all cases where the offence can be committed. This supposes two things: 1. That the offence is such as admits of an adequate compensation: 2. That such a compensation is sure to be forthcoming. Of these suppositions, the latter will be found to be a merely ideal one: a supposition that cannot, in the universality here given to it, be verified by fact. It cannot, therefore, in practice, be numbered amongst the grounds of absolute impunity. It may, however, be admitted as a ground for an abatement of that punishment, which other considerations, standing by themselves, would seem to dictate.[e]

§ iii. *Cases in which punishment must be inefficacious*

These are,

1. Where the penal provision comes too late: as in, 1. An ex-post-facto law. 2. An ultra-legal sentence

7. (1) Where the penal provision is *not established* until after the act is done. Such are the cases, 1. Of an *ex-post-facto* law; where the legislator himself appoints not a punishment till after the act is done. 2. Of a sentence beyond the law; where the judge, of his own authority, appoints a punishment which the legislator had not appointed.

2. Or is not made known: as in a law not sufficiently promulgated

8. (2) Where the penal provision, though established, is *not conveyed* to the notice of the person on whom it seems intended that it should operate. Such is the case where the law has omitted to employ any of the expedients which are necessary, to make sure that every person whatsoever, who is within the reach of the law, be apprized of all the cases whatsoever, in which (being in the station of life he is in) he can be subjected to the penalties of the law.[f]

[d] See Book I. tit. (Justifications).

Hence the favour shewn to the offences of responsible offenders: such as simple mercantile frauds

[e] This, for example, seems to have been one ground, at least, of the favour shewn by perhaps all systems of laws, to such offenders as stand upon a footing of responsibility: shewn, not directly indeed to the persons themselves; but to such offences as none but responsible persons are likely to have the opportunity of engaging in. In particular, this seems to be the reason why embezzlement, in certain cases, has not commonly been punished upon the footing of theft: nor mercantile frauds upon that of common sharping.*

[f] See B. II. Appendix. tit. iii (Promulgation).[1]

* See tit. (Simple merc. Defraudment).

[1] It was presumably material originally intended for this part of the Appendix to the *Plan of a Penal Code* that was used by Dumont for that part of the *Traités de Législation* (1802) which was edited in English for the Bowring edition by Richard Smith as *Essay on the Promulgation of Laws and the Reasons Thereof; with Specimen of a Penal Code* (Bowring, i, 155–68).

9. (3) Where the penal provision, though it were conveyed to a man's notice, *could produce no effect* on him, with respect to the preventing him from engaging in any act of the *sort* in question. Such is the case, 1. In extreme *infancy*; where a man has not yet attained that state or disposition of mind in which the prospect of evils so distant as those which are held forth by the law, has the effect of influencing his conduct. 2. In *insanity*; where the person, if he has attained to that disposition, has since been deprived of it through the influence of some permanent though unseen cause. 3. In *intoxication*; where he has been deprived of it by the transient influence of a visible cause: such as the use of wine, or opium, or other drugs, that act in this manner on the nervous system: which condition is indeed neither more nor less than a temporary insanity produced by an assignable cause.[g]

3. Where the will cannot be deterred from any act: as in, Infancy

Insanity

Intoxication

10. (4) Where the penal provision (although, being conveyed to the party's notice, it might very well prevent his engaging in acts of the sort in question, provided he knew that it related to those acts) could not have this effect, with regard to the *individual* act he is about to engage in: to wit, because he knows not that it is of the number of those to which the penal provision relates. This may happen, 1. In the case of *unintentionality*; where he intends not to engage, and thereby knows not that he is about to engage, in the *act* in which eventually he is about to engage.[h] 2. In the case of *unconsciousness*; where, although he may know that he is about to engage in the *act* itself, yet, from not knowing all the material

4. Or not from the individual act in question, as in,

Unintentionality

Unconsciousness

[g] Notwithstanding what is here said, the cases of infancy and intoxication (as we shall see hereafter) cannot be looked upon in practice as affording sufficient grounds for absolute impunity. But this exception in point of practice is no objection to the propriety of the rule in point of theory. The ground of the exception is neither more nor less than the difficulty there is of ascertaining the matter of fact: viz. whether at the requisite point of time the party was actually in the state in question; that is, whether a given case comes really under the rule. Suppose the matter of fact capable of being perfectly ascertained, without danger or mistake, the impropriety of punishment would be as indubitable in these cases as in any other.*

In infancy and intoxication the case can hardly be proved to come under the rule

The reason that is commonly assigned for the establishing an exemption from punishment in favour of infants, insane persons, and persons under intoxication, is either false in fact, or confusedly expressed. The phrase is, that the will of these persons concurs not with the act; that they have no vicious will; or, that they have not the free use of their will. But suppose all this to be true? What is it to the purpose? Nothing: except in as far as it implies the reason given in the text.

The reason for not punishing in these three cases is commonly put upon a wrong footing

[h] See Ch. viii (Intentionality).

* See B. I. tit. iv (Exemptions) and tit. vii (Extenuations).

circumstances attending it, he knows not of the *tendency* it has to produce that mischief, in contemplation of which it has been made penal in most instances. 3. In the case of *mis-supposal*; where, although he may know of the tendency the act has to produce that degree of mischief, he supposes it, though mistakenly, to be attended with some circumstance, or set of circumstances, which, if it had been attended with, it would either not have been productive of that mischief, or have been productive of such a greater degree of good, as has determined the legislator in such a case not to make it penal.[1]

Missupposal

11. (5) Where, though the penal clause might exercise a full and prevailing influence, were it to act alone, yet by the *predominant* influence of some opposite cause upon the will, it must necessarily be ineffectual; because the evil which he sees[1] himself about to undergo, in the case of his *not* engaging in the act, is so great, that the evil denounced by the penal clause, in case of his engaging in it, cannot appear greater. This may happen, 1. In the case of *physical danger*; where the evil is such as appears likely to be brought about by the unassisted powers of *nature*. 2. In the case of a *threatened mischief*; where it is such as appears likely to be brought about through the intentional and conscious agency of *man*.[j]

5. Or is acted on by an opposite superior force: as by,

Physical danger

Threatened mischief

12. (6) Where (though the penal clause may exert a full and prevailing influence over the *will* of the party) yet his *physical faculties* (owing to the predominant influence of some physical cause) are not in a condition to follow the determination of the will insomuch that the act is absolutely *involuntary*. Such is the case of physical *compulsion* or *restraint*, by whatever means brought about; where the man's hand, for instance, is pushed against some object which his will disposes him *not* to touch; or tied down from touching some object which his will disposes him to touch.

6. –or the bodily organs cannot follow its determination: as under

Physical compulsion or restraint

[1] See Ch. IX (Consciousness).

[j] The influences of the *moral* and *religious* sanctions, or, in other words, of the motives of *love of reputation* and *religion*, are other causes, the force of which may, upon particular occasions, come to be greater than that of any punishment which the legislator is *able*, or at least which he will *think proper*, to apply. These, therefore, it will be proper for him to have his eye upon. But the force of these influences is variable and different in different times and places: the force of the foregoing influences is constant and the same, at all times and every where. These, therefore, it can never be proper to look upon as safe grounds for establishing absolute impunity: owing (as in the abovementioned cases of infancy and intoxication) to the impracticability of ascertaining the matter of fact.

Why the influence of the moral and religious sanctions is not mentioned in the same view

[1] Thus 1789. The 1823 text, followed by the Bowring and later editions mistakenly reads 'sets'.

§ iv. *Cases where punishment is unprofitable*

These are,

13. (1) Where, on the one hand, the nature of the offence, on the other hand, that of the punishment, are, *in the ordinary state of things,* such, that when compared together, the evil of the latter will turn out to be greater than that of the former.

14. Now the evil of the punishment divides itself into four branches, by which so many different sets of persons are affected. 1. The evil of *coercion* or *restraint*: or the pain which it gives a man not to be able to do the act, whatever it be, which by the apprehension of the punishment he is deterred from doing. This is felt by those by whom the law is *observed*. 2. The evil of *apprehension*: or the pain which a man, who has exposed himself to punishment, feels at the thoughts of undergoing it. This is felt by those by whom the law has been *broken*, and who feel themselves in *danger* of its being executed upon them. 3. The evil of *sufferance*[k]: or the pain which a man feels, in virtue of the punishment itself, from the time when he begins to undergo it. This is felt by those by whom the law is broken, and upon whom it comes actually to be executed. 4. The pain of sympathy, and the other *derivative* evils resulting to the persons who are in *connection* with the several classes of original sufferers just mentioned.[1] Now of these four lots of evil, the first will be greater or less, according to the nature of the act from which the party is restrained: the second and third according to the nature of the punishment which stands annexed to that offence.

15. On the other hand, as to the evil of the offence, this will also, of course, be greater or less, according to the nature of each offence. The proportion between the one evil and the other will therefore be different in the case of each particular offence. The cases, therefore, where punishment is unprofitable on this ground, can by no other means be discovered, than by an examination of each particular offence; which is what will be the business of the body of the work.

16. (2) Where, although in the *ordinary state* of things, the evil resulting from the punishment is not greater than the benefit which is likely to result from the force with which it operates, during the same space of time, towards the excluding the evil of the offence, yet it may have been rendered so by the influence of some *occasional circumstances.* In the number of these circumstances may

Side notes:

1. Where, in the sort *of case in question, the punishment would produce more evil than the offence would*

Evil producible by a punishment – its four branches – viz. Restraint

Apprehension

Sufferance

Derivative evils

(The evil of the offence being different, according to the nature of the offence, cannot be represented here)

2.–Or in the individual *case in question: by reason of*

---

[k] See Ch. v (Pleasures and Pains).

[1] See Ch. xii (Consequences) 4.

be, 1. The multitude of delinquents at a particular juncture; being such as would increase, beyond the ordinary measure, the *quantum* of the second and third lots, and thereby also of a part of the fourth

lot, in the evil of the punishment. 2. The extraordinary value of the services of some one delinquent; in the case where the effect of the punishment would be to deprive the community of the benefit of

those services. 3. The displeasure of the *people*; that is, of an indefinite number of the members of the *same* community, in cases where (owing to the influence of some occasional incident) they happen to conceive, that the offence or the offender ought not to be punished at all, or at least ought not to be punished in the way

in question. 4. The displeasure of *foreign powers*; that is, of the governing body, or a considerable number of the members of some *foreign* community or communities, with which the community in question, is connected.

§ v. *Cases where punishment is needless*

These are,[1]

*1. Where the
mischief is to
be prevented
at a cheaper
rate: as,*

*By instruc-
tion*
17. (1) Where the purpose of putting an end to the practice may be attained as effectually at a cheaper rate: by instruction, for instance, as well as by terror: by informing the understanding, as well as by exercising an immediate influence on the will. This seems to be the case with respect to all those offences which consist in the disseminating pernicious principles in matters of *duty*; of whatever kind the duty be; whether political, or moral, or religious. And this, whether such principles be disseminated *under*, or even *without*, a sincere persuasion of their being beneficial. I say, even *without*: for though in such a case it is not instruction that can prevent the writer from endeavouring to inculcate his principles, yet it may the readers from adopting them: without which, his endeavouring to inculcate them will do no harm. In such a case, the sovereign will commonly have little need to take an active part: if it be the interest of *one* individual to inculcate principles that are pernicious, it will as surely be the interest of *other* individuals to expose them. But if the sovereign must needs take a part in the controversy, the pen is the proper weapon to combat error with, not the sword.

[1] Bentham evidently intended to deal with a number of examples under this heading, as in previous sections, but did not in fact proceed beyond the first case.

CHAPTER XIV

OF THE PROPORTION BETWEEN PUNISHMENTS AND OFFENCES

1. We have seen that the general object of all laws is to prevent mischief; that is to say, when it is worth while; but that, where there are no other means of doing this than punishment, there are four cases in which it is *not* worth while. *Recapitulation*

2. When it *is* worth while, there are four subordinate designs or objects, which, in the course of his endeavours to compass, as far as may be, that one general object, a legislator, whose views are governed by the principle of utility, comes naturally to propose to himself. *Four objects of punishment*

3. (1) His first, most extensive, and most eligible object, is to prevent, in as far as it is possible, and worth while, all sorts of offences whatsoever[a]: in other words, so to manage, that no offence whatsoever may be committed. *1st Object— to prevent all offences*

4. (2) But if a man must needs commit an offence of some kind or other, the next object is to induce him to commit an offence *less* mischievous, *rather* than one *more* mischievous: in other words, to choose always the *least* mischievous, of two offences that will either of them suit his purpose. *2d Object— to prevent the worst*

5. (3) When a man has resolved upon a particular offence, the next object is to dispose him to do *no more* mischief than is *necessary* to his purpose: in other words, to do as little mischief as is consistent with the benefit he has in view. *3d Object— to keep down the mischief*

6. (4) The last object is, whatever the mischief be, which it is proposed to prevent, to prevent it at as *cheap* a rate as possible. *4th Object— to act at the least expense*

7. Subservient to these four objects, or purposes, must be the rules or canons by which the proportion of punishments[b] to offences is to be governed. *Rules of proportion between punishments and offences*

[a] By *offences* I mean, at present, acts which appear to him to have a tendency to produce mischief.

[b] (Punishments). The same rules (it is to be observed) may be applied, with little variation, to rewards as well as punishment: in short, to motives in general, which, according as they are of the pleasurable or painful kind, are of the nature of *reward* or *punishment*: and, according as the act they are applied to produce is of the positive or negative kind, are styled impelling or restraining. See Ch. x (Motives) 43. *The same rule applicable to motives in general*

Rule 1. Outweigh the profit of the offence

8. The first object, it has been seen, is to prevent, in as far as it is worth while, all sorts of offences; therefore,

The value of the punishment must not be less in any case than what is sufficient to outweigh that of the profit[c] *of the offence.*[d]

If it be, the offence (unless some other considerations, independent of the punishment, should intervene and operate efficaciously in the character of tutelary motives[e]) will be sure to be committed notwithstanding[f]: the whole lot of punishment will be thrown away: it will be altogether *inefficacious*.[g]

Profit may be of any other kind, as well as pecuniary

[c] (Profit). By the profit of an offence, is to be understood, not merely the pecuniary profit, but the pleasure or advantage, of whatever kind it be, which a man reaps, or expects to reap, from the gratification of the desire which prompted him to engage in the offence.[*]

Impropriety of the notion that the punishment ought not to increase with the temptation

It is the profit (that is, the expectation of the profit) of the offence that constitutes the *impelling* motive, or, where there are several, the sum of the impelling motives, by which a man is prompted to engage in the offence. It is the punishment, that is, the expectation of the punishment, that constitutes the *restraining* motive, which, either by itself, or in conjunction with others, is to act upon him in a *contrary* direction, so as to induce him to abstain from engaging in the offence. Accidental circumstances apart, the strength of the temptation is as the force of the seducing, that is, of the impelling motive or motives. To say then, as authors of great merit and great name have said that the punishment ought not to increase with the strength of the temptation, is as much as to say in mechanics, that the moving force or *momentum* of the *power* need not increase in proportion to the momentum of the *burthen*.

[d] Beccaria, dei delitti, § 6. id. trad. par Morellet, § 23.[1]

[e] See Ch. xi (Dispositions) 29.

[f] It is a well-known adage, though it is to be hoped not a true one, that every man has his price. It is commonly meant of a man's virtue. This saying, though in a very different sense, was strictly verified by some of the Anglo-saxon laws: by which a fixed price was set, not upon a man's virtue indeed, but upon his life: that of the sovereign himself among the rest. For 200 shillings you might have killed a peasant: for six times as much, a nobleman: for six-and-thirty times as much you might have killed the king.[†] A king in those days was worth exactly 7,200 shillings. If then the heir to the throne, for example, grew weary of waiting for it, he had a secure and legal way of gratifying his impatience: he had but to kill the king with one hand, and pay himself with the other,

[g] [See next page.]

[*] See Ch. x (Motives) § i.

[†] Wilkin's Leg. Anglo-sax. p. 71, 72. See Hume, vol. i. app. i. p. 219.

[1] Cesare Beccaria, Marchese de Beccaria-Bonesana (1738–94), *Dei delitti e delle pene* (1764). The French translation by André Morellet (1727–1819) which Bentham cites was published in 1766 as *Traité des délits et des peines*. It may be noted that the 1789 edition, followed without correction in later editions, printed *diletti* for *delitti* in the Italian title.

[2] David Wilkins (1685–1745) published *Leges Anglo-Saxonicae Ecclesiasticae et Civiles* in 1721. Hume cites this in his *History of Great Britain* when describing the institution of *wergild*.

9. The above rule has been often objected to, on account of its seeming harshness: but this can only have happened for want of its being properly understood. The strength of the temptation, *cæteris paribus*, is as the profit of the offence: the quantum of the punishment must rise with the profit of the offence: *cæteris paribus*, it must therefore rise with the strength of the temptation. This there is no disputing. True it is, that the stronger the temptation, the less conclusive is the indication which the act of delinquency affords of the depravity of the offender's disposition.[h] So far then as the absence of any aggravation, arising from extraordinary depravity of disposition, may operate, or at the utmost, so far as the presence of a ground of extenuation, resulting from the innocence or beneficence of the offender's disposition, can operate, the strength of the temptation may operate in abatement of the demand for punishment. But it can never operate so far as to indicate the propriety of making the punishment ineffectual, which it is sure to be when brought below the level of the apparent profit of the offence.

The propriety of taking the strength of the temptation for a ground of abatement, no objection to this rule

The partial benevolence which should prevail for the reduction of it below this level, would counteract as well those purposes which such a motive would actually have in view, as those more extensive purposes which benevolence ought to have in view: it would be cruelty not only to the public, but to the very persons in whose behalf it pleads: in its effects, I mean, however opposite in its intention. Cruelty to the public, that is cruelty to the innocent, by suffering them, for want of an adequate protection, to lie exposed to the

and all was right. An earl Godwin, or a duke Streon, could have bought the lives of a whole dynasty. It is plain, that if ever a king in those days died in his bed, he must have had something else, besides this law, to thank for it. This being the production of a remote and barbarous age, the absurdity of it is presently recognized: but, upon examination, it would be found, that the freshest laws of the most civilized nations are continually falling into the same error.* This, in short, is the case wheresoever the punishment is fixed while the profit of delinquency is indefinite: or, to speak more precisely, where the punishment is limited to such a mark, that the profit of delinquency may reach beyond it.

  [g] See Ch. XIII (Cases unmeet) § i.

  [h] See Ch. XI (Dispositions) 42.

  * See in particular the *English Statute laws* throughout, *Bonaparte's* Penal Code, and the recently enacted or not enacted *Spanish* Penal Code.[1]

Note by the Author, July, 1822

  [1] The Napoleonic Penal Code was promulgated between 1808 and 1810. The Spanish Penal Code, in which Bentham was greatly interested (cf. esp. his *Letters to Count Toreno,* Bowring, viii, 487–554), was the work of the short-lived liberal administration of the early 1820's and was discussed by the Cortes between September 1821 and February 1822.

mischief of the offence: cruelty even to the offender himself, by punishing him to no purpose, and without the chance of compassing that beneficial end, by which alone the introduction of the evil of punishment is to be justified.

Rule 2. Venture more against a great offence than a small one

10. But whether a given offence shall be prevented in a given degree by a given quantity of punishment, is never any thing better than a chance; for the purchasing of which, whatever punishment is employed, is so much expended in advance. However, for the sake of giving it the better chance of outweighing the profit of the offence,

The greater the mischief of the offence, the greater is the expence, which it may be worth while to be at, in the way of punishment.[1]

Rule 3. Cause the least of two offences to be preferred

11. The next object is, to induce a man to choose always the least mischievous of two offences; therefore

Where two offences come in competition, the punishment for the greater offence must be sufficient to induce a man to prefer the less.[j]

Rule 4. Punish for each particle of the mischief

12. When a man has resolved upon a particular offence, the next object is, to induce him to do no more mischief than what is necessary for his purpose: therefore

The punishment should be adjusted in such manner to each particular offence, that for every part of the mischief there may be a motive to restrain the offender from giving birth to it.[k]

Example.— Incendiarism and coining

[1] For example, if it can ever be worth while to be at the expence of so horrible a punishment as that of burning alive, it will be more so in the view of preventing such a crime as that of murder or incendiarism, than in the view of preventing the uttering of a piece of bad money. See B. I. tit. (Defraudment touching the Coin) and (Incendiarism).

[j] Espr. des Loix, L. vi. c. 16.[1]

Example.— In blows given, and money stolen

[k] If any one have any doubt of this, let him conceive the offence to be divided into as many separate offences as there are distinguishable parcels of mischief that result from it. Let it consist for example, in a man's giving you ten blows, or stealing from you ten shillings. If then, for giving you ten blows, he is punished no more than for giving you five, the giving you five of these ten blows is an offence for which there is no punishment at all: which being understood, as often as a man gives you five blows, he will be sure to give you five more, since he may have the pleasure of giving you these five for nothing. In like manner, if for stealing from you ten shillings, he is punished no more than for stealing five, the stealing of the remaining five of those ten shillings is an offence for which there is no punishment at all. This rule is violated in almost every page of every body of laws I have ever seen.

The profit, it is to be observed, though frequently, is not constantly, pro-

[1] This chapter of Montesquieu's *De l'esprit des lois* begins as follows: 'Il est essentiel que les peines aient de l'harmonie entr'elles, parce qu'il est essentiel que l'on évite plutot un grand crime qu'un moindre, ce qui attaque plus la société, que ce qui choque moins.'

13. The last object is, whatever mischief is guarded against, to guard against it at as cheap a rate as possible: therefore

The punishment ought in no case to be more than what is necessary to bring it into conformity with the rules here given.

Rule 5. Punish in no degree without special reason

14. It is further to be observed, that owing to the different manners and degrees in which persons under different circumstances are affected by the same exciting cause, a punishment which is the same in name will not always either really produce, or even so much as appear to others to produce, in two different persons the same degree of pain: therefore,

That the quantity actually inflicted on each individual offender may correspond to the quantity intended for similar offenders in general, the several circumstances influencing sensibility ought always to be taken into account.[1]

Rule 6. Attend to circumstances influencing sensibility

15. Of the above rules of proportion, the four first, we may perceive, serve to mark out the limits on the side of diminution; the limits *below* which a punishment ought not to be *diminished*: the fifth, the limits on the side of increase; the limits *above* which it ought not to be *increased*. The five first are calculated to serve as guides to the legislator: the sixth is calculated, in some measure, indeed, for the same purpose; but principally for guiding the judge in his endeavours to conform, on both sides, to the intentions of the legislator.

Comparative view of the above rules

16. Let us look back a little. The first rule, in order to render it more conveniently applicable to practice, may need perhaps to be a little more particularly unfolded. It is to be observed, then, that for the sake of accuracy, it was necessary, instead of the word *quantity* to make use of the less perspicuous term *value*. For the word *quantity* will not properly include the circumstances either of certainty or proximity: circumstances which, in estimating the value of a lot of pain or pleasure, must always be taken into the account.[m] Now, on the one hand, a lot of punishment is a lot of pain; on the other hand, the profit of an offence is a lot of pleasure, or what is equivalent to it. But the profit of the offence *is* commonly more *certain* than the punishment, or, what comes to the same thing, *appears* so at least to the offender. It is at any rate commonly more *immediate*. It follows, therefore, that, in order to maintain its super-

Into the account of the value of a punishment must be taken its deficiency in point of certainty and proximity

portioned to the mischief: for example, where a thief, along with the things he covets, steals others which are of no use to him. This may happen through wantonness, indolence, precipitation, etc. etc.

[1] See Ch. vi (Sensibility).

[m] See Ch. iv (Value).

iority over the profit of the offence, the punishment must have its value made up in some other way, in proportion to that whereby it falls short in the two points of *certainty* and *proximity*. Now there is no other way in which it can receive any addition to its *value*, but by receiving an addition in point of *magnitude*. Wherever then the value of the punishment falls short, either in point of *certainty*, or of *proximity*, of that of the profit of the offence, it must receive a proportionable addition in point of *magnitude*.[n]

Also, into the account of the mischief, and profit of the offence, the mischief and profit of other offences of the same habit

17. Yet farther. To make sure of giving the value of the punishment the superiority over that of the offence, it may be necessary, in some cases, to take into the account the profit not only of the *individual* offence to which the punishment is to be annexed, but also of such *other* offences of the *same sort* as the offender is likely to have already committed without detection. This random mode of calculation, severe as it is, it will be impossible to avoid having recourse to, in certain cases: in such, to wit, in which the profit is pecuniary, the chance of detection very small, and the obnoxious act of such a nature as indicates a habit: for example, in the case of frauds against the coin. If it be *not* recurred to, the practice of committing the offence will be sure to be, upon the balance of the account, a gainful practice. That being the case, the legislator will be absolutely sure of *not* being able to suppress it, and the whole punishment that is bestowed upon it will be thrown away. In a word (to keep to the same expressions we set out with) that whole quantity of punishment will be *inefficacious*.

Rule 7. Want of certainty must be made up in magnitude

18. These things being considered, the three following rules may be laid down by way of supplement and explanation to Rule 1.

To enable the value of the punishment to outweigh that of the profit of the offence, it must be increased, in point of magnitude, in proportion as it falls short in point of certainty.

Rule 8. So also want of proximity

Rule 9. For acts indicative of a habit punish as for the habit

19. *Punishment must be further increased in point of magnitude, in proportion as it falls short in point of proximity.*

20. *Where the act is conclusively indicative of a habit, such an encrease must be given to the punishment as may enable it to outweigh the profit not only of the individual offence, but of such other like offences as are likely to have been committed with impunity by the same offender.*

The remaining rules are of less importance

21. There may be a few other circumstances or considerations which may influence, in some small degree, the demand for punishment: but as the propriety of these is either not so demonstrable,

---

[n] It is for this reason, for example, that simple compensation is never looked upon as sufficient punishment for theft or robbery.

or not so constant, or the application of them not so determinate, as that of the foregoing, it may be doubted whether they be worth putting on a level with the others.

22. *When a punishment, which in point of quality is particularly well calculated to answer its intention, cannot exist in less than a certain quantity, it may sometimes be of use, for the sake of employing it, to stretch a little beyond that quantity which, on other accounts, would be strictly necessary.*

Rule 10. For the sake of quality, increase in quantity

23. *In particular, this may sometimes be the case, where the punishment proposed is of such a nature as to be particularly well calculated to answer the purpose of a moral lesson.*[o]

Rule 11. Particularly for a moral lesson

24. The tendency of the above considerations is to dictate an augmentation in the punishment: the following rule operates in the way of diminution. There are certain cases (it has been seen[p]) in which, by the influence of accidental circumstances, punishment may be rendered unprofitable in the whole: in the same cases it may chance to be rendered unprofitable as to a part only. Accordingly,

Rule 12. Attend to circumstances which may render punishment unprofitable

In adjusting the quantum of punishment, the circumstances, by which all punishment may be rendered unprofitable, ought to be attended to.

25. It is to be observed, that the more various and minute any set of provisions are, the greater the chance is that any given article in them will not be borne in mind: without which, no benefit can ensue from it. Distinctions, which are more complex than what the conceptions of those whose conduct it is designed to influence can take in, will even be worse than useless. The whole system will present a confused appearance: and thus the effect, not only of the proportions established by the articles in question, but of whatever is connected with them, will be destroyed.[q] To draw a precise line of

Rule 13. For simplicity's sake, small disproportions may be neglected

[o] A punishment may be said to be calculated to answer the purpose of a moral lesson, when, by reason of the ignomy it stamps upon the offence, it is calculated to inspire the public with sentiments of aversion towards those pernicious habits and dispositions with which the offence appears to be connected; and thereby to inculcate the opposite beneficial habits and dispositions.

A punishment applied by way of moral lesson, what

It is this, for example, if anything, that must justify the application of so severe a punishment as the infamy of a public exhibition, hereinafter proposed, for him who lifts up his hand against a woman, or against his father. See B. I. tit. (Simp. corporal injuries.)

Example.– In simple corporal injuries

It is partly on this principle, I suppose, that military legislators have justified to themselves the inflicting death on the soldier who lifts up his hand against his superior officer.

Example.– In military laws

[p] See Ch. XIII (Cases unmeet). § iv.

[q] See B. II. tit. (Purposes). Append. tit. (Composition).[1]

[1] For the second reference cf. above 72 n. 1.

direction in such case seems impossible. However, by way of memento, it may be of some use to subjoin the following rule.

Among provisions designed to perfect the proportion between punishments and offences, if any occur, which, by their own particular good effects, would not make up for the harm they would do by adding to the intricacy of the Code, they should be omitted.[r]

Auxiliary force of the physical, moral, and religious sanction, not here allowed for—why

26. It may be remembered, that the political sanction, being that to which the sort of punishment belongs, which in this chapter is all along in view, is but one of four sanctions, which may all of them contribute their share towards producing the same effects. It may be expected, therefore, that in adjusting the quantity of political punishment, allowance should be made for the assistance it may meet with from those other controlling powers. True it is, that from each of these several sources a very powerful assistance may sometimes be derived. But the case is, that (setting aside the moral sanction, in the case where the force of it is expressly adopted into and modified by the political[s]) the force of those other powers is never determinate enough to be depended upon. It can never be reduced, like political punishment, into exact lots, nor meted out in number, quantity, and value. The legislator is therefore obliged to provide the full complement of punishment, as if he were sure of not receiving any assistance whatever from any of those quarters. If he does, so much the better: but lest he should not, it is necessary he should, at all events, make that provision which depends upon himself.

Recapitulation

27. It may be of use, in this place, to recapitulate the several circumstances, which, in establishing the proportion betwixt punishments and offences, are to be attended to. These seem to be as follows:

I. *On the part of the offence:*

1. The profit of the offence;

2. The mischief of the offence;

3. The profit and mischief of other greater or lesser offences, of different sorts, which the offender may have to choose out of;

Proportionality carried very far in the present work—why

[r] Notwithstanding this rule, my fear is, that in the ensuing model, I may be thought to have carried my endeavours at proportionality too far. Hitherto scarce any attention has been paid to it. Montesquieu seems to have been almost the first who has had the least idea of any such thing.[1] In such a matter, therefore, excess seemed more eligible than defect. The difficulty is to invent; that done, if any thing seems superfluous, it is easy to retrench.

[s] See B. I. tit. (Punishments).

[1] *De l'esprit des lois,* VI.

4. The profit and mischief of other offences, of the same sort, which the same offender may probably have been guilty of already.

II. *On the part of the punishment:*

5. The magnitude of the punishment: composed of its intensity and duration;

6. The deficiency of the punishment in point of certainty;

7. The deficiency of the punishment in point of proximity;

8. The quality of the punishment;

9. The accidental advantage in point of quality of a punishment, not strictly needed in point of quantity;

10. The use of a punishment of a particular quality, in the character of a moral lesson.

III. *On the part of the offender:*

11. The responsibility of the class of persons in a way to offend;

12. The sensibility of each particular offender;

13. The particular merits or useful qualities of any particular offender, in case of punishment which might deprive the community of the benefit of them;

14. The multitude of offenders on any particular occasion.

IV. *On the part of the public*, at any particular conjuncture:

15. The inclinations of the people, for or against any quantity or mode of punishment;

16. The inclinations of foreign powers.

V. *On the part of the law*: that is, of the public for a continuance:

17. The necessity of making small sacrifices, in point of proportionality, for the sake of simplicity.

28. There are some, perhaps, who, at first sight, may look upon the nicety employed in the adjustment of such rules, as so much labour lost: for gross ignorance, they will say, never troubles itself about laws, and passion does not calculate. But the evil of ignorance admits of cure[t]: and as to the proposition that passion does not calculate, this like most of these very general and oracular propositions, is not true. When matters of such importance as pain and pleasure are at stake, and these in the highest degree (the only matters, in short, that can be of importance) who is there that does not calculate? Men calculate, some with less exactness, indeed, *The nicety here observed vindicated from the charge of inutility*

[t] See Append. tit. (Promulgation).[1]

[1] See above 160 n. 1.

some with more: but all men calculate. I would not say, that even a madman does not calculate.[u] Passion calculates, more or less, in every man: in different men, according to the warmth or coolness of their dispositions: according to the firmness or irritability of their minds: according to the nature of the motives by which they are acted upon. Happily, of all passions, that is the most given to calculation, from the excesses of which, by reason of its strength, constancy, and universality, society has most to apprehend[v]: I mean that which corresponds to the motive of pecuniary interest: so that these niceties, if such they are to be called, have the best chance of being efficacious, where efficacy is of the most importance.

[u] There are few madmen but what are observed to be afraid of the strait waistcoat.
[v] See Ch. XII (Consequences) 33.

CHAPTER XV

OF THE PROPERTIES TO BE GIVEN TO A LOT OF PUNISHMENT

1. It has been shown what the rules are, which ought to be observed in adjusting the proportion between the punishment and the offence. The properties to be given to a lot of punishment, in every instance, will of course be such as it stands in need of, in order to be capable of being applied, in conformity to those rules: the *quality* will be regulated by the *quantity*. *Properties are to be governed by proportion*

2. The first of those rules, we may remember, was, that the quantity of punishment must not be less, in any case, than what is sufficient to outweigh the profit of the offence: since, as often as it is less, the whole lot (unless by accident the deficiency should be supplied from some of the other sanctions) is thrown away: it is *inefficacious*. The fifth was, that the punishment ought in no case to be more than what is required by the several other rules: since, if it be, all that is above that quantity is *needless*. The fourth was, that the punishment should be adjusted in such manner to each individual offence, that every part of the mischief of that offence may have a penalty (that is, a tutelary motive) to encounter it: otherwise, with respect to so much of the offence as has not a penalty to correspond to it, it is as if there were no punishment in the case. Now to none of those rules can a lot of punishment be conformable, unless, for every variation in point of quantity, in the mischief of the species of offence to which it is annexed, such lot of punishment admits of a correspondent variation. To prove this, let the profit of the offence admit of a multitude of degrees. Suppose it, then, at any one of these degrees: if the punishment be less than what is suitable to that degree, it will be *inefficacious*; it will be so much thrown away: if it be more, as far as the difference extends, it will be *needless*; it will therefore be thrown away also in that case. *Property 1. Variability*

The first property, therefore, that ought to be given to a lot of punishment, is that of being variable in point of quantity, in conformity to every variation which can take place in either the profit or mischief of the offence. This property might, perhaps, be termed, in a single word, *variability.*

3. A second property, intimately connected with the former, may be styled *equability*. It will avail but little, that a mode of *Property 2. Equability*

175

punishment (proper in all other respects) has been established by the legislator; and that capable of being screwed up or let down to any degree that can be required; if, after all, whatever degree of it be pitched upon, that same degree shall be liable, according to circumstances, to produce a very heavy degree of pain, or a very slight one, or even none at all. In this case, as in the former, if circumstances happen one way, there will be a great deal of pain produced which will be *needless*: if the other way, there will be no pain at all applied, or none that will be *efficacious*. A punishment, when liable to this irregularity, may be styled an unequable one: when free from it, an equable one. The quantity of pain produced by the punishment will, it is true, depend in a considerable degree upon circumstances distinct from the nature of the punishment itself: upon the condition which the offender is in, with respect to the circumstances by which a man's sensibility is liable to be influenced. But the influence of these very circumstances will in many cases be reciprocally influenced by the nature of the punishment: in other words, the pain which is produced by any mode of punishment, will be the joint effect of the punishment which is applied to him, and the circumstances in which he is exposed to it. Now there are some punishments, of which the effect may be liable to undergo a greater alteration by the influence of such foreign circumstances, than the effect of other punishments is liable to undergo. So far, then, as this is the case, equability or unequability may be regarded as properties belonging to the punishment itself.

Punishments which are apt to be deficient in this respect

4. An example of a mode of punishment which is apt to be unequable, is that of *banishment,* when the *locus a quo* (or place the party is banished from) is some determinate place appointed by the law, which perhaps the offender cares not whether he ever see or no. This is also the case with *pecuniary,* or *quasi-pecuniary* punishment, when it respects some particular species of property, which the offender may have been possessed of, or not, as it may happen. All these punishments may be split down into parcels, and measured out with the utmost nicety: being divisible by time, at least, if by nothing else. They are not, therefore, any of them defective in point of variability: and yet, in many cases, this defect in point of equability may make them as unfit for use as if they were.[a]

[a] By the English law, there are several offences which are punished by a total forfeiture of moveables, not extending to immoveables. This is the case with suicide, and with certain species of theft and homicide. In some cases, this is the principal punishment: in others, even the only one. The consequence is, that if a man's fortune happens to consist in moveables, he is ruined; if in immoveables, he suffers nothing.

5. The third rule of proportion was, that where two offences come in competition, the punishment for the greater offence must be sufficient to induce a man to prefer the less. Now, to be sufficient for this purpose, it must be evidently and uniformly greater: greater, not in the eyes of some men only, but of all men who are liable to be in a situation to take their choice between the two offences; that is, in effect, of all mankind. In other words, the two punishments must be perfectly *commensurable*. Hence arises a third property, which may be termed *commensurability*: to wit, with reference to other punishments.[b]

Property 3. Commensurability to other punishments

6. But punishments of different kinds are in very few instances uniformly greater one than another; especially when the lowest degrees of that which is ordinarily the greater, are compared with the highest degrees of that which is ordinarily the less: in other words, punishments of different kinds are in few instances uniformly commensurable. The only certain and universal means of making two lots of punishment perfectly commensurable, is by making the lesser an ingredient in the composition of the greater. This may be done in either of two ways. 1. By adding to the lesser punishment another quantity of punishment of the same kind. 2. By adding to it another quantity of a different kind. The latter mode is not less certain than the former: for though one cannot always be absolutely sure, that to the same person a given punishment will appear greater than another given punishment; yet one may be always absolutely sure, that any given punishment, so as it does but come into contemplation, will appear greater than none at all.

How two lots of punishment may be rendered perfectly commensurable

7. Again: Punishment cannot act any farther than in as far as

Property 4. Characteristicalness

[b] See *View of the Hard-Labour Bill*. Lond. 1778. p. 100.[1]
For the idea of this property, I must acknowledge myself indebted to an anonymous letter in the St James's Chronicle, of the 27th of September 1777; the author of which is totally unknown to me. If any one should be disposed to think lightly of the instruction, on account of the channel by which it was first communicated, let him tell me where I can find an idea more ingenious or original.[2]

[1] Cf. Bowring, iv, 29: 'I cannot help entertaining some doubt of the expediency of capital punishment in case of escapes. Punishments that a man has occasion to choose out of should be commensurable.'

[2] This letter, signed 'Peter Hint' appeared in the *St James's Chronicle or British Evening Post*, no. 2581, 25–27 September 1777. The writer, commenting on an incident where two men were sentenced to work on the Thames for ten years for stealing goods from a waggon, objects to 'Legislature . . . changing the Mode of Punishment to render it so severe as to tempt Criminals rather to get sure of being hanged, than undergo a much worse punishment . . .' The word 'commensurability' itself does not occur.

the idea of it, and of its connection with the offence, is present in the mind. The idea of it, if not present, cannot act at all; and then the punishment itself must be *inefficacious*. Now, to be present, it must be remembered, and to be remembered it must have been learnt. But of all punishments that can be imagined, there are none of which the connection with the offence is either so easily learnt, or so efficaciously remembered, as those of which the idea is already in part associated with some part of the idea of the offence: which is the case when the one and the other have some circumstance that belongs to them in common. When this is the case with a punishment and an offence, the punishment is said to bear an *analogy* to, or to be *characteristic* of, the offence.[c] *Characteristicalness* is, therefore, a fourth property, which on this account ought to be given, whenever it can conveniently be given, to a lot of punishment.

The mode of punishment the most eminently characteristic, is that of retaliation

8. It is obvious, that the effect of this contrivance will be the greater, as the analogy is the closer. The analogy will be the closer, the more *material*[d] that circumstance is, which is in common. Now the most material circumstance that can belong to an offence and a punishment in common, is the hurt or damage which they produce. The closest analogy, therefore, that can subsist between an offence and the punishment annexed to it, is that which subsists between them when the hurt or damage they produce is of the same nature: in other words, that which is constituted by the circumstance of identity in point of damage.[e] Accordingly, the mode of punishment, which of all others bears the closest analogy to the offence, is that which in the proper and exact sense of the word is termed *retaliation*. Retaliation, therefore, in the few cases in which it is practicable, and not too expensive, will have one great advantage over every other mode of punishment.

Property 5. Exemplarity

9. Again: It is the idea only of the punishment (or, in other words, the *apparent* punishment) that really acts upon the mind; the punishment itself (the *real* punishment) acts not any farther than as giving

[c] See Montesq. Esp. des Loix. L. xii. ch. iv. He seems to have the property of characteristicalness in view; but that the idea he had of it was very indistinct, appears from the extravagant advantages he attributes to it.[1]

[d] See Ch. vii (Actions) 3.

[e] Besides this, there are a variety of other ways in which the punishment may bear an analogy to the offence. This will be seen by looking over the table of punishments.

[1] Book xii, Ch. iv of *De l'esprit des lois* is entitled 'Que la liberté est favorisée par la nature des peines, et leur proportion' and opens with the sentence: 'C'est le triomphe de la liberté, lorsque les lois criminelles tirent chaque peine de la nature particulière du crime.'

rise to that idea. It is the apparent punishment, therefore, that does all the service, I mean in the way of example, which is the principal object.[f] It is the real punishment that does all the mischief.[g] Now the ordinary and obvious way of increasing the magnitude of the apparent punishment, is by increasing the magnitude of the real. The apparent magnitude, however, may to a certain degree be increased by other less expensive means: whenever, therefore, at the same time that these less expensive means would have answered that purpose, an additional real punishment is employed, this additional real punishment is *needless*. As to these less expensive means, they consist, 1. In the choice of a particular mode of punishment, a punishment of a particular quality, independent of the quantity.[h] 2. In a particular set of *solemnities* distinct from the punishment itself, and accompanying the execution of it.[i]

10. A mode of punishment, according as the appearance of it bears a greater proportion to the reality, may be said to be the more *exemplary*. Now as to what concerns the choice of the punishment itself, there is not any means by which a given quantity of punishment can be rendered more exemplary, than by choosing it of such a sort as shall bear an *analogy* to the offence. Hence another reason for rendering the punishment analogous to, or in other words characteristic of, the offence. *The most effectual way of rendering a punishment exemplary is by means of analogy*

11. Punishment, it is still to be remembered, is in itself an expence: it is in itself an evil.[j] Accordingly the fifth rule of proportion is, not to produce more of it than what is demanded by the other rules. But this is the case as often as any particle of pain is produced, which contributes nothing to the effect proposed. Now if any mode of punishment is more apt than another to produce any such superfluous and needless pain, it may be styled *unfrugal*; if less, it may be styled *frugal*. *Frugality*, therefore, is a sixth property to be wished for in a mode of punishment. *Property 6. Frugality*

12. The perfection of frugality, in a mode of punishment, is where not only no superfluous pain is produced on the part of the person punished, but even that same operation, by which he is subjected to pain, is made to answer the purpose of producing pleasure on the part of some other person. Understand a profit or stock of pleasure of the self-regarding kind: for a pleasure of the *Frugality belongs in perfection to pecuniary punishment*

[f] See Ch. xiii (Cases unmeet) § i, 2 note.

[g] Ibid. § iv, par. 3.

[h] See B. I. tit. (Punishments).

[i] See B. II. tit. (Execution).

[j] Ch. xiii (Cases unmeet) par. 2.

dissocial kind is produced almost of course, on the part of all persons in whose breasts the offence has excited the sentiment of ill-will. Now this is the case with pecuniary punishment, as also with such punishments of the *quasi-pecuniary* kind as consist in the substraction of such a species of possession as is transferable from one party to another. The pleasure, indeed, produced by such an operation, is not in general equal to the pain[k]: it may, however, be so in particular circumstances, as where he, from whom the thing is taken, is very rich, and he, to whom it is given, very poor: and, be it what it will, it is always so much more than can be produced by any other mode of punishment.

Exemplarity and frugality in what they differ and agree

13. The properties of exemplarity and frugality seem to pursue the same immediate end, though by different courses. Both are occupied in diminishing the ratio of the real suffering to the apparent: but exemplarity tends to increase the apparent; frugality to reduce the real.

Other properties of inferior importance

14. Thus much concerning the properties to be given to punishments in general, to whatsoever offences they are to be applied. Those which follow are of less importance, either as referring only to certain offences in particular, or depending upon the influence of transitory and local circumstances.

In the first place, the four distinct ends into which the main and general end of punishment is divisible,[1] may give rise to so many distinct properties, according as any particular mode of punishment appears to be more particularly adapted to the compassing of one or of another of those ends. To that of *example*, as being the principal one, a particular property has already been adapted. There remain the three inferior ones of *reformation, disablement,* and *compensation.*

Property 7. Subserviency to reformation

15. A seventh property, therefore, to be wished for in a mode of punishment, is that of *subserviency to reformation,* or *reforming tendency.* Now any punishment is subservient to reformation in proportion to its *quantity*: since the greater the punishment a man has experienced, the stronger is the tendency it has to create in him an aversion towards the offence which was the cause of it: and that with respect to all offences alike. But there are certain punishments which, with regard to certain offences, have a particular tendency to produce that effect by reason of their *quality*: and where this is the case, the punishments in question, as applied to the offences in question, will *pro tanto* have the advantage over all others. This

[k] Ibid. note.
[1] See Ch. XIII (Cases unmeet) par. 2 note.

influence will depend upon the nature of the motive which is the cause of the offence: the punishment most subservient to reformation will be the sort of punishment that is best calculated to invalidate the force of that motive.

16. Thus, in offences originating from the motive of ill-will,[m] that punishment has the strongest reforming tendency, which is best calculated to weaken the force of the irascible affections. And more particularly, in that sort of offence which consists in an obstinate refusal, on the part of the offender, to do something which is lawfully required of him,[n] and in which the obstinacy is in great measure kept up by his resentment against those who have an interest in forcing him to compliance, the most efficacious punishment seems to be that of confinement to spare diet. *–applied to offences originating in ill-will*

17. Thus, also, in offences which owe their birth to the joint influence of indolence and pecuniary interest, that punishment seems to possess the strongest reforming tendency, which is best calculated to weaken the force of the former of those dispositions. And more particularly, in the cases of theft, embezzlement, and every species of defraudment, the mode of punishment best adapted to this purpose seems, in most cases, to be that of penal labour. *–to offences originating in indolence joined to pecuniary interest*

18. An eighth property to be given to a lot of punishment in certain cases, is that of *efficacy with respect to disablement*, or, as it might be styled more briefly, *disabling efficacy.* This is a property which may be given in perfection to a lot of punishment; and that with much greater certainty than the property of subserviency to reformation. The inconvenience is, that this property is apt, in general, to run counter to that of frugality: there being, in most cases, no certain way of disabling a man from doing mischief, without, at the same time, disabling him, in a great measure, from doing good, either to himself or others. The mischief therefore of the offence must be so great as to demand a very considerable lot of punishment, for the purpose of example, before it can warrant the application of a punishment equal to that which is necessary for the purpose of disablement. *Property 8. Efficacy with respect to disablement*

19. The punishment, of which the efficacy in this way is the greatest, is evidently that of death. In this case the efficacy of it is certain. This accordingly is the punishment peculiarly adapted to those cases in which the name of the offender, so long as he lives, may be sufficient to keep a whole nation in a flame. This will now and then be the case with competitors for the sovereignty, and *–is most conspicuous in capital punishment*

[m] See Ch. x (Motives).

[n] See B. I. tit. (Offences against Justice).

leaders of the factions in civil wars: though, when applied to offences of so questionable a nature, in which the question concerning criminality turns more upon success than any thing else; an infliction of this sort may seem more to savour of hostility than punishment. At the same time this punishment, it is evident, is in an eminent degree *unfrugal*; which forms one among the many objections there are against the use of it, in any but very extraordinary cases.[o]

Other punishments iu which it is to be found

20. In ordinary cases the purpose may be sufficiently answered by one or other of the various kinds of confinement and banishment: of which, imprisonment is the most strict and efficacious. For when an offence is so circumstanced that it cannot be committed but in a certain place, as is the case, for the most part, with offences against the person, all the law has to do, in order to disable the offender from committing it, is to prevent his being in that place. In any of the offences which consist in the breach or the abuse of any kind of trust, the purpose may be compassed at a still cheaper rate, merely by forfeiture of the trust: and in general, in any of those offences which can only be committed under favour of some relation in which the offender stands with reference to any person, or sets of persons, merely by forfeiture of that relation: that is, of the right of continuing to reap the advantages belonging to it. This is the case, for instance, with any of those offences which consist in an abuse of the privileges of marriage, or of the liberty of carrying on any lucrative or other occupation.

Property 9. Subserviency to compensation

21. The *ninth* property is that of *subserviency to compensation*. This property of punishment, if it be *vindictive* compensation that is in view, will, with little variation, be in proportion to the quantity: if *lucrative*, it is the peculiar and characteristic property of pecuniary punishment.

Property 10. Popularity

22. In the rear of all these properties may be introduced that of *popularity*; a very fleeting and indeterminate kind of property, which may belong to a lot of punishment one moment, and be lost by it the next. By popularity is meant the property of being acceptable, or rather not unacceptable, to the bulk of the people, among whom it is proposed to be established. In strictness of speech, it should rather be called *absence of unpopularity*: for it cannot be expected, in regard to such a matter as punishment, that any species or lot of it should be positively acceptable and grateful to the people: it is sufficient, for the most part, if they have no decided aversion to the thoughts of it. Now the property of characteristicalness, above noticed, seems to go as far towards conciliating

[o] See B. I. tit. (Punishments).

the approbation of the people to a mode of punishment, as any; insomuch that popularity may be regarded as a kind of secondary quality, depending upon that of characteristicalness.[p] The use of inserting this property in the catalogue, is chiefly to make it serve by way of memento to the legislator not to introduce, without a cogent necessity, any mode or lot of punishment, towards which he happens to perceive any violent aversion entertained by the body of the people.

23. The effects of unpopularity in a mode of punishment are analogous to those of unfrugality. The unnecessary pain which denominates a punishment unfrugal, is most apt to be that which is produced on the part of the offender. A portion of superfluous pain is in like manner produced when the punishment is unpopular: but in this case it is produced on the part of persons altogether innocent, the people at large. This is already one mischief; and another is, the weakness which it is apt to introduce into the law. When the people are satisfied with the law, they voluntarily lend their assistance in the execution: when they are dissatisfied, they will naturally withhold that assistance; it is well if they do not take a positive part in raising impediments. This contributes greatly to the uncertainty of the punishment; by which, in the first instance, the frequency of the offence receives an increase. In process of time that deficiency, as usual, is apt to draw on an increase in magnitude: an addition of a certain quantity which otherwise would be *needless*.[q]

Mischiefs resulting from the unpopularity of a punishment—discontent among the people, and weakness in the law

24. This property, it is to be observed, necessarily supposes, on the part of the people, some prejudice or other, which it is the business of the legislator to endeavour to correct. For if the aversion to the punishment in question were grounded on the principle of utility, the punishment would be such as, on other accounts, ought not to be employed: in which case its popularity or unpopularity would never be worth drawing into question. It is properly therefore a property not so much of the punishment as of the people: a disposition to entertain an unreasonable dislike against an object which merits their approbation. It is the sign also of another property, to wit, indolence or weakness, on the part of the legislator: in suffering the people, for the want of some instruction, which ought

This property supposes a prejudice which the legislator ought to cure

[p] The property of characteristicalness, therefore, is useful in a mode of punishment in three different ways: 1. It renders a mode of punishment, before infliction, more easy to be borne in mind: 2. It enables it, especially after infliction, to make the stronger impression, when it is there; that is, renders it the more *exemplary*. 3. It tends to render it more acceptable to the people, that is, it renders it the more *popular*.

[q] See Ch. XIII (Cases unmeet) § v.

Characteristicalness renders a punishment, 1. memorable: 2. exemplary: 3. popular

to be and might be given them, to quarrel with their own interest. Be this as it may, so long as any such dissatisfaction subsists, it behoves the legislator to have an eye to it, as much as if it were ever so well grounded. Every nation is liable to have its prejudices and its caprices, which it is the business of the legislator to look out for, to study, and to cure.[r]

Property 11.
Remissibility

25. The eleventh and last of all the properties that seem to be requisite in a lot of punishment, is that of *remissibility*.[s] The general presumption is, that when punishment is applied, punishment is needful: that it ought to be applied, and therefore cannot want to be *remitted*. But in very particular, and those always very deplorable cases, it may by accident happen otherwise. It may happen that punishment shall have been inflicted, where, according to the intention of the law itself, it ought not to have been inflicted: that is, where the sufferer is innocent of the offence. At the time of the sentence passed he appeared guilty: but since then, accident has brought his innocence to light. This being the case, so much of the destined punishment as he has suffered already, there is no help for. The business is then to free him from as much as is yet to come. But *is* there any yet to come? There is very little chance of their being any, unless it be so much as consists of *chronical* punishment: such as imprisonment, banishment, penal labour, and the like. So much as consists in *acute* punishment, to wit where the penal process itself is over presently, however permanent the punishment may be in its effects, may be considered as *ir*remissible. This is the case, for example, with whipping, branding, mutilation, and capital punishment. The most perfectly irremissible of any is capital punishment. For though other punishments cannot, when they are over, be remitted, they may be compensated for; and although the unfortunate victim cannot be put into the same condition, yet possibly means may be found of putting him into as good a condition, as he would have been in if he had never suffered. This may in general be done very effectually where the punishment has been no other than pecuniary.

There is another case in which the property of remissibility may appear to be of use: this is, where, although the offender has been justly punished, yet on account of some good behaviour of his, displayed at a time subsequent to that of the commencement of the punishment, it may seem expedient to remit a part of it. But this it

[r] See Ch. XIII (Cases unmeet) § iv par. 4.
[s] See View of the Hard Labour Bill, p. 109.[1]

[1] Cf. Bowring, iv, 32. Bentham's reference is of course to the 1778 edition.

can scarcely be, if the proportion of the punishment is, in other respects, what it ought to be. The purpose of example is the more important object, in comparison of that of reformation.[t] It is not very likely, that less punishment should be required for the former purpose than for the latter. For it must be rather an extraordinary case, if a punishment, which is sufficient to deter a man who has only thought of it for a few moments, should not be sufficient to deter a man who has been feeling it all the time. Whatever, then, is required for the purpose of example, must abide at all events: it is not any reformation on the part of the offender, that can warrant the remitting of any part of it: if it could, a man would have nothing to do but to reform immediately, and so free himself from the greatest part of that punishment which was deemed necessary. In order, then, to warrant the remitting of any part of a punishment upon this ground, it must first be supposed that the punishment at first appointed was more than was necessary for the purpose of example, and consequently that a part of it was *needless* upon the whole. This, indeed, is apt enough to be the case, under the imperfect systems that are as yet on foot: and therefore, during the continuance of those systems, the property of remissibility may, on this second ground likewise, as well as on the former, be deemed a useful one. But this would not be the case in any new-constructed system, in which the rules of proportion above laid down should be observed. In such a system, therefore, the utility of this property would rest solely on the former ground.

26. Upon taking a survey of the various possible modes of punishment, it will appear evidently, that there is not any one of them that possesses all the above properties in perfection. To do the best that can be done in the way of punishment, it will therefore be necessary upon most occasions, to compound them, and make them into complex lots, each consisting of a number of different modes of punishment put together: the nature and proportions of the constituent parts of each lot being different, according to the nature of the offence which it is designed to combat. *To obtain all these properties punishments must be mixed*

27. It may not be amiss to bring together, and exhibit in one view, the eleven properties above established. They are as follows: *The foregoing properties recapitulated*

Two of them are concerned in establishing a proper proportion between a single offence and its punishment; viz.

1. Variability.
2. Equability.

[t] See Ch. xiii (Cases unmeet) 2 note.

One, in establishing a proportion, between more offences than one, and more punishments than one; viz.

    3. Commensurability.

A fourth contributes to place the punishment in that situation in which alone it can be efficacious; and at the same time to be bestowing on it the two farther properties of exemplarity and popularity; viz.

    4. Characteristicalness.

Two others are concerned in excluding all useless punishment; the one indirectly, by heightening the efficacy of what is useful; the other in a direct way; viz.

    5. Exemplarity.
    6. Frugality.

Three others contribute severally to the three inferior ends of punishment; viz.

    7. Subserviency to reformation.
    8. Efficacy in disabling.
    9. Subserviency to compensation.

Another property tends to exclude a collateral mischief, which a particular mode of punishment is liable accidentally to produce; viz.

    10. Popularity.

The remaining property tends to palliate a mischief, which all punishment, as such, is liable accidentally to produce; viz.

    11. Remissibility.

The properties of commensurability, characteristicalness, exemplarity, subserviency to reformation, and efficacy in disabling, are more particularly calculated to augment the *profit* which is to be made by punishment: frugality, subserviency to compensation, popularity, and remissibility, to diminish the *expense*: variability and equability are alike subservient to both those purposes.

Connection of this with the ensuing chapter **28.** We now come to take a general survey of the system of *offences*: that is, of such *acts* to which, on account of the mischievous *consequences* they have a *natural* tendency to produce, and in the view of putting a stop to those consequences, it may be proper to annex a certain *artificial* consequence, consisting of punishment, to be inflicted on the authors of such acts, according to the principles just established.

CHAPTER XVI

DIVISION OF OFFENCES

§ i. *Classes of offences*

1. [a]It is necessary, at the outset, to make a distinction between such

[a] This chapter is an attempt to put our ideas of offences into an exact method. The particular uses of *method* are various: but the general one is, to enable men to understand the things that are the subjects of it. To understand a thing, is to be acquainted with its qualities or properties. Of these properties, some are common to it with other things; the rest, peculiar. But the qualities which are peculiar to any one sort of thing are few indeed, in comparison with those which are common to it with other things. To make it known in respect of its *difference*, would, therefore be doing little, unless it were made known also by its genus. To understand it perfectly, a man must therefore be informed of the points in which it agrees, as well as of those in which it disagrees, with all other things. When a number of objects, composing a logical whole, are to be considered together, all of these possessing with respect to one another a certain congruency or agreement denoted by a certain name, there is but one way of giving a perfect knowledge of their nature; and that is, by distributing them into a system of parcels, each of them a part, either of some other parcel, or, at any rate, of the common whole. This can only be done in the way of *bipartition*, dividing each superior branch into two, and but two, immediately subordinate ones; beginning with the logical whole, dividing that into two parts, then each of those parts into two others; and so on. These first-distinguished parts agree in respect of those properties which belong to the whole: they differ in respect of those properties which are peculiar to each. To divide the whole into more than two parcels at once, for example into three, would not answer the purpose; for, in fact, it is but two objects that the mind can compare together exactly at the same time. Thus then, let us endeavour to deal with offences; or rather, strictly speaking, with acts which possess such properties as seem to indicate them fit to be constituted offences. The task is arduous; and, as *yet* at least, perhaps *for ever*, above our force. There is no speaking of objects but by their names: but the business of giving them names has always been prior to the true and perfect knowledge of their natures. Objects the most dissimilar have been spoken of and treated as if their properties were the same. Objects the most similar have been spoken of and treated as if they had scarce any thing in common. Whatever discoveries may be made concerning them, how different soever their real[1] congruencies and disagreements may be found to be from those which are indicated by their current[2] names, it is not without the utmost difficulty that any means can be

[1] The word 'real' was inserted by Bentham in the sheet of corrections and additions printed in 1783. It was overlooked in the 1823 edition, but was inserted in the Bowring edition (i, 97n.).

[2] The word 'current', another 1783 insertion, was overlooked both in 1823 and in the Bowring edition.

acts as *are* or *may* be, and such as *ought* to be offences. Any act *may* be an offence, which they whom the community are in the habit of obeying shall be pleased to make one: that is, any act which they shall be pleased to prohibit or to punish. But, upon the principle of utility, such acts alone *ought* to be made offences, as the good of the community requires should be made so.

No act ought to be an offence but what is detrimental to the community

2. The good of the community cannot require, that any act should be made an offence, which is not liable, in some way or other, to be detrimental to the community. For in the case of such an act, all punishment is *groundless*.[b]

To be so, it must be detrimental to some one or more of its members

3. But if the whole assemblage of any number of individuals be considered as constituting an imaginary compound *body*, a community or political state; any act that is detrimental to any one or more of those *members* is, as to so much of its effects, detrimental to the *state*.

These may be assignable or not

4. An act cannot be detrimental to a *state*, but by being detrimental to some one or more of the *individuals* that compose it. But these individuals may either be *assignable*[c] or *unassignable*.

If assignable, the offender himself, or others

5. When there is any assignable individual to whom an offence is detrimental, that person may either be a person *other* than the offender, or the offender *himself*.

Class 1. Private offences

6. Offences that are detrimental, in the first instance, to assignable persons other than the offender, may be termed by one common name, *offences against individuals*. And of these may be composed the 1st class of offences. To contrast them with offences of the 2d and 4th classes, it may also sometimes be convenient to style them *private* offences. To contrast them at the same time with

found out of expressing those discoveries by other more apposite denominations.[1] Change the import of the old names, and you are in perpetual danger of being misunderstood: introduce an entire new set of names, and you are sure not to be understood at all. Complete success, then, is, as yet at least, unattainable. But an attempt, though imperfect, may have its use: and, at the worst, it may accelerate the arrival of that perfect system, the possession of which will be the happiness of some maturer age. Gross ignorance descries no difficulties; imperfect knowledge finds them out, and struggles with them: it must be perfect knowledge that overcomes them.

[b] See Ch. XIII (Cases unmeet) § ii 1.

Persons assignable, how

[c] (Assignable). That is, either by name, or at least by description, in such manner as to be sufficiently distinguished from all others; for instance, by the circumstance of being the owner or occupier of such and such goods. See B. I. tit. (Personation). Supra, Ch. XII (Consequences) 15.

[1] The words 'other more apposite denominations' were substituted for 'a conformable set of names' in the 1783 sheet: the substitution was overlooked in 1823 but was carried out in the Bowring edition (i, 97n.).

offences of the 3d class, they may be styled *private extra-regarding* offences.

7. When it appears, in general, that there are persons to whom the act in question may be detrimental, but such persons cannot be individually assigned, the circle within which it appears that they may be found, is either of less extent than that which comprizes the whole community, or not. If of less, the persons comprized within this lesser circle may be considered for this purpose as composing a body of themselves; comprized within, but distinguishable from, the greater body of the whole community. The circumstance that constitutes the union between the members of this lesser body, may be either their residence within a particular place, or, in short, any other less explicit principle of union, which may serve to distinguish them from the remaining members of the community. In the first case, the act may be styled an *offence against a neighbourhood*: in the second, an offence against a particular *class* of persons in the community. Offences, then, against a class or neighbourhood, may, together, constitute the 2d class of offences.[d] To contrast them with private offences on the one hand, and public on the other, they may also be styled *semi-public* offences.

Class 2. Semi-public offences

8. Offences, which in the first instance are detrimental to the offender himself, and to no one else, unless it be by their being detrimental to himself, may serve to compose a third class. To contrast them the better with offences of the first, second, and fourth classes, all which are of a *transitive* nature, they might be styled *intransitive*[e] offences; but still better, *self-regarding*.

Class 3. Self-regarding offences

9. The fourth class may be composed of such acts as ought to be made offences, on account of the distant mischief which they threaten to bring upon an unassignable indefinite multitude of the whole number of individuals, of which the community is composed: although no particular individual should appear more likely to be

Class 4. Public offences

[d] With regard to offences against a class or neighbourhood, it is evident, that the fewer the individuals are, of which such class is composed, and the narrower that neighbourhood is, the more likely are the persons, to whom the offence is detrimental, to become assignable; insomuch that, in some cases, it may be difficult to determine concerning a given offence, whether it be an offence against individuals, or against a class or neighbourhood. It is evident also, that the larger the class or neighbourhood is, the more it approaches to a coincidence with the great body of the state. The three classes, therefore, are liable, to a certain degree, to run into one another, and be confounded. But this is no more than what is the case, more or less, with all those ideal compartments under which men are wont to distribute objects for the convenience of discourse.

Limits between private, semi-public, and public offences, are, strictly speaking, undistinguishable

[e] See Ch. VII (Actions) 13.

a sufferer by them than another. These may be called *public* offences, or offences against the *state*.

Class 5. Multiform offences, viz. 1. Offences by falsehood 2. Offences against trust

10. A fifth class, or appendix, may be composed of such acts as, according to the circumstances in which they are committed, and more particularly according to the purposes to which they are applied, may be detrimental in any one of the ways in which the act of one man can be detrimental to another. These may be termed *multiform*, or *heterogeneous offences*.[f] Offences that are in this case

The imperfections of language an obstacle to arrangement

[f] This class will appear, but too plainly, as a kind of botch in comparison of the rest. But such is the fate of science, and more particularly of the moral branch; the distribution of things must in a great measure be dependent on their names: arrangement, the work of mature reflection, must be ruled by nomenclature, the work of popular caprice.

In the book of the laws, offences must therefore be treated of as much as possible under their accustomed names. Generical terms, which are in continual use, and which express ideas for which there are no other terms in use, cannot safely be discarded. When any such occur, which cannot be brought to quadrate with such a plan of classification as appears to be most convenient upon the whole, what then is to be done? There seems to be but one thing; which is, to retain them, and annex them to the regular part of the system in the form of an appendix. Though they cannot, when entire, be made to rank under any of the classes established in the rest of the system, the divisions to which they give title may be broken down into lesser divisions, which may not be alike intractable. By this means, how discordant soever with the rest of the system they may appear to be at first sight, on a closer inspection they may be found conformable.

Irregularity of this class

This must inevitably be the case with the names of offences, which are so various and universal in their nature, as to be capable, each of them, of doing whatever mischief can be done by any other kind or kinds of offences whatsoever. Offences of this description may well be called anomalous.

–which could not be avoided on any other plan

Such offences, it is plain, cannot but shew themselves equally intractable under every kind of system. Upon whatever principle the system be constructed, they cannot, any of them, with any degree of propriety, be confined to any one division. If therefore, they constitute a blemish in the present system, it is such a blemish as could not be avoided but at the expense of a greater. The class they are here thrown into will traverse, in its subordinate ramifications, the other classes and divisions of the present system: true, but so would they of any other. An irregularity, and that but a superficial one, is a less evil than continual error and contradiction. But even this slight deviation, which the fashion of language seemed to render unavoidable at the outset, we shall soon find occasion to correct as we advance. For though the first great parcels into which the offences of this class are divided are not referable, any of them, to any of the former classes, yet the subsequent lesser subdivisions *are*.[1]

[1] In the 1823 and later editions, note *f* is combined with and added to note g. The latter is however an addition of January 1789 reflecting, as Bentham himself says, his 'maturer views'; and his intentions seem to be better fulfilled, while the evolution of his ideas is certainly made clearer, by separating the two notes.

may be reduced to two great heads: 1. Offences by *falsehood*: and, 2. Offences against *trust*.[g]

§ i. *Divisions and sub-divisions*

11. Let us see by what method these classes may be farther sub-divided. First, then, with regard to offences against individuals.

In the present period of existence, a man's being and well-being, his happiness and his security; in a word, his pleasures and his immunity from pains, are all dependent, more or less, in the first place, upon his *own person*; in the next place, upon the *exterior objects* that surround him. These objects are either *things*, or other *persons*. Under one or other of these classes must evidently be comprised every sort of exterior object, by means of which his interest can be affected. If then, by means of any offence, a man should on any occasion become a sufferer, it must be in one or other of two ways: 1. *absolutely*, to wit, immediately in his own person; in which case the offence may be said to be an offence against his person: or, 2. *relatively* by reason of some *material*[h] relation[i]

Divisions of Class 1.
1. Offences against person. 2.—Property. 3.—Reputation. 4.—Condition. 5.—Person and property. 6.—Person and reputation

[g] (*Multiform or heterogeneous* offences.[1] 1. Offences by *falsehood*: 2. Offences against *trust*). See also par. 20 to 30 and par. 66.[2] Maturer views have suggested the feasibility, and the means, of ridding the system of this anomalous excrescence. Instead of considering these as so many *divisions* of offences, divided into *genera*, correspondent and collateral to the several *genera* distinguished by other appellations, they may be considered as so many specific differences, respectively applicable to those *genera*. Thus, in the case of a *simple personal injury*, in the operation of which a plan of falsehood has been employed: it seems more simple and more natural, to consider the offence thus committed as a particular *species* or *modification* of the *genus* of offence termed a *simple personal injury*, than to consider the simple personal injury, when effected by such means, as a modification of the *division* of offences entitled *Offences through falsehood*. By this means the circumstances of the intervention of falsehood as an instrument, and of the existence of a particular obligation of the nature of a trust, will be reduced to a par with various other classes of circumstances capable of affording grounds of modification, commonly of *aggravation* or *extenuation*, to various genera of offences: instance, *premeditation*, and *conspiracy*, on the one hand; *provocation received*, and *intoxication*, on the other.

[h] See Ch. VII (Actions) 3 and 24.

[i] If, by reason of the word *relation*,[3] this part of the division should appear

[1] These first four words are omitted in the 1823 and later editions. Cf. 190 n. 1 for the placing of note g (added in January 1789).

[2] The 1789 edition also gives page-references (omitted in later editions) for these paragraphs: cf. below, 203–22, 279–80.

[3] In the 1789 and 1823 editions the indicator for note i precedes the word 'relation', being thus juxtaposed to the indicator for note h. The Bowring edition (i, 99n.) combines the two notes; but this is not entirely satisfactory, since the first note is concerned with the term *material*, while the second deals with what Bentham calls 'the unknown term' *relation*.

In what manner pleasure and pain depend upon the relation a man bears to exterior objects

which the beforementioned exterior objects may happen to bear, in the way of *causality* (see Ch. VII (Actions) par. 24) to his happiness.[1] Now in as far as a man is in a way to derive either happiness or security from any object which belongs to the class of *things*, such thing is said to be his *property*, or at least he is said to have a *property* or an *interest* therein: an offence, therefore, which tends to lessen the facility he might otherwise have of deriving happiness or security from an object which belongs to the class of things, may be styled an offence against his property. With regard to persons, in as far as, from objects of this class, a man is in a way to derive happiness or security, it is in virtue of their *services*: in virtue of some services, which, by one sort of inducement or another, they may be disposed to render him.[j] Now, then, take any man, by way

obscure, the unknown term may be got rid of in the following manner. Our ideas are derived, all of them, from the senses; pleasurable and painful ones, therefore, among the rest: consequently, from the operation of sensible objects upon our senses. A man's happiness, then, may be said to depend more or less upon the *relation* he bears to any sensible object, when such object[2] stands a chance,[3] greater or less, of producing to him, or averting from him, pain or pleasure. Now this, if at all, it must do in one or other of two ways; 1. In an *active* way, properly so called; viz. by motion: or, 2. In a *passive* or quiescent way, by being moved to, or acted upon: and in either case, either, 1. in an *immediate* way, by acting upon, or being acted on by, the organs of sense, without the intervention of any other external object: or, 2. in a more or less *remote* way, by acting upon, or being acted on by, some other external object, which (with the intervention of a greater or less number of such objects, and at the end of more or less considerable intervals of time) will come at length to act upon, or be acted upon by, those organs. And this is equally true, whether the external objects in question be things or persons. It is also equally true of pains and pleasures of the mind, as of those of the body: all the difference is, that in the production of these, the pleasure or pain may result immediately from the perception which it accompanies: in the production of those of the mind, it cannot result from the action of an object of sense, any otherwise than by *association*; to wit, by means of some connection which the perception has contracted with certain prior ones, lodged already in the memory.*

[j] See Ch. x (Motives).

* See Ch. v (Pleasures and Pains) 15, 31. Ch. x (Motives) 39 note.

[1] The text as printed in 1780 reads: '2. *relatively*, by reason of some *material* relation he bears to the before-mentioned exterior objects.' The reading in the present text was substituted in the 1783 sheet of corrections and additions; but the 1823 edition, owing to a misunderstanding of Bentham's instructions, produced a meaningless conflation of the two versions. The Bowring edition (i, 99) corrected the mistake.

[2] 1823 edn., 'subject'. This slip, which is reproduced in the Bowring edition (i, 99n.), is corrected in Harrison, 316n.

[3] The text originally (1780) read: 'when such object is in a way that stands a chance . . .'. The deletion of the words 'is in a way that' was one of the corrections made in the 1789 errata list; but neither the 1823 nor any later edition made the correction.

of example, and the disposition, whatever it may be, which he may be in to render you service, either has no other connection to give birth or support to it, than the general one which binds him to the whole species, or it has some other connection more particular. In the latter case, such a connection may be spoken of as constituting, in your favour, a kind of fictitious or incorporeal object of property, which is styled your *condition*. An offence, therefore, the tendency of which is to lessen the facility you might otherwise have of deriving happiness from the services of a person thus specially connected with you, may be styled an offence against your condition in life, or simply against your condition. Conditions in life must evidently be as various as the relations by which they are constituted. This will be seen more particularly farther on. In the mean time, those of husband, wife, parent, child, master, servant, citizen of such or such a city, natural-born subject of such or such a country, may answer the purpose of examples.

Where there is no such particular connection, or (what comes to the same thing) where the disposition, whatever it may be, which a man is in to render you service, is not considered as depending upon such connection, but simply upon the good-will he bears to you; in such case, in order to express what chance you have of deriving a benefit from his services, a kind of fictitious object of property is spoken of, as being constituted in your favour, and is called your *reputation*. An offence, therefore, the tendency of which is to lessen the facility you might otherwise have had of deriving happiness or security from the services of persons at large, whether connected with you or not by any special tie, may be styled an offence against your *reputation*. It appears, therefore, that if by any offence an individual becomes a sufferer, it must be in one or other of the four points above-mentioned; viz. his person, his property, his condition in life, or his reputation. These sources of distinction, then, may serve to form so many subordinate divisions. If any offences should be found to affect a person in more than one of these points at the same time, such offences may respectively be put under so many separate divisions; and such compound divisions may be subjoined to the preceding simple ones. The several divisions (simple and compound together) which are hereinafter established, stand as follows: 1. Offences against person. 2. Offences against reputation. 3. Offences against property.[1] 4. Offences against con-

---

[1] In the original (1780) text items 2 and 3 in this list appear in the reverse order, property being placed before reputation. The change was one of the corrections and additions printed in 1783.

dition. 5. Offences against person and property together. 6. Offences against person and reputation together.[k]

Divisions of
Class 2.
1. Offences
through
calamity

12. Next with regard to semi-public offences. Pain, considered with reference to the time of the act from which it is liable to issue, must, it is evident, be either present, past, or future. In as far as it is either present or past, it cannot be the result of any act which comes under the description of a semi-public offence: for if it be present or past, the individuals who experience, or who have experienced, it are *assignable*.[1] There remains that sort of mischief, which, if it ever come to exist at all, is as yet but future: mischief, thus circumstanced, takes the name of *danger*.[m] Now, then, when by means of the act of any person a whole neighbourhood, or other class of persons, are exposed to danger, this danger must either be *intentional* on his part, or *unintentional*.[n] If unintentional, such danger, when it is converted into actual mischief, takes the name of a *calamity*: offences, productive of such danger, may be styled *semi-public offences operating through calamity*; or, more briefly, *offences through calamity*. If the danger be intentional, insomuch that it might be produced, and might convert itself into actual mischief, without the concurrence of any calamity, it may be said to originate in *mere delinquency*: offences, then, which, without the concurrence of any calamity, tend to produce such danger as disturbs the security of a local, or other subordinate class of persons, may be styled *semi-public offences operating merely by delinquency*, or more briefly, *offences of mere delinquency*.

Sub-divisions
of offences
through
calamity,
dismissed

13. With regard to any farther sub-divisions, offences [through][1] calamity will depend upon the nature of the several calamities to which man, and the several things that are of use to him, stand exposed. These will be considered in another place.[o]

[k] Subsequent consideration has here suggested several alternations. The necessity of adding, to *property, power*, in the character of a distinguishable as well as valuable object or subject-matter of possession, has presented itself to view: and in regard to the fictitious entity here termed *condition* (for shortness instead of saying *condition in life*,) it has been observed to be a sort of composite object, compounded of *property, reputation, power*, and *right* to *services*. For this *composite* object the more proper place was therefore at the tail of the several *simple* ones.—*Note by the Editor, July*, 1822.[2]

[1] Supra, 4 note.   [m] See Ch. XII (Consequences).

[n] See Ch. VIII (Intentionality).

[o] See B. I. tit. (Semi-public offences.) In the mean time that of *pestilence* may

[1] 1789, 1823 and Bowring all mistakenly read 'against' for 'through'. The correction is made in Harrison (p. 319).

[2] In the index of the Bowring edition (xi, p. cccxlviii) this note is attributed to Richard Smith (cf. Introduction, above, xl nn. 1, 4).

14. Semi-public offences of mere delinquency, will follow the *Offences of mere delin-quency,* method of division applied to offences against individuals. It will easily be conceived, that whatever pain or inconvenience any given *how they* individual may be made to suffer, to the danger of that pain or *correspond with the di-* inconvenience may any number of individuals, assignable or not *visions of* assignable, be exposed. Now there are four points or articles, as we *private of-* have seen, in respect to which an individual may be made to suffer *fences* pain or inconvenience. If then, with respect to any one of them, the connection of causes and effects is such, that to the danger of suffering in that article a number of persons, who individually are not assignable, may, by the delinquency of one person, be exposed, such article will form a ground of distinction on which a particular sub-division of semi-public offences may be established: if, with respect to any such article, no such effect can take place, that ground of distinction will lie for the present unoccupied: ready, however, upon any change of circumstances, or in the manner of viewing the subject, to receive a correspondent subdivision of offences, if ever it should seem necessary that any such offences should be created.

15. We come next to self-regarding offences; or, more properly, *Divisions of Class 3. co-incide with* to acts productive in the first instance of no other than a self-regarding mischief: acts which, if in any instance it be thought fit to *those of* constitute them offences, will come under the denomination of *Class 1* offences against one's self. This class will not for the present give us much trouble. For it is evident, that in whatever points a man is vulnerable by the hand of another, in the same points may he be conceived to be vulnerable by his own. Whatever divisions therefore will serve for the first class, the same will serve for this. As to the questions, What acts are productive of a mischief of this stamp? and, among such as *are*, which it may, and which it may not, be *worth while*[p] to treat upon the footing of offences? these are points, the latter of which at least is, too unsettled, and too open to controversy, to be laid down[1] with that degree of confidence which is

serve as an example. A man, without any intention of giving birth to such a calamity, may expose a neighbourhood to the danger of it, by breaking *quarantine* or violating any of those other preventive regulations which governments, at certain conjunctures, may find it expedient to have recourse to, for the purpose of guarding against such danger. See infra 33 note.[2]

[p] See Ch. XIII (Cases unmeet) § iv.

[1] 1789 reads 'decided' for 'laid down'.
[2] This reference (to the long note at the end of par. 33: 224–5 n. z2 below) was omitted in the 1823 and later editions.

implied in the exhibition of properties which are made use of as[1] the groundwork of an arrangement. Properties for this purpose ought to be such as shew themselves at first glance, and appear to belong to the subject beyond dispute.

Divisions of Class 4.

16. Public offences may be distributed under eleven divisions.[q] 1. Offences against *external* security. 2. Offences against *justice*. 3. Offences against the *preventive* branch of the *police*. 4. Offences against the public *force*. 5. Offences against the *positive* increase of the national *felicity*. 6. Offences against the public *wealth*. 7. Offences against *population*. 8. Offences against the *national wealth*. 9. Offences against the *sovereignty*. 10. Offences against *religion*. 11. Offences against the national *interest* in general. The way in which these several sorts of offences connect with one another, and with the interest of the public, that is, of an unassignable multitude of the individuals of which that body is composed, may be thus conceived.

Connection of the nine first divisions one with another

17. Mischief by which the interest of the public as above defined may be affected, must, if produced at all, be produced either by means of an influence exerted on the operations of government, or by other means, without the exertion of such influence.[r] To begin

Exhaustive method departed from

[q] In this part of the analysis, I have found it necessary to deviate in some degree from the rigid rules of the exhaustive method I set out with. By me, or by some one else, this method may, perhaps, be more strictly pursued at some maturer period of the science. At present, the benefit that might result from the unrelaxed observance of it, seemed so precarious, that I could not help doubting whether it would pay for the delay and trouble. Doubtless such a method is eminently instructive: but the fatigue of following it out is so great, not only to the author, but probably also to the reader, that if carried to its utmost length at the first attempt, it might perhaps do more disservice in the way of disgust, than service in the way of information. For knowledge, like physic, how salutary soever in itself, becomes no longer of any use, when made too unpalatable to be swallowed. Mean time, it cannot but be a mortifying circumstance to a writer, who is sensible of the importance of his subject, and anxious to do it justice, to find himself obliged to exhibit what he perceives to be faulty, with any view, how indistinct soever, of something more perfect before his eyes. If there be any thing new and original in this work, it is to the exhaustive method so often aimed at that I am indebted for it. It will, therefore, be no great wonder if I should not be able to quit it without reluctance. On the other hand, the marks of stiffness which will doubtless be perceived in a multitude of places, are chiefly owing to a solicitous, and not perfectly successful, pursuit of this same method. New instruments are seldom handled at first with perfect ease.

[r] The idea of government, it may be observed, is introduced here without any preparation. The fact of its being established I assume as notorious, and the

[1] 1789 'made to serve as' for 'made use of as'.

with the latter case: mischief, be it what it will, and let it happen to whom it will, must be produced either by the unassisted powers of the agent in question, or by the instrumentality of some other agents. In the latter case, these agents will be either persons or things. Persons again must be either not members of the community in question, or members. Mischief produced by the instrumentality of persons, may accordingly be produced by the instrumentality either of *external* or of *internal* adversaries. Now when it is produced by the agent's own unassisted powers, or by the instrumentality of internal adversaries, or only by the instrumentality of things, it is seldom that it can show itself in any other shape (setting aside any influence it may exert on the operations of government) than either that of an offence against assignable individuals, or that of an offence against a local or other subordinate class of persons. If there should be a way in which mischief can be produced, by any of these means, to individuals altogether unassignable, it will scarcely be found conspicuous or important enough to occupy a title by itself: it may accordingly be referred to the miscellaneous head of *offences against the national interest in general*.[s] The only mischief, of any considerable account, which can be made to impend indiscriminately over the whole number of members in the community, is that complex kind of mischief which results from a state of war, and is produced by the instrumentality of external adversaries; by their being provoked, for instance, or invited, or encouraged to invasion. In this way may a man very well bring down a mischief, and that a very heavy one, upon the whole community in general, and that without taking a part in any of the injuries which came in consequence to be offered to particular individuals.

Next with regard to the mischief which an offence may bring upon the public by its influence on the operations of the government. This it may occasion either, 1. In a more immediate way, by its influence on those *operations* themselves: 2. In a more remote way, by its influence on the *instruments* by or by the help of which

necessity of it as alike obvious and incontestible. Observations indicating that necessity, if any such should be thought worth looking at in this view, may be found by turning to a passage in a former chapter, where they were incidentally adduced for the purpose of illustration. See Ch. XII (Consequences) 17.

[s] See infra, 54 note. Even this head, ample as it is, and vague as it may seem to be, will not, when examined by the principle of utility, serve, any more than another, to secrete any offence which has no title to be placed there. To show the pain or loss of pleasure which is likely to ensue, is a problem, which before a legislator can justify himself in adding the act to the catalogue of offences, he may in this case, as in every other, be called upon to solve.

those operations should be performed: or 3. In a more remote way still, by its influence on the *sources* from whence such instruments are to be derived. First then, as to the operations of government, the tendency of these, in as far as it is conformable to what on the principle of utility it ought to be, is in every case either to avert mischief from the community, or to make an addition to the sum of positive good.[t] Now mischief we have seen, must come either from external adversaries, from internal adversaries, or from calamities. With regard to mischief from external adversaries, there requires no further division. As to mischief from internal adversaries, the expedients employed for averting it may be distinguished into such as may be applied *before* the discovery of any mischievous design in particular, and such as can not be employed but in consequence of the discovery of some such design: the former of these are commonly referred to a branch which may be styled the *preventive* branch of the *police*: the latter to that of justice.[u] Second,

[t] For examples, see infra, 54 note. This branch of the business of government, a sort of work of supererogation, as it may be called, in the calendar of political duty, is comparatively but of recent date. It is not for this that the untutored many could have originally submitted themselves to the dominion of the few. It was the dread of evil, not the hope of good, that first cemented societies together. Necessaries come always before luxuries. The state of language marks the progress of ideas. Time out of mind the military department has had a name: so has that of justice: the power which occupies itself in preventing mischief, not till lately, and that but a loose one, the police: for the power which takes for its object the introduction of positive good, no peculiar name, however inadequate, seems yet to have been devised.

[u] The functions of justice, and those of the police, must be apt in many points to run one into another: especially as the business would be very badly managed if the same persons, whose more particular duty it is to act as officers of the police, were not upon occasion to act in the capacity of officers of justice. The ideas, however, of the two functions may still be kept distinct: and I see not where the line of separation can be drawn, unless it be as above.

As to the word *police*, though of Greek extraction, it seems to be of French growth: it is from France, at least, that it has been imported into Great Britain, where it still retains its foreign garb: in Germany, if it did not originate there, it has at least been naturalized. Taken all together, the idea belonging to it seems to be too multifarious to be susceptible of any single definition. Want of words obliged me to reduce the two branches here specified into one. Who would have endured in this place to have seen two such words as the *phthano-paranomic* or *crime-preventing*, and the *phthano-symphoric* or *calamity-preventing*, branches of the police? The inconveniences[1] of uniting the two branches under the same denomination, are however, the less, inasmuch as the

[1] 1780 text, 'inconvenience'. The correction to the plural was made in the 1789 errata, but this was not followed by either the 1823 or the Bowring edition. Harrison (p. 323n.) has the correct reading, but follows the 1823 text in omitting the capital in 'The' at the beginning of the sentence.

198

as to the *instruments* which government, whether in the averting of evil or in the producing of positive good, can have to work with, these must be either *persons* or *things*. Those which are destined to the particular function of guarding against mischief from adversaries in general, but more particularly from external adversaries,[v] may be distinguished from the rest under the collective appellation of the *public military force*, and, for conciseness sake, the *military force*. The rest may be characterised by the collective appellation of the *public wealth*. Thirdly, with regard to the sources or funds from whence these instruments, howsoever applied, must be derived, such of them as come under the denomination of *persons* must be taken out of the whole number of persons that are in the community, that is, out of the total *population* of the state: so that the greater the population, the greater may *cæteris paribus* be this branch of the public wealth; and the less the less. In like manner, such as come under the denomination of *things* may be, and most of them commonly are, taken out of the sum total of those things which are the separate properties of the several members of the community: the sum of which properties may be termed *the national wealth*[w]: so that the greater the national wealth, the greater

operations requisite to be performed for the two purposes will in many cases be the same. Other functions, commonly referred to the head of police, may be referred either to the head of that power which occupies itself in promoting in a positive way the increase of the national felicity, or of that which employs itself in the management of the public wealth. See infra, 54 note.

[v] It is from abroad that those pernicious enterprises are most apt to originate, which come backed with a greater quantity of physical force than the persons who are in a more particular sense the officers of justice are wont to have at their command. Mischief the perpetration of which is ensured by a force of such magnitude, may therefore be looked upon in general as the work of *external* adversaries. Accordingly, when the persons by whom it is perpetrated, are in such force as to bid defiance to the ordinary efforts of justice, they loosen themselves from their original denomination in proportion as they increase in force, till at length they are looked upon as being no longer members of the state, but as standing altogether upon a footing with external adversaries. Give force enough to robbery, and it swells into rebellion: give permanence enough to rebellion, and it settles into hostility.

[w] It must be confessed, that in common speech the distinction here established between the public wealth and the national wealth is but indifferently settled: nor is this to be wondered at; the ideas themselves, though here necessary to be distinguished, being so frequently convertible. But I am mistaken if the language will furnish any other two words that would express the distinction better. Those in question will, I imagine, be allowed to be thus far well chosen, that if they were made to change their places, the import given to them would not appear to be quite so proper as that which is given to them as they stand at present.

ceteris paribus, may be this remaining branch of the public wealth; and the less, the less. It is here to be observed, that if the influence exerted on any occasion by any individual over the operations of the government be pernicious, it must be in one or other of two ways: 1. by causing, or tending to cause, operations *not* to be performed which *ought* to be performed; in other words, by *impeding* the operations of government. Or, 2. by causing operations to *be* performed which ought *not* to be performed; in other words, by *misdirecting* them. Last, to the total assemblage of the persons by whom the several political operations above-mentioned come to be performed, we set out with applying the collective appellation of *the government.* Among these persons there *commonly*[x] is some one person, or body of persons, whose office it is to assign and distribute to the rest their several departments, to determine the conduct to be pursued by each in the performance of the particular set of operations that belongs to him, and even upon occasion to exercise his function in his stead. Where there is any such person, or body of persons, *he* or *it* may, according as the turn of the phrase requires, be termed *the sovereign,* or the *sovereignty.* Now it is evident, that to impede or misdirect the operations of the sovereign, as here described, may be to impede or misdirect the operations of the several departments of government as described above.

From this analysis, by which the connection between the several above-mentioned heads of offences is exhibited, we may now collect a definition for each article. By *offences against external security,* we may understand such offences whereof the tendency is to bring upon the public a mischief resulting from the hostilities of foreign adversaries. By *offences against justice,* such offences whereof the tendency is to impede or misdirect the operations of that power which is employed in the business of guarding the public against the mischiefs resulting from the delinquency of internal adversaries, as far as it is to be done by expedients, which do not come to be applied in any case till *after* the discovery of some particular design of the sort of those which they are calculated to prevent. By *offences against the preventive branch of the police,* such offences whereof the tendency is to impede or misdirect the operations of that power which is employed in guarding against mischiefs result-

---

[x] I should have been afraid to have said *necessarily.* In the United Provinces, in the Helvetic, or even in the Germanic body, where is that one assembly in which an absolute power over the whole resides? where was there in the Roman Commonwealth? I would not undertake for certain to find an answer to all these questions.

ing from the delinquency of internal adversaries, by expedients that come to be applied *before-hand*; or of that which is employed in guarding against the mischiefs that might be occasioned by physical calamities. By *offences against the public force*, such offences whereof the tendency is to impede or misdirect the operations of that power which is destined to guard the public from the mischiefs which may result from the hostility of foreign adversaries, and, in case of necessity, in the capacity of ministers of justice, from mischiefs of the number of those which result from the delinquency of internal adversaries. By *offences against the increase of the national felicity*, such offences whereof the tendency is to impede or misapply the operations of those powers that are employed in the conducting of various establishments, which are calculated to make, in so many different ways, a *positive* addition to the stock of public happiness. By *offences against the public wealth*, such offences whereof the tendency is to diminish the amount or misdirect the application of the money, and other articles of wealth, which the government reserves as a fund, out of which the stock of instruments employed in the service above-mentioned may be kept up. By *offences against population*, such offences whereof the tendency is to diminish the numbers or impair the political value of the sum total of the members of the community. By *offences against the national wealth* such offences whereof the tendency is to diminish the quantity, or impair the value, of the things which compose the separate properties or estates of the several members of the community.

18. In this deduction, it may be asked, what place is left for *religion*? This we shall see presently. For combating the various kinds of offences above enumerated, that is, for combating all the offences (those not excepted which we are now about considering) which it is in man's nature to commit, the state has two great engines, *punishment* and *reward*: punishment, to be applied to all, and upon all ordinary occasions: reward, to be applied to a few, for particular purposes, and upon extraordinary occasions. But whether or no a man has done the act which renders him an object meet for punishment or reward, the eyes of those, whosoever they be, to whom the management of these engines is entrusted cannot always see, nor, where it is punishment that is to be administered, can their hands be always sure to reach him. To supply these deficiencies in point of power, it is thought necessary, or at least *useful*, (without which the *truth* of the doctrine would be nothing to the purpose) to inculcate into the minds of the people the belief of the

Connection of offences against religion with the foregoing ones

existence of a power applicable to the same purposes, and not liable to the same deficiencies: the power of a supreme invisible being, to whom a disposition of contributing to the same ends to which the several institutions already mentioned are calculated to contribute, must for this purpose be ascribed. It is of course expected that this power will, at one time or other, be employed in the promoting of those ends: and to keep up and strengthen this expectation among men, is spoken of as being the employment of a kind of allegorical personage, feigned, as before,[y] for convenience of discourse, and styled *religion*. To diminish, then, or misapply the influence of religion, is *pro tanto* to diminish or misapply what power the state has of combating with effect any of the before enumerated kinds of offences; that is, all kinds of offences whatsoever. Acts that appear to have this tendency may be styled *offences against religion*. Of these then may be composed the tenth division of the class of offences against the state.[z]

Connection of offences against the national interest in general with the rest

19. If there be any acts which appear liable to affect the state in any one or more of the above ways, by operating in prejudice of the external security of the state, or of its internal security; of the public force; of the increase of the national felicity; of the public

[y] See par. 17 with regard to *justice*.

[z] It may be observed, that upon this occasion I consider religion in no other light, than in respect of the influence it may have on the happiness of, the *present* life. As to the effects it may have in assuring us of and preparing us for, a better life to come, this is a matter which comes not within the cognizance of the legislator. See tit. (Offences against religion).[1]

I say offences against *religion*, the fictitious entity: not offences against God, the real being. For, what sort of pain should the act of a feeble mortal occasion to a being unsusceptible of pain? How should an offence affect him? Should it be an offence against his person, his property, his reputation, or his condition?

It has commonly been the way to put offences against religion foremost. The idea of precedence is naturally enough connected with that of reverence. Εκ Διος αρχωμεσθα.[2] But for expressing reverence, there are other methods enough that are less equivocal. And in point of method and perspicuity, it is evident, that with regard to offences against religion, neither the nature of the mischief which it is their tendency to produce, nor the reason there may be for punishing them, can be understood, but from the consideration of the several mischiefs which result from the several other sorts of offences. In a political view, it is only because those others are mischievous, that offences against religion are so too.

[1] Bentham felt considerable doubt as to whether offences against religion should or should not be explicitly dealt with in his *Plan of a Penal Code*. Cf. his letter of 30 March 1779 to Franz Ludwig Tribolet (*Correspondence*, in *CW*, ii, 252).

[2] Theocritus, *Idylls*, xvii.1: Ἐκ Διὸς ἀρχώμεσθα καὶ ’ες Δία λήγετε, Μοῦσαι (Let us with Zeus begin, and end, O Muse, with Zeus).

wealth; of the national population, of the national wealth; of the sovereignty; or of religion; at the same time that it is not clear in which of all these ways they will affect it most, nor but that, according to contingencies, they may affect it in one of these ways only or in another; such acts may be collected together under a miscellaneous division by themselves, and styled *offences against the national interest in general.* Of these then may be composed the eleventh and last division of the class of offences against the state.

20. We come now to class the fifth: consisting of *multiform* offences. These, as has been already intimated, are either offences by *falsehood*, or offences concerning *trust*. Under the head of offences by falsehood, may be comprehended, 1. Simple falsehoods. 2. Forgery. 3. Personation. 4. Perjury.[a2] Let us observe in what particulars these four kinds of falsehood agree, and in what they differ. *Sub-divisions of Class 5 enumerated. 1. Divisions of offences by falsehood*

21. Offences by falsehood, however diversified in other particulars, have this in common, that they consist in some abuse of the faculty of discourse, or rather as we shall see hereafter, of the faculty of influencing the sentiment of belief in other men,[b2] whether by discourse or otherwise. The use of discourse is to influence belief, and that in such manner as to give other men to understand that things are as they are really. Falsehoods, of whatever kind they be, agree in this: that they give men to understand that things are otherwise than as in reality they are. *Offences by falsehood, in what they agree with one another*

22. Personation, forgery, and perjury, are each of them distinguished from other modes of uttering falsehood by certain special circumstances. When a falsehood is not accompanied by any *–in what they differ*

[a2] This division of falsehoods, it is to be observed, is not regularly drawn out: that being what the nature of the case will not here admit of. Falsehood may be infinitely diversified in other ways than these. In a particular case, for instance, simple falsehood when uttered by writing, is distinguished from the same falsehood when uttered by word of mouth; and has had a particular name given to it accordingly. I mean, where it strikes against reputation; in which case, the instrument it has been uttered by has been called a *libel.* Now it is obvious, that in the same manner it might have received a distinct name in all other cases where it is uttered by writing. But there has not happened to be any thing in particular that has disposed mankind in those cases to give it such a name. The case is, that among the infinity of circumstances by which it might have been diversified, those which constitute it a libel, happen to have engaged a peculiar share of attention on the part of the institutors of language; either in virtue of the influence which these circumstances have on the tendency of the act, or in virtue of any particular degree of force with which on any other account they may have disposed it to strike upon the imagination.

[b2] See B. I. tit. (Falsehoods).

of those circumstances, it may be styled simple falsehood. These circumstances are, 1. The *form* in which the falsehood is uttered. 2. The circumstance of its relating or not to the identity of the *person* of him who utters it. 3. The solemnity of the *occasion* on which it is uttered.[c2] The particular application of these distinctive characters may more commodiously be reserved for another place.[d2]

Sub-divisions of offences by falsehood are determined by the divisions of the preceding classes

23. We come now to the sub-divisions of offences by falsehood. These will bring us back into the regular track of analysis, pursued, without deviation, through the four preceding classes.

By whatever means a mischief is brought about, whether falsehood be or be not of the number, the individuals liable to be affected by it must either be assignable or unassignable. If assignable, there are but four material articles in respect to which they can be affected: to wit, their persons their properties, their reputations, and their conditions in life. The case is the same, if, though unassignable, they are comprisable in any class subordinate to that which is composed of the whole number of members of the state. If the falsehood tend to the detriment of the whole state, it can only be by operating in one or other of the characters, which every act that is an offence against the state must assume; viz. that of an offence against external security, against justice, against the preventive branch of the police, against the public force, against the encrease of the national felicity, against the public wealth, against the national population, against the national wealth, against the sovereignty of the state, or against its religion.

Offences of this class in some instances change their names: in others not

24. It is the common property, then, of the offences that belong to this division, to run over the same ground that is occupied by those of the preceding classes. But some of them, as we shall see, are apt, on various occasions, to drop or change the names which bring them under this division: this is chiefly the case with regard to simple falsehoods. Others retain their names unchanged; and even thereby supersede the names which would otherwise belong to the offences which they denominate: this is chiefly the case with regard to personation, forgery, and perjury. When this circumstance then, the circumstance of falsehood, intervenes, in some

---

[c2] There are two other circumstances still more material; viz. 1. The parties whose interest is affected by the falsehood. 2. The point or article in which that interest is affected. These circumstances, however, enter not into the composition of the generical character. Their use is, as we shall see, to characterize the several species of each genus. See B. I. tit. (Falsehoods).

[d2] Ibid.

cases the name which takes the lead, is that which indicates the offence by its effect; in other cases, it is that which indicates the expedient or instrument as it were by the help of which the offence is committed. Falsehood, take it by itself, consider it as not being accompanied by any other material circumstances, nor therefore productive of any material effects, can never, upon the principle of utility, constitute any offence at all. Combined with other circumstances, there is scarce any sort of pernicious effect which it may not be instrumental in producing. It is therefore rather in compliance with the laws of language, than in consideration of the nature of the things themselves, that falsehoods are made separate mention of under the name and in the character of distinct offences. All this would appear plain enough, if it were now a time for entering into particulars: but that is what can not be done, consistently with any principle of order or convenience, until the inferior divisions of those other classes shall have been previously exhibited.

25. We come now to offences against trust. A trust is, where there is any particular act which one party, in the exercise of some *power*, or some *right*,[e2] which is conferred on him, is bound to

A trust, what

[e2] Powers, though not a species of rights (for the two sorts of fictitious entities, termed a *power* and a *right*, are altogether disparate) are yet so far included under rights, that wherever the word *power* may be employed, the word *right* may also be employed: The reason is, that wherever you may speak of a person as having a power, you may also speak of him as having a right to such power: but the converse of this proposition does not hold good: there are cases in which, though you may speak of a man as having a right, you can not speak of him as having a power, or in any other way make any mention of that word. On various occasions you have a *right* for instance, to the services of the magistrate: but if you are a private person, you have no *power* over him: all the power is on his side. This being the case, as the word *right* was employed, the word *power* might, perhaps, without any deficiency in the sense, have been omitted. On the present occasion however, as in speaking of trusts this word is commonly made more use of than the word *right*, it seemed most eligible, for the sake of perspicuity, to insert them both.

It may be expected that, since the word *trust* has been here expounded, the words *power* and *right*, upon the meaning of which the exposition of the word *trust* is made to depend, should be expounded also: and certain it is, that no two words can stand more in need of it than these do. Such exposition I accordingly set about to give, and indeed have actually drawn up: but the details into which I found it necessary to enter for this purpose, were of such length as to take up more room than could consistently be allotted to them in this place. With respect to these words, therefore, and a number of others, such as *possession, title*, and the like, which in point of import are inseparably connected with them, instead of exhibiting the exposition itself, I must content

Power and right, why no complete definition is here given of them

205

e² cont.

myself with giving a general idea of the plan which I have pursued in framing it: and as to every thing else, I must leave the import of them to rest upon whatever footing it may happen to stand upon in the apprehension of each reader. Power and right, and the whole tribe of fictitious entities of this stamp, are all of them in the sense which belongs to them in a book of jurisprudence, the results of some manifestation or other of the legislator's will with respect to such or such an act. Now every such manifestation is either a prohibition, a command, or their respective negations; viz. a permission, and the declaration which the legislator makes of his will when on any occasion he leaves an act uncommanded. Now, to render the expression of the rule more concise, the commanding of a positive act may be represented by the prohibition of the negative act which is opposed to it. To know then how to expound a right, carry your eye to the act which, in the circumstances in question, would be a violation of that right: the law creates the right by prohibiting that act. Power, whether over a man's own person, or over other persons, or over things, is constituted in the first instance by permission: but in as far as the law takes an active part in corroborating it, it is created by prohibition, and by command: by prohibition of such acts (on the part of other persons) as are judged incompatible with the exercise of it; and upon occasion, by command of such acts as are judged to be necessary for the removal of such or such obstacles of the number of those which may occur to impede the exercise of it. For every right which the law confers on one party, whether that party be an individual, a subordinate class of individuals, or the public, it thereby imposes on some other party a *duty* or *obligation*. But there may be laws which command or prohibit acts, that is, impose duties, without any other view than the benefit of the agent: these generate no rights: duties, therefore, may be either *extra-regarding* or *self-regarding*: extra-regarding have rights to correspond to them: self-regarding, none.

That the exposition of the words *power* and *right* must, in order to be correct, enter into a great variety of details, may be presently made appear. One branch of the system of rights and powers, and but one, are those of which property is composed: to be correct, then, it must, among other things, be applicable to the whole tribe of modifications of which property is susceptible. But the commands and prohibitions, by which the *powers* and *rights* that compose those several modifications are created, are of many different forms: to comprize the exposition in question within the compass of a single paragraph, would therefore be impossible: to take as many paragraphs for it as would be necessary, in order to exhibit these different forms, would be to engage in a detail so ample, that the analysis of the several possible species of property would compose only a part of it. This labour, uninviting as it was, I have accordingly undergone: but the result of it, as may well be imagined, seemed too voluminous and minute to be exhibited in an outline like the present. Happily it is not necessary, except only for the scientific purpose of arrangement to the understanding of any thing that need be said on the penal branch of the art of legislation. In a work which should treat of the civil branch of that art, it would find its proper place: and in such a work, if conducted upon the plan of the present one, it would be indispensable. Of the limits which seem to separate the one of these branches from the other, a pretty ample description will be found in the next chapter: from which some further lights respecting the course to be taken for developing the notions to be annexed to the words perform for the benefit of another. Or, more fully, thus: A party is said to be invested with a trust, when, being invested with a *power*, or with a *right*, there is a certain behaviour which, in the exercise of that power, or of that right, he is bound to maintain for the benefit of some other party. In such case, the party first mentioned is styled a trustee: for the other party, no name has ever yet been found: for want of a name, there seems to be no other resource than to give a new and more extensive sense to the word *beneficiary*, or to say at length *the party to be benefitted*.[f2]

e2 cont.

right and *power*, may incidentally be collected. See in particular, § iii and iv.[1] See also par. 55 of the present chapter.

I might have cut this matter very short, by proceeding in the usual strain, and saying, that a power was a faculty, and that a right was a privilege, and so on, following the beaten track of definition. But the inanity of such a method in cases like the present, has been already pointed out*: a power is not a— any thing: neither is a right a—any thing: the case is, they have neither of them any superior genus: these, together with *duty*, *obligation*, and a multitude of others of the same stamp being of the number of those fictitious entities, of which the import can by no other means be illustrated than by showing the relation which they bear to real ones.

[f2] The first of these parties is styled in the law language, as well as in common speech, by the name here given to him. The other is styled, in the technical language of the English law, a *cestuy que trust*: in common speech, as we have observed, there is, unfortunately, no name for him. As to the law phrase, it is antiquated French, and though complex, it is still elliptical, and to the highest degree obscure. The phrase in full length would run in some such manner as this: *cestuy al use de qui le trust est créé*: he to whose use the trust or benefit is created. In a particular case, a *cestuy que trust* is called by the Roman law, *fideicommissarius*. In imitation of this, I have seen him somewhere or other called in English a *fide-committee*. This term however, seems not very expressive. A fide-committee, or, as it should have been, a *fidei*-committee, seems, literally speaking, to mean one who is committed to the good faith of another. Good faith seems to consist in the keeping of a promise. But a trust may be created without any promise in the case. It is indeed common enough to exact a promise, in order the more effectually to oblige a man to do that which he is made to promise he will do. But this is merely an accidental circumstance. A trust may be created without any such thing. What is it that constitutes a legal obligation in any case? A command, express or virtual, together with punishment appointed for the breach of it. By the same means may an obligation be constituted in this case as well as any other. Instead of the word *beneficiary*, which I found it necessary to adopt, the sense would be better

* See Fragment of Government, Ch. v, § 6, note.[2]

[1] These sections of Ch. xvii were never in fact completed in the form of parts of that chapter: they are part of what eventually grew into the work published in this edition as *Of Laws in General* (cf. the editorial introduction to that work in *CW*, xxxi ff.).

[2] Cf. Bowring, i, 292–4n. This is the long note in which Bentham develops his concept of definition by way of 'paraphrasis'.

The trustee is also said to have a trust *conferred* or *imposed* upon him, to be *invested* with a trust, to have had a trust given him to execute, to perform, to discharge, or to fulfil. The party to be benefitted, is said to have a trust established or created in his favour: and so on through a variety of other phrases.

Offences against trust, condition, and property, why ranked under separate divisions

26. Now it may occur, that a *trust* is oftentimes spoken of as a species of *condition*[g2]: that a trust is also spoken of as a species of *property*: and that a condition itself is also spoken of in the same light. It may be thought, therefore, that in the first class, the division of offences against condition should have been included under that of the offences against property: and that at any rate, so much of the fifth class now before us as contains offences against trust, should have been included under one or other of those two divisions of the first class. But upon examination it will appear, that no one of these divisions could with convenience, nor even perhaps with propriety, have been included under either of the other two. It will appear at the same time, that there is an intimate connection subsisting amongst them all: insomuch that of the lists of the offences to which they are respectively exposed, any one may serve in great measure as a model for any other. There are certain offences to which all trusts as such are exposed: to all these offences every sort of condition will be found exposed: at the same time that particular species of the offences against trust will, upon their application to particular conditions, receive different particular denominations. It will appear also, that of the two groups of offences into which the list of those against trust will be found naturally to divide itself, there is one, and but one, to which property, taken in its proper and more confined sense, stands exposed: and that these,

expressed by some such word as *beneficiendary*, (a word analogous in its formation to *referendary*) were it such an one as the ear could bring itself to endure. This would put it more effectually out of doubt, that the party meant was the party who *ought* to receive the benefit, whether he actually receives it or no: whereas the word *beneficiary* might be understood to intimate, that the benefit was *actually* received: while in offences against trust the mischief commonly is, that such benefit is reaped not by the person it was designed for, but by some other: for instance, the trustee.

[g2] It is for shortness' sake that the proposition is stated as it stands in the text. If critically examined, it might be found, perhaps, to be scarcely justifiable by the laws of language. For the fictitious entities, characterized by the two abstract terms, *trust* and *condition*, are not subalternate but disparate. To speak with perfect precision, we should say that he who is invested with a trust, is, on that account, spoken of as being invested with a condition: viz. the condition of a trustee. We speak of the condition of a trustee as we speak of the condition of a husband or a father.

208

in their application to the subject of property, will be found susceptible of distinct modifications, to which the usage of language,
and the occasion there is for distinguishing them in point of treatment, make it necessary to find names.

In the first place, as there are, or at least may be (as we shall see)
conditions which are not trusts,[h2] so there are trusts of which the
idea would not be readily and naturally understood to be included
under the word *condition*: add to which, that of those conditions
which do include a trust, the greater number include other ingredients along with it: so that the idea of a condition, if on the one
hand it stretches beyond the idea of a trust, does on the other hand
fall short of it. Of the several sorts of trusts, by far the most important are those in which it is the public that stands in the relation of
beneficiary. Now these trusts, it should seem, would hardly present
themselves at first view upon the mention of the word *condition*.
At any rate, what is more material, the most important of the
offences against these kinds of trust would not seem to be included
under the denomination of offences against condition. The offences
which by this latter appellation would be brought to view, would be
such only as seemed to affect the interests of an individual: of him,
for example, who is considered as being invested with that condition. But in offences against public trust, it is the influence they
have on the interests of the public that constitutes by much the most
material part of their pernicious tendency: the influence they have
on the interests of any individual, the only part of their influence
which would be readily brought to view by the appellation of offences against condition, is comparatively as nothing. The word
trust directs the attention at once to the interests of that party for
whom the person in question is trustee: which party, upon the
addition of the epithet public, is immediately understood to be the
body composed of the whole assemblage, or an indefinite portion of
the whole assemblage of the members of the state. The idea presented by the words *public trust* is clear and unambiguous: it is but an
obscure and ambiguous garb that that idea could be expressed in
by the words *public condition*. It appears, therefore, that the principal
part of the offences, included under the denomination of offences
against trust, could not, commodiously at least, have been included
under the head of offences against condition.

It is evident enough, that for the same reasons neither could they
have been included under the head of offences against property.
It would have appeared preposterous, and would have argued a

[h2] Infra, 55.

209

total inattention to the leading principle of the whole work, the principle of utility, to have taken the most mischievous and alarming part of the offences to which the public stands exposed, and forced them into the list of offences against the property of an individual: of that individual, to wit, who in that case would be considered as having in him the property of that public trust, which by the offences in question is affected.

Nor would it have been less improper to have included conditions, all of them, under the head of property: and thereby the whole catalogue of offences against condition, under the catalogue of offences against property. True it is, that there are offences against condition, which perhaps with equal propriety, and without any change in their nature, might be considered in the light of offences against property: so extensive and so vague are the ideas that are wont to be annexed to both these objects. But there are other offences which though with unquestionable propriety they might be referred to the head of offences against condition, could not, without the utmost violence done to language, be forced under the appellation of offences against property. Property, considered with respect to the proprietor, implies invariably a benefit, and nothing else: whatever obligations or burthens may, by accident, stand annexed to it, yet in itself it can never be otherwise than beneficial. On the part of the proprietor, it is created not by any commands that are laid on him, but by his being left free to do with such or such an article as he likes. The obligations it is created by, are in every instance laid upon other people. On the other hand, as to conditions, there are several which are of a mixed nature, importing as well a burthen to him who stands invested with them as a benefit: which indeed is the case with those conditions which we hear most of under that name, and which make the greatest figure. There are even conditions which import nothing but burthen, without any spark of benefit. Accordingly, when between two parties there is such a relation, that one of them stands in the place of an object of property with respect to the other, the word *property* is applied only on one side; but the word *condition* is applied alike to both: it is but one of them that is said on that account to be possessed of a property; but both of them are alike spoken of as being possessed of or being invested with a condition: it is the master alone that is considered as possessing a property, of which the servant, in virtue of the services he is bound to render, is the object: but the servant, not less than the master, is spoken of as possessing or being invested with a condition.

The case is, that if a man's condition is ever spoken of as con-stituting an article of his *property*, it is in the same loose and in-definite sense of the word in which almost every other offence that could be imagined might be reckoned into the list of offences against property. If the language indeed were in every instance, in which it made use of the phrase, *object of property*,[1] perspicuous enough to point out under that appellation the material and really existent body, the *person* or the *thing* in which those acts terminate, by the performance of which the property is said to be *enjoyed*; if, in short, in the import given to the phrase *object of property*, it made no other use of it than the putting it to signify what is now called a corporeal *object*, this difficulty and this confusion would not have occurred. But the import of the phrase *object of property*, and in consequence the import of the word *property*, has been made to take a much wider range. In almost every case in which the law does any thing for a man's benefit or advantage, men are apt to speak of it, on some occasion or other, as conferring on him a sort of property. At the same time, for one reason or other, it has in several cases been not practicable, or not agreeable, to bring to view, under the appellation of *the object of his property*, the thing in which the acts, by the performance of which the property is said to be enjoyed, have their termination, or the person in whom they have their commencement. Yet something which could be spoken of under that appellation, was absolutely requisite.[12] The

[12] It is to be observed, that in common speech, in the phrase *the object of a man's property*, the words *the object of* are commonly left out; and by an ellip-sis, which, violent as it is, is now become more familiar than the phrase at length, they have made that part of it which consists of the words *a man's property*, perform the office of the whole. In some cases then it was only on a *part* of the object that the acts in question might be performed: and to say, on this account, that the object was a man's property, was as much as to intimate that they might be performed on any part. In other cases it was only certain particular acts that might be exercised on the object: and to say of the object that it was his property, was as much as to intimate that any acts whatever might be exercised on it. Sometimes the acts in question were not to be exercised but at a future *time*, nor then, perhaps, but in the case of the happening of a particular event, of which the happening was *uncertain*: and to say of an object that it was his property, was as much as to intimate that the acts in question might be exercised on it at any time. Sometimes the object on which the acts in question were to have their termination, or their com-mencement, was a human creature: and to speak of one human creature as being the property of another is what would shock the ear every where but

[1] At this point Bentham made the following Ms. marginal note in the copy of the 1789 edition now in the British Museum: 'For *object* of property say now A° 1827 *subject matter*.' In Bowring (i, 108n.) this was inserted as a footnote to the text.

expedient then has been to create, as it were, on every occasion, an ideal being, and to assign to a man this ideal being for the object of his property: and these are the sort of objects to which men of science, in taking a view of the operations of the law in this behalf, came, in process of time, to give the name of *incorporeal*. Now of these incorporeal objects of property the variety is prodigious. Fictitious entities of this kind have been fabricated almost out of every thing: not *conditions* only (that of a trustee included) but even *reputation* have been of the number. Even *liberty* has been considered in this same point of view: and though on so many occasions it is contrasted with *property*, yet on other occasions, being reckoned into the catalogue of possessions, it seems to have been considered as a branch of property. Some of these applications of the words *property, object of property*, (the last, for instance) are looked upon, indeed, as more figurative, and less proper than the rest: but since the truth is, that where the immediate object is incorporeal, they are all of them improper, it is scarce practicable any where to draw the line.

Notwithstanding all this latitude, yet, among the relations in virtue of which you are said to be possessed of a condition, there is one at least which can scarcely, by the most forced construction, be said to render any other man, or any other thing, the object of your property. This is the right of persevering in a certain course of action; for instance, in the exercising of a certain trade. Now to confer on you this right, in a certain degree at least, the law has nothing more to do than barely to abstain from forbidding you to exercise it. Were it to go farther, and, for the sake of enabling you to exercise your trade to the greater advantage, prohibit others from exercising the like, then, indeed, persons might be found, who in a certain sense, and by a construction rather forced than otherwise, might be spoken of as being the objects of your property: viz. by being made to render you that sort of negative service which consists in the forbearing to do those acts which would lessen the profits of your trade. But the ordinary right of exercising any such

where slavery is established, and even there, when applied to persons in any other condition than that of slaves. Among the first Romans, indeed, the wife herself was the property of her husband; the child, of his father; the servant, of his master. In the civilized nations of modern times, the two first kinds of property are altogether at an end: and the last, unhappily not yet at an end, but however verging, it is to be hoped, towards extinction. The husband's property, is now the company* of his wife; the father's the guardianship and service of his child; the master's the service of his servant.

* The *consortium*, says the English Law.

trade or profession, as is not the object of a monopoly, imports no such thing; and yet, by possessing this right, a man is said to possess a condition: and by forfeiting it, to forfeit his condition.[1]

After all, it will be seen, that there must be cases in which, according to the usage of language, the same offence may, with more or less appearance of propriety, be referred to the head of offences against condition, or that of offences against property indifferently. In such cases the following rule may serve for drawing the line. Wherever, in virtue of your possessing a property, or being the object of a property possessed by another, you are characterised, according to the usage of language, by a particular name, such as master, servant, husband, wife, steward, agent, attorney, or the like, there the word *condition* may be employed in exclusion of the word *property*: and an offence in which, in virtue of your bearing such relation, you are concerned, either in the capacity of an offender, or in that of a party injured, may be referred to the head of offences against condition, and not to that of offences against property. To give an example: Being bound, in the capacity of land steward to a certain person, to oversee the repairing of a certain bridge, you forbear to do so: in this case, as the services you are bound to render are of the number of those which give occasion to the party, from whom they are due, to be spoken of under a certain generical name, viz. that of land steward, the offence of withholding them may be referred to the class of offences against condition. But suppose that, without being engaged in that general and miscellaneous course of service, which with reference to a particular person would denominate you his land steward, you were bound, whether by usage or by contract, to render him that single sort of service which consists in the providing, by yourself or by others, for the repairing of that bridge: in this case, as there is not any such current denomination to which, in virtue of your being bound to render this service, you stand aggregated (for that of architect, mason, or the like, is not here in question) the offence you commit by withholding such service can not with propriety be referred to the class of offences against condition: it can only therefore be referred to the class of offences against property.

By way of further distinction, it may be remarked, that where a

---

[1] At this point in his copy of the 1789 edition Bentham inserted the following Ms. note: 'To condition in this case should be added the words *in life* to form a tri-compound analogous to *end-in-view art-and-science* etc.'. No use was made of this note in the 1823 edition (it may, like the note mentioned above on 211, n. 1, have been written at a later date). In the Bowring edition (i, 109n.) the first twelve words were inserted as a footnote.

man, in virtue of his being bound to render, or of others being bound to render him, certain services, is spoken of as possessing a condition, the assemblage of services is generally so considerable, in point of duration, as to constitute a course of considerable length so as on a variety of occasions to come to be varied and repeated: and in most cases, when the condition is not of a domestic nature, sometimes for the benefit of one person, sometimes for that of another. Services which come to be rendered to a particular person on a particular occasion, especially if they be of short duration, have seldom the effect of occasioning either party to be spoken of as being invested with a condition. The particular occasional services which one man may come, by contract or otherwise, to be bound to render to another, are innumerably various: but the number of conditions which have names may be counted, and are, comparatively, but few.

If after all, notwithstanding the rule here given for separating conditions from articles of property, any object should present itself which should appear to be referable, with equal propriety, to either head, the inconvenience would not be material; since in such cases, as will be seen a little farther on, whichever appellation were adopted, the list of the offences, to which the object stands exposed, would be substantially the same.

These difficulties being cleared up, we now proceed to exhibit an analytical view of the several possible offences against trust.

Offences against trust – their connection with each other

27. Offences against trust may be distinguished, in the first place, into such as concern the *existence* of the trust in the hands of such or such a person, and such as concern the *exercise* of the functions that belong to it.[12] First then, with regard to such as relate

[12] We shall have occasion, a little farther on, to speak of the person in whose hands the trust exists, under the description of the person who possesses, or is in possession of it, and thence of the possession of the trust abstracted from the consideration of the possessor. However different the expression, the import is in both cases the same. So irregular and imperfect is the structure of language on this head, that no one phrase can be made to suit the idea on all the occasions on which it is requisite it should be brought to view: the phrase must be continually shifted, or new modified: so likewise in regard to conditions, and in regard to property. The being invested with, or possessing a condition: the being in possession of an article of property, that is, if the object of the property be corporeal; the having a legal title (defeasible or indefeasible) to the physical possession of it, answers to the being in possession of a trust, or the being the person in whose hands a trust exists. In like manner, to the *exercise* of the *functions* belonging to a trust, or to a condition, corresponds the *enjoyment* of an article of property; that is, if the object of it be corporeal, the *occupation*. These verbal discussions are equally tedious and indispensable.

to its existence. An offence of this description, like one of any other description, if an offence it ought to be, must to some person or other import a prejudice. This prejudice may be distinguished into two branches: 1. That which may fall on such persons as are or should be invested with the trust: 2. That which may fall on the persons for whose sake it is or should be instituted, or on other persons at large. To begin with the former of these branches. Let any trust be conceived. The consequences which it is in the nature of it to be productive of to the possessor, must, in as far as they are *material*,[k2] be either of an advantageous or of a disadvantageous nature: in as far as they are advantageous, the trust may be considered as a *benefit* or privilege: in as far as they are disadvantageous, it may be considered as a *burthen*.[12] To consider it then upon the footing of a benefit. The trust either is of the number of those which ought by law to subsist[m2]; that is, which the legislator

Striving to cut a new road through the wilds of jurisprudence, I find myself continually distressed, for want of tools that are fit to work with. To frame a complete set of new ones is impossible. All that can be done is, to make here and there a new one in cases of absolute necessity, and for the test, to patch up from time to time the imperfections of the old.

As to the bipartition which this paragraph sets out with, it must be acknowledged not to be of the nature of those which to a first glance afford a sort of intuitive proof of their being exhaustive. There is not that marked connection and opposition between the terms of it, which subsists between contradictory terms and between terms that have the same common genus. I imagine, however, that upon examination it would be found to be exhaustive notwithstanding: and that it might even be demonstrated so to be. But the demonstration would lead us too far out of the ordinary track of language.

[k2] See Ch. VII (Actions) 3.

[12] If advantageous, it will naturally be on account of the *powers* or *rights* that are annexed to the trust: if disadvantageous, on account of the *duties*.

[m2] It may seem a sort of anachronism to speak on the present occasion of a trust, condition, or other possession, as one of which it may happen that a man ought or ought not to have had possession given him by the law. For the plan here set out upon is to give such a view all along of the laws that are proposed, as shall be taken from the reasons which there are for making them: the reason then it would seem should subsist before the law: not the law before the reason. Nor is this to be denied: for, unquestionably, upon the principle of utility, it may be said with equal truth of those operations by which a trust, or any other article of property, is instituted, as of any other operations of the law, that it never can be expedient they should be performed, unless some reason for performing them, deduced from that principle, can be assigned. To give property to one man, you must impose obligation on another: you must oblige him to do something which he may have a mind not to do, or to abstain from doing something which he may have a mind to do: in a word, you must in some way or other expose him to inconvenience. Every such law, therefore, must at any rate be mischievous in the first instance; and if no good effects

meant should be established; or is not. If it *is*, the possession which at any time you may be deprived of, with respect to it, must at that time be either present or to come: if to come (in which case it may be regarded either as certain or as contingent) the investitive event, or event from whence your possession of it should have taken its commencement, was either an event in the production of which the will of the offender should have been instrumental, or any other event at large: in the former case, the offence may be termed *wrongful non-investment of trust*: in the latter case, *wrongful interception of trust*.[n2] If at the time of the offence whereby you are

can be produced to set against the bad, it must be mischievous upon the whole. Some reasons, therefore, in this case, as in every other, there ought to be. The truth is, that in the case before us, the reasons are of too various and complicated a nature to be brought to view in an analytical outline like the present. Where the offence is of the number of those by which *person* or *reputation* are affected, the reasons for prohibiting it lie on the surface, and apply to every man alike. But *property*, before it can be offended against, must be created, and at the instant of its creation distributed, as it were, into parcels of different sorts and sizes, which require to be assigned, some to one man and some to another, for reasons, of which many lie a little out of sight, and which being different in different cases, would take up more room than could consistently be allotted to them here. For the present purpose, it is sufficient if it appear, that for the carrying on of the several purposes of life, there are trusts, and conditions, and other articles of property, which must be possessed by somebody: and that it is not every article that can, nor every article that ought, to be possessed by every body. What articles ought to be created, and to what persons and in what cases they ought to be respectively assigned, are questions which cannot be settled here. Nor is there any reason for wishing that they could, since the settling them one way or another is what would make no difference in the nature of any offence whereby any party may be exposed, on the occasion of any such institution to sustain a detriment.

[n2] In the former case it may be observed, the act is of the negative kind: in the latter, it will commonly be of the positive kind.

As to the expression *non-investment of trust*, I am sensible that it is not perfectly consonant to the idiom of the language: the usage is to speak of a person as being invested (that is clothed) with a trust, not of a trust as of a thing, that is itself *invested*, or *put on*. The phrase at length would be, *the non-investment of a person with a trust*: but this phrase is by much too long-winded to answer the purpose of an appellative. I saw, therefore, no other resource than to venture upon the ellipsis here employed. The ancient lawyers, in the construction of their appellatives, have indulged themselves in much harsher ellipsises without scruple. See above, 25 note. It is already the usage to speak of a trust as a thing that *vests*, and as a thing that may be *divested*.

(Investment and Divestment)[1]. More simply and characteristically, as well

[1] This note on the terms investment and divestment was added by Bentham in 1789. It is not entirely clear where he meant it to be placed, but it seems most convenient to treat it as a continuation of n. *n*2. The addition was overlooked in the 1823, Bowring and later editions.

deprived of it, you were already in possession of it, the offence may be styled *wrongful divestment of trust*. In any of these cases, the effect of the offence is either to put somebody else into the trust, or not: if not, it is wrongful divestment,[1] wrongful interception, or wrongful divestment, and nothing more: if it be, the person put in possession is either the wrong doer himself, in which case it may be styled *usurpation of trust*; or some other person, in which case it may be styled *wrongful investment*, or attribution, *of trust*. If the trust in question is *not* of the number of those which ought to subsist, it depends upon the manner in which one man deprives another of it, whether such deprivation shall or shall not be an offence, and, accordingly, whether non-investment, interception, or divestment, shall or shall not be wrongful. But the putting any body into it must at any rate be an offence: and this offence may be either usurpation or wrongful investment, as before.

In the next place, to consider it upon the footing of a burthen. In this point of view, if no other interest than that of the persons liable to be invested with it were considered, it is what ought not, upon the principle of utility, to subsist: if it ought, it can only be for the sake of the persons in whose favour it is established. If then it ought *not* on any account to subsist, neither non-investment, interception, nor divestment, can be wrongful with relation to the persons first-mentioned, whatever they may be on any other account, in respect of the manner in which they happen to be performed: for usurpation, though not likely to be committed, there is the same room as before: so likewise is there for wrongful investment; which, in as far as the trust is considered as a burthen, may be styled *wrongful imposition of trust*. If the trust, being still of the burthensome kind, is of the number of those which *ought* to subsist, any offence that can be committed, with relation to the existence of it, must consist either in causing a person to *be* in possession of it, who ought *not* to be, or in causing a person *not* to be in possession of it who *ought* to be: in the former case, it must be either usurpation or wrongful divestment, as before: in the latter case, the person

as more commodiously for grammatical construction, collation and ablation. So afterwards, p. 227, par. 35,[2] instead of *investitive* and *divestitive events*, *collative* and *ablative*. But on different occasions, each of these different sets of terms may have its use.

[1] Thus all editions; but to complete the enumeration of the possibilities in the order followed above it seems necessary to read 'non-investment' for 'divestment' at this point.

[2] Bentham of course gives a page-reference to the 1780 text here; and the paragraph number appears in Roman numerals.

who is caused to be not in possession, is either the wrong-doer himself, or some other: if the wrong-doer himself, either at the time of the offence he was in possession of it, or he was not: if he was, it may be termed *wrongful abdication* of trust; if not, *wrongful detrectation*[o2] or *non-assumption*: if the person, whom the offence causes not to be in the trust, is any other person, the offence must be either wrongful divestment, wrongful non-investment, or wrongful interception, as before: in any of which cases, to consider the trust in the light of a burthen, it might also be styled *wrongful exemption from trust.*

Lastly, with regard to the prejudice which the persons for whose benefit the trust is instituted, or any other persons whose interests may come to be affected by its existing or not existing in such or such hands, are liable to sustain. Upon examination it will appear, that by every sort of offence whereby the persons who are or should be in possession of it are liable, in that respect, to sustain a prejudice, the persons now in question are also liable to sustain a prejudice. The prejudice, in this case, is evidently of a very different nature from what it was of in the other: but the same general names will be applicable in this case as in that. If the beneficiaries, or persons whose interests are at stake upon the exercise of the trust, or any of them, are liable to sustain a prejudice, resulting from the quality of the person by whom it may be filled, such prejudice must result from the one or the other of two causes: 1. From a person's having the possession of it who ought not to have it: or 2. From a person's not having it who ought: whether it be a benefit or burthen to the possessor, is a circumstance that to this purpose makes no difference. In the first of these cases the offences from which the prejudice takes its rise are those of usurpation of trust, wrongful attribution of trust, and wrongful imposition of trust: in the latter, wrongful non-investment of trust, wrongful interception of trust, wrongful divestment of trust, wrongful abdication of trust, and wrongful detrectation of trust.

So much for the offences which concern the existence or possession of a trust: those which concern the exercise of the functions that

[o2] (Detrectation). I do not find that this word has yet been received into the English language.[1] In the Latin, however, it is very expressive, and is used in a sense exactly suitable to the sense here given to it. *Militiam detrectare*, to endeavour to avoid serving in the army, is a phrase not unfrequently met with in the Roman writers.

[1] In fact, though rare, the word was not unknown in English: the *O.E.D.* cites instances from 17th-century authors. The words 'or *non-assumption*' following 'detrectation' were an insertion of 1783.

belong to it may be thus conceived. You are in possession of a trust: the time then for your acting in it must, on any given occasion, neglecting, for simplicity's sake, the then present instant) be either past or yet to come. If past, your conduct on that occasion must have been either conformable to the purposes for which the trust was instituted, or unconformable: if conformable, there has been no mischief in case: if unconformable, the fault has been either in yourself alone, or in some other person, or in both: in as far as it has lain in yourself, it has consisted either in your *not* doing something which you ought to do, in which case it may be styled *negative breach of trust*; or in your *doing* something which you ought *not* to do: if in the doing something which you ought not to do, the party to whom the prejudice has accrued is either the same for whose benefit the trust was instituted, or some other party at large: in the former of these cases, the offences may be styled *positive breach of trust*; in the other *abuse of trust*.p2 In as far as the fault lies in another person, the offence on his part may be styled *disturbance of trust*. Supposing the time for your acting in the trust to be yet to come, the effect of any act which tends to render your conduct unconformable to the purposes of the trust, may be either to render it actually and eventually unconformable, or to produce a chance of its being so. In the former of these cases, it can do no otherwise than take one or other of the shapes that have just been mentioned. In the latter case, the blame must lie either in yourself alone, or in some other person, or in both together, as before. If in another person, the acts whereby he may tend to render your conduct un-

p2 What is here meant by abuse of trust, is the exercise of a power usurped over strangers, under favour of the powers properly belonging to the trust. The distinction between what is here meant by breach of trust, and what is here meant by abuse of trust, is not very steadily observed in common speech: and in regard to public trusts, it will even in many cases be imperceptible. The two offences are, however, in themselves perfectly distinct: since the persons, by whom the prejudice is suffered, are in many cases altogether different. It may be observed, perhaps, that with regard to abuse of trust, there is but one species here mentioned[1]; viz. that which corresponds to positive breach of trust: none being mentioned as corresponding to negative breach of trust. The reason of this distinction will presently appear. In favour of the parties, for whose benefit the trust was created, the trustee is bound to act; and therefore merely by his doing nothing they may receive a prejudice: but in favour of other persons at large he is not bound to act: and therefore it is only from some positive act on his part that any prejudice can ensue to them.

[1] In the 1789 text this sentence begins as follows: 'It may be noticed, perhaps, for a moment, as an omission, that of abuse of trust, no more than one species is here mentioned . . .'

conformable, must be exercised either on yourself, or on other objects at large. If exercised on yourself, the influence they possess must either be such as operates immediately on your body, or such as operates immediately on your mind. In the latter case, again, the tendency of them must be to deprive you either of the knowledge, or of the power, or of the inclination,[q2] which would be necessary to your maintaining such a conduct as shall be conformable to the purposes in question. If they be such, of which the tendency is to deprive you of the inclination in question, it must be by applying to your will the force of some *seducing* motive.[r2] Lastly, this motive must be either of the *coercive*, or of the *alluring* kind; in other words, it must present itself either in the shape of a mischief or of an advantage. Now in none of all the cases that have been mentioned, except the last, does the offence receive any new denomination; according to the event it is either a disturbance of trust, or an abortive attempt to be guilty of that offence. In this last it is termed *bribery*; and it is that particular species of it which may be termed *active* bribery, or *bribe-giving*. In this case, to consider the matter on your part, either you accept of the bribe, or you do not: if not, and you do not afterwards commit, or go about to commit, either a breach or an abuse of trust, there is no offence, on your part, in the case: if you do accept it, whether you eventually do or do not commit the breach or the abuse which it is the bribe-givers intention you should commit, you at any rate commit an offence which is also termed bribery: and which, for distinction sake may be termed *passive* bribery, or *bribe-taking*.[s2] As to any farther distinctions, they will depend upon the nature of the particular sort of trust in question, and therefore belong not to the present place. And thus we have thirteen sub-divisions of offences against trust: viz. 1. Wrongful non-investment of trust. 2. Wrongful interception of trust. 3. Wrongful divestment of trust. 4. Usur-

---

[q2] See infra; and Ch. xviii (Indirect Legislation).[1]

[r2] See Ch. xi (Dispositions) 29.

[s2] To bribe a trustee, as such, is in fact neither more nor less than to *suborn* him to be guilty of a breach or an abuse of trust. Now subornation is of the number of those *accessory* offences which every principal offence, one as well as another, is liable to be attended with. See infra, and B. I. tit. (Accessory offences.) This particular species of subornation however, being one that, besides its having a specific name framed to express it, is apt to engage a particular share of attention, and to present itself to view in company with other offences against trust, it would have seemed an omission not to have included it in that catalogue.

[1] See above 124 n. 1.

pation of trust. 5. Wrongful investment or attribution of trust. 6. Wrongful abdication of trust. 7. Wrongful detrectation of trust. 8. Wrongful imposition of trust. 9. Negative breach of trust. 10. Positive breach of trust. 11. Abuse of trust. 12. Disturbance of trust. 13. Bribery.

28. From what has been said, it appears that there cannot be any other offences, on the part of a trustee, by which a *beneficiary* can receive on any particular occasion any assignable specific prejudice. One sort of acts, however, there are by which a trustee may be put in some *danger* of receiving a prejudice, although neither the nature of the prejudice, nor the occasion on which he is in danger of receiving it, should be assignable. These can be no other than such acts, whatever they may be, as dispose the trustee to be acted upon by a given bribe with greater effect than any with which he could otherwise be acted upon: or in other words, which place him in such circumstances as have a tendency to encrease the quantum of his sensibility to the action of any motive of the sort in question.[t2] Of these acts, there seem to be no others, that will admit of a description applicable to all places and times alike, than acts of *prodigality* on the part of the trustee. But in acts of this nature the prejudice to the *beneficiary* is contingent only and unliquidated; while the prejudice to the trustee himself is certain and liquidated. If therefore on any occasion it should be found advisable to treat it on the footing of an offence, it will find its place more naturally in the class of self-regarding ones.

Prodigality in trustees dismissed to Class 3

29. As to the sub-divisions of offences against trust, these are perfectly analogous to those of offences by falsehood. The trust may be private, semi-public, or public: it may concern property, person, reputation, or condition; or any two or more of those articles at a time: as will be more particularly explained in another place. Here too the offence, in running over the ground occupied by the three prior classes, will in some instances change its name, while in others it will not.

The sub-divisions of offences against trust are also determined by the divisions of the preceding classes

30. Lastly, if it be asked, what sort of relation there subsists between falsehoods on one hand, and offences concerning trust on the other hand; the answer is, they are altogether disparate. Falsehood is a circumstance that may enter into the composition of any sort of offence, those concerning trust, as well as any other: in some as an accidental, in others as an essential instrument. Breach or abuse of trust are circumstances which, in the character of accidental concomitants, may enter into the composition of any

Connection between offences by falsehood and offences against trust

[t2] See Ch. VI (Sensibility) 2.

other offences (those against falsehood included) besides those to which they respectively give name.

iii.[1] *Genera of Class* I

Analysis into genera pursued no farther than Class 1

31. Returning now to class the first, let us pursue the distribution a step farther, and branch out the several divisions of that class, as above exhibited, into their respective *genera*, that is, into such minuter divisions as are capable of being characterised by denominations of which a great part are already current among the people.[u2] In this place the analysis must stop. To apply it in the same regular form to any of the other classes seems scarcely practicable: to semi-public, as also to public offences, on account of the interference of local circumstances: to self-regarding ones, on account of the necessity it would create of deciding prematurely upon points which may appear liable to controversy: to offences by falsehood, and offences against trust, on account of the dependence there is between this class and the three former. What remains to be done in this way, with reference to these four classes, will require discussion, and will therefore be introduced with more propriety in the body of the work, than in a preliminary part, of which the business is only to draw outlines.

Offences against an individual may be simple in their effects, or complex

32. An act, by which the happiness of an individual is disturbed, is either *simple* in its effects or *complex*. It may be styled simple in its effects, when it affects him in one only of the articles or points in which his interest, as we have seen, is liable to be affected: complex, when it affects him in several of those points at once. Such as are simple in their effects must of course be first considered.

Offences against person – their genera

33. In a simple way, that is in one way at a time, a man's happiness is liable to be disturbed either 1. by actions referring to his own person itself; or 2. by actions referring to such external objects on which his happiness is more or less dependent. As to his own person, it is composed of two different parts, or reputed parts,[2] his

---

[u2] In the enumeration of these genera, it is all along to be observed, that offences of an accessory nature are not mentioned; except unless it be here and there where they have obtained current names which seemed too much in vogue to be omitted. Accessory offences are those which, without being the very acts from which the mischief in question takes its immediate rise, are, in the way of causality, connected with those acts. See Ch. vii (Actions) 24 and B. I. tit. (Accessory offences).

[1] The number of this section is omitted in the 1789, 1823, and Bowring editions. It is supplied in the Harrison edition (p. 347); and the numbering of § iv (270 below) shows that this is correct.

[2] The words 'or reputed parts' are an 1823 addition.

body and his mind. Acts which exert a pernicious influence on his person, whether it be on the corporeal or on the mental part of it, will operate thereon either immediately, and without affecting his will, or mediately, through the intervention of that faculty: viz. by means of the influence which they cause his will to exercise over his body. If with the intervention of his will, it must be by *mental coercion*: that is, by causing him to *will* to maintain, and thence actually to maintain, a certain conduct which it is disagreeable, or in any other way pernicious, to him to maintain. This conduct may either be positive or negative[v2]: when positive, the coercion is styled *compulsion* or *con*straint: when negative, *re*straint. Now the way in which the coercion is disagreeable to him, may be by producing either pain of body, or only pain of mind. If pain of body is produced by it, the offence will come as well under this as under other denominations, which we shall come to presently. Moreover, the conduct which a man, by means of the coercion, is forced to maintain, will be determined either specifically, and originally by the determination of the particular acts themselves, which he is forced to perform or to abstain from, or generally and incidentally, by means of his being forced to be or not to be in such or such a place. But if he is prevented from being in one place, he is confined thereby to another. For the whole surface of the earth, like the surface of any greater or lesser body, may be conceived to be divided into two, as well as into any other number of parts or spots. If the spot then, which he is confined to, be smaller than the spot which he is excluded from, his condition may be called *confinement*: if larger, *banishment*.[w2] Whether an act, the effect of which is to exert a pernicious influence on the person of him who suffers by it, operates with or without the intervention of an act of his will, the mischief it produces will either be *mortal* or *not mortal*. If not mortal, it will either be *reparable*, that is temporary; or *irreparable*, that is perpetual. If reparable, the mischievous act may be termed a *simple corporal injury*; if irreparable, an *irreparable corporal injury*. Lastly, a pain that a man experiences in his mind will either be a pain of actual *sufferance*, or a pain of *apprehension*. If a pain of apprehension, either the offender himself is represented as intending to bear a part in the production of it, or he is not. In the former

[v2] Ch. vii (Actions) 8.

[w2] Of these, and the several other leading expressions which there is occasion to bring to view in the remaining part of this analysis, ample definitions will be found in the body of the work, conceived *in terminis legis*. To give particular references to these definitions, would be encumbering the page to little purpose.

case the offence may be styled *menacement*: in the latter case, as also where the pain is a pain of actual sufferance, a *simple mental injury*. And thus we have nine *genera* or kinds of personal injuries; which, when ranged in the order most commodious for examination, will stand as follows; viz. 1. Simple corporal injuries. 2. Irreparable corporal injuries. 3. Simple injurious restrainment. 4. Simple injurious compulsion.^{x2} 5. Wrongful confinement. 6. Wrongful banishment. 7. Wrongful homicide. 8. Wrongful menacement.^{y2} 9. Simple mental injuries.^{z2}

^{x2} Injurious restrainment at large, and injurious compulsion at large, are here styled *simple*, in order to distinguish them from confinement, banishment, robbery, and extortion; all which are, in many cases, but so many modifications of one or other of the two first-mentioned offences.

To constitute an offence an act of simple injurious restrainment, or simple injurious compulsion, it is sufficient if the influence it exerts be, in the first place, pernicious; in the next place, exerted on the person by the medium of the will: it is not necessary that that part of the person on which it is exerted be the part to which it is pernicious: it is not even necessary that it should immediately be pernicious to either of these parts, though to one or other of them it must be pernicious in the long-run, if it be pernicious at all. An act in which the body, for example, is concerned, may be very disagreeable, and thereby pernicious to him who performs it, though neither disagreeable nor pernicious to his body: for instance, to stand or sit in public with a label on his back, or under any other circumstances of ignominy.

^{y2} It may be observed, that wrongful menacement is included as well in simple injurious restrainment, as in[1] simple injurious compulsion, except in the rare case where the motives by which one man is prevented by another from doing a thing that would have been materially to his advantage, or induced to do a thing that is materially to his prejudice, are of the *alluring* kind.

^{z2} Although, for reasons that have been already given, (supra 31) no complete catalogue, nor therefore any exhaustive view, of either semi-public or self-regarding offences, can be exhibited in this chapter, it may be a satisfaction, however, to the reader, to see some sort of list of them, if it were only for the sake of having examples before his eyes. Such lists cannot any where be placed to more advantage than under the heads of the several divisions of private extra-regarding offences, to which the semi-public and self-regarding offences in question respectively correspond. Concerning the two latter, however, and the last more particularly, it must be understood that all I mean by inserting them here, is to exhibit the mischief, if any, which it is of the nature of them respectively to produce, without deciding upon the question, whether it would be *worth while* (See Ch. XIII Cases unmeet) in every instance, for the sake of combating that mischief, to introduce the evil of punishment. In the course of this detail, it will be observed, that there are several heads of extra-regarding private offences, to which the correspondent heads, either of semi-public or self-regarding offences, or of both, are wanting. The reasons of these deficiencies will probably, in most instances, be evident enough upon the face of them. Lest they should not, they are however specified in the body of

[1] The 1823 and later editions mistakenly read 'and' for 1789 'as in'.

34. We come now to offences against reputation merely. These *Offences* require but few distinctions. In point of reputation there is but one *against* way of suffering, which is by losing a portion of the good-will of *reputation* others. Now, in respect of the good-will which others bear you, you may be a loser in either of two ways: 1. by the manner in which you are thought to behave *yourself*; and 2. by the manner in which

the work. They would take up too much room were they to be inserted here.

I. SEMI-PUBLIC OFFENCES through calamity. Calamities, by which the persons or properties of men, or both, are liable to be affected, seem to be as follows: 1. Pestilence or contagion. 2. Famine, and other kinds of scarcity. 3. Mischiefs producible by persons deficient in point of understanding, such as infants, idiots, and maniacs, for want of their being properly taken care of. 4. Mischief producible by the ravages of noxious animals, such as beasts of prey, locusts, etc. etc. 5. Collapsion, or fall of large masses of solid matter, such as decayed buildings, or rocks, or masses of snow. 6. Inundation or submersion. 7. Tempest. 8. Blight. 9. Conflagration. 10. Explosion. In as far as a man may contribute, by any imprudent act of his, to give birth to any of the above calamities, such act may be an offence. In as far as a man may fail to do what is incumbent on him to do towards preventing them, such failure may be an offence.

II. SEMI-PUBLIC OFFENCES of mere delinquency. A whole neighbourhood may be made to suffer, 1. Simple corporal injuries: in other words, they may be made to suffer in point of health, by offensive or dangerous trades or manufactures: by selling or falsely puffing off unwholesome medicines or provisions: by poisoning or drying up of springs, destroying of aqueducts, destroying woods, walls, or other fences against wind and rain: by any kinds of artificial scarcity; or by any other calamities intentionally produced. 2. and 3. Simple injurious restrainment, and simple injurious compulsion: for instance, by obliging a whole neighbourhood, by dint of threatening hand-bills, or threatening discourses, publicly delivered, to join, or forbear to join, in illuminations, acclamations, outcries, invectives, subscriptions, undertakings, processions, or any other mode of expressing joy or grief, displeasure or approbation; or, in short, in any other course of conduct whatsoever. 4. and 5. Confinement and banishment: by the spoiling of roads, bridges, or ferry-boats: by destroying or unwarrantably pre-occupying public carriages, or houses of accommodation. 6. By menacement: as by incendiary letters, and tumultuous assemblies: by newspapers or hand-bills, denouncing vengeance against persons of particular denominations: for example, against Jews, Catholics, Protestants, Scotchmen, Gascons, Catalonians, etc. 7. Simple mental injuries: as by distressful, terrifying, obscene, or irreligious exhibitions; such as exposure of sores by beggars, exposure of dead bodies, exhibitions or reports of counterfeit witchcrafts or apparitions, exhibition of obscene or blasphemous prints: obscene or blasphemous discourses held in public; spreading false news of public defeats in battle, or of other misfortunes.

III. SELF-REGARDING OFFENCES against person. 1. Fasting, abstinence from venery, self-flagellation, self-mutilation, and other self-denying and self-tormenting practices. 2. Gluttony, drunkenness, excessive venery, and other species of intemperance. 3. Suicide.

others behave, or are thought to behave, towards you. To cause people to think that you yourself have so behaved, as to have been guilty of any of those acts which cause a man to possess less than he did before of the good-will of the community, is what may be styled *defamation*. But such is the constitution of human nature, and such the force of prejudice, that a man merely by manifesting his own want of good-will towards you, though ever so unjust in itself, and ever so unlawfully expressed, may in a manner force others to withdraw from you a part of theirs. When he does this by words, or by such actions as have no other effect than in as far as they stand in the place of words, the offence may be styled *vilification*. When it is done by such actions as, besides their having this effect, are injuries to the person, the offence may be styled a *personal insult*: if it has got the length of reaching the body, a *corporal insult*: if it stopped short before it reached that length, it may be styled *insulting menacement*. And thus we have two *genera* or kinds of offences against reputation merely; to wit, 1. Defamation: and, 2. Vilification, or revilement.[1][a3] As to corporal insults, and insulting menacement, they belong to the compound title of offences against person and reputation both together.

Offences against property

35. If the property of one man suffers by the delinquency of another, such property either was in trust with the offender, or it was not: if it was in trust, the offence is a breach of trust, and of whatever nature it may be in other respects, may be styled *dissipation in breach of trust*, or *dissipation of property in trust*. This is a particular case: the opposite one is the more common: in such case the several ways in which property may, by possibility, become the object of an offence, may be thus conceived. Offences against property, of whatever kind it be, may be distinguished, as hath been already intimated,[b3] into such as concern the legal possession of it, or right to it, and such as concern only the enjoyment of it, or, what is the same thing, the exercise of that right. Under the former of these heads come, as hath been already intimated,[c3] the several offences of *wrongful non-investment, wrongful interception, wrongful divestment, usurpation,* and *wrongful attribution*. When in the commission of any of these offences a falsehood has served as an instrument, and that, as it is commonly called, a *wilful*, or as it might

[a3] I. SEMI-PUBLIC OFFENCES. 1. Calumniation and vilification of particular denominations of persons; such as Jews, Catholics, etc.
    II. SELF-REGARDING OFFENCES. 1. Incontinence in females. 2. Incest.
[b3] Supra 27.
[c3] Ibid.
[1] The words 'or revilement' were added in 1783.

more properly be termed, an *advised*[d3] one, the epithet *fraudulent* may be prefixed to the name of the offence, or substituted in the room of the word *wrongful.* The circumstance of fraudulency then may serve to characterise a particular species, comprisable under each of those generic heads: in like manner the circumstance of *force*, of which more a little farther on, may serve to characterise another. With respect to wrongful interception in particular, the *investitive event* by which the title to the thing in question should have accrued to you, and for want of which such title is, through the delinquency of the offender, as it were, *intercepted*, is either an act of his own, expressing it as his will, that you should be considered by the law as the person who is legally in possession of it, or it is any other event at large: in the former case, if the thing, of which you should have been put into possession, is a sum of money to a certain amount, the offence is that which has received the name of *insolvency*; which branch of delinquency, in consideration of the importance and extent of it, may be treated on the footing of a distinct genus of itself.[e3]

[d3] See Ch. ix (Consciousness) 2.

[e3] The light in which the offence of insolvency is here exhibited, may per- *Payment,* haps at first consideration be apt to appear not only novel but improper. It *what* may naturally enough appear, that when a man owes you a sum of money, for instance, the right to the money is yours already, and that what he with- holds from you by not paying you, is not the legal title to it, possession of it, or power over it, but the physical possession of it, or power over it, only. But upon a more accurate examination this will be found not to be the case. What is meant by payment, is always an act of investitive power, as above explained, an expression of an act of the will, and not a physical act: it is an act exercised *with relation* indeed *to* the thing said to be *paid*, but not in a physical sense exercised *upon* it. A man who owes you ten pounds, takes up a handful of silver to that amount, and lays it down on a table at which you are sitting. If then by words, or gestures, or any means whatever, addressing himself to you, he intimates it to be his will that you should take up the money, and do with it as you please, he is said to have *paid* you: but if the case was, that he laid it down not for that purpose, but for some other, for instance, to count it and examine it, meaning to take it up again himself, or leave it for somebody else, he has *not* paid you: yet the physical acts, exercised upon the pieces of money in question, are in both cases the same. Till he does express a will to that purport, what you have is not, properly speaking, the legal possession of the money, or a right to the money, but only a right to have him, or in his default perhaps a minister of justice, compelled to render you that sort of service, by the rendering of which he is said to pay you: that is, to express such will as above-mentioned, with regard to some corporeal article, or other of a certain species, and of value equal to the amount of what he owes you: or, in other words, to exercise in your favour an act of investitive power with relation to some such article.

Next, with regard to such of the offences against property as concern only the enjoyment of the object in question. This object must be either a service, or set of services,[f3] which should have been rendered by some *person*, or else an article belonging to the class of *things*. In the former case, the offence may be styled *wrongful withholding of services*.[g3] In the latter case it may admit of farther

True it is, that in certain cases a man may perhaps not be deemed, according to common acceptation, to have *paid* you, without rendering you a further set of services, and those of another sort: a set of services, which are rendered by the exercising of certain acts of a physical nature upon the very thing with which he is said to pay you: to wit, by transferring the thing to a certain place where you may be sure to find it, and where it may be convenient for you to receive it. But these services, although the obligation of rendering them should be annexed by law to the obligation of rendering those other services, in the performance of which the operation of payment properly consists, are plainly acts of a distinct nature: nor are they essential to the operation: by themselves they do not constitute it, and it may be performed without them. It *must* be performed without them wherever the thing to be transferred happens to be already as much within the reach, physically speaking, of the creditor, as by any act of the debtor it can be made to be.

This matter would have appeared in a clearer light had it been practicable to enter here into a full examination of the nature of property, and the several modifications of which it is susceptible: but every thing cannot be done at once.

[f3] Supra 26.

[g3] Under wrongful withholding of services is included *breach of contract*: for the obligation to render services may be grounded either on contract, or upon other titles: in other words, the event of a man's engaging in a contract is one out of many other investitive events from which the right of receiving them may take its commencement.[1]

Were the word *services* to be taken in its utmost latitude (negative included as well as positive) this one head would be enough to[2] cover the whole law. To this place then are to be referred such services only, the withholding of which does not coincide with any of the other offences, for which separate denominations have been provided.

There are some services, we may observe, the withholding of which may affect the person, and by that means come under the negative branches of the several *genera* of corporal *injuries* such as services due from a surgeon, an innkeeper, etc.[3]

[1] In the text as printed in 1780 this paragraph ends with the following reference: 'See Ch. xvii (Limits) §iv.' In 1783 Bentham indicated that this reference (to a section of Ch. xvii which had by then become part of the great extension of *An Introduction to the Principles* published in the present edition as *Of Laws in General*) should be deleted. But the deletion was not made in the 1823 edition nor in the Bowring and later editions.

[2] The words 'be enough to' were an insertion of 1783, overlooked in 1823 and later editions following that text, but duly made in the Bowring edition (i, 117n.).

[3] This third paragraph was added to the note in 1783, but the addition was not made in 1823. The Bowring text makes the insertion.

modifications, which may be thus conceived: When any object which you have had the physical occupation or enjoyment of, ceases, in any degree, in consequence of the act of another man, and without any change made in so much of that power as depends upon the intrinsic physical condition of your person, to be subject to that power; this cessation is either owing to change in the intrinsic condition of the thing itself, or in its exterior situation with respect to you, that is, to its being situated out of your reach. In the former case, the nature of the change is either such as to put it out of your power to make any use of it at all, in which case the thing is said to be *destroyed*, and the offence whereby it is so treated may be termed *wrongful destruction*: or such only as to render the uses it is capable of being put to of less value than before, in which case it is said to be *damaged*, or to have sustained damage, and the offence may be termed *wrongful endamagement*. Moreover, in as far as the value which a thing is of to you is considered as being liable to be in some degree impaired, by any act on the part of any other person exercised upon that thing, although on a given occasion no perceptible damage should ensue, the exercise of any such act is commonly treated on the footing of an offence, which may be termed *wrongful using or occupation*.

If the cause of the thing's failing in its capacity of being of use to you, lies in the exterior situation of it with relation to you, the offence may be styled *wrongful detainment*[h3] or *detention*.[1] Wrongful detainment, during any given period of time, may either be accompanied with the intention of detaining the thing for ever, (that is for an indifferent time) or not: if it be, and if it be accompanied at the same time with the intention of not being amenable to law for what is done, it seems to answer to the idea commonly annexed

[h3] In the English law, *detinue* and *detainer*: detinue applied chiefly to moveables; detainer, to immoveables. Under detinue and detainer cases are also comprised, in which the offence consists in forbearing to transfer the legal possession of the thing: such cases may be considered as coming under the head of wrongful non-investment. The distinction between mere physical possession and legal possession, where the latter is short-lived and defeasible, seems scarcely hitherto to have been attended to. In a multitude of instances they are confounded under the same expressions. The cause is, that probably under all laws, and frequently for very good reasons, the legal possession, with whatever certainty defeasible upon the event of a trial, is, down to the time of that event, in many cases annexed to the appearance of the physical.

[1] The words 'or *detention*' were added in 1783. There is some ambiguity in Bentham's instruction, and the 1823 edition made the insertion after the next occurrence of the word 'detainment'. The insertion was made as above in the Bowring edition (i, 117).

to the word *embezzlement,* an offence which is commonly accompanied with breach of trust.[13] In the case of wrongful occupation, the physical faculty of occupying may have been obtained with or without the assistance or consent of the proprietor, or other person appearing to have a right to afford such assistance or consent. If without such assistance or consent, and the occupation be accompanied with the intention of detaining the thing for ever, together with the intention of not being amenable to law for what is done, the offence seems to answer to the idea commonly annexed to the word *theft* or *stealing.* If in the same circumstances a force is put upon the body of any person who uses, or appears to be disposed to use, any endeavours to prevent the act, this seems to be one of the cases in which the offence is generally understood to come under the name of *robbery.*

If the physical faculty in question was obtained with the assistance or consent of a proprietor, or other person above spoken of, and still the occupation of the thing is an offence, it may have been either because the assistance or consent was not fairly, or because it was not freely obtained. If not *fairly* obtained, it was obtained by falsehood, which, if *advised,* is in such a case termed *fraud:* and the offence, if accompanied with the intention of not being amenable to law, may be termed *fraudulent obtainment* or *defraudment.*[13] If not *freely* obtained, it was obtained by *force:* to wit, either by a force put upon the body, which has been already mentioned, or by a force put upon the mind. If by a force put upon the mind, or in other words, by the application of coercive motives,[k3] it must be by producing the apprehension of some evil: which evil, if the act is an offence, must be some evil to which on the occasion in question the one person has no right to expose the other. This is one case, in which, if the offence be accompanied with the intention of detaining the thing for ever, whether it be or be not accompanied with the intention of not being amenable to law, it seems

[13] In attempting to exhibit the import belonging to this and other names of offences in common use, I must be understood to speak all along with the utmost diffidence. The truth is, the import given to them is commonly neither determinate nor uniform: so that in the nature of things, no definition that can be given of them by a private person can be altogether an exact one. To fix the sense of them belongs only to the legislator.

[13] The remaining cases come under the head of usurpation, or wrongful investment of property. The distinction seems hardly hitherto to have been attended to: it turns like another, mentioned above, upon the distinction between legal possession and physical. The same observation may be applied to the case of extortion hereafter following.

[k3] See supra 27.

to agree with the idea of what is commonly meant by *extortion*. Now the part a man takes in exposing another to the evil in question, must be either a positive or a negative part. In the former case, again, the evil must either be present or distant. In the case then where the assistance or consent is obtained by a force put upon the body, or where, if by a force put upon the mind, the part taken in the exposing a man to the apprehension of the evil is positive, the evil present, and the object of it his person, and if at any rate the extortion, thus applied, be accompanied with the intention of not being amenable to law, it seems to agree with the remaining case of what goes under the name of *robbery*.

As to dissipation in breach of trust, this, when productive of a pecuniary profit to the trustee, seems to be one species of what is commonly meant by *peculation*. Another, and the only remaining one, seems to consist in acts of occupation exercised by the trustee upon the things which are the objects of the fiduciary property, for his own benefit, and to the damage of the beneficiary. As to robbery, this offence, by the manner in which the assistance or consent is obtained, becomes an offence against property and person at the same time. Dissipation in breach of trust, and peculation, may perhaps be more commodiously treated of under the head of offences against trust.[13] After these exceptions, we have [nineteen][1] genera or principal kinds of offences against property, which, when ranged in the order most commodious for examination, may stand as follows, viz. 1. Wrongful non-investment of property. 2. Wrongful interception of property. 3. Wrongful divestment of property. 4. Usurpation of property. 5. Wrongful investment of property. 6. Wrongful withholding of services. 7. Insolvency. 8. Wrongful interception of services. 9. Wrongful obtainment of services. 10. Wrongful imposition of services. 11. Wrongful imposition of expense. 12. Wrongful destruction or endamagement. 13. Wrongful

---

[13] Usury, which, if it must be an offence, is an offence committed with consent, that is, with the consent of the party supposed to be injured, cannot merit a place in the catalogue of offences, unless the consent were either unfairly obtained or unfreely: in the first case, it coincides with defraudment; in the other, with extortion.

[1] The 1780 text reads 'thirteen' at this point, and the list below originally comprised thirteen items, corresponding to nos. 1–6, 12–14, 16–19 ('detainment' was used for 'detention', and the order of the entries 'Theft' and 'Embezzlement' was reversed). In the 1783 sheet of corrections and additions Bentham provided the revised list printed above. This revision was ignored in 1823 and imperfectly followed in the Bowring edition (i, 118): there, the heading 'Wrongful interception of services' is omitted, leaving a list of eighteen items, and the order followed departs at several points from that indicated by Bentham.

occupation. 14. Wrongful detention. 15. Wrongful disturbance of proprietary rights. 16. Theft. 17. Embezzlement. 18. Defraudment. 19. Extortion.[m3]

We proceed now to consider offences which are complex in their effects. Regularly, indeed, we should come to offences against condition; but it will be more convenient to speak first of offences by which a man's interest is affected in two of the preceeding points at once.

Offences against person and reputation

36. First then, with regard to offences which affect person and reputation together. When any man, by a mode of treatment which affects the person, injures the reputation of another, his end and purpose must have been either his own immediate pleasure, or that sort of reflected pleasure, which in certain circumstances may be reaped from the suffering of another. Now the only immediate pleasure worth regarding, which any one can reap from the person of another, and which at the same time is capable of affecting the reputation of the latter, is the pleasure of the sexual appetite.[n3] This pleasure, then, if reaped at all, must have been reaped either against the consent of the party, or with consent. If with consent, the consent must have been obtained either freely and fairly both, or freely but not fairly, or else not even freely; in which case the fairness is out of the question. If the consent be altogether wanting, the offence is called *rape*: if not fairly obtained, *seduction* simply: if not freely, it may be called *forcible seduction*. In any case, either the offence has gone the length of consummation, or has stopped short of that period; if it has gone that length, it takes one or other of the names just mentioned: if not, it may be included alike in all cases under the denomination of a *simple lascivious injury*. Lastly, to take the case where a man injuring you in your reputation, by proceedings that regard your person, does it for the sake of that sort of pleasure which will sometimes result from

[m3] I. SEMI-PUBLIC OFFENCES. 1. Wrongful divestment, interception, usurpation, etc. of valuables, which are the property of a corporate body; or which are in the indiscriminate occupation of a neighbourhood; such as parish churches, altars, relics, and other articles appropriated to the purposes of religion: or things which are in the indiscriminate occupation of the public at large; such as mile-stones, market-houses, exchanges, public gardens, and cathedrals. 2. Setting on foot what have been called *bubbles*, or fraudulent partnership, or gaming adventures; propagating false news, to raise or sink the value of stocks, or of any other denomination of property.

II. SELF-REGARDING OFFENCES. 1. Idleness. 2. Gaming. 3. Other species of prodigality.

[n3] See Ch. v (Pleasures and Pains).

the contemplation of another's pain. Under these circumstances either the offence has actually gone the length of a corporal injury, or it has rested in menacement: in the first case it may be styled a *corporal insult*; in the other, it may come under the name of *insulting menacement*. And thus we have six genera, or kinds of offences, against person and reputation together; which, when ranged in the order most commodious for consideration, will stand thus: 1. Corporal insults. 2. Insulting menacement. 3. Seduction. 4. Rape. 5. Forcible seduction. 6. Simple lascivious injuries.[o3]

37. Secondly, with respect to those which affect person and property together. That a force put upon the person of a man may be among the means by which the title to property may be unlawfully taken away or acquired, has been already stated.[p3] A force of this sort then is a circumstance which may accompany the offences of wrongful interception, wrongful divestment, usurpation, and wrongful investment. But in these cases the intervention of this circumstance does not happen to have given any new denomination to the offence.[q3] In all or any of these cases, however, by prefixing the epithet *forcible*, we may have so many names of offences, which may either be considered as constituting so many species of the genera belonging to the division of offences against property, or as so many genera belonging to the division now before us. Among the offences that concern the enjoyment of the thing, the case is the same with wrongful destruction and wrongful endamagement; as also with wrongful occupation and wrongful detainment. As to the offence of wrongful occupation, it is only in the case where the thing occupied belongs to the class of immoveables, that, when accompanied by the kind of force in question, has obtained a particular name which is in common use: in this case it is called *forcible entry*: forcible detainment, as applied also to immoveables, but only to immoveables, has obtained, among lawyers at least, the name of *forcible detainer*.[r3] As to robbery, the relation which it bears to

Offences against person and property

[o3] I. SEMI-PUBLIC OFFENCES—none.

II. SELF-REGARDING OFFENCES. 1. Sacrifice of virginity. 2. Indecencies not public.

[p3] Supra.[1]

[q3] In the technical language of the English law, property so acquired is said to be acquired by *duress*.

[r3] Applied to moveables, the circumstance of force has never, at least by the technical part of the language, been taken into account: no such combination of terms as *forcible occupation* is in current use. The word *detinue* is applied to moveables only: and (in the language of the law) the word *forcible* has never

[1] The reference is apparently to para. 35 (226 ff. above).

these other offences, and the claims which it has to a place in the division now before us, have been already stated (supra, 35).[1] And thus we may distinguish 10 *genera*, or kinds of offences, against person and property together, which, omitting for conciseness sake the epithet *wrongful*, will stand thus: 1. Forcible interception of property. 2. Forcible divestment of property. 3. Forcible usurpation. 4. Forcible investment. 5. Forcible destruction or endamagement. 6. Forcible occupation of moveables. 7. Forcible entry. 8. Forcible detainment of moveables. 9. Forcible detainment of immoveables. 10. Robbery.[s3]

Offences against condition. – Conditions, domestic or civil

38. We come now to offences against *condition*. A man's condition or station in life is constituted by the legal relation he bears to the persons who are about him; that is, as we have already had occasion to shew,[t3] by *duties*, which, by being imposed on one side, give birth to *rights* or *powers* on the other. These relations, it is evident, may be almost infinitely diversified. Some means, however, may be found of circumscribing the field within which the varieties of them are displayed. In the first place, they must either be such as are capable of displaying themselves within the circle of a private family, or such as require a larger space. The conditions constituted by the former sort of relations may be styled *domestic*: those constituted by the latter, *civil*.

Domestic conditions grounded on natural relationships

39. As to domestic conditions, the legal relations by which they are constituted may be distinguished into 1. Such as are super-added to relations purely natural: and 2. Such as, without any such natural basis, subsist purely by institution. By relations purely natural, I mean those which may be said to subsist between certain persons in virtue of the concern which they themselves, or certain other persons, have had in the process which is necessary to the continuance of the species. These relations may be distinguished, in the first place, into contiguous and uncontiguous. The uncontiguous

---

been combined with it. The word applied to immoveables is *detainer*: this is combined with the word *forcible*: and what is singular, it is scarcely in use without that word. It was impossible to steer altogether clear of this technical nomenclature, on account of the influence which it has on the body of the language.

[s3] I. SEMI-PUBLIC OFFENCES. 1. Incendiarism. 2. Criminal[2] inundation.

II. SELF-REGARDING OFFENCES—none.

[t3] Supra 25 note.

[1] This sentence, though essential to the construction of the list which follows, was omitted in the 1823 and later editions.

[2] 1783 correction for 1780 'Wrongful'.

subsist through the intervention of such as are contiguous. The contiguous may be distinguished, in the first place, into *connubial*, and *post-connubial*.[u3] Those which may be termed connubial are two: 1. That which the male bears towards the female: 2. That which the female bears to the male.[v3] The post-connubial are either *productive* or *derivative*. The productive is that which the male and female above-mentioned bear each of them towards the children who are the immediate fruit of their union; this is termed the relation of *parentality*. Now as the parents must be, so the children may be, of different sexes. Accordingly the relation of parentality may be distinguished into four species: 1. That which a father bears to his son: this is termed *paternity*. 2. That which a father bears to his daughter: this also is termed paternity. 3. That which a mother bears to her son: this is called *maternity*. 4. That which a mother bears to her daughter: this also is termed maternity. Uncontiguous natural relations may be distinguished into *immediate* and *remote*. Such as are immediate, are what one person bears to another in consequence of their bearing each of them one simple relation to some third person. Thus the paternal grandfather is related to the paternal grandson by means of the two different relations, of different kinds, which together they bear to the father: the brother on the father's side, to the brother by means of the two relations of the same kind, which together they bear to the father. In the same man-

---

[u3] By the terms *connubial* and *post-connubial*, all I mean at present to bring to view is, the mere physical union, apart from the ceremonies and legal engagements that will afterwards be considered as accompanying it.

[v3] The vague and undetermined nature of the fictitious entity, called a *relation*, is, on occasions like the present, apt to be productive of a good deal of confusion. A relation is either said to be *borne by* one of the objects which are parties to it, to the other, or to *subsist between* them. The latter mode of phraseology is, perhaps, rather the more common. In such case the idea seems to be, that from the consideration of the two objects there results but one relation, which belongs as it were in common to them both. In some cases, this perhaps may answer the purpose very well: it will not, however, in the present case. For the present purpose it will be necessary we should conceive two relations as resulting from the two objects, and *borne*, since such is the phrase, *by* the one of them to or towards the other: one relation borne by the first object to the second: another relation borne by the second object to the first. This is necessary on two accounts: 1. Because for the relations themselves there are in many instances separate names: for example, the relations of guardianship and wardship: in which case, the speaking of them as if they were but one, may be productive of much confusion. 2. Because the two different relationships give birth to so many conditions: which conditions are so far different, that what is predicated and will hold good of the one, will, in various particulars, as we shall see, not hold good of the other.

Relations – two result from every two objects

ner we might proceed to find places in the system for the infinitely-diversified relations which result from the combinations that may be formed by mixing together the several sorts of relationships by *ascent,* relationships by *descent, collateral* relationships, and relationships by *affinity*: which latter, when the union between the two parties through whom the affinity takes place is sanctioned by matrimonial solemnities, are termed relationships by *marriage.* But this, as it would be a most intricate and tedious task, so happily is it, for the present purpose, an unnecessary one. The only natural relations to which it will be necessary to pay any particular attention, are those which, when sanctioned by law, give birth to the conditions of husband and wife, the two relations comprized under the head of parentality, and the corresponding relations comprized under the head filiality or filiation.

What then are the relations of a legal kind which can be superinduced upon the above-mentioned natural relations? They must be such as it is the nature of law to give birth to and establish. But the relations which subsist purely by institution exhaust, as we shall see, the whole stock of relationships which it is in the nature of the law to give birth to and establish. The relations then which can be superinduced upon those which are purely natural, cannot be in themselves any other than what are of the number of those which subsist purely by institution: so that all the difference there can be between a legal relation of the one sort, and a legal relation of the other sort, is, that in the former case the circumstance which gave birth to the natural relation serves as a mark to indicate where the legal relation is to fix: in the latter case, the place where the legal relation is to attach is determined not by that circumstance but by some other. From these considerations it will appear manifestly enough, that for treating of the several sorts of conditions, as well natural as purely conventional, in the most commodious order, it will be necessary to give the precedence to the latter. Proceeding throughout upon the same principle, we shall all along give the priority, not to those which are first by nature, but to those which are most simple in point of description. There is no other way of avoiding perpetual anticipations and repetitions.

Domestic relations which are purely of legal institution

40. We come now to consider the domestic or family relations, which are purely of legal institution. It is to these in effect, that both kinds of domestic conditions, considered as the work of law, are indebted for their origin. When the law, no matter for what purpose, takes upon itself to operate, in a matter in which it has not operated before, it can only be by imposing *obligation*.[w3] Now when a legal obligation is imposed on any man, there are but two ways in which it can in the first instance be enforced. The one is by giving the power of enforcing it to the party in whose favour it is imposed: the other is by reserving that power to certain third persons, who, in virtue of their possessing it, are styled ministers of justice. In the first case, the party favoured is said to possess not only a *right* as against the party obliged, but also a *power* over him: in the second case, a *right* only, uncorroborated by power. In the first case, the party favoured may be styled a *superior*, and as they are both members of the same family, a *domestic superior*, with reference to the party obliged: who, in the same case, may be styled a *domestic inferior*, with reference to the party favoured. Now in point of possibility, it is evident, that domestic conditions, or a kind of fictitious possession analogous to domestic conditions, might have been looked upon as constituted, as well by rights alone, without powers on either side, as by powers. But in point of utility[x3] it does not

---

[w3] See Ch. xvii (Limits) § iii.[1]

[x3] Two persons, who by any means stand engaged to live together, can never live together long, but one of them will choose that some act or other should be done, which the other will choose should not be done. When this is the case, how is the competition to be decided? Laying aside generosity and good-breeding, which are the tardy and uncertain fruits of long-established laws, it is evident that there can be no certain means of deciding it but physical power: which indeed is the very means by which family, as well as other competitions, must have been decided long before any such office as that of legislator had existence. This then being the order of things which the legislator finds established by nature, how should he do better than to acquiesce in it? The persons who by the influence of causes that prevail every where, stand engaged to live together, are, 1. Parent and child, during the infancy of the latter: 2. Man and wife: 3. Children of the same parents. Parent and child, by necessity: since, if the child did not live with the parent (or with somebody standing in the place of the parent) it could not live at all: husband and wife, by a choice approaching to necessity: children of the same parents, by the necessity of their living each of them with the parents. As between parent and child, the necessity there is of a power on the part of the parent for the preservation of the child supersedes all farther reasoning. As between man and wife, that necessity does not subsist. The only reason that applies to this case is, the necessity of putting an end to competition. The man would have the meat roasted, the woman boiled: shall they both fast till the judge comes in to dress it for them? The woman would have the child dressed in green; the man, in blue: shall the child be naked till the judge comes in to clothe it? This affords a reason for giving a power to one or other of the parties: but it affords none for giving the power to the one rather than to the other. How then shall the

---

[1] The third section of Ch. xvii was never written in that form: it became part of the continuation of the present work published in this edition as *Of Laws in General*.

seem expedient: and in point of fact, probably owing to the invariable perception which men must have had of the inexpediency, no such conditions seem ever to have been constituted by such feeble bands. Of the legal relationships then, which are capable of being made to subsist within the circle of a family, there remain those only in which the obligation is enforced by power. Now then, wherever any such power is conferred, the end or purpose for which it was conferred (unless the legislator can be supposed to act without a motive) must have been the producing of a benefit to somebody: in other words, it must have been conferred for the *sake* of somebody. The person then, for whose sake it is conferred, must either be one of the two parties just mentioned, or a third party: if one of these two, it must be either the superior or the inferior. If the superior, such superior is commonly called a *master*; and the inferior is termed his *servant*: and the power may be termed a *beneficial* one. If it be for the sake of the inferior that the power is established, the superior is termed a *guardian*; and the inferior his *ward*: and the power, being thereby coupled with a trust, may be termed a *fiduciary* one. If for the sake of a third party, the superior may be termed a *superintendent*; and the inferior his *subordinate*. This third party will either be an assignable individual or set of individuals, or a set of unassignable individuals. In this latter

legislator determine? Supposing it equally easy to give it to either, let him look ever so long for a reason why he should give it to the one rather than to the other, and he may look in vain. But how does the matter stand already? for there were men and wives (or, what comes to the same thing, male and female living together as man and wife) before there were legislators. Looking round him then, he finds almost every where the male the stronger of the two; and therefore possessing already, by purely physical means, that power which he is thinking of bestowing on one of them by means of law. How then can he do so well as by placing the legal power in the same hands which are beyond comparison the more likely to be in possession of the physical? in this way, few transgressions, and few calls for punishment: in the other way, perpetual transgressions, and perpetual calls for punishment. Solon is said to have transferred the same idea to the distribution of state powers. Here then was *generalization*: here was the work of genius. But in the disposal of domestic power, every legislator, without any effort of genius, has been a Solon. So much for *reasons**[1]: add to which, in point of *motives*,† that legislators seem all to have been of the male sex, down to the days of Catherine. I speak here of those who frame laws, not of those who touch them with a sceptre.

* Social motives: sympathy for the public: love of reputation, etc.

† Self-regarding motives: or social motives, which are social in a less extent: sympathy for persons of a particular description: persons of the same sex.

[1] Thus 1789, followed by Harrison (p. 364 n.). 1823 and Bowring (i, 121 n.) read '*reason*'.

case the trust is either a public or a semi-public one: and the condition which it constitutes is not of the domestic, but of the civil kind. In the former case, this third party or *principal*, as he may be termed, either has a beneficial power over the superintendent, or he has not: if he has, the superintendent is his servant, and consequently so also is the subordinate: if not, the superintendent is the master of the subordinate; and all the advantage which the principal has over his superintendent, is that of possessing a set of rights, uncorroborated by power; and therefore, as we have seen[y3] not fit to constitute a condition of the domestic kind. But be the condition what it may which is constituted by these rights, of what nature can the obligations be, to which the superintendent is capable of being subjected by means of them? They are neither more nor less than those which a man is capable of being subjected to by powers. It follows, therefore, that the functions of a principal and his superintendent coincide with those of a master and his servant; and consequently that the offences relative to the two former conditions will coincide with the offences relative to the two latter.

41. Offences to which the condition of a master, like any other kind of condition, is exposed, may, as hath been already intimated,[z3] be distinguished into such as concern the existence of the condition itself, and such as concern the performance of the functions of it, while subsisting. First then, with regard to such as affect its existence. It is obvious enough that the services of one man may be a benefit to another: the condition of a master may therefore be a beneficial one. It stands exposed, therefore, to the offences of *wrongful non-investment, wrongful interception, usurpation, wrongful investment,* and *wrongful divestment.* But how should it stand exposed to the offences of *wrongful abdication, wrongful detrectation,* and *wrongful imposition?* Certainly it cannot of itself; for services, when a man has the power of exacting them or not, as he thinks fit, can never be a burthen. But if to the powers, by which the condition of a master is constituted, the law thinks fit to annex any obligation on the part of the master; for instance, that of affording maintenance or giving wages, to the servant, or paying money to any body else, it is evident, that in virtue of such obligation the condition *may* become a burthen. In this case, however, the condition possessed by the master will not, properly speaking, be the pure and simple condition of a master: it will be a kind of complex object, resolvable into the beneficial condition of a master, and the

Offences touching the condition of a master

[y3] Supra, note, page 237.

[z3] See supra 27.

burthensome obligation which is annexed to it. Still however, if the nature of the obligation lies within a narrow compass, and does not, in the manner of that which constitutes a trust, interfere with the exercise of those powers by which the condition of the superior is constituted, the latter, notwithstanding this foreign mixture, will still retain the name of mastership.[a4] In this case, therefore, but not otherwise, the condition of a master may stand exposed to the offences of *wrongful abdication, wrongful detrectation*, and *wrongful imposition*. Next as to the behaviour of persons, with reference to this condition, while considered as subsisting. In virtue of its being a benefit, it is exposed to *disturbance*. This disturbance will either be the offence of a stranger, or the offence of the servant himself. Where it is the offence of a stranger, and is committed by taking the person of the servant, in circumstances in which the taking of an object belonging to the class of things would be an act of theft, or (what is scarcely worth distinguishing from theft) an act of embezzlement, it may be termed *servant-stealing*. Where it is the offence of the servant himself, it is styled *breach of duty*. Now the most flagrant species of breach of duty, and that which includes indeed every other, is that which consists in the servant's withdrawing himself from the place in which the duty should be performed. This species of breach of duty is termed *elopement*. Again, in virtue of the power belonging to this condition, it is liable, on the part of the master, to *abuse*. But this power is not coupled with a trust. The condition of a master is therefore not exposed to any offence which is analogous to breach of trust. Lastly, on account of its being exposed to abuse, it may be conceived to stand, in point of possibility, exposed to *bribery*. But considering how few, and how insignificant, the persons are who are liable to be subject to the power here in question, this is an offence which, on account of the want of temptation, there will seldom be any example of in practice. We may therefore reckon thirteen sorts of offences to which the condition of a master is exposed; viz. 1. Wrongful non-investment of mastership. 2. Wrongful interception of mastership. 3. Wrongful divestment of mastership. 4. Usurpation of mastership. 5. Wrongful investment of mastership. 6. Wrongful abdication of mastership.

[a4] In most civilized nations there is a sort of domestic condition, in which the superior is termed a master, while the inferior is termed sometimes indeed a servant, but more particularly and more frequently an *apprentice*. In this case, though the superior is, in point of usage, known by no other name than that of a master, the relationship is in point of fact a mixed one, compounded of that of *master* and that of *guardian*.

7. Wrongful detrectation of mastership. 8. Wrongful imposition of mastership. 9. Abuse of mastership. 10. Disturbance of mastership. 11. Breach of duty in servants. 12. Elopement of servants. 13. Servant-stealing.

42. As to the *power* by which the condition of a master is constituted, this may be either *limited* or *unlimited*. When it is altogether unlimited, the condition of the servant is styled *pure slavery*. But as the rules of language are as far as can be conceived from being steady on this head, the term slavery is commonly made use of wherever the limitations prescribed to the power of the master are looked upon as inconsiderable. Whenever any such limitation is prescribed, a kind of fictitious entity is thereby created, and, in quality of an incorporeal object of possession, is bestowed upon the servant: this object is of the class of those which are called *rights*: and in the present case is termed, in a more particular manner, a *liberty*: and sometimes a *privilege*, an *immunity* or an *exemption*. Now those limitations on the one hand, and these liberties on the other, may, it is evident, be as various as the acts (positive or negative) which the master may or may not have the power of obliging the servant to submit to or to perform. Correspondent then to the infinitude of these liberties, is the infinitude of the modifications which the condition of mastership (or, as it is more common to say in such a case, that of servitude) admits of. These modifications, it is evident, may, in different countries, be infinitely diversified. In different countries, therefore, the offences characterised by the above names will, if specifically considered, admit of very different descriptions. If there be a spot upon the earth so wretched as to exhibit the spectacle of pure and absolutely unlimited slavery, on that spot there will be no such thing as any abuse of mastership; which means neither more nor less than that no abuse of mastership will there be treated on the footing of an offence. As to the question, Whether any, and what, modes of servitude ought to be established or kept on foot? this is a question, the solution of which belongs to the civil branch of the art of legislation.

Various modes of servitude

43. Next, with regard to the offences that may concern the condition of a servant. It might seem at first sight, that a condition of this kind could not have a spark of benefit belonging to it: that it could not be attended with any other consequences than such as rendered it a mere burthen. But a burthen itself may be a benefit, in comparison of a greater burthen. Conceive a man's situation then to be such, that he must, at any rate, be in a state of pure slavery. Still may it be material to him, and highly material, who the person

Offences touching the condition of a servant

is whom he has for his master. A state of slavery then, under one master, may be a beneficial state to him, in comparison with a state of slavery under another master. The condition of a servant then is exposed to the several offences to which a condition, in virtue of its being a beneficial one, is exposed.[b4] More than this, where the power of the master is limited, and the limitations annexed to it, and thence the liberties of the servant, are considerable, the servitude may even be positively eligible. For amongst those limitations may be such as are sufficient to enable the servant to possess property of his own: being capable then of possessing property of his own, he may be capable of receiving it from his master: in short, he may receive *wages*, or other emoluments, from his master; and the benefit resulting from these wages may be so considerable as to outweigh the burthen of the servitude, and, by that means, render that condition more beneficial upon the whole, and more eligible, than that of one who is not in any respect under the control of any such person as a master. Accordingly, by these means the condition of the servant may be so eligible, that his entrance into it, and his continuance in it, may have been altogether the result of his own choice.

That the nature of the two conditions may be the more clearly understood, it may be of use to shew the sort of correspondency there is between the offences which affect the existence of the one, and those which affect the existence of the other. That this correspondency cannot but be very intimate is obvious at first sight. It is not, however, that a given offence in the former catalogue coincides with an offence of the same name in the latter catalogue: usurpation of servantship with usurpation of mastership, for example. But the case is, that an offence of one denomination in the one catalogue coincides with an offence of a different denomination in the other catalogue. Nor is the coincidence constant and certain: but liable to contingencies, as we shall see. First, then, wrongful non-investment[1] of the condition of a servant, if it be the offence of one who

[b4] It may seem at first, that a person who is in the condition of a slave,

[1] An Ms. note here by Bentham in his copy of the 1789 edition proposes to substitute 'non-collation' for 'non-investment' and, below, 'ablation' for 'divestment'. These substitutions were not made in 1823, but the Bowring edition does make the changes in this passage (i, 124), just as that edition also followed Bentham's 1789 suggestion (cf. 216 n. n2 above) that 'collative' and 'ablative' might replace 'investitive' and 'divestitive' near the beginning of par. 35 (cf. 227 above and Bowring, i, 116). But there is no consistent substitution: the Bowring text leaves the terms 'non-investment' and 'divestment' unchanged at the end of the present paragraph. Nor is it clear that Bentham intended a systematic change: his view in 1789 was that each set of terms 'on different occasions . . . may have its use' (217 n. n2 above).

should have been the master, coincides with wrongful detrectation of mastership: if it be the offence of a third person, it involves in it non-investment of mastership, which, provided the mastership be in the eyes of him who should have been master a beneficial thing, but not otherwise is wrongful. 2. Wrongful interception of the condition of a servant, if it be the offence of him who should have been master, coincides with wrongful detrectation of mastership: if it be the offence of a third person, and the mastership be a beneficial thing, it involves in it wrongful interception of mastership. 3. Wrongful divestment of servantship, if it be the offence of the master, but not otherwise, coincides with wrongful abdication of mastership: if it be the offence of a stranger, it involves in it divestment of mastership, which, in as far as the mastership is a beneficial thing, is wrongful. 4. Usurpation of servantship coincides necessarily with wrongful imposition of mastership: it will be apt to involve in it wrongful divestment of mastership: but this only in the case where the usurper, previously to the usurpation, was in a state of servitude under some other master. 5. Wrongful investment of servantship (the servantship being considered as a beneficial thing) coincides with imposition of mastership; which, if in the eyes of the pretended master the mastership should chance to be a burthen, will be wrongful. 6. Wrongful abdication of servantship coincides with wrongful divestment of mastership. 7. Wrongful detrectation of servantship, with wrongful non-investment of mastership. 8. Wrongful imposition of servantship, if it be the offence of the pretended master, coincides with usurpation of mastership: if it be the offence of a stranger, it involves in it imposition of mastership, which, if in the eyes of the pretended master the mastership should be a burthen, will be wrongful. As to abuse of mastership, disturbance of mastership, breach of duty in servants, elopement of servants, and servant-stealing, these are offences which, without any change of denomination, bear equal relation to both conditions. And thus we may reckon thirteen sorts of offences to which the condition of a servant stands exposed: viz. 1. Wrongful non-investment of servantship. 2. Wrongful interception of servantship.

could not have it in his power to engage in such course of proceeding as would be necessary, in order to give him an apparent title to be reckoned among the slaves of another master. But though a slave in point of *right*, it may happen that he has eloped for instance, and is not a slave in point of *fact*: or, suppose him a slave in point of fact, and ever so vigilantly guarded, still a person connected with him by the ties of sympathy, might do that for him which, though willing and assenting, he might not be able to do for himself: might forge a deed of donation, for example, from the one master to the other.

3. Wrongful divestment of servantship. 4. Usurpation of servant-ship. 5. Wrongful investment of servantship. 6. Wrongful abdication of servantship. 7. Wrongful detrectation of servantship. 8. Wrongful imposition of servantship. 9. Abuse of mastership. 10. Disturbance of mastership. 11. Breach of duty in servants. 12. Elopement of servants. 13. Servant-stealing.

Guardian-ship, what— Necessity of the institu-tion

44. We now come to the offences to which the condition of a guardian is exposed. A guardian is one who is invested with power over another, living within the compass of the same family, and called a ward; the power being to be exercised for the benefit of the ward. Now then, what are the cases in which it can be for the benefit of one man, that another, living within the compass of the same family, should exercise power over him? Consider either of the parties by himself, and suppose him, in point of understanding, to be on a level with the other, it seems evident enough that no such cases can ever exist.[c4] To the production of happiness on the part of any given person (in like manner as to the production of any other effect which is the result of human agency) three things it is necessary should concur: knowledge, inclination, and physical power. Now as there is no man who is so sure of being *inclined*, on all occasions, to promote your happiness as you yourself are, so neither is there any man who upon the whole can have had so good opportunities as you must have had of *knowing* what is most conducive to that purpose. For who should know so well as you do what it is that gives you pain or pleasure?[d4] Moreover, as to power, it is manifest that no superiority in this respect, on the part of a stranger, could, for a constancy, make up for so great a deficiency as he must lie under in respect of two such material points as knowledge and inclination. If then there be a case where it can be for the advantage of one man to be under the power of another, it must be on account of some palpable and very considerable deficiency, on the part of the former, in point of intellects, or (which is the same thing in other words) in point of knowledge or understanding. Now there are two cases in which such palpable deficiency is known to take place. These are, 1. Where a man's intellect is not yet arrived at that state in which it is capable of directing his own inclination in the pursuit

[c4] Consider them *together* indeed, take the sum of the two interests, and the case, as we have seen (supra 40) is then the reverse. That case, it is to be remembered, proceeds only upon the supposition that the two parties are obliged to live together; for suppose it to be at their option to part, the necessity of establishing the power ceases.

[d4] Ch. xvii (Limits) § i.

of happiness: this is the case of *infancy*.[e4] 2. Where by some particular known or unknown circumstance his intellect has either never arrived at that state, or having arrived at it has fallen from it: which is the case of *insanity*.

By what means then is it to be ascertained whether a man's intellect is in that state or no? For exhibiting the quantity of sensible heat in a human body we have a very tolerable sort of instrument, the thermometer; but for exhibiting the quantity of intelligence, we have no such instrument. It is evident, therefore, that the line which separates the quantity of intelligence which *is* sufficient for the purposes of self-government from that which is *not* sufficient, must be, in a great measure, arbitrary. Where the insufficiency is the result of want of age, the sufficient quantity of intelligence, be it what it may, does not accrue to all at the same period of their lives. It becomes therefore necessary for legislators to cut the gordian knot, and fix upon a particular period, at which and not before, truly or not, every person whatever shall be deemed, as far as depends upon age, to be in possession of this sufficient quantity.[f4] In this case then a line is drawn which may be the same for every man, and in the description of which, such as it is, whatever persons are concerned may be certain of agreeing: the circumstance of time affording a mark by which the line in question may be traced with the utmost degree of nicety. On the other hand, where the insufficiency is the result of insanity, there is not even this resource: so that here the legislator has no other expedient than to appoint some particular person or persons to give a particular determination of the question, in every instance in which it occurs, according to his or their particular and arbitrary discretion. Arbitrary enough it must be at any rate, since the only way in which it can be exercised is by considering whether the share of intelligence possessed

[e4] See Ch. xiii (Cases unmeet) § iii.

[f4] In certain nations, women, whether married or not, have been placed in a state of perpetual wardship: this has been evidently founded on the notion of a decided inferiority in point of intellects on the part of the female sex, analogous to that which is the result of infancy or insanity on the part of the male. This is not the only instance in which tyranny has taken advantage of its own wrong, alleging as a reason for the domination it exercises, an imbecility, which, as far as it has been real, has been produced by the abuse of that very power which it is brought to justify. Aristotle, fascinated by the prejudice of the times, divides mankind into two distinct species, that of freemen, and that of slaves.[1] Certain men were born to be slaves, and ought to be slaves.—Why? Because they are so.

[1] Aristotle, *Politics*, i.v.

by the individual in question does or does not come up to the loose and indeterminate idea which persons so appointed may chance to entertain with respect to the quantity which is deemed sufficient.

Duration to be given to it

45. The line then being drawn, or supposed to be so, it is expedient to a man who cannot, with safety to himself, be left in his own power, that he should be placed in the power of another. How long then should he remain so? Just so long as his inability is supposed to continue: that is, in the case of infancy, till he arrives at that period at which the law deems him to be of full age: in the case of insanity, till he be of sound mind and understanding. Now it is evident, that this period, in the case of infancy, may not arrive for a considerable time: and in the case of insanity, perhaps never. The duration of the power belonging to this trust must therefore, in the one case, be very considerable; in the other case, indefinite.

Powers that may, and duties that ought to be annexed to it

46. The next point to consider, is what *may* be the extent of it? for as to what *ought* to be, that is a matter to be settled, not in a general analytical sketch, but in a particular and circumstantial dissertation. By possibility, then, this power may possess any extent that can be imagined: it may extend to any acts which, physically speaking, it may be in the power of the ward to perform himself, or be the object of if exercised by the guardian. Conceive the power, for a moment, to stand upon this footing: the condition of the ward stands now exactly upon a footing with pure slavery. Add the obligation by which the power is turned into a trust: the limits of the power are now very considerably narrowed. What then is the purport of this obligation? Of what nature is the course of conduct it prescribes? It is such a course of conduct as shall be best calculated for procuring to the ward the greatest quantity of happiness which his faculties, and the circumstances he is in, will admit of: saving always, in the first place, the regard which the guardian is permitted to shew to his own happiness; and, in the second place, that which he is obliged, as well as permitted, to shew to that of other men. This is, in fact, no other than that course of conduct which the ward, did he but know how, ought, in point of *prudence*, to maintain of himself: so that the business of the former is to govern the latter precisely in the manner in which this latter ought to govern himself. Now to instruct each individual in what manner to govern his own conduct in the details of life, is the particular business of private ethics: to instruct individuals in what manner to govern the conduct of those whose happiness, during non-age, is committed to their charge, is the business of the art of private education. The details, therefore, of the rules to be given for that purpose, any more than the acts which are capable of being committed in violation of those rules, belong not to the art of legislation: since, as will be seen more particularly hereafter,[g4] such details could not, with any chance of advantage, be provided for by the legislator. Some general outlines might indeed be drawn by his authority: and, in point of fact, some are in every civilized state. But such regulations, it is evident, must be liable to great variation: in the first place, according to the infinite diversity of civil conditions which a man may stand invested with in any given state: in the next place, according to the diversity of local circumstances that may influence the nature of the conditions which may chance to be established in different states. On this account, the offences which would be constituted by such regulations could not be comprised under any concise and settled denominations, capable of a permanent and extensive application. No place, therefore, can be allotted to them here.

47. By what has been said, we are the better prepared for taking an account of the offences to which the condition in question stands exposed. Guardianship being a private trust, is of course exposed to those offences, and no others, by which a private trust is liable to be affected. Some of them, however, on account of the special quality of the trust, will admit of some further particularity of description. In the first place, breach of this species of trust may be termed *mismanagement* of guardianship: in the second[1] place, of whatever nature the duties are, which are capable of being annexed to this condition, it must often happen, that in order to fulfil them, it is necessary the guardian should be at a certain particular place. Mismanagement of guardianship, when it consists in the not being, on the occasion in question, at the place in question, may be termed *desertion* of guardianship. Third, it is manifest enough, that the object which the guardian ought to propose to himself, in the exercise of the powers to which those duties are annexed, is to procure for the ward the greatest quantity of happiness which can be procured for him, consistently with the regard which is due to the other interests that have been mentioned: for this is the object which the ward would have proposed to himself, and might and ought to have been allowed to propose to himself, had he been capable of governing his own conduct. Now, in order to procure this happiness, it is necessary that he should possess a

Offences touching the condition of a guardian

[g4] See Ch. XVII (Limits) § i.

[1] 1789 'next'.

certain power over the objects on the use of which such happiness depends. These objects are either the person of the ward himself, or other objects that are extraneous to him. These other objects are either things or persons. As to *things* then, objects of this class, in as far as a man's happiness depends upon the use of them, are styled his *property*. The case is the same with the services of any *persons* over whom he may happen to possess a beneficial power, or to whose services he may happen to possess a beneficial right. Now when property of any kind, which is in trust, suffers by the delinquency of him with whom it is in trust, such offence, of whatever nature it is in other respects, may be styled *dissipation* in breach of trust: and if it be attended with a profit to the trustee, it may be styled *peculation*.[h4] Fourth, for one person to exercise a power of any kind over another, it is necessary that the latter should either perform certain acts, upon being commanded so to do by the former, or at least should suffer certain acts to be exercised upon himself. In this respect a ward must stand upon the footing of a servant: and the condition of a ward must, in this respect, stand exposed to the same offences to which that of a servant stands exposed: that is, on the part of a stranger, to *disturbance*, which in particular circumstances, will amount to *theft*: on the part of the ward, to *breach of duty*: which, in particular circumstances, may be effected by *elopement*. Fifth, there does not seem to be any offence concerning guardianship that corresponds to *abuse of trust*: I mean in the sense to which the last-mentioned denomination has been here confined.[i4] The reason is, that guardianship, being a trust of a private nature, does not, as such, confer upon the trustee any power, either over the persons or over the property of any party, other than the *beneficiary* himself. If by accident it confers on the trustee a power over any persons whose services constitute a part of the property of the beneficiary, the trustee becomes thereby, in certain respects, the master of such servants.[j4] Sixth, bribery also is a sort of offence to which, in this case, there is not commonly much temptation. It is an offence, however, which by possibility is capable of taking this direction: and must therefore be aggregated to the number of the offences to which the condition of a guardian stands exposed. And thus we have in all seventeen of these offences: viz. 1. Wrongful non-investment of guardianship. 2. Wrongful interception of guardianship. 3. Wrongful divestment of guardianship.

[h4] Supra 35.
[14] See supra 25.
[j4] See supra 40.

4. Usurpation of guardianship. 5. Wrongful investment of guardianship. 6. Wrongful abdication of guardianship. 7. Detrectation of
guardianship. 8. Wrongful imposition of guardianship. 9. Mismanagement of guardianship. 10. Desertion of guardianship.
11. Dissipation in prejudice of wardship. 12. Peculation in prejudice of wardship. 13. Disturbance of guardianship. 14. Breach of
duty to guardians. 15. Elopement from guardians. 16. Ward-
stealing. 17. Bribery in prejudice of wardship.

48. Next, with regard to offences to which the condition of ward- *Offences*
ship is exposed. Those which first affect the existence of the con- *touching the*
dition itself are as follows: 1. Wrongful non-investment of the *condition of*
condition of a ward. This, if it be the offence of one who should *a ward*
have been guardian, coincides with wrongful detrectation of guardianship: if it be the offence of a third person, it involves in it non-
investment of guardianship, which, provided the guardianship is,
in the eyes of him who should have been guardian, a desirable thing,
is wrongful. 2. Wrongful interception of wardship. This, if it be the
offence of him who should have been guardian, coincides with wrongful detrectation of guardianship: if it be the offence of a third person, it involves in it interception of guardianship, which, provided
the guardianship is, in the eyes of him who should have been
guardian, a desirable thing, is wrongful. 3. Wrongful divestment of
wardship. This, if it be the offence of the guardian, but not otherwise, coincides with wrongful abdication of guardianship: if it be
the offence of a third person, it involves in it divestment of guardianship, which, if the guardianship is, in the eyes of the guardian,
a desirable thing, is wrongful. 4. Usurpation of the condition of a
ward: an offence not very likely to be committed. This coincides
at any rate with wrongful imposition of guardianship; and if the
usurper were already under the guardianship of another guardian,
it will involve in it wrongful divestment of such guardianship.[k4]
5. Wrongful investment of wardship: (the wardship being considered as a beneficial thing) this coincides with imposition of
guardianship, which, if in the eyes of the pretended guardian the
guardianship should be a burthen, will be wrongful. 6. Wrongful

[k4] This effect it may be thought will not necessarily take place: since a ward
may have two guardians. One man then is guardian by right: another man
comes and makes himself so by usurpation. This may very well be, and yet
the former may continue guardian notwithstanding. How then (it may be
asked) is he divested of his guardianship?—The answer is—Certainly not of the
whole of it: but, however, of a part of it: of such part as is occupied, if one
may so say, that is, of such part of the powers and rights belonging to it as are
exercised, by the usurper.

abdication of wardship. This coincides with wrongful divestment of guardianship. 7. Wrongful detrectation of wardship. This coincides with wrongful interception of guardianship. 8. Wrongful imposition of wardship. This, if the offender be the pretended guardian, coincides with usurpation of guardianship: if a stranger, it involves in it wrongful imposition of guardianship. As to such of the offences relative to this condition, as concern the consequences of it while subsisting, they are of such a nature that, without any change of denomination, they belong equally to the condition of a guardian, and that of a ward. We may therefore reckon seventeen sorts of offences relative to the condition of a ward: 1. Wrongful non-investment of wardship. 2. Wrongful interception of wardship. 3. Wrongful divestment of wardship. 4. Usurpation of wardship. 5. Wrongful investment of wardship. 6. Wrongful abdication of wardship. 7. Wrongful detrectation of wardship. 8. Wrongful imposition of wardship. 9. Mis-management of guardianship. 10. Desertion of guardianship. 11. Dissipation in prejudice of wardship. 12. Peculation in prejudice of wardship. 13. Disturbance of guardianship. 14. Breach of duty to guardians. 15. Elopement from guardians. 16. Ward-stealing. 17. Bribery in prejudice of wardship.

Offences touching the condition of a parent

49. We come now to the offences to which the condition of a parent stands exposed: and first, with regard to those by which the very existence of the condition is affected. On this occasion, in order to see the more clearly into the subject, it will be necessary to distinguish between the natural relationship, and the legal relationship, which is superinduced as it were upon the natural one. The natural one being constituted by a particular event, which, either on account of its being already past, or on some other account, is equally out of the power of the law, neither is, nor can be made, the subject of an offence. *Is* a man your father? It is not any offence of mine that can make you not his son. Is he *not* your father? It is not any offence of mine that can render him so. But although he does in fact bear that relation to you, I, by an offence of mine, may perhaps so manage matters, that he shall not be *thought* to bear it: which, with respect to any legal advantages which either he or you could derive from such relationship, will be the same thing as if he did not. In the capacity of a witness, I may cause the judges to believe that he is not your father, and to decree accordingly: or, in the capacity of a judge, I may myself decree him not to be your father. Leaving then the purely natural relationship as an object equally out of the reach of justice and injustice, the legal condition, it is evident, will stand exposed to the same offences, neither more nor less, as every other condition, that is capable of being either beneficial or burthensome, stands exposed to. Next, with regard to the exercise of the functions belonging to this condition, considered as still subsisting. In parentality there must be two persons concerned, the father and the mother. The condition of a parent includes, therefore, two conditions; that of a father, and that of a mother, with respect to such or such a child. Now it is evident, that between these two parties, whatever beneficiary powers, and other rights, as also whatever obligations, are annexed to the condition of a parent, may be shared in any proportions that can be imagined. But if in these several objects of legal creation, each of these two parties have severally a share, and if the interests of all these parties are in any degree provided for, it is evident that each of the parents will stand, with relation to the child, in two several capacities: that of a master, and that of a guardian. The condition of a parent then, in as far as it is the work of law, may be considered as a complex condition, compounded of that of a guardian, and that of a master. To the parent then, in quality of guardian, results a set of duties, involving, as necessary to the discharge of them, certain powers: to the child, in the character of a ward, a set of rights corresponding to the parent's duties, and a set of duties corresponding to his powers. To the parent again, in quality of master, a set of beneficiary powers, without any other necessary limitation (so long as they last) than what is annexed to them by the duties incumbent on him in quality of a guardian: to the child, in the character of a servant, a set of duties corresponding to the parent's beneficiary powers, and without any other necessary limitation (so long as they last) than what is annexed to them by the rights which belong to the child in his capacity of ward. The condition of a parent will therefore be exposed to all the offences to which either that of a guardian or that of a master are exposed: and, as each of the parents will partake, more or less, of both those characters, the offences to which the two conditions are exposed may be nominally, as they will be substantially, the same. Taking them then all together, the offences to which the condition of a parent is exposed will stand as follows: 1. Wrongful non-investment of parentality.[14] 2. Wrongful inter-

---

[14] At first view it may seem a solecism to speak of the condition of parentality as one which a man can have need to be invested with. The reason is, that it is not common for any ceremony to be required as necessary to a man's being deemed in law the father of such or such a child. But the institution of such a ceremony, whether advisable or not, is at least perfectly conceivable. Nor are there wanting cases in which it has actually been exemplified. By an article in

ception of parentality. 3. Wrongful divestment of parentality. 4. Usurpation of parentality. 5. Wrongful investment of parentality. 6. Wrongful abdication of parentality. 7. Wrongful detrectation of parentality. 8. Wrongful imposition of parentality. 9. Mismanagement of parental guardianship. 10. Desertion of parental guardianship. 11. Dissipation in prejudice of filial wardship. 12. Peculation in prejudice of filial wardship. 13. Abuse of parental powers. 14. Disturbance of parental guardianship. 15. Breach of duty to parents. 16. Elopement from parents. 17. Child-stealing. 18. Bribery in prejudice of filial wardship.

Offences touching the filial condition

50. Next with regard to the offences to which the *filial* condition,[m4] the condition of a son or daughter stands exposed. The principles to be pursued in the investigation of offences of this description, have already been sufficiently developed. It will be sufficient, therefore, to enumerate them without further discussion. The only peculiarities by which offences relative to the condition in question stand distinguished from the offences relative to all the preceding conditions, depend upon this one circumstance; viz. that it is certain every one must have had a father and a mother: at the same time that it is not certain that every one must have had a master, a servant, a guardian, or a ward. It will be observed all along, that where a person, from whom, if alive, the benefit would be taken, or on whom the burthen would be imposed, be dead, so much of the mischief is extinct along with the object of the offence. There still, however, remains so much of the mischief as depends upon the advantage or disadvantage which might accrue to persons related, or supposed to be related, in the several remoter degrees, to him in question. The catalogue then of these offences stand as

the Roman law, adopted by many modern nations, an illegitimate child is rendered legitimate by the subsequent marriage of his parents. If then a priest, or other person whose office it was, were to refuse to join a man and woman in matrimony, such refusal, besides being a wrongful non-investment with respect to the two matrimonial conditions, would be a wrongful non-investment of parentality and filiation, to the prejudice of any children who should have been legitimated.

[m4] In English we have no word that will serve to express with propriety the person who bears the relation opposed to that of parent. The word *child* is ambiguous, being employed in another sense, perhaps more frequently than in this: more frequently in opposition to *a person of full age*, and *adult*, than in correlation to a *parent*. For the condition itself we have no other word than *filiation*: an ill-contrived term, not analogous to *paternity* and *maternity*: the proper term would have been *filiality*: the word filiation is as frequently, perhaps, and more consistently, put for the act of establishing a person in the possession of the condition of filiality.

252

follows: 1. Wrongful non-investment of filiation. This, if it be the offence of him or her who should have been recognized as the parent, coincides with wrongful detrectation of parentality: if it be the offence of a third person, it involves in it non-investment of parentality, which, provided the parentality is, in the eyes of him or her who should have been recognized as the parent, a desirable thing, is wrongful. 2. Wrongful interception of filiation. This, if it be the offence of him or her who should have been recognised as the parent, coincides with wrongful detrectation of parentality: if it be the offence of a third person, it involves in it interception of parentality, which, provided the parentality is, in the eyes of him or her who should have been recognized as parent, a desirable thing, is wrongful. 3. Wrongful divestment of filiation. This, if it be the offence of him or her who should be recognised as parent, coincides with wrongful abdication of parentality: if it be the offence of a third person, it involves in it divestment of parentality: to wit, of paternity, or of maternity, or of both: which, if the parentality is, in the eyes of him or her who should be recognised as parent, a desirable thing, are respectively wrongful. 4. Usurpation of filiation. This coincides with wrongful imposition of parentality; to wit, either of paternity, or of maternity or of both: and necessarily involves in it divestment of parentality, which, if the parentality thus divested were, in the eyes of him or her who are thus divested of it, a desirable thing, is wrongful. 5. Wrongful investment of filiation: (the filiation being considered as a beneficial thing.) This coincides with imposition of parentality, which, if in the eyes of the pretended father or mother the parentality should be an undesirable thing, will be wrongful. 6. Wrongful abdication of filiation. This necessarily coincides with wrongful divestment of parentality; it also is apt to involve in it wrongful imposition of parentality; though not necessarily either to the advantage or to the prejudice of any certain person. For if a man, supposed at first to be your son, appears afterwards not to be yours, it is certain indeed that he is the son of some other man, but it may not appear who that other man is. 7. Wrongful detrectation of filiation. This coincides with wrongful non-investment or wrongful interception of parentality. 8. Wrongful imposition of filiation. This, if it be the offence of the pretended parent, coincides necessarily with usurpation of parentality: if it be the offence of a third person, it necessarily involves imposition of parentality; as also divestment of parentality: either or both of which, according to the circumstance above-mentioned, may or may not be wrongful. 9. Mismanagement of parental guardianship. 10. Desertion of parental guardianship. 11. Dissipation in prejudice of filial wardship. 12. Peculation in prejudice of filial wardship. 13. Abuse of parental power. 14. Disturbance of parental guardianship. 15. Breach of duty to parents. 16. Elopement from parents. 17. Child-stealing. 18. Bribery in prejudice of parental guardianship.

Condition of a husband – Powers, duties, and rights, that may be annexed to it

51. We shall now be able to apply ourselves with some advantage to the examination of the several offences to which the marital condition, or condition of a husband, stands exposed. A husband is a man, between whom and a certain woman, who in this case is called his wife, there subsists a legal obligation for the purpose of their living together, and in particular for the purpose of a sexual[1] intercourse to be carried on between them. This obligation will naturally be considered in four points of view: 1. In respect of its commencement. 2. In respect of the placing it. 3. In respect of the nature of it. 4. In respect of its duration. First then, it is evident, that in point of possibility, one method of commencement is as conceivable as another: the time of its commencement might have been marked by one sort of event (by one sort of *signal*, as it may here be called) as well as by another. But in practice the signal has usually been, as in point of utility it ought constantly to be, a contract entered into by the parties: that is, a set of signs, pitched upon by the law, as expressive of their *mutual consent*, to take upon them this condition. Second, and third, with regard to the placing of the obligations which are the result of the contract, it is evident that they must rest either[2] solely on one side, or mutually on both. On the first supposition, the condition is not to be distinguished from pure slavery. In this case, either the wife must be the slave of the husband, or the husband of the wife. The first of these suppositions has perhaps never been exemplified; the opposing influence of physical causes being too universal to have ever been surmounted: the latter seems to have been exemplified but too often; perhaps among the first Romans; at any rate, in many barbarous nations. Thirdly, With regard to the nature of the obligations. If they are not suffered to rest all on one side, certain rights are thereby given to the other. There must, therefore, be rights on both sides. Now, where there are mutual rights possessed by two persons, as against each other, either there are powers annexed to those rights, or not. But the persons in question are, by the supposition, to live together:

[1] Thus, exceptionally, 1789 (instead of Bentham's then usual 'venereal').
[2] 1823 and Bowring editions omit 'either', which is restored in Harrison (p. 382).

in which case we have shewn,[n4] that it is not only expedient, but in a manner necessary, that on one side there should be powers. Now it is only on one side that powers can be: for suppose them on both sides, and they destroy one another. The question is then, In which of the parties these powers shall be lodged? We have shewn, that on the principle of utility they ought to be lodged in the husband. The powers then which subsist being lodged in the husband, the next question is, Shall the interest of one party only, or of both, be consulted in the exercise of them? It is evident, that on the principle of utility the interests of both ought alike to be consulted: since in two persons, taken together, more happiness is producible than in one. This being the case, it is manifest, that the legal relation which the husband will bear to the wife will be a complex one: compounded of that of master and that of guardian.

52. The offences then to which the condition of a husband will be exposed, will be the sum of those to which the two conditions of master and guardian are exposed. Thus far the condition of a husband, with respect to the general outlines of it, stands upon the same footing as that of a parent. But there are certain reciprocal services, which being the main subject of the matrimonial contract, constitute the essence of the two matrimonial relations, and which neither a master nor guardian, as such, nor a parent, at any rate, have usually been permitted to receive. These must of course have been distinguished from the indiscriminate train of services at large which the husband in his character of master is impowered to exact, and of those which in his character of guardian he is bound to render. Being thus distinguished, the offences relative to the two conditions have, in many instances, in as far as they have reference to these peculiar services, acquired particular denominations. In the first place, with regard to the contract, from the celebration of which the legal condition dates its existence. It is obvious that in point of possibility, this contract might, on the part of either sex, subsist with respect to several persons of the other sex at the same time: the husband might have any number of wives: the wife might have any number of husbands: the husband might enter into the contract with a number of wives at the same time: or, if with only one at a time, he might reserve to himself a right of engaging in a similar contract with any number, or with only such or such a number of other women afterwards, during the continuance of each

Offences touching the condition of a husband

[n4] Supra (40 note).[1]

[1] In the 1823 and Bowring editions this note reads simply 'Supra'. Harrison (p. 381) restores the 1789 reading, as here.

former contract. This latter accordingly is the footing upon which, as is well known, marriage is and has been established in many extensive countries: particularly in all those which profess the Mahometan religion. In point of possibility, it is evident that the like liberty might be reserved on the part of the wife: though in point of practice no examples of such an arrangement seem ever to have occurred. Which of all these arrangements is, in point of utility, the most expedient, is a question which would require too much discussion to answer in the course of an analytical process like the present, and which belongs indeed to the civil branch of legislation, rather than to the penal.[o4] In Christian countries, the solemnization of any such contract is made to exclude the solemnization of any subsequent one during the continuance of a former: and the solemnization of any such subsequent contract is accordingly treated as an offence, under the name of *Polygamy*. Polygamy then is at any rate, on the part of the man, a particular modification of that offence which may be styled usurpation of the condition of a husband. As to its other effects, they will be different, according as it was the man only, or the woman only, or both, that were in a state of matrimony at the time of the commission of the offence. If the man only, then his offence involves in it *pro tanto* that of wrongful divestment of the condition of a wife, in prejudice of his prior wife.[p4] If the woman only, then it involves in it *pro tanto* that of wrongful divestment of the condition of a husband, in prejudice of her prior husband. If both were already married, it of course involves both the wrongful divestments which have just been mentioned. And on the other hand also, the converse of all this may be observed with regard to polygamy on the part of the woman. Second, As the engaging not to enter into any subsequent engagement of the like kind during the continuance of the first, is one of the conditions on which the law lends its sanction to the first; so another is, the inserting as one of the articles of this engagement, an undertaking not to render to, or accept from, any other person the services which form the characteristic object of it: the rendering or acceptance of any such services is accordingly treated as an offence, under the name of *adultery*: under which name is also comprised the offence of the stranger, who, in the commission of the above

[o4] See Ch. xvii (Limits) § iv.[1]

[p4] In this case also, if the woman knew not of the prior marriage, it is besides a species of seduction; and, in as far as it affects her, belongs to another division of the offences of this class. See supra 36.

[1] See above 207 n. 1.

offence, is the necessary accomplice. Third, Disturbing either of the parties to this engagement, in the possession of these characteristic services, may, in like manner, be distinguished from the offence of disturbing them in the enjoyment of the miscellaneous advantages derivable from the same condition; and on whichever side the blame rests, whether that of the party, or that of a third person, may be termed *wrongful withholding of connubial services*. And thus we have one-and-twenty sorts of offences to which, as the law stands at present in Christian countries, the condition of a husband stands exposed: viz. 1. Wrongful non-investment of the condition of a husband. 2. Wrongful interception of the condition of a husband. 3. Wrongful divestment of the condition of a husband. 4. Usurpation of the condition of a husband. 5. Polygamy. 6. Wrongful investment of the condition of a husband. 7. Wrongful abdication of the condition of a husband. 8. Wrongful detrectation of the condition of a husband. 9. Wrongful imposition of the condition of a husband. 10. Mismanagement of marital guardianship. 11. Desertion of marital guardianship. 12. Dissipation in prejudice of matrimonial wardship. 13. Peculation in prejudice of matrimonial wardship. 14. Abuse of marital power. 15. Disturbance of marital guardianship. 16. Wrongful withholding of connubial services. 17. Adultery. 18. Breach of duty to husbands. 19. Elopement from husbands. 20. Wife-stealing. 21. Bribery in prejudice of marital guardianship.[q4]

53. Next with regard to the offences to which the condition of a wife stands exposed. From the patterns that have been exhibited already, the coincidences and associations that take place between the offences that concern the existence of this condition and those which concern the existence of the condition of a husband, may easily enough be apprehended without farther repetitions. The catalogue of those now under consideration will be precisely the same in every article as the catalogue last exhibited. *Offences touching the condition of a wife*

54. Thus much for the several sorts of offences relative to the several sorts of domestic conditions: those which are constituted by such natural relations as are contiguous being included. There *[Uncontiguous domestic relations]*[1]

[q4] I. SEMI-PUBLIC OFFENCES. Falsehoods contesting, or offences against justice destroying, the validity of the marriages of people of certain descriptions: such as Jews, Quakers, Hugonots, etc. etc.

II. SELF-REGARDING OFFENCES. Improvident marriage on the part of minors.

[1] Bentham did not provide a marginal heading for para. 54, though its subject-matter is quite distinct from para. 53 and para. 55. A heading has therefore been editorially supplied.

remain those which are uncontiguous: of which, after so much as has been said of the others, it will naturally be expected that some notice should be taken. These, however, do not afford any of that matter which is necessary to constitute a condition. In point of fact, no power seems ever to be annexed to any of them. A grandfather, perhaps, may be called by the law to take upon him the guardianship of his orphan grandson: but then the power he has belongs to him not as grandfather, but as guardian. In point of possibility, indeed, power might be annexed to these relations, just as it might to any other. But still no new sort of domestic condition would result from it: since it has been shewn that there can be no others, that, being constituted by power, shall be distinct from those which have been already mentioned. Such as they are, however, they have this in common with the beforementioned relations, that they are capable of importing either benefit or burthen: they therefore stand exposed to the several offences whereby those or any other relations are liable to be affected in point of existence. It might be expected, therefore, that in virtue of these offences, they should be added to the list of the relations which are liable to be objects of delinquency. But the fact is, that they already stand included in it: and although not expressly named, yet as effectually as if they were. On the one hand, it is only by affecting such or such a contiguous relation that any offence, affecting uncontiguous relations can take place. On the other hand, neither can any offence, affecting the existence of the contiguous relations, be committed, without affecting the existence of an indefinite multitude of such as are uncontiguous. A false witness comes, and causes it to be believed that you are the son of a woman, who, in truth, is not your mother. What follows? An endless tribe of other false persuasions—that you are the grandson of the father and of the mother of this supposed mother: that you are the son of some husband of her's, or, at least, of some man with whom she has cohabited: the grandson of his father and his mother; and so on: the brother of their other children, if they have any: the brother-in-law of the husbands and wives of those children, if married: the uncle of the children of those children: and so on.— On the other hand, that you are not the son of your real mother, nor of your real father: that you are not the grandson of either of your real grandfathers or grandmothers; and so on without end: all which persuasions result from, and are included in, the one original false persuasion of your being the son of this your pretended mother.

It should seem, therefore, at first sight, that none of the offences against these uncontiguous relations could ever come expressly into question: for by the same rule that one ought, so it might seem ought a thousand others: the offences against the uncontiguous being merged as it were in those which affect the contiguous relations. So far, however, is this from being the case, that in speaking of an offence of this stamp, it is not uncommon to hear a great deal said of this or that uncontiguous relationship which it affects, at the same time that no notice at all shall be taken of any of those which are contiguous. How happens this? Because, to the uncontiguous relation are annexed perhaps certain remarkable advantages or disadvantages, while to all the intermediate relations none shall be annexed which are in comparison worth noticing. Suppose Antony or Lepidus to have contested the relationship of Octavius (afterwards Augustus) to Caius Julius Cæsar. How could it have been done? It could only have been by contesting, either Octavius's being the son of Atia, or Atia's being the daughter of Julia, or Julia's being the daughter of Lucius Julius Cæsar, or Lucius Julius Cæsar's being the father of Caius.[1] But to have been the son of Atia, or the grandson of Julia, or the great grandson of Lucius Julius Cæsar, was, in comparison of small importance. Those intervening relationships were, comparatively speaking, of no other use to him than in virtue of their being so many necessary links in the genealogical chain which connected him with the sovereign of the empire.

As to the advantages and disadvantages which may happen to be annexed to any of those uncontiguous relationships, we have seen already that no powers over the correlative person, nor any corresponding obligations, are of the number. Of what nature then can they be? They are, in truth, no other than what are the result either of local and accidental institutions, or of some spontaneous bias that has been taken by the moral sanction. It would, therefore, be to little purpose to attempt tracing them out *a priori* by an exhaustive process: all that can be done is, to pick up and lay together some of the principal articles in each catalogue by way of specimen. The advantages which a given relationship is apt to impart, seem to be referable chiefly to the following heads: 1. Chance of succession to the property, or a part of the property, of the correlative person. 2. Chance of pecuniary support, to be yielded by the correlative person, either by appointment of law, or by spontaneous dona-

---

[1] Octavius's maternal grandmother, Julia, was the sister of Julius Caesar. Mark Antony and Lepidus were Octavius's colleagues in the second triumvirate following the assassination of Caesar.

tion. 3. Accession of legal rank; including any legal privileges which may happen to be annexed to it: such as capacity of holding such and such beneficial offices; exemption from such and such burthensome obligations; for instance, paying taxes, serving burthensome offices, &c. &c. 4. Accession of rank by courtesy; including the sort of reputation which is customarily and spontaneously annexed to distinguished birth and family alliance: whereon may depend the chance of advancement in the way of marriage, or in a thousand other ways less obvious. The disadvantages which a given relation is liable to impart, seem to be referable chiefly to the following heads: 1. Chance of being obliged, either by law, or by force of the moral sanction, to yield pecuniary support to the correlative party. 2. Loss of legal rank: including the legal disabilities, as well as the burthensome obligations, which the law is apt to annex, sometimes with injustice enough, to the lower stations. 3. Loss of rank by courtesy: including the loss of the advantages annexed by custom to such rank. 4. Incapacity of contracting matrimony with the correlative person, where the supposed consanguinity or affinity lies within the prohibited degrees.[r4]

[r4] In pursuance of the plan adopted with relation to semi-public and self-regarding offences, it may here be proper to exhibit such a catalogue as the nature of the design will admit, of the several genera or inferior divisions of public offences.

I. OFFENCES against the EXTERNAL SECURITY of the state. 1. Treason (in favour of foreign enemies.) It may be positive or negative (negative consisting, for example, in the not opposing the commission of positive.) 2. *Espionage* (in favour of foreign rivals not yet enemies.) 3. Injuries to foreigners at large (including piracy.) 4. Injuries to privileged foreigners (such as ambassadors.)

II. OFFENCES against JUSTICE. 1. Offences against judicial trust: viz. Wrongful non-investment of judicial trust, wrongful interception of judicial trust, wrongful divestment of judicial trust, usurpation of judicial trust, wrongful investment of judicial trust, wrongful abdication of judicial trust, wrongful detrectation of judicial trust, wrongful imposition of judicial trust, breach of judicial trust, abuse of judicial trust, disturbance of judicial trust, and bribery in prejudice of judicial trust.

Breach and abuse of judicial trust may be either intentional or unintentional. Intentional is culpable at any rate. Unintentional will proceed either from inadvertence, or from mis-supposal: if the inadvertence be coupled with heedlessness, or the mis-supposal with rashness, it is culpable: if not, blameless. For the particular acts by which the exercise of judicial trust may be *disturbed* see B. I. tit. (Offences against justice.) They are too multifarious, and too ill provided with names, to be examined[1] here.

If a man fails in fulfilling the duties of this trust, and thereby comes either to break or to abuse it, it must be through some deficiency in the three requisite

[1] Thus 1823 and Bowring editions. 1789, followed by Harrison (p. 389 n.) 'exhibited'.

r4 cont.

and only requisite endowments, of knowledge, inclination, and power. (See supra 27.) A deficiency in any of those points, if any person be in fault, may proceed either from his own fault, or from the fault of those who should act with or under him. If persons who are in fault are persons invested with judicial trust, the offence comes under the head of breach or abuse of trust: if other persons, under that of disturbance of trust.

The ill effects of any breach, abuse, or disturbance of judicial trust, will consist in the production of some article or articles in the list of the mischiefs which it ought to be the original purpose of judicial procedure to remedy or avert, and of those which it ought to be the incidental purpose of it to avoid producing. These are either primary (that is immediate) or remote: remote are of the 2d, 3d, or 4th order, and so on. The primary are those which import actual pain to persons assignable, and are therefore mischievous in themselves: the secondary are mischievous on account of the tendency they have to produce some article or articles in the catalogue of those of the first order; and are therefore mischievous in their effects. Those of the 3d order are mischievous only on account of the connection they have in the way of productive tendency, as before, with those of the 2d order: and so on.

Primary inconveniences, which it ought to be the object of procedure to provide against, are, 1. The continuance of the individual offence itself, and thereby the increase as well as continuance of the mischief of it. 2. The continuance of the whole mischief of the individual offence. 3. The continuance of a part of the mischief of the individual offence. 4. Total want of amends on the part of persons injured by the offence. 5. Partial want of amends on the part of persons injured by the offence. 6. Superfluous punishment of delinquents. 7. Unjust punishment of persons accused. 8. Unnecessary labour, expense, or other suffering or danger, on the part of superior judicial officers. 9. Unnecessary labour, expense, or other suffering or danger, on the part of ministerial or other subordinate judicial officers. 10. Unnecessary labour, expense, or other suffering or danger, on the part of persons whose co-operation is requisite *pro re natâ*, in order to make up the necessary complement of knowledge and power on the part of judicial officers, who are such by profession. 11. Unnecessary labour, expense, or other suffering or danger, on the part of persons at large, coming under the sphere of the operations of the persons above-mentioned.

Secondary inconveniences are, in the purely civil branch of procedure, 1. Misadjudication. In the penal branch,[1] 2. Total impunity of delinquents: (as favouring the production of other offences of the like nature.) 3. Partial impunity of delinquents. 4. Application of punishment improper *in specie*, though perhaps not in degree (this lessening the beneficial efficacy of the quantity employed.) 5. Uneconomical application of punishment, though proper, perhaps, as well *in specie* as in degree. 6. Unnecessary pecuniary expense on the part of the state.

[1] In the text as printed in 1780 the opening of this paragraph reads as follows: 'Second inconveniences are, in the consultative, pre-interpretative (or purely civil) branch of procedure, 1. Mis-interpretation, or adjudication. In the executive (including the penal) branch . . .' The corrections were made in 1783 but overlooked in 1823 (and editions following that text). In the Bowring edition (i, 133n.) the corrections were made, but under '1.' the words 'Misinterpretation or', deleted by Bentham in 1783, were left in before 'misadjudication'.

^{r4} cont.

Inconveniences of the 3d order are, 1. Unnecessary delay. 2. Unnecessary intricacy.

Inconveniences of the 4th order are, 1. Breach, 2. Abuse, 3. Disturbance, of judicial trust, as above: viz. in as far as these offences are preliminary to and distinct from those of the 2d and 3d orders.

Inconveniences of the 5th order are, Breach of the several regulations of procedure, or other regulations, made in the view of obviating the inconveniences above enumerated: viz. if preliminary and distinct as before.

III. OFFENCES against the PREVENTIVE branch of the POLICE. 1. Offences against *phthano-paranomic* trust: (φθανω, to prevent; παρανομια, an offence.) 2. Offences against *phthano-symphoric* trust: συμφορα, a calamity. The two trusts may be termed by the common appellation of *prophylactic*: (προ, beforehand, and φυλαττω, to guard against.)

IV. OFFENCES against the PUBLIC FORCE. 1. Offences against military trust, corresponding to those against judicial trust. Military desertion is a breach of military duty, or of military trust. Favouring desertion is a disturbance of it. 2. Offences against that branch of public trust which consists in the management of the several sorts of *things* appropriated to the purposes of war: such as arsenals, fortifications, dock-yards, ships of war, artillery, ammunition, military magazines, and so forth. It might be termed *polemo-tamieutic*: from πολεμος, war; and ταμιευς, a steward.*

V. OFFENCES against the POSITIVE INCREASE of the NATIONAL FELICITY. 1. Offences against *epistemo-threptic* trust: (επιστημη, knowledge; and τρεφω, to nourish or promote.) 2. Offences against *eupædagogic* trust: ευ, well; and παιδαγωγεω, to educate. 3. Offences against *noso-comial* trust: νοσος, a disease; and κομιζω, to take care of. 4. Offences against *moro-comial* trust: (μωρος, an insane person.) 5. Offences against *ptocho-comial* trust: (πτωχοι, the poor.) 6. Offences against *antembletic* trust: (αντεμβαλλω, to bestow in reparation of a loss.) 7. Offences against *hedonarchic* trust: (ηδοναι, pleasures; and αρχομαι, to preside over.) The above are examples of the principal establishments which should or might be set on foot for the purpose of making, in so many different ways, a positive addition to the stock of national felicity. To exhibit an exhaustive analysis of the possible total of these establishments would not be a very easy task: nor on the present occasion is it a necessary one; for be they of what nature and in what number they may, the offences to which they stand exposed will, in as far as they are offences against trust, be in point of denomination the same: and as to what turns upon the particular nature of each trust, they will be of too local a nature to come within the present plan.

All these trusts might be comprized under some such general name as that of *agatho-poieutic* trust: (αγαθοποιεω, to do good to any one.)

VI. OFFENCES against the PUBLIC WEALTH. 1. Non-payment of forfeitures. 2. Non-payment of taxes, including smuggling. 3. Breach of the several regulations made to prevent the evasion of taxes. 4. Offences against fiscal trust: the same as offences against judicial and military trusts. Offences against the origi-

* A number of different branches of public trust, none of which have yet been provided with appellatives, have here been brought to view: which then were best? to coin new names for them out of the Greek; or, instead of a word, to make use of a whole sentence? In English, and in French, there is no other alternative; no more than in any of the other southern languages. It rests with the reader to determine.

r4 cont.

nal revenue, not accruing either from taxes or forfeitures, such as that arising from the public demesnes, stand upon the same footing as offences against private property. 5. Offences against *demosio-tamieutic* trust: (δημοσια, things belonging to the public; and ταμιευς, a steward) viz. against that trust, of which the object is to apply to their several destinations such articles of the public wealth as are provided for the indiscriminate accommodation of individuals: such as public roads and waters, public harbours, post-offices, and packet-boats, and the stock belonging to them; market-places, and other such public buildings; race-grounds, public walks, and so forth. Offences of this description will be apt to coincide with offences against *agatho-poieutic* trust as above, or with offences against *ethno-plutistic* trust hereafter mentioned, according as the benefit in question is considered in itself, or as resulting from the application of such or such a branch or portion of the public wealth.

VII. OFFENCES against POPULATION. 1. Emigration. 2. Suicide. 3. Procurement of impotence or barrenness. 4. Abortion. 5. Unprolific coition. 6. Celibacy.

VIII. OFFENCES against the NATIONAL WEALTH. 1. Idleness. 2. Breach of the regulations made in the view of preventing the application of industry to purposes less profitable, in prejudice of purposes more profitable. 3. Offences against *ethno-plutistic* trust; (εθνος, the nation at large; πλουτιζω, to enrich.

IX. OFFENCES against the SOVEREIGNTY. 1. Offences against sovereign trust: corresponding to those against judicial, prophylactic, military, and fiscal trusts. Offensive rebellion includes wrongful interception, wrongful divestment, usurpation, and wrongful investment, of sovereign trust, with the offences accessary thereto. Where the trust is in a single person, wrongful interception, wrongful divestment, usurpation, and wrongful investment, cannot any of them, be committed without rebellion; abdication and detrectation can never be deemed wrongful; breach and abuse of sovereign trust can scarcely be punished: no more can bribe-taking: wrongful imposition of it is scarce practicable. When the sovereignty is shared among a number, wrongful interception, wrongful divestment, usurpation, and wrongful investment, may be committed without rebellion: none of the offences against this trust are impracticable: nor is there any of them but might be punished. Defensive rebellion is disturbance of this trust. Political tumults, political defamation, and political vilification, are offences accessory to such disturbance.

Sovereign power (which, upon the principle of utility, can never be other than fiduciary) is exercised either by rule or without rule: in the latter case it may be termed *autocratic*: in the former case it is divided into two branches, the *legislative* and the *executive*.* In either case, where the designation of the person by whom the power is to be possessed, depends not solely upon mere physical events, such as that of natural succession, but in any sort upon the will of another person, the latter possesses an *investitive* power, or right of investiture, with regard to the power in question: in like manner may any person also possess a *divestitive* power. The powers above enumerated, such as judicial power, military power, and so forth, may therefore be exercisable by a man, either directly, *propriâ manu*; or indirectly, *manu alienâ*. †Power to be

* See Ch. XVII (Limits) § iii.[1]

† In the former case, the power might be termed in one word, *autochirous*: in the latter, *heterochirous*: (αυτος, a man's own; χειρ, a hand: ετερος another's.)

[1] See above 207 n. 1.

Civil
conditions

55. We come now to civil conditions: these, it may well be ima-gined, may be infinitely various: as various as the acts which a man may be either commanded or allowed, whether for his own benefit, or that of others, to abstain from or to perform. As many different denominations as there are of persons distinguished with a view to such commands and allowances (those denominations only except-ed which relate to the conditions above spoken of under the name of domestic ones) so many civil conditions one might enumerate. Means however, more or less explicit, may be found out of circum-scribing their infinitude.

What the materials are, if so they may be called, of which con-ditions, or any other kind of legal possession, can be made up, we have already seen: beneficial powers, fiduciary powers, beneficial rights, fiduciary rights, relative duties, absolute duties. But as many conditions as import a power or right of the fiduciary kind, as possessed by the person whose condition is in question, belong to the head of trusts. The catalogue of the offences to which these condi-

r4 cont.

exercised *manu alienâ* is investitive, which may or may not be accompanied by divestitive. Of sovereign power, whether autocratic, legislative, or executive, the several public trusts above-mentioned form so many subordinate branches. Any of these powers may be placed, either, 1. in an individual; or, 2. in a body politic: who may be either supreme or subordinate. Subordination on the part of a magistrate is established, 1. Where he is made punishable: 2. Where he is made removable: 3. When his orders are made reversible: 4. When the good or evil which he has it in its power to produce on the part of the common subordinate is less in value than the good or evil which the superior has it in his power to produce on the part of the same subordinate.[1]

x. OFFENCES against RELIGION. 1. Offences tending to weaken the force of the religious sanction: including blasphemy and profaneness. 2. Offences tend-ing to misapply the force of the religious sanction: including false prophecies, and other pretended revelations; also heresy, where the doctrine broached is pernicious to the temporal interests of the community. 3. Offences against religious trust, where any such is thought fit to be established.

xi. OFFENCES against the NATIONAL INTEREST in general. 1. Immoral publi-cations. 2. Offences against the trust of an ambassador; or, as it might be termed, *presbeutic* trust. 3. Offences against the trust of a privy-counsellor; or, as it might be termed, *symbouleutic* trust. 4. In pure or mixed monarchies, prodigality on the part of persons who are about the person of the sovereign, though without being invested with any specific trust. 5. Excessive gaming on the part of the same persons. 6. Taking presents from rival powers without leave.

[1] In the text as printed in 1780 the last sentence of this paragraph reads as follows: 'Subordination on the part of a magistrate may be established, 1. By the person's being punishable: 2. By his being removeable: 3. By the orders being reversible.' The changes made by Bentham in 1783 were overlooked in 1823 (and editions follow-ing that text), but were inserted in the Bowring edition (i, 134n.) except for the omis-sion of the word 'made' before 'punishable' under item 1.

tions are exposed, coincides therefore exactly with the catalogue of offences against trust: under which head they have been considered in a general point of view under the head of offences against trust: and such of them as are of a domestic nature, in a more particular manner in the character of offences against the several domestic conditions. Conditions constituted by such duties of the relative kind, as have for their counterparts trusts constituted by fiduciary powers, as well as rights on the side of the correlative party, and those of a private nature, have also been already discussed under the appellation of domestic conditions. The same observation may be applied to the conditions constituted by such powers of the beneficial kind over persons as are of a private nature: as also to the subordinate correlative conditions constituted by the duties corresponding to those rights and powers. As to absolute duties, there is no instance of a condition thus created, of which the institution is upon the principle of utility to be justified; unless the several religious conditions of the monastic kind should be allowed of as examples. There remain, as the only materials out of which the conditions which yet remain to be considered can be composed, conditions constituted by beneficial powers over things; conditions constituted by beneficial rights to things (that is, rights to powers over things) or by rights to those rights, and so on; conditions constituted by rights to services; and conditions constituted by the duties corresponding to those respective rights. Out of these are to be taken those of which the materials are the ingredients of the several modifications of property, the several conditions of proprietorship. These are the conditions, if such for a moment they may be styled, which having but here and there any specific names, are not commonly considered on the footing of conditions: so that the acts which, if such conditions were recognized, might be considered as offences against those conditions, are not wont to be considered in any other light than that of offences against property.

Now the case is, as hath been already intimated,[s4] that of these civil conditions, those which are wont to be considered under that name, are not distinguished by any uniform and explicit line from those of which the materials are wont to be carried to the head of property: a set of rights shall, in one instance be considered as constituting an article of property rather than a condition: while, in another instance, a set of rights of the same stamp is considered as constituting rather a condition than an article of property. This will probably be found to be the case in all languages: and the usage

[s4] Supra 17.

is different again in one language from what it is in another. From these causes it seems to be impracticable to subject the class of civil conditions to any exhaustive method: so that for making a complete collection of them there seems to be no other expedient than that of searching the language through for them, and taking them as they come. To exemplify this observation, it may be of use to lay open the structure as it were of two or three of the principal sorts or classes of conditions, comparing them with two or three articles of property which appear to be nearly of the same complexion: by this means the nature and generation, if one may so call it, of both these classes of ideal objects may be the more clearly understood.

The several sorts of civil conditions that are not fiduciary may all, or at least the greater part of them, be comprehended under the head of *rank*, or that of *profession*; the latter word being taken in its most extensive sense, so as to include not only what are called the liberal professions, but those also which are exercised by the several sorts of traders, artists, manufacturers, and other persons of whatsoever station, who are in the way of making a profit by their labour. Among ranks then, as well as professions, let us, for the sake of perspicuity, take for examples such articles as stand the clearest from any mixture of either fiduciary or beneficial power. The rank of knighthood is constituted, how? by prohibiting all other persons from performing certain acts, the performance of which is the symbol of the order, at the same time that the knight in question, and his companions, are permitted: for instance, to wear a ribbon of a certain colour in a certain manner: to call himself by a certain title: to use an armorial seal with a certain mark on it. By laying all persons but the knight under this prohibition, the law subjects them to a set of duties: and since from the discharge of these duties a benefit results to the person in whose favour they are created, to wit, the benefit of enjoying such a share of extraordinary reputation and respect as men are wont to yield to a person thus distinguished, to discharge them is to render him a service: and the duty being a duty of the negative class, a duty consisting in the performance of certain acts of the negative kind,[t4] the service is what may be called *a service of forbearance*. It appears then, that to generate this condition there must be two sorts of services: that which is the immediate cause of it, a service of the negative kind, to be rendered by the community at large: that which is the cause again of this service, a service of the positive kind, to be rendered by the law.

[t4] See Ch. VII (Actions) 8.

The condition of a professional man stands upon a narrower footing. To constitute this condition there needs nothing more than a permission given him on the part of the legislator to perform those acts, in the performance of which consists the exercise of his profession: to give or sell his advice or assistance in matters of law or physic: to give or sell his services as employed in the executing or overseeing of a manufacture or piece of work of such or such a kind: to sell a commodity of such or such a sort. Here then we see there is but one sort of service requisite; a service which may be merely of the negative kind, to be rendered by the law: the service of permitting him to exercise his profession: a service which, if there has been no prohibition laid on before, is rendered by simply forbearing to prohibit him.

Now the ideal objects, which in the cases above specified are said to be conferred upon a man by the services that are respectively in question, are in both cases not articles of property but conditions. By such a behaviour on the part of the law, as shall be the reverse of that whereby they were respectively produced, a man may be made to forfeit them: and what he is then said to forfeit is in neither case his property; but in one case, his rank or dignity: in the other case, his trade or his profession: and in both cases, his condition.

Other cases there are again in which the law, by a process of the same sort with that by which it constituted the former of the two above-mentioned conditions, confers on him an ideal object, which the laws of language have placed under the head of property. The law permits a man to sell books: that is, all sorts of books in general. Thus far all that it has done is to invest him with a condition: and this condition he would equally possess, although every body else in the world were to sell books likewise. Let the law now take an active part in his favour, and prohibit all other persons from selling books of a certain description, he remaining at liberty to sell them as before. It thereby confers on him a sort of exclusive privilege or monopoly, which is called a *copy-right*. But by investing him with this right, it is not said to invest him with any new sort of condition; and what it invests him with is spoken of as an article of property; to wit, of that sort of property which is termed incorporeal[u4]: and so on in the case of an engraving, a mechanical engine, a medicine; or, in short, of a saleable article of any other sort. Yet when it gave

[u4] The reason probably why an object of the sort here in question is referred to the head of property, is, that the chief value of it arises from its being capable of being made a source of property in the more ordinary acceptations of the word; that is, of money, consumable commodities, and so forth.

him an exclusive right of wearing a particular sort of ribbon, the object which it was then considered as conferring on him was not an article of property but a condition.

By forbearing to subject you to certain disadvantages, to which it subjects an alien, the law confers on you the condition of a natural-born subject: by subjecting him to them, it imposes on him the condition of an alien: by conferring on you certain privileges or rights, which it denies to a *roturier*, the law confers on you the condition of a *gentilhomme*; by forbearing to confer on him those privileges, it imposes on him the condition of a *roturier*.[v4] The rights, out of which the two advantageous conditions here exemplified are both of them as it were composed, have for their counterpart a sort of services of forbearance, rendered, as we have seen, not by private individuals, but by the law itself. As to the duties which it creates in rendering you these services, they are to be considered as duties imposed by the legislator on the ministers of justice.

It may be observed, with regard to the greater part of the conditions here comprised under the general appellation of *civil*, that the relations corresponding to those by which they are respectively constituted, are not provided with appellatives. The relation which has a name, is that which is borne by the party favoured to the party bound: that which is borne by the party bound to the party favoured has not any. This is a circumstance that may help to distinguish them from those conditions which we have termed domestic. In the domestic conditions, if on the one side the party *to* whom the power is given is called a master; on the other side, the party *over* whom that power is given, the party who is the object of that power, is termed a *servant*. In the civil conditions this is not the case. On the one side, a man, in virtue of certain services of forbearance, which the rest of the community are bound to render him, is denominated a *knight* of such or such an order: but on the other side, these services do not bestow any particular denomination on the persons from whom such services are due. Another man, in virtue of the legislator's rendering that sort of negative service which consists in the not prohibiting him from exercising a trade, invests him at his option with the condition of a trader: it accordingly denominates him a *farmer*, a *baker*, a *weaver*, and so on: but the ministers of the law do not, in virtue of their rendering the man this sort of negative service, acquire for themselves any particular name. Suppose even that the trade you have the right of

[v4] The conditions themselves having nothing that corresponds to them in England, it was necessary to make use of foreign terms.

exercising happens to be the object of a monopoly, and that the legislator, besides rendering you himself those services which you derive from the permission he bestows on you, obliges other persons to render you those farther services which you receive from their forbearing to follow the same trade; yet neither do they, in virtue of their being thus bound, acquire any particular name.

After what has been said of the nature of the several sorts of civil conditions that have names, the offences to which they are exposed may, without much difficulty, be imagined. Taken by itself, every condition which is thus constituted by a permission granted to the possessor, is of course of a beneficial nature: it is, therefore, exposed to all those offences to which the possession of a benefit is exposed. But either on account of a man's being obliged to persevere when once engaged in it, or on account of such other obligations as may stand annexed to the possession of it, or on account of the comparative degree of disrepute which may stand annexed to it by the moral sanction, it may by accident be a burthen: it is on this account liable to stand exposed to the offences to which, as hath been seen, every thing that partakes of the nature of a burthen stands exposed. As to any offences which may concern the exercise of the functions belonging to it, if it happens to have any duties annexed to it, such as those, for instance, which are constituted by regulations touching the exercise of a trade, it will stand exposed to so many breaches of duty; and lastly, whatsoever are the functions belonging to it, it will stand exposed at any rate to *disturbance.*

In the forming however of the catalogue of these offences, exactness is of the less consequence, inasmuch as an act, if it should happen not to be comprised in this catalogue, and yet is in any respect of a pernicious nature, will be sure to be found in some other division of the system of offences: if a baker sells bad bread for the price of good, it is a kind of *fraud* upon the buyer; and perhaps an injury of the *simple corporal* kind done to the health of an individual, or a neighbourhood: if a clothier sells bad cloth for good at home, it is a fraud; if to foreigners abroad, it may, over and above the fraud put upon the foreign purchaser, have pernicious effects perhaps in the prosperity of the trade at home, and become thereby an offence against the *national wealth.* So again with regard to *disturbance*: if a man be disturbed in the exercise of his trade, the offence will probably be a wrongful *interception of the profit* he might be presumed to have been in a way to make by it: and were it even to appear in any case that a man exercised a trade, or what is less unlikely, a liberal profession, without having profit in his view, the offence will still be reducible to the head of *simple injurious restrainment*, or *simple injurious compulsion.*

§ iv. *Advantages of the present method*

*General
idea of the
method here
pursued*

56. A few words, for the purpose of giving a general view of the method of division here pursued, and of the advantages which it possesses, may have their use. The whole system of offences, we may observe, is branched out into five classes. In the three first, the subordinate divisions are taken from the same source; viz. from the consideration of the different points, in respect whereof the interest of an individual is exposed to suffer. By this uniformity, a considerable degree of light seems to be thrown upon the whole system; particularly upon the offences that come under the third class: objects which have never hitherto been brought into any sort of order. With regard to the fourth class, in settling the precedence between its several subordinate divisions, it seemed most natural and satisfactory to place those first, the connection whereof with the welfare of individuals seemed most obvious and immediate. The mischievous effects of those offences, which tend in an immediate way to deprive individuals of the protection provided for them against the attacks of one another, and of those which tend to bring down upon them the attacks of foreign assailants, seem alike obvious and palpable. The mischievous quality of such as tend to weaken the force that is provided to combat those attacks, but particularly the latter, though evident enough, is one link farther off in the chain of causes and effects. The ill effects of such offences as are of disservice only by diminishing the particular fund from whence that force is to be extracted, such effects, I say, though indisputable, are still more distant and out of sight. The same thing may be observed with regard to such as are mischievous only by affecting the universal fund. Offences against the sovereignty in general would not be mischievous, if offences of the several descriptions preceding were not mischievous. Nor in a temporal view are offences against religion mischievous, except in as far as, by removing, or weakening, or misapplying one of the three great incentives to virtue, and checks to vice, they tend to open the door to the several mischiefs, which it is the nature of all those other offences to produce. As to the fifth class, this, as hath already been observed, exhibits, at first view, an irregularity, which however seems to be unavoidable. But this irregularity is presently corrected, when the analysis returns back, as it does after a step or two, into the path from which the tyranny of language had forced it a while to deviate.

It was necessary that it should have two purposes in view: the one, to exhibit, upon a scale more or less minute, a systematical enumeration of the several possible modifications of delinquency, denominated or undenominated; the other, to find places in the list for such names of offences as were in current use: for the first purpose, nature was to set the law; for the other, custom. Had the nature of the things themselves been the only guide, every such difference in the manner of perpetration, and such only, should have served as a ground for a different denomination, as was attended with a difference in point of effect. This however of itself would never have been sufficient; for as on one hand the new language, which it would have been necessary to invent, would have been uncouth, and in a manner unintelligible: so on the other hand the names, which were before in current use, and which, in spite of all systems, good or bad, must have remained in current use, would have continued unexplained. To have adhered exclusively to the current language, would have been as bad on the other side; for in that case the catalogue of offences, when compared to that of the mischiefs that are capable of being produced, would have been altogether broken and uncomplete.

To reconcile these two objects, in as far as they seemed to be reconcileable, the following course has therefore been pursued. The logical whole, constituted by the sum total of possible offences, has been bisected in as many different directions as were necessary, and the process in each direction carried down to that stage at which the particular ideas thus divided found names in current use in readiness to receive them. At that period I have stopped; leaving any minuter distinctions to be enumerated in the body of the work, as so many species of the genus characterized by such or such a name, If in the course of any such process I came to a mode of conduct which, though it required to be taken notice of, and perhaps had actually been taken notice of, under all laws, in the character of an offence, had hitherto been expressed under different laws, by different circumlocutions, without ever having received any name capable of occupying the place of a substantive in a sentence, I have frequently ventured so far as to fabricate a new name for it, such an one as the idiom of the language, and the acquaintance I happened to have with it, would admit of. These names consisting in most instances, and that unavoidably, of two or three words brought together, in a language too which admits not, like the German and the Greek, of their being melted into one, can never be upon a par, in point of commodiousness, with those univocal appellatives which make part of the established stock.

In the choice of names in current use, care has been taken to avoid all such as have been grounded on local distinctions, ill founded, perhaps, in the nation in which they received their birth, and at any rate not applicable to the circumstances of other countries.

The analysis, as far as it goes, is as applicable to the legal concerns of one country as of another: and where, if it had descended into further details, it would have ceased to be so, there I have taken care always to stop: and thence it is that it has come to be so much more particular in the class of offences against individuals, than in any of the other classes. One use then of this arrangement, if it should be found to have been properly conducted, will be its serving to point out in what it is that the legal interests of all countries agree, and in what it is that they are liable to differ: how far a rule that is proper for one, will serve, and how far it will not serve, for another. That the legal interests of different ages and countries have nothing in common, and they have every thing, are suppositions equally distant from the truth.[w4]

Its advantages.
– 1. It is convenient for the apprehension and the memory

57. A natural method, such as it hath been here attempted to exhibit, seems to possess four capital advantages; not to mention others of inferior note. In the first place, it affords such assistance to the apprehension and to the memory, as those faculties would in vain look for in any technical arrangement.[x4] That arrangement of the objects of any science may, it should seem, be termed a *natural* one, which takes such properties to characterize them by, as men in general are, by the common constitution of man's nature, independently of any accidental impressions they may have received from the influence of any local or other particular causes, accustomed to attend to: such, in a word, as *naturally*, that is readily, and at first sight, engage, and firmly fix, the attention of any one to whom they have once been pointed out. Now by what other means should an object engage, or fix a man's attention, unless by interesting him? and what circumstance belonging to any

[w4] The above hints are offered to the consideration of the few who may be disposed to bend their minds to disquisitions of this uninviting nature: to sift the matter to the bottom, and engage in the details of illustration, would require more room than could in this place be consistently allowed.

[x4] See Fragment on Government, pref. p. xlv. edit. 1776.—pref. p. xlvii. edit. 1823.[1]

[1] *Fragment on Government*, Preface, para. 52 (Bowring, i, 237).

action can be more interesting, or rather what other circumstance belonging to it can be at all interesting to him, than that of the influence it promises to have on his own happiness, and the happiness of those who are about him? By what other mark then should he more easily find the place which any offence occupies in the system, or by what other clue should he more readily recall it?

58. In the next place, it not only gives at first glance a general intimation of the nature of each division of offences, in as far as that nature is determined by some one characteristic property, but it gives room for a number of general propositions to be formed concerning the particular offences that come under that division, in such manner as to exhibit a variety of other properties that may belong to them in common. It gives room, therefore, for the framing of a number of propositions concerning them, which, though very general, because predicated of a great number of articles, shall be as generally true.[y4]

– 2. It gives room for general propositions

59. In the third place, it is so contrived, that the very place which any offence is made to occupy, suggests the reason of its being put there. It serves to indicate not only that such and such acts *are* made offences, but *why* they *ought* to be. By this means, while it addresses itself to the understanding, it recommends itself, in some measure, to the affections. By the intimation it gives of the nature

– 3. It points out the reason of the law

[y4] Imagine what a condition a science must be in, when as yet there shall be no such thing as forming any extensive proposition relative to it, that shall be at the same time a true one: where, if the proposition shall be true of some of the particulars contained under it, it shall be false with regard to others. What a state would botany, for example, be in, if the classes were so contrived, that no common characters could be found for them? Yet in this state, and no better, seems every system of penal law to be, authoritative or unauthoritative that has ever yet appeared. Try if it be otherwise, for instance, with the *delicta privata et publica*, and with the *publica ordinaria*, and *publica extra-ordinaria* of the Roman law.* All this for want of method: and hence the necessity of endeavouring to strike out a new one.

Nor is this want of method to be wondered at. A science so new as that of penal legislation, could hardly have been in any better state. Till objects are distinguished, they cannot be arranged. It is thus that *truth* and *order* go on hand in hand. It is only in proportion as the former is discovered, that the latter can be improved. Before a certain order is established, truth can be put imperfectly announced: but until a certain proportion of truth has been developed and brought to light, that order cannot be established. The discovery of truth leads to the establishment of order: and the establishment of order fixes and propagates the discovery of truth.

* See Heinecc. Elem. p. vii. § 79, 80.[1]

[1] i.e. Johann Gottlieb Heineccius, *Elementa Iuris Civilis secundum ordinem Pandectarum* (1731), part vii, lib. xlvii, tit. I, *De privatis delictis*, sects. 79–80.

and tendency of each obnoxious act, it accounts for, and in some measure vindicates, the treatment which it may be thought proper to bestow upon that act in the way of punishment. To the subject then it is a kind of perpetual apology: shewing the necessity of every defalcation, which, for the security and prosperity of each individual, it is requisite to make from the liberty of every other. To the legislator it is a kind of perpetual lesson: serving at once as a corrective to his prejudices, and as a check upon his passions. Is there a mischief which has escaped him? in a natural arrangement, if at the same time an exhaustive one, he cannot fail to find it. Is he tempted ever to force innocence within the pale of guilt? the difficulty of finding a place for it advertises him of his error. Such are the uses of a map of universal delinquency, laid down upon the principle of utility: such the advantages, which the legislator as well as the subject may derive from it. Abide by it, and every thing that is arbitrary in legislation vanishes. An evil-intentioned or prejudiced legislator durst not look it in the face. He would proscribe it, and with reason: it would be a satire on his laws.

–4. It is alike applicable to the laws of all nations

60. In the fourth place, a natural arrangement, governed as it is by a principle which is recognized by all men, will serve alike for the jurisprudence of all nations. In a system of proposed law, framed in pursuance of such a method, the language will serve as a glossary by which all systems of positive law might be explained, while the matter serves as a standard by which they might be tried. Thus illustrated, the practice of every nation might be a lesson to every other: and mankind might carry on a mutual interchange of experiences and improvements as easily in this as in every other walk of science. If any one of these objects should in any degree be attained, the labour of this analysis, severe as it has been, will not have been thrown away.

§ v. *Characters of the five classes*

Characters of the classes, how deducible from the above method

61. It has been mentioned (supra, 58) as an advantage possessed by this method, and not possessed by any other, that the objects comprised under it are cast into groups, to which a variety of propositions may be applied in common. A collection of these propositions, as applied to the several classes, may be considered as exhibiting the distinctive characters of each class. So many of these propositions as can be applied to the offences belonging to any given class, so many properties are they found to have in common: so many of these common properties as may respectively be attributed to them, so many properties may be set down to serve as *characters* of the class. A collection of these characters it may here be proper to exhibit. The more of them we can bring together, the more clearly and fully will the nature of the several classes, and of the offences they are composed of, be understood.

62. Characters of Class 1; composed of PRIVATE offences, or offences against assignable *individuals*.

Characters of Class 1

1. When arrived at their last stage (the stage of *consummation*)[z4] they produce, all of them, a primary mischief as well as a secondary.[a5]

2. The individuals whom they affect in the first instance,[b5] are constantly *assignable*. This extends to all; to *attempts* and *preparations*, as well as to such as have arrived at the stage of consummation.[c5]

3. Consequently they admit of *compensation*[d5]: in which they differ from the offences of all the other classes, as such.

4. They admit[e5] also of *retaliation*[f5]; in which also they differ from the offences of all the other classes.

5. There is always some person who has a natural and peculiar interest to prosecute them. In this they differ from self-regarding offences: also from semi-public and public ones; except in as far as the two latter may chance to involve a private mischief.

6. The mischief they produce is obvious: more so than that of semi-public offences: and still more so than that of self-regarding ones, or even public.

7. They are every where, and must ever be, obnoxious to the censure of the world: more so than semi-public offences as such; and still more so than public ones.

8. They are more *constantly* obnoxious to the censure of the world than self-regarding offences: and would be so universally, were it not for the influence of the two false principles; the principle of asceticism, and the principle of antipathy.[g5]

9. They are less apt than semi-public and public offences to re-

---

[z4] Ch. VII (Actions) 14.

[a5] See Ch. XII (Consequences) 3.

[b5] (First Instance.) That is, by their primary mischief.

[c5] See supra, and B. I. tit. (Accessory offences).

[d5] See Ch. XIII (Cases unmeet) 2 note.

[e5] (Admit.) I mean, that retaliation is *capable* of being applied in the cases in question; not that it *ought* always to be employed. Nor is it capable of being applied in every *individual* instance of each offence, but only in some individual instance of each *species* of offence.

[f5] See Ch. XV (Properties) 8.

[g5] Ch. II (Principles adverse).

quire different descriptions[h5] in different states and countries: in which respect they are much upon a par with self-regarding ones.

10. By certain circumstances of aggravation, they are liable to be transformed into semi-public offences: and by certain others, into public.

11. There can be no ground for punishing them, until they can be proved to have occasioned, or to be about to occasion, some particular mischief to some particular individual. In this they differ from semi-public offences, and from public.

12. In slight cases, *compensation* given to the individual affected by them, may be a sufficient ground for remitting punishment: for if the primary mischief has not been sufficient to produce any alarm, the whole of the mischief may be cured by compensation. In this also they differ from semi-public offences, and from public ones.

Characters of Class 2 **63.** Characters of Class 2; composed of SEMI-PUBLIC offences, or offences affecting a whole subordinate *class* of persons.

1. As such, they produce no primary mischief. The mischief they produce consists of one or other or both branches of the secondary mischief produced by offences against individuals, without the primary.

2. In as far as they are to be considered as belonging to this class, the persons whom they affect in the first instance are not individually assignable.

3. They are apt, however, to involve or terminate in some primary mischief of the first order, which when they do, they advance into the first class, and become private offences.

4. They admit not, as such, of compensation.

5. Nor of retaliation.

6. As such, there is never any one particular individual whose exclusive interest it is to prosecute them: a circle of persons may, however, always be marked out, within which may be found some who have a greater interest to prosecute than any who are out of that circle have.

7. The mischief they produce is in general pretty obvious; not so much so indeed as that of private offences, but more so upon the whole than that of self-regarding and public ones.

[h5] (Different descriptions.) It seems to be from their possessing these three last properties, that the custom has arisen of speaking of them, or at least of many of them, under the name of offences against the *law of nature*: a vague expression, and productive of a multitude of inconveniences. See Ch. II (Principles adverse).

8. They are rather less obnoxious to the censure of the world than private offences; but they are more so than public ones: they would also be more so than self-regarding ones, were it not for the influence of the two false principles, the principle of sympathy and antipathy, and that of asceticism.

9. They are more apt than private and self-regarding offences to require different descriptions in different countries: but less so than public ones.

10. There may be ground for punishing them before they have been proved to have occasioned, or to be about to occasion, mischief to any particular individual; which is not the case with private offences.

11. In no cases can satisfaction given to any particular individual, affected by them be a sufficient ground for remitting punishment: for by such satisfaction it is but a part of the mischief of them that is cured. In this they differ from private offences; but agree with public.

64. Characters of Class 3; consisting of SELF-REGARDING offences: offences against *one's self*.

Characters of Class 3

1. In individual instances it will often be questionable, whether they are productive of any primary[15] mischief at all: secondary, they produce none.

2. They affect not any other individuals, assignable or not assignable, except in as far as they affect the offender himself; unless by possibility in particular cases; and in a very slight and distant manner the whole state.

3. They admit not, therefore, of *compensation*.

4. Nor of *retaliation*.

5. No person has naturally any peculiar interest to prosecute them; except in as far as in virtue of some *connection* he may have with the offender, either in point of *sympathy* or of *interest*,[15] a mischief of the *derivative* kind[k5] may happen to devolve upon him.[15]

6. The mischief they produce is apt to be unobvious, and in

---

[15] Because the person, who in general is most likely to be sensible to the mischief (if there is any) of any offence, viz. the person whom it most affects, shews by his conduct that he is not sensible of it.

[15] See Ch. vi (Sensibility) 25, 26.

[k5] See Ch. xii (Consequences) 4.

[15] Among the offences, however, which belong to this class, there are some which in certain countries it is not uncommon for persons to be disposed to prosecute without any artificial inducement, and merely on account of an *antipathy*, which such acts are apt to excite. See Ch. ii (Principles adverse) 11.

general more questionable than that of any of the other classes.[m5]

7. They are however apt, many of them, to be more obnoxious to the censure of the world than public offences; owing to the influence of the two false principles; the principle of asceticism, and the principle of antipathy. Some of them more even than semi-public, or even than private offences.

8. They are less apt than offences of any other class to require different descriptions in different states and countries.[n5]

9. Among the inducements[o5] to punish them, antipathy against the offender is apt to have a greater share than sympathy for the public.

10. The best plea for punishing them is founded on a faint probability there may be of their being productive of a mischief, which, if real, will place them in the class of public ones: chiefly in those divisions of it which are composed of offences against population, and offences against the national wealth.

Characters of Class 4

65. Characters of Class 4; consisting of PUBLIC offences, or offences against *the state* in general.

1. As such, they produce not any primary mischief; and the secondary mischief they produce, which consists frequently of danger without alarm, though great in *value*, is in *specie* very indeterminate.

2. The individuals whom they affect, in the first instance, are constantly unassignable; except in as far as by accident they happen to involve or terminate in such or such offences against individuals.

3. Consequently they admit not of compensation.

4. Nor of retaliation.

5. Nor is there any person who has naturally any particular interest to prosecute them; except in as far as they appear to affect the power, or in any other manner the private interest, of some person in authority.

6. The mischief they produce, as such, is comparatively unobvious; much more so than that of private offences, and more so likewise, than that of semi-public ones.

7. They are, as such, much less obnoxious to the censure of the world, than private offences; less even than semi-public, or even

[m5] See note i5 in the preceding page.

[n5] Accordingly, most of them are apt to be ranked among offences against the law of nature. See supra, Characters of the 1st class, 62 note.

[o5] (Inducements). I mean the considerations, right or wrong, which induce or dispose the legislator to treat them on the footing of offences.

than self-regarding offences; unless in particular cases, through sympathy to certain persons in authority, whose private interests they may appear to affect.

8. They are more apt than any of the other classes to admit of different descriptions, in different states and countries.

9. They are constituted, in many cases, by some circumstances of aggravation superadded to a private offence: and therefore, in these cases, involve the mischief, and exhibit the other characters belonging to both classes. They are, however, even in such cases, properly enough ranked in the 4th class, inasmuch as the mischief they produce in virtue of the properties which aggregate them to that class, eclipses and swallows up that which they produce in virtue of those properties which aggregate them to the 1st.

10. There may be sufficient ground for punishing them, without their being proved to have occasioned, or to be about to occasion, any particular mischief to any particular individual. In this they differ from private offences, but agree with semi-public ones. Here, as in semi-public offences, the *extent* of the mischief makes up for the *uncertainty* of it.

11. In no case can satisfaction, given to any particular individual affected by them, be a sufficient ground for remitting punishment. In this they differ from private offences; but agree with semi-public.

66. Characters of Class 5, or appendix: composed of MULTIFORM or ANOMALOUS offences; and containing offences by FALSEHOOD, and offences concerning trust. *Characters of Class 5*

1. Taken collectively, in the parcels marked out by their popular appellations, they are incapable of being aggregated to any systematical method of distribution, grounded upon the mischief of the offence.

2. They may, however, be thrown into subdivisions, which may be aggregated to such a method of distribution.

3. These sub-divisions will naturally and readily rank under the divisions of the several preceding classes of this system.

4. Each of the two great divisions of this class spreads itself in that manner over all the preceding classes.

5. In some acts of this class, the distinguishing circumstance which constitutes the essential character of the offence, will in some instances enter necessarily, in the character of a criminative circumstance, into the constitution of the offence; insomuch that, without the intervention of this circumstance, no offence at all, of that denomination, can be committed.[p5] In other instances, the offence

---

[p5] Instance, offences by falsehood, in the case of *defraudment*.

may subsist without it; and where it interferes, it comes in as an accidental independent circumstance, capable of constituting a ground of aggravation.[q5]

[q5] Instance, offences by falsehood, in the case of simple corporal injuries, and other offences against person.

CHAPTER XVII

OF THE LIMITS OF THE PENAL BRANCH OF JURISPRUDENCE

§ i. *Limits between private ethics and the art of legislation*

1. So much for the division of offences in general. Now an offence *Use of this* is an act prohibited, or (what comes to the same thing) an act of *chapter* which the contrary is commanded by the law: and what is it that the law can be employed in doing, besides prohibiting and commanding? It should seem then, according to this view of the matter, that were we to have settled what may be proper to be done with relation to offences, we should thereby have settled every thing that may be proper to be done in the way of law. Yet that branch which concerns the method of dealing with offences, and which is termed sometimes the *criminal*, sometimes the *penal*, branch, is universally understood to be but one out of two branches which compose the whole subject of the art of legislation; that which is termed the *civil* being the other.[a] Between these two branches then, it is evident enough, there cannot but be a very intimate connection; so intimate is it indeed, that the limits between them are by no means easy to mark out. The case is the same in some degree between the whole business of legislation (civil and penal branches taken together) and that of private ethics. Of these several limits however it will be in a manner necessary to exhibit some idea: lest, on the one hand, we should seem to leave any part of the subject that *does* belong to us untouched, or, on the other hand, to deviate on any side into a track which does *not* belong to us.

[a] And the *constitutional* branch, what is become of it? Such is the question which many a reader will be apt to put. An answer that might be given is— that the matter of it might without much violence be distributed under the two other heads. But, as far as recollection serves, that branch, notwithstanding its importance, and its capacity of being lodged separately from the other matter, had at that time scarcely presented itself to my view in the character of a distinct one: the thread of my enquiries had not as yet reached it. But in the concluding note of this same chapter, in paragraphs 22 to the end, the omission may be seen in some measure supplied.[1]

[1] Note added by Bentham to the 1823 edition. His attention had been drawn to the apparent omission of constitutional law very soon after the completion of the 1780 text: cf. his letter to Lord Shelburne of 18 July 1781 and several drafts for that letter in the University College collection (to be published in *Correspondence*, iii, in *CW*).

In the course of this enquiry, that part of it I mean which concerns the limits between the civil and the penal branch of law, it will be necessary to settle a number of points, of which the connection with the main question might not at first sight be suspected. To ascertain what sort of a thing *a* law is; what the *parts* are that are to be found in it; what it must contain in order to be *complete*; what the connection is between that part of a body of laws which belongs to the subject of *procedure*; and the rest of the law at large: —All these, it will be seen, are so many problems, which must be solved before any satisfactory answer can be given to the main question above mentioned.

Nor is this their only use: for it is evident enough, that the notion of a complete law must first be fixed, before the legislator can in any case know what it is he has to do, or when his work is done.

Ethics in general, what

2. Ethics at large may be defined, the art of directing men's actions to the production of the greatest possible quantity of happiness, on the part of those whose interest is in view.

Private ethics

3. What then are the actions which it can be in a man's power to direct? They must be either his own actions, or those of other agents. Ethics, in as far as it is the art of directing a man's own actions, may be styled the *art of self-government*, or *private ethics*.

The art of government: that is, of legislation and administration

4. What other agents then are there, which, at the same time that they are under the influence of man's direction, are susceptible of happiness? They are of two sorts: 1. Other human beings who are styled persons. 2. Other animals, which on account of their interests having been neglected by the insensibility of the ancient jurists, stand degraded into the class of *things*.[b] As to other human

Interests of the inferior animals improperly neglected in legislation

[b] Under the Gentoo[1] and Mahometan religions, the interests of the rest of the animal creation seem to have met with some attention. Why have they not, universally, with as much as those of human creatures, allowance made for the difference in point of sensibility? Because the laws that are have been the work of mutual fear; a sentiment which the less rational animals have not had the same means as man has of turning to account. Why *ought* they not? No reason can be given. If the being eaten were all, there is very good reason why we should be suffered to eat such of them as we like to eat: we are the better for it, and they are never the worse. They have none of those long-protracted anticipations of future misery which we have. The death they suffer in our hands commonly is, and always may be, a speedier, and by that means a less painful one, than that which would await them in the inevitable course of nature. If the being killed were all, there is very good reason why we should be suffered to kill such as molest us; we should be the worse for their living, and they are never the worse for being dead. But is there any reason

[1] This term for Hindu seems to have become obsolete during the first half of the 19th century.

282

beings, the art of directing their actions to the above end is what we mean, or at least the only thing which, upon the principle of utility, we *ought* to mean, by the art of government: which, in as far as the measures it displays itself in are of a permanent nature, is generally distinguished by the name of *legislation*: as it is by that of *administration*, when they are of a temporary nature, determined by the occurrences of the day.

5. Now human creatures, considered with respect to the maturity of their faculties, are either in an *adult*, or in a *non-adult* state. The art of government, in as far as it concerns the direction of the actions of persons in a non-adult state, may be termed the art of *education*. In as far as this business is entrusted with those who, in virtue of some private relationship, are in the main the best disposed to take upon them, and the best able to discharge, this office, it may be termed the art of *private education*: in as far as it is exercised by those whose province it is to superintend the conduct of the whole community, it may be termed the art of *public education*. *Art of education*

6. As to ethics in general, a man's happiness will depend, in the *Ethics exhibits the rules of, 1. Prudence. 2. Probity. 3. Beneficence*

why we should be suffered to torment them? Not any that I can see. Are there any why we should *not* be suffered to torment them? Yes, several. See B. I. tit. (Cruelty to animals.) The day has been, I grieve to say in many places it is not yet past, in which the greater part of the species, under the denomination of slaves, have been treated by the law exactly upon the same footing, as, in England for example, the inferior races of animals are still. The day *may* come, when the rest of the animal creation may acquire those rights which never could have been withholden from them but by the hand of tyranny. The French have already discovered that the blackness of the skin is no reason why a human being should be abandoned without redress to the caprice of a tormentor.* It may come one day to be recognized, that the number of the legs, the villosity of the skin, or the termination of the *os sacrum*, are reasons equally insufficient for abandoning a sensitive being to the same fate? What else is it that should trace the insuperable line? Is it the faculty of reason, or, perhaps, the faculty of discourse? But a full-grown horse or dog, is beyond comparison a more rational, as well as a more conversible animal, than an infant of a day, or a week, or even a month, old. But suppose the case were otherwise, what would it avail? the question is not, Can they *reason*? nor, Can they *talk*? but, Can they *suffer*?

* See Lewis XIVth's Code Noir.[1]

[1] This code, begun under Colbert, completed by Seignelay, and issued in March 1685, regulated the status of slaves in the French West Indies. It forbade the killing of slaves by their masters, and gave the royal authorities the power to protect slaves from maltreatment. It also provided that a slave freed in the West Indies should become a French citizen without formal naturalisation.

first place, upon such parts of his behaviour as none but himself are interested in; in the next place, upon such parts of it as may affect the happiness of those about him. In as far as his happiness depends upon the first-mentioned part of his behaviour, it is said to depend upon his *duty to himself*. Ethics then, in as far as it is the art of directing a man's actions in this respect, may be termed the art of discharging one's duty to one's self: and the quality which a man manifests by the discharge of this branch of duty (if duty it is to be called) is that of *prudence*. In as far as his happiness, and that of any other person or persons whose interests are considered, depends upon such parts of his behaviour as may affect the interests of those about him, it may be said to depend upon his *duty to others*; or, to use a phrase now somewhat antiquated, his *duty to his neighbour*. Ethics then, in as far as it is the art of directing a man's actions in this respect, may be termed the art of discharging one's duty to one's neighbour. Now the happiness of one's neighbour may be consulted in two ways: 1. In a negative way, by forbearing to diminish it. 2. In a positive way, by studying to increase it. A man's duty to his neighbour is accordingly partly negative and partly positive: to discharge the negative branch of it, is *probity*: to discharge the positive branch, *beneficence*.

Probity and beneficence how they connect with prudence

7. It may here be asked, How it is that upon the principle of private ethics, legislation and religion out of the question, a man's happiness depends upon such parts of his conduct as affect, immediately at least, the happiness of no one but himself: this is as much as to ask, What motives (independent of such as legislation and religion may chance to furnish) can one man have to consult the happiness of another? by what motives, or, which comes to the same thing, by what obligations, can he be bound to obey the dictates of *probity* and *beneficence*? In answer to this, it cannot but be admitted, that the only interests which a man at all times and upon all occasions is sure to find *adequate* motives for consulting, are his own. Notwithstanding this, there are no occasions in which a man has not some motives for consulting the happiness of other men. In the first place, he has, on all occasions, the purely social motive of sympathy or benevolence: in the next place, he has, on most occasions, the semi-social motives of love of amity and love of reputation. The motive of sympathy will act upon him with more or less effect, according to the *bias* of his sensibility[c]: the two other motives, according to a variety of circumstances, principally according to the strength of his intellectual powers, the firmness and

[c] Ch. VI (Sensibility) 3.

284

steadiness of his mind, the quantum of his moral sensibility, and the characters of the people he has to deal with.

8. Now private ethics has happiness for its end: and legislation can have no other. Private ethics concerns every member, that is, the happiness and the actions of every member of any community that can be proposed; and legislation can concern no more. Thus far, then, private ethics and the art of legislation go hand in hand. The end they have, or ought to have, in view, is of the same nature. The persons whose happiness they ought to have in view, as also the persons whose conduct they ought to be occupied in directing, are precisely the same. The very acts they ought to be conversant about, are even in a *great measure* the same. Where then lies the difference? In that the acts which they ought to be conversant about, though in a great measure, are not *perfectly and throughout* the same. There is no case in which a private man ought not to direct his own conduct to the production of his own happiness, and of that of his fellow-creatures: but there are cases in which the legislator ought not (in a direct way at least, and by means of punishment applied immediately to particular *individual* acts) to attempt to direct the conduct of the several other members of the community. Every act which promises to be beneficial upon the whole to the community (himself included) each individual ought to perform of himself: but it is not every such act that the legislator ought to compel him to perform. Every act which promises to be pernicious upon the whole to the community (himself included) each individual ought to abstain from of himself: but it is not every such act that the legislator ought to compel him to abstain from.

Every act which is a proper object of ethics is not of legislation

9. Where then is the line to be drawn?—We shall not have far to seek for it. The business is to give an idea of the cases in which ethics ought, and in which legislation ought not (in a direct manner at least) to interfere. If legislation interferes in a direct manner, it must be by punishment.[d] Now the cases in which punishment, meaning the punishment of the political sanction, ought not to be inflicted, have been already stated.[e] If then there be any of these cases in which, although legislation ought not, private ethics does or ought to interfere, these cases will serve to point out the limits between the two arts or branches of science. These cases, it may be

The limits between the provinces of private ethics and legislation, marked out by the cases unmeet for punishment

[d] I say nothing in this place of reward: because it is only in a few extraordinary cases that it can be applied, and because even where it is applied, it may be doubted perhaps whether the application of it can, properly speaking, be termed an act of legislation. See infra, § iii.[1]

[e] Ch. XIII (Cases unmeet).   [1] See above, 207 n. 1.

remembered, are of four sorts: 1. Where punishment would be groundless. 2. Where it would be inefficacious. 3. Where it would be unprofitable. 4. Where it would be needless. Let us look over all these cases, and see whether in any of them there is room for the interference of private ethics, at the same time that there is none for the direct interference of legislation.

1. Neither ought to apply where punishment is groundless

10. (1) First then, as to the cases where punishment would be *groundless*. In these cases it is evident, that the restrictive interference of ethics would be groundless too. It is because, upon the whole, there is no evil in the act, that legislation ought not to endeavour to prevent it. No more, for the same reason, ought private ethics.

2. How far private ethics can apply in the cases where punishment would be inefficacious

11. (2) As to the cases in which punishment would be *inefficacious*. These, we may observe, may be divided into two sets or classes. The first do not depend at all upon the nature of the act: they turn only upon a defect in the timing of the punishment. The punishment in question is no more than what, for any thing that appears, ought to have been applied to the act in question. It ought, however, to have been applied at a different time; viz. not till after it had been properly denounced. These are the cases of an *ex-post-facto* law; of a judicial sentence beyond the law; and of a law not sufficiently promulgated. The acts here in question then might, for any thing that appears, come properly under the department even of coercive legislation: of course do they under that of private ethics. As to the other set of cases, in which punishment would be inefficacious; neither do these depend upon the nature of the act, that is, of the *sort* of act: they turn only upon some extraneous *circumstances*, with which an act of *any* sort may chance to be accompanied. These, however, are of such a nature as not only to exclude the application of legal punishment, but in general to leave little room for the influence of private ethics. These are the cases where the will could not be deterred from any act, even by the extraordinary force of artificial punishment: as in the cases of extreme infancy, insanity, and perfect intoxication: of course, therefore, it could not by such slender and precarious force as could be applied by private ethics. The case is in this respect the same, under the circumstances of unintentionality with respect to the event of the action, unconsciousness with regard to the circumstances, and missupposal with regard to the existence of circumstances which have not existed; as also where the force, even of extraordinary punishment, is rendered inoperative by the superior force of a physical danger or threatened mischief. It is evident, that in these cases, if the thunders of the law prove impotent, the whispers of simple morality can have but little influence.

12. (3) As to the cases where punishment would be *unprofitable.* These are the cases which constitute the great field for the exclusive interference of private ethics. When a punishment is unprofitable, or in other words too expensive, it is because the evil of the punishment exceeds that of the offence. Now the evil of the punishment, we may remember,[f] is distinguishable into four branches: 1. The evil of coercion, including constraint or restraint, according as the act commanded is of the positive kind or the negative. 2. The evil of apprehension. 3. The evil of sufferance. 4. The derivative evils resulting to persons in *connection* with those by whom the three above-mentioned original evils are sustained. Now with respect to those original evils, the persons who lie exposed to them may be two very different sets of persons. In the first place, persons who may have actually committed, or been prompted to commit, the acts really meant to be prohibited. In the next place, persons who may have performed, or been prompted to perform, such other acts as they fear may be in danger of being involved in the punishment designed only for the former. But of these two sets of acts, it is the former only that are pernicious: it is, therefore, the former only that it can be the business of private ethics to endeavour to prevent. The latter being by the supposition not mischievous, to prevent them is what it can no more be the business of ethics to endeavour at, than of legislation. It remains to shew how it may happen, that there should be acts really pernicious, which, although they may very properly come under the censure of private ethics, may yet be no fit objects for the legislator to control.

How far, where it would be unprofitable

13. Punishment then, as applied to delinquency, may be unprofitable in both or either of two ways: 1. By the expense it would amount to, even supposing the application of it to be confined altogether to delinquency: 2. By the danger there may be of its involving the innocent in the fate designed only for the guilty. First then, with regard to the cases in which the expense of the punishment, as applied to the guilty, would outweigh the profit to be made by it. These cases, it is evident, depend upon a certain proportion between the evil of the punishment and the evil of the offence. Now were the offence of such a nature, that a punishment which, in point of *magnitude*, should but just exceed the profit of it, would be sufficient to prevent it, it might be rather difficult perhaps to find an instance in which such punishment would clearly appear to be un-

Which it may be, 1. Although confined to the guilty

[f] See Ch. XIII (Cases unmeet) § iv.

profitable. But the fact is, there are many cases in which a punishment, in order to have any chance of being efficacious, must, in point of magnitude, be raised a great deal above that level. Thus it is, wherever the danger of detection is, or, what comes to the same thing, is likely to appear to be, so small, as to make the punishment appear in a high degree uncertain. In this case it is necessary, as has been shewn,[g] if punishment be at all applied, to raise it in point of magnitude as much as it falls short in point of certainty. It is evident, however, that all this can be but guess-work: and that the effect of such a proportion will be rendered precarious, by a variety of circumstances: by the want of sufficient promulgation on the part of the law[h]: by the particular circumstances of the temptation[i]: and by the circumstances influencing the sensibility of the several individuals who are exposed to it.[j] Let the *seducing* motives be strong, the offence then will at any rate be frequently committed. Now and then indeed, owing to a coincidence of circumstances more or less extraordinary, it will be detected, and by that means punished. But for the purpose of example, which is the principal one, an act of punishment, considered in itself, is of no use: what use it can be of, depends altogether upon the expectation it raises of similar punishment, in future cases of similar delinquency. But this future punishment, it is evident, must always depend upon detection. If then the want of detection is such as must in general (especially to eyes fascinated by the force of the seducing motives) appear too improbable to be reckoned upon, the punishment, though it should be inflicted, may come to be of no use. Here then will be two opposite evils running on at the same time, yet neither of them reducing the quantum of the other: the evil of the disease and the evil of the painful and inefficacious remedy. It seems to be partly owing to some such considerations, that fornication, for example, or the illicit commerce between the sexes, has commonly either gone altogether unpunished, or been punished in a degree inferior to that in which, on other accounts, legislators might have been disposed to punish it.

2. By enveloping the innocent

14. Second, with regard to the cases in which political punishment, as applied to delinquency, may be unprofitable, in virtue of the danger there may be of its involving the innocent in the fate

[g] Ch. xiv (Proportion) 18. Rule 7.
[h] Ch. xiii (Cases unmeet) § iii. Append. tit. (Promulgation).[1]
[i] Ch. xi (Disposition) 35 etc.
[j] Ch. vi (Sensibility).

[1] See above 160 n. 1.

designed only for the guilty. Whence should this danger then arise? From the difficulty there may be of fixing the idea of the guilty action: that is, of subjecting it to such a definition as shall be clear and precise enough to guard effectually against misapplication. This difficulty may arise from either of two sources: the one permanent, to wit, the nature of the *actions* themselves: the other occasional, I mean the qualities of the *men* who may have to deal with those actions in the way of government. In as far as it arises from the latter of these sources, it may depend partly upon the use which the *legislator* may be *able* to make of language; partly upon the use which, according to the apprehension of the legislator, the *judge* may be *disposed* to make of it. As far as legislation is concerned, it will depend upon the degree of perfection to which the arts of language may have been carried, in the first place, in the nation in general; in the next place, by the *legislator* in particular. It is to a sense of this difficulty as it should seem, that we may attribute the caution with which most legislators have abstained from subjecting to censure, on the part of the law, such actions as come under the notion of rudeness, for example, or treachery, or ingratitude. The attempt to bring acts of so vague and questionable a nature under the control of law, will argue either a very immature age, in which the difficulties, which give birth to that danger are not descried; or a very enlightened age, in which they are overcome.[k]

15. For the sake of obtaining the clearer idea of the limits between the art of legislation and private ethics, it may now be time to call to mind the distinctions above established with regard to ethics in general. The degree in which private ethics stands in need of the assistance of legislation, is different in the three branches of duty above distinguished. Of the rules of moral duty, those which seem to stand least in need of the assistance of legislation, are the rules of *prudence*. It can only be through some defect on the part of the understanding, if a man be ever deficient in point of duty to himself. If he does wrong, there is nothing else that it can be owing to but either some *inadvertence*[1] or some *missupposal*,[1] with regard

Legislation how far necessary for the enforcement of the dictates of prudence

[k] In certain countries, in which the voice of the people has a more especial control over the hand of the legislator, nothing can exceed the dread which they are under of seeing any effectual provision made against the offences which come under the head of *defamation*, particularly that branch of it which may be styled the *political*. This dread seems to depend partly upon the apprehension they may think it prudent to entertain of a defect in point of ability or integrity on the part of the legislator, partly upon a similar apprehension of a defect in point of integrity on the part of the judge.

[1] See Ch. ix (Consciousness).

to the circumstances on which his happiness depends. It is a standing topic of complaint, that a man knows too little of himself.
Be it so: but is it so certain that the legislator must know more[m] [n]?
It is plain, that of individuals the legislator can know nothing: concerning those points of conduct which depend upon the particular
circumstances of each individual, it is plain, therefore, that he can
determine nothing to advantage. It is only with respect to those
broad lines of conduct in which all persons, or very large and permanent descriptions of persons, may be in a way to engage, that he
can have any pretence for interfering; and even here the propriety
of his interference will, in most instances, lie very open to dispute.
At any rate, he must never expect to produce a perfect compliance
by the mere force of the sanction of which he is himself the author.
All he can hope to do, is to increase the efficacy of private ethics,
by giving strength and direction to the influence of the moral sanction. With what chance of success, for example, would a legislator
go about to extirpate drunkenness and fornication, by dint of legal
punishment? Not all the tortures which ingenuity could invent
would compass it: and, before he had made any progress worth
regarding, such a mass of evil would be produced by the punishment, as would exceed, a thousand-fold, the utmost possible mischief of the offence. The great difficulty would be in the procuring
evidence; an object which could not be attempted, with any probability of success, without spreading dismay through every family,[o]
tearing the bonds of sympathy asunder,[p] and rooting out the influence of all the social motives. All that he can do then, against
offences of this nature, with any prospect of advantage, in the way
of direct legislation, is to subject them, in cases of notoriety, to a
slight censure, so as thereby to cover them with a slight shade of
artificial disrepute.

*– Apt to go
too far in
this respect*

16. It may be observed, that with regard to this branch of duty,
legislators have, in general, been disposed to carry their inter-

[m] On occasions like this, the legislator should never lose sight of the well-
known story of the oculist and the sot. A countryman who had hurt his eyes
by drinking, went to a celebrated oculist for advice. He found him at table,
with a glass of wine before him. 'You must leave off drinking', said the oculist.
'How so', says the countryman? '*You* don't, and yet methinks your own eyes
are none of the best'.—'That's very true, friend', replied the oculist: 'but you
are to know, I love my bottle better than my eyes.'

[n] Ch. XVI (Division) 52.

[o] Evil of apprehension: third branch of the evil of a punishment. Ch. XIII
§ iv.

[p] Derivative evils: fourth branch of the evil of a punishment. Ibid.

ference full as far as is expedient. The great difficulty here is, to persuade them to confine themselves within bounds. A thousand little passions and prejudices have led them to narrow the liberty of the subject in this line, in cases in which the punishment is either attended with no profit at all, or with none that will make up for the expense.

17. The mischief of this sort of interference is more particularly conspicuous in the article of religion. The reasoning, in this case, is of the following stamp. There are certain errors, in matters of belief, to which all mankind are prone: and for these errors in judgment, it is the determination of a Being of infinite benevolence, to punish them with an infinity of torments. But from these errors the legislator himself is necessarily free: for the men, who happen to be at hand for him to consult with, being men perfectly enlightened, unfettered, and unbiassed, have such advantages over all the rest of the world, that when they sit down to enquire out the truth relative to points so plain and so familiar as those in question, they cannot fail to find it. This being the case, when the sovereign sees his people ready to plunge headlong into an abyss of fire, shall he not stretch out a hand to save them? Such, for example, seems to have been the train of reasoning, and such the motives, which led Lewis the XIVth into those coercive measures which he took for the conversion of heretics, and the confirmation of true believers.[1] The ground-work, pure sympathy and loving-kindness: the superstructure, all the miseries which the most determined malevolence could have devised.[q] But of this more fully in another place.[r]

– Particularly in matters of religion

[q] I do not mean but that other motives of a less social nature might have introduced themselves, and probably, in point of fact, did introduce themselves, in the progress of the enterprise. But in point of possibility, the motive above mentioned, when accompanied with such a thread of reasoning, is sufficient, without any other, to account for all the effects above alluded to. If any others interfere, their interference, how natural soever, may be looked upon as an accidental and inessential circumstance, not necessary to the production of the effect. Sympathy, a concern for the danger they appear to be exposed to, gives birth to the wish of freeing them from it: that wish shews itself in the shape of a command: this command produces disobedience: disobedience on the one part, produces disappointment on the other: the pain of disappointment produces ill-will towards those who are the authors of it. The affections will often make this progress in less time than it would take to describe it. The sentiment of wounded pride, and other modifications of the love of reputation and the love of power, add fuel to the flame. A kind of revenge exasperates the severities of coercive policy.

[r] See B. I. tit. (Self-regarding offences).

[1] The revocation of the Edict of Nantes in 1685.

– *How far
necessary
for the en-
forcement of
the dictates
of probity*

18. The rules of *probity* are those, which in point of expediency stand most in need of assistance on the part of the legislator, and in which, in point of fact, his interference has been most extensive. There are few cases in which it *would* be expedient to punish a man for hurting *himself*: but there are few cases, if any, in which it would *not* be expedient to punish a man for injuring his neighbour. With regard to that branch of probity which is opposed to offences against property, private ethics depends in a manner for its very existence upon legislation. Legislation must first determine what things are to be regarded as each man's property, before the general rules of ethics, on this head, can have any particular application. The case is the same with regard to offences against the state. Without legislation there would be no such thing as a *state*: no particular persons invested with powers to be exercised for the benefit of the rest. It is plain, therefore, that in this branch the interference of the legislator cannot any where be dispensed with. We must first know what are the dictates of legislation, before we can know what are the dictates of private ethics.[s]

19. As to the rules of beneficence, these, as far as concerns matters of detail, must necessarily be abandoned in great measure to the jurisdiction of private ethics. In many cases the beneficial quality of the act depends essentially upon the disposition of the agent; that is, upon the motives by which he appears to have been prompted to perform it: upon their belonging to the head of sympathy, love of amity, or love of reputation; and not to any head of self-regarding motives, brought into play by the force of political constraint: in a word, upon their being such as denominate his conduct *free* and *voluntary*, according to one of the many senses given to those ambiguous expressions.[t] The limits of the law on

---

[s] But suppose the dictates of legislation *are* not what they *ought to be*: what are then, or (what in this case comes to the same thing) what ought to be, the dictates of private ethics? Do they coincide with the dictates of legislation, or do they oppose them, or do they remain neuter? a very interesting question this, but one that belongs not to the present subject. It belongs exclusively to that of private ethics. Principles which may lead to the solution of it may be seen in A Fragment on Government, p. 150. Lond. edit. 1776—and p. 114. edit. 1823.[1]

[t] If we may believe M. Voltaire,* there was a time when the French ladies

* Quest. sur l'Encyclop. tom. 7. art. Impuissance.[2]

[1] Bentham is referring to para. 21 ff. of Ch. IV of the *Fragment* (Bowring, i, 287 ff.).
[2] Bentham refers to the 1770–1 edition of Voltaire's *Questions sur l'Encyclopédie*.

this head seem, however, to be capable of being extended a good deal farther than they seem ever to have been extended hitherto. In particular, in cases where the person is in danger, why should it not be made the duty of every man to save another from mischief, when it can be done without prejudicing himself, as well as to abstain from bringing it on him? This accordingly is the idea pursued in the body of the work.[u]

20. To conclude this section, let us recapitulate and bring to a point the difference between private ethics, considered as an art or science, on the one hand, and that branch of jurisprudence which contains the art or science of legislation, on the other. Private ethics teaches how each man may dispose himself to pursue the course most conducive to his own happiness, by means of such motives as offer of themselves: the art of legislation (which may be considered as one branch of the science of jurisprudence) teaches how a multitude of men, composing a community, may be disposed to pursue that course which upon the whole is the most conducive to the happiness of the whole community, by means of motives to be applied by the legislator. *Difference between private ethics and the art of legislation recapitulated*

We come now to exhibit the limits between penal and civil jurisprudence. For this purpose it may be of use to give a distinct though summary view of the principal branches into which jurisprudence, considered in its utmost extent, is wont to be divided.

§ ii. *Jurisprudence, its branches*

21. Jurisprudence is a fictitious entity: nor can any meaning be found for the word, but by placing it in company with some word that shall be significative of a real entity. To know what is meant by jurisprudence, we must know, for example, what is meant by a book of jurisprudence. A book of jurisprudence can have but *Jurisprudence, expository — censorial*

who thought themselves neglected by their husbands, used to petition *pour être embesoignées*: the technical word, which, he says, was appropriated to this purpose. These sort of law-proceedings seem not very well calculated to answer the design: accordingly we hear nothing of them now-a-days. The French ladies of the present age seem to be under no such difficulties.

[u] A woman's head-dress catches fire: water is at hand: a man, instead of assisting to quench the fire, looks on, and laughs at it. A drunken man, falling with his face downwards into a puddle, is in danger of suffocation: lifting his head a little on one side would save him: another man sees this and lets him lie. A quantity of gunpowder lies scattered about a room: a man is going into it with a lighted candle: another knowing this, lets him go in without warning. Who is there that in any of these cases would think punishment misapplied?

one or the other of two objects: 1. to ascertain what the *law*[v] is:
2. to ascertain what it ought to be. In the former case it may be styled
a book of *expository* jurisprudence; in the latter, a book of *censorial*
jurisprudence: or, in other words, a book on the *art of legislation*.

Expository jurisprudence, authoritative – unauthoritative

22. A book of expository jurisprudence is either *authoritative* or
unauthoritative. It is styled authoritative, when it is composed by
him who, by representing the state of the law to be so and so, cau-
seth it so to be; that is, of the legislator himself: unauthoritative,
when it is the work of any other person at large.

Sources of the distinctions yet remaining

23. Now *law*, or *the law*, taken indefinitely, is an abstract and
collective term; which, when it means any thing, can mean neither
more nor less than the sum total of a number of individual laws
taken together.[w] It follows, that of whatever other modifications
the subject of a book of jurisprudence is susceptible, they must all
of them be taken from some circumstance or other of which such
individual laws, or the assemblages into which they may be sorted,
are susceptible. The circumstances that have given rise to the principal branches of jurisprudence we are wont to hear of, seem to be
as follow: 1. The *extent* of the laws in question in point of dominion.
2. The *political quality* of the persons whose conduct they undertake to regulate. 3. The *time* of their being in force. 4. The manner
in which they are *expressed*. 5. The concern which they have with
the article of *punishment*.

Jurisprudence, local – universal

24. In the first place, in point of extent, what is delivered concerning the laws in question, may have reference either to the laws
of such or such a nation or nations in particular, or to the laws of all
nations whatsoever: in the first case, the book may be said to relate
to *local*, in the other, to *universal jurisprudence*.

[v] The word *law* itself which stands so much in need of a definition, must
wait for it awhile, (see § iii[1]): for there is no doing every thing at once. In the
mean time every reader will understand it according to the notion he has been
accustomed to annex to it.

[w] In most of the European languages there are two different words for distinguishing the abstract and the concrete senses of the word *law*: which words
are so wide asunder as not even to have any etymological affinity. In Latin, for
example, there is *lex* for the concrete sense, *jus* for the abstract: in Italian,
legge and *diritto*: in French, *loi* and *droit*: in Spanish, *ley* and *derecho*: in German, *gesetz* and *recht*. The English is at present destitute of this advantage.

In the Anglo-Saxon, besides *lage*, and several other words, for the concrete
sense, there was the word *right*, answering to the German *recht*, for the abstract; as may be seen in the compound *folc-right*, and in other instances. But
the word *right* having long ago lost this sense, the modern English no longer
possesses this advantage.

[1] See above, 207 n. 1.

Now of the infinite variety of nations there are upon the earth, there are no two which agree exactly in their laws: certainly not in the whole; perhaps not even in any single article; and let them agree to-day, they would disagree to-morrow. This is evident enough with regard to the *substance* of the laws: and it would be still more extraordinary if they agreed in point of *form*; that is, if they were conceived in precisely the same strings of words. What is more, as the languages of nations are commonly different, as well as their laws, it is seldom that, strictly speaking, they have so much as a single *word* in common. However, among the words that are appropriated to the subject of law, there are some that in all languages are pretty exactly correspondent to one another: which comes to the same thing nearly as if they were the same. Of this stamp, for example, are those which correspond to the words *power, right, obligation, liberty*, and many others.

It follows, that if there are any books which can, properly speaking, be styled books of universal jurisprudence, they must be looked for within very narrow limits. Among such as are expository, there can be none that are authoritative: nor even, as far as the *substance* of the laws is concerned, any that are unauthoritative. To be susceptible of an universal application, all that a book of the expository kind can have to treat of, is the import of words: to be, strictly speaking, universal, it must confine itself to terminology. Accordingly the definitions which there has been occasion here and there to intersperse in the course of the present work, and particularly the definition hereafter given of the word *law*, may be considered as matter belonging to the head of universal jurisprudence. Thus far in strictness of speech: though in point of usage, where a man, in laying down what he apprehends to be the law, extends his views to a few of the nations with which his own is most connected, it is common enough to consider what he writes as relating to universal jurisprudence.

It is in the censorial line that there is the greatest room for disquisitions that apply to the circumstances of all nations alike: and in this line what regards the substance of the laws in question is as susceptible of an universal application, as what regards the words. That the laws of all nations, or even of any two nations, should coincide in all points, would be as ineligible as it is impossible: some leading points, however, there seem to be, in respect of which the laws of all civilized nations might, without inconvenience, be the same. To mark out some of these points will, as far as it goes, be the business of the body of this work.

25. In the second place, with regard to the *political quality* of the persons whose conduct is the object of the law. These may, on any given occasion, be considered either as members of the same state, or as members of different states: in the first case, the law may be referred to the head of *internal*, in the second case, to that of *international*[x] jurisprudence.

Now as to any transactions which may take place between individuals who are subjects of different states, these are regulated by the internal laws, and decided upon by the internal tribunals, of the one or the other of these states: the case is the same where the sovereign of the one has any immediate transactions with a private member of the other: the sovereign reducing himself, *pro re natâ*, to the condition of a private person, as often as he submits his cause to either tribunal; whether by claiming a benefit, or defending himself against a burthen. There remain then the mutual transactions between sovereigns as such, for the subject of that branch of jurisprudence which may be properly and exclusively termed *international*.[y]

[x] The word *international*, it must be acknowledged, is a new one; though, it is hoped, sufficiently analogous and intelligible. It is calculated to express, in a more significant way, the branch of law which goes commonly under the name of the *law of nations*: an appellation so uncharacteristic, that, were it not for the force of custom, it would seem rather to refer to internal jurisprudence. The chancellor D'Aguesseau[1] has already made, I find, a similar remark: he says, that what is commonly called *droit* des *gens*, ought rather to be termed *droit* entre *les gens*.*

[y] In the times of James I of England, and Philip III of Spain, certain merchants at London happened to have a claim upon Philip, which his ambassador Gondemar did not think fit to satisfy. They applied for counsel to Selden, who advised them to sue the Spanish monarch in the court of King's Bench, and prosecute him to an outlawry. They did so: and the sheriffs of London were accordingly commanded in the usual form, to take the body of the defendant Philip, wherever it was to be found within their bailiwick. As to the sheriffs, Philip, we may believe, was in no great fear of them: but, what answered the same purpose, he happened on his part to have demands upon some other merchants, whom, so long as the outlawry remained in force, there was no proceeding against. Gondemar paid the money.†[2] This was internal juris-

* Oeuvres, Tom. ii. p. 337, Edit. 1773, 12mo.
† Selden's Table-Talk, tit. Law.[3]

[1] Henri-Francois Daguesseau (1668–1751) was Chancellor of France under Louis XIV.

[2] Diego Sarmiento de Acuna (1567–1626), Conde de Gondomar, came to England as ambassador of Philip III (1598–1621) in 1613 and remained until 1622. John Selden (1584–1654), the jurist, was called to the bar in 1612.

[3] The *Table Talk* of John Selden (see n. 2 above) was posthumously published in 1689.

With what degree of propriety rules for the conduct of persons of this description can come under the appellation of *laws*, is a question that must rest till the nature of the thing called *a law* shall have been more particularly unfolded.

It is evident enough, that international jurisprudence may, as well as internal, be censorial as well as expository, unauthoritative as well as authoritative.

26. Internal jurisprudence, again, may either concern all the members of a state indiscriminately, or such of them only as are connected in the way of residence, or otherwise, with a particular district. Jurisprudence is accordingly sometimes distinguished into *national* and *provincial*. But as the epithet *provincial* is hardly applicable to districts so small as many of those which have laws of their own are wont to be, such as towns, parishes, and manors; the term *local* (where universal jurisprudence is plainly out of the question) or the term *particular*, though this latter is not very characteristic, might either of them be more commodious.ᶻ

Internal jurisprudence, national and provincial, local or particular

27. Third, with respect to *time*. In a work of the expository kind, the laws that are in question may either be such as are still in force at the time when the book is writing, or such as have ceased to be in force. In the latter case the subject of it might be termed *ancient*; in the former, *present* or *living* jurisprudence: that is, if the substantive *jurisprudence*, and no other, must at any rate be employed, and that with an epithet in both cases. But the truth is, that a book of the former kind is rather a book of history than a book of jurisprudence; and, if the word *jurisprudence* be expressive of the subject, it is only with some such words as *history* or *antiquities* prefixed. And as the laws which are any where in question are supposed,

Jurisprudence, ancient–living

prudence: if the dispute had been betwixt Philip and James himself, it would have been international.

As to the word *international*, from this work, or the first of the works edited in French by Mr Dumont, it has taken root in the language. Witness Reviews and Newspapers.[1]

ᶻ The term *municipal* seemed to answer the purpose very well, till it was taken by an English author of the first eminence, to signify internal law in general, in contradistinction to international law, and the imaginary law of nature.[2] It might still be used in this sense, without scruple, in any other language.

[1] Paragraph added in 1823. The first of Dumont's works based on Bentham's manuscripts was *Traités de législation civile et pénale* (Paris, 1802).

[2] If, as seems likely, Bentham has Blackstone in mind here, his comment is questionable; for the usage he criticises seems to have been established at a much earlier period.

if nothing appears to the contrary, to be those which are in force, no such epithet as that of *present* or *living* commonly appears.

Where a book is so circumstanced, that the laws which form the subject of it, though in force at the time of its being written, are in force no longer, that book is neither a book of living jurisprudence, nor a book on the history of jurisprudence: it is no longer the former, and it never was the latter. It is evident that, owing to the changes which from time to time must take place, in a greater or less degree, in every body of laws, every book of jurisprudence, which is of an expository nature, must, in the course of a few years, come to partake more or less of this condition.

The most common and most useful object of a history of jurisprudence, is to exhibit the circumstances that have attended the establishment of laws actually in force. But the exposition of the dead laws which have been superseded, is inseparably interwoven with that of the living ones which have superseded them. The great use of both these branches of *science,* is to furnish examples for the *art* of legislation.[a2]

Jurisprudence, statutory – customary

28. Fourthly, in point of *expression,* the laws in question may subsist either in the form of *statute* or in that of *customary* law.

As to the difference between these two branches (which respects only the article of form or expression) it cannot properly be made appear till some progress has been made in the definition of *a* law.

Jurisprudence, civil – penal – criminal

29. Last, The most intricate distinction of all, and that which comes most frequently on the carpet, is that which is made between

---

[a2] Of what stamp are the works of Grotius, Puffendorf, and Burlamaqui?[1] Are they political or ethical, historical or juridical, expository or censorial?— Sometimes one thing, sometimes another: they seem hardly to have settled the matter with themselves. A defect this to which all books must almost unavoidably be liable, which take for their subject the pretended *law of nature*; an obscure phantom, which, in the imaginations of those who go in chase of it, points sometimes to *manners,* sometimes to *laws*; sometimes to what law *is,* sometimes to what it *ought* to be.* Montesquieu sets out upon the censorial plan: but long before the conclusion, as if he had forgot his first design, he throws off the censor, and puts on the antiquarian. The Marquis Beccaria's book,[2] the first of any account that is uniformly censorial, concludes as it sets out with penal jurisprudence.

* See Ch. II (Principles adverse) 14.

[1] Hugo Grotius (1583–1645): *De jure belli ac pacis* (1625). Samuel Puffendorf (1632–94): *Elementa jurisprudentiae universalis* (1661); *De jure naturae et gentium* (1672). Jean Jacques Burlamaqui (1694–1748): *Principes du droit naturel* (1747); *Principes du droit politique* (1751).
[2] *Dei delitti e delle pene* (1764). Cf. above, 166 n. 1.

the *civil* branch of jurisprudence and the *penal*, which latter is wont, in certain circumstances, to receive the name of *criminal*.

What is a penal code of laws? What a civil code? Of what nature are their contents? Is it that there are two sorts of laws, the one penal the other civil, so that the laws in a penal code are all penal laws, while the laws in a civil code are all civil laws? Or is it, that in every law there is some matter which is of a penal nature, and which therefore belongs to the penal code and at the same time other matter which is of a civil nature, and which therefore belongs to the civil code? Or is it, that some laws belong to one code or the other exclusively, while others are divided between the two?[b2] To answer these questions in any manner that shall be tolerably satisfactory, it will be necessary to ascertain what *a law* is; meaning one entire but single law: and what are the parts into which a law, as such, is capable of being distinguished: or, in other words, to ascertain what the properties are that are to be found in every object

Question, concerning the distinction between the civil branch and the penal, stated

[b2] To anyone who should come new to the subject the questions mentioned in the text will naturally appear to be the very A B C of Jurisprudence: they must long ago, he would think, have met with a full and satisfactory solution: to say anything at all about them here would therefore appear idle: to say anything new, impossible. So many ages as have been spent in the study of the laws, so many libraries-full as have been written on them, not know yet what a law is? So many laws as have been made, not know the ingredients they are made of? Incredible—and yet nothing is more true. To write to any purpose a man must begin *ab ovo*: I see no fund open that he can draw from: what he makes use of he must make.

The wonder will cease when it comes to be perceived that the idea of a law, meaning one single but entire law, is in a manner inseparably connected with that of a complete body of laws: so that what is a law and what are the contents of a complete body of the laws are questions of which neither can well be answered without the other. A body of laws is a vast and complicated piece of mechanism, of which no part can be fully explained without the rest. To understand the functions of a balance-wheel you must take to pieces the whole watch: to understand the nature of a law you must take to pieces the whole code.

The subject we are now entering upon belongs to a particular branch of logic, untouched by Aristotle. The main and ultimate business of the school-logic of which that philosopher was the father, is to exhibit the several forms of *argumentation*: the business of the branch now before us is to exhibit the several forms of *imperation*: or (to take the subject in its utmost extent) of sentences expressive of volition: a leaf which seems to be yet wanting in the book of science.

All language whatsoever, every sentence whatsoever, inasmuch as it *expresses* something must *assert* something: something expressive of the state and condition, real or pretended, of the mind of him whose language it is: that is either of his understanding or his will: for at bottom, whatever is said even of external events resolves itself into this. In the first case the sentence expressive of

which can with propriety receive the appellation of *a law*. This then will be the business of the third and fourth sections: what concerns the import of the word *criminal,* as applied to law, will be discussed separately in the fifth.

it has been styled exclusively a *sentence of assertion*: in the other case, a *sentence of volition** of which latter, a *sentence of interrogation* is a particular species.† 'The robber is killed':—'Kill the robber':—'Is the robber killed?'—This is as much as to say, 'I *understand* or I believe that the robber is killed.'—'My *will* is that you kill the robber': 'My *will* is that you tell me whether the robber be killed or no': that is, that if the robber is killed, you tell me he is killed: if not, that he is not killed. Now it is to sentences of the assertive kind that the logic of the schools has confined itself: those which concern volition it has left untouched. The demesnes of the logical branch of science appear then to be more extensive than has commonly been suspected: the language of the will being a new and unexplored province which, neglected as it has been hitherto, might be cultivated, it is probable to at least as good a purpose as the old. It is the branch here in question that is more particularly applicable to the business of government: that subdivision which concerns the forms of imperation at large having a more particular regard to legislation; that which concerns the forms of interrogation, to the less dignified but not less necessary business of collecting verbal information: a process subservient to the business as well of the legislative as of the executive departments.

Had Aristotle happened to turn his view this way, as many pens might perhaps have been employed on this branch of logic as on the other: like that it might have had its algebraical method of notation, its graphical schemes, and its *memoriter* verses: the *Asserit A negat B . . .*': the '*Barbara, celarent, darii, ferioque*' of the schoolmen might have found their parodies: and every piece of intellectual machinery which the ingenuity of those subtle speculatists has ever invented for the accommodation or affrightment of beginners might here have been initiated and improved.

Had this happened to be the case the subject we are entering upon would it is to be presumed by this time have stood in a much clearer light than that in which in the course of a cursory review, I have been able to place it: the business of a great part of the following pages might in that case have been dispatched by a few references. As it is I mean not to descend any deeper into the subject than is absolutely necessary in order to find the requisite materials for the task actually in hand: content with opening the mine, I leave the working of it out to others.[1]

* Harris's Hermes B. 5 Ch. 2 p. 17.[2]
† Ibid.

[1] For the insertion here of this note on the 'logic of the will', see above, Introduction, xlii.

[2] James Harris (1709–80) published in 1751 his *Hermes, or a philosophical enquiry concerning universal grammar.* For some comments on it by Bentham, see his letter to Samuel Bentham of 9 December 1774 (*Correspondence,* in *CW*, i, 221–2).

CONCLUDING NOTE[1]

1. Here ends the original work, in the state into which it was brought in November 1780. What follows is now added in January, 1789.

Occasion and purpose of this concluding note

The third, fourth, and fifth sections intended, as expressed in the text, to have been added to this chapter, will not here, nor now be given; because to give them in a manner tolerably complete and satisfactory, might require a considerable volume. This volume will form a work of itself, closing the series of works mentioned in the preface.[2]

What follows here may serve to give a slight intimation of the nature of the task, which such a work will have to achieve, it will at the same time furnish, not any thing like a satisfactory answer to the questions mentioned in the text, but a slight and general indication of the course to be taken for giving them such an answer.

2. What is a law? What the parts of a law? The subject of these questions, it is to be observed, is the *logical*, the *ideal*, the *intellectual* whole, not the *physical* one: the *law* and not the *statute*. An inquiry directed to the latter sort of object, could neither admit of difficulty nor afford instruction. In this sense whatever is given for law by the person or persons recognized as possessing the power of making laws, is *law*. The Metamorphoses of Ovid, if thus given, would be law. So much as was embraced by one and the same act of authentication, so much as received the touch of the sceptre at one stroke, is *one* law: a whole law, and nothing more. A statute of George II made to substitute an *or* instead of an *and* in a former statute is a complete law; a statute containing an entire body of laws, perfect in all its parts, would not be more so. By the word *law* then, as often as it occurs in the succeeding pages, is meant that ideal object, of which the part, the whole, or the multiple, or an assemblage of parts, wholes, and multiples mixed together, is exhibited by a statute; not the statute which exhibits them.

By a law here is not meant a statute

---

[1] The origin of this long note is explained in its opening paragraph. Printed in all previous editions as a footnote, it has rather the character of an appendix, and its length, interest and importance alike warrant its treatment, typographically, as part of the text.

[2] Above, 6.

3. Every law, when complete, is either of a *coercive* or *uncoercive* nature.

Every law is either a command or a revocation of one

A coercive law is a *command*.

An uncoercive, or rather a *discoercive*, law is the *revocation*, in whole, or in part, of a coercive law.

4. What has been termed a *declaratory* law, so far as it stands distinguished from either a coercive or a discoercive law, is not properly speaking a law. It is not the expression of an act of the will exercised at the time: it is a mere notification of the existence of a law, either of the coercive or the discoercive kind, as already subsisting: of the existence of some document expressive of some act of the will, exercised, not at the time, but at some former period. If it does any thing more than give information of this fact, viz. of the prior existence of a law of either the coercive or the discoercive kind, it ceases *pro tanto* to be what is meant by a declaratory law, and assuming either the coercive or the discoercive quality.

A declaratory law is not, properly speaking, a law

5. Every coercive law creates an *offence*, that is, converts an act of some sort or other into an offence. It is only by so doing that it can *impose obligation*, that it can *produce coercion*.

Every coercive law creates an offence

6. A law confining itself to the creation of an offence, and a law commanding a punishment to be administered in case of the commission of such an offence, are two distinct laws; not parts (as they seem to have been generally accounted hitherto) of one and the same law. The acts they command are altogether different; the persons they are addressed to are altogether different. Instance, *Let no man steal;* and, *Let the judge cause whoever is convicted of stealing to be hanged.*

A law creating an offence, and one appointing punishment are distinct laws

They might be styled; the former, a *simple imperative* law; the other, a *punitory;* but the punitory, if it commands the punishment to be inflicted, and does not merely permit it, is as truly *imperative* as the other: only it is punitory besides, which the other is not.

7. A law of the discoercive kind, considered in itself, can have no punitory law belonging to it; to receive the assistance and support of a punitory law, it must first receive that of a simply imperative or coercive law, and it is to this latter that the punitory law will attach itself, and not to the discoercive one. Example; discoercive law. *The sheriff has power to hang all such as the judge, proceeding in due course of law, shall order him to hang.* Example of a coercive law, made in support of the above discoercive one. *Let no man hinder the sheriff from hanging such as the judge, proceeding in due course of law, shall order him to hang.* Example of a punitory law, made in support of the above coercive one. *Let the judge cause to be*

A discoercive law can have no punitory one appertaining to it but through the intervention of a coercive one

imprisoned whosoever attempts to hinder the sheriff from hanging one, whom the judge, proceeding in due course of law, has ordered him to hang.

8. But though a simply imperative law, and the punitory law attached to it, are so far distinct laws, that the former contains nothing of the latter, and the latter, in its direct tenor, contains nothing of the former; yet by *implication*, and that a necessary one, the punitory does involve and include the import of the simple imperative law to which it is appended. To say to the judge, *Cause to be hanged whoever in due form of law is convicted of stealing*, is, though not a direct, yet as intelligible a way of intimating to men in general that they must not steal, as to say to them directly, *Do not steal*: and one sees, how much more likely to be efficacious. *But a punitory law involves the simply imperative one it belongs to*

9. It should seem then, that, wherever a simply imperative law is to have a punitory one appended to it, the former might be spared altogether: in which case, saving the exception, (which naturally should seem not likely to be a frequent one) of a law capable of answering its purpose without such an appendage, there should be no occasion in the whole body of the law for any other than punitory, or in other words than *penal*, laws. And this, perhaps, would be the case, were it not for the necessity of a large quantity of matter of the *expository* kind of which we come now to speak. *The simply imperative one might therefore be spared, but for its expository matter*

10. It will happen in the instance of many, probably of most, possibly of all commands endued with the force of a public law, that, in the expression given to such a command, it shall be necessary to have recourse to terms too complex in their signification, to exhibit the requisite ideas, without the assistance of a greater or less quantity of matter of an expository nature. Such terms, like the symbols used in algebraical notation, are rather substitutes and indexes to the terms capable of themselves of exhibiting the ideas in question, than the real and immediate representatives of those ideas. *Nature of such expository matter*

Take for instance the law, *Thou shalt not steal*: Such a command, were it to rest there, could never sufficiently answer the purpose of a law. A word of so vague and unexplicit a meaning can no otherwise perform this office, than by giving a general intimation of a variety of propositions, each requiring, to convey it to the apprehension, a more particular and ample assemblage of terms. Stealing, for example, (according to a definition not accurate enough for use, but sufficiently so for the present purpose) is *the taking of a thing which is another's, by one who has no* TITLE *so to do, and is conscious of his having none*. Even after this exposition, supposing it a correct one, can the law be regarded as completely expressed? Certainly not. For what is meant by *a man's having a* TITLE *to take a thing*? To be complete, the law must have exhibited, amongst a multitude of other things, two catalogues; the one of events to which it has given the quality of *conferring title* in such a case; the other of the events to which it has given the quality of *taking it away*. What follows? That for a man to have *stolen*, for a man to *have had no title to what he took*, either no one of the articles contained in the first of those lists must have happened in his favour, or if there has, some one of the number of those contained in the second, must have happened to his prejudice.

The vastness of its comparative bulk is not peculiar to legislative commands   **11.** Such then is the nature of a general law, that while the imperative part of it, the *punctum saliens* as it may be termed, of this artificial body, shall not take up above two or three words, its expository appendage, without which that imperative part could not rightly perform its office, may occupy a considerable volume.

But this may equally be the case with a private order given in a family. Take for instance one from a bookseller to his foreman. *Remove, from this shop to my new one, my whole stock, according to this printed catalogue.—Remove, from this shop to my new one, my whole stock*, is the imperative matter of this order; the catalogue referred to contains the expository appendage.

The same mass of expository matter may serve in common for many laws   **12.** The same mass of expository matter may serve in common for, may appertain in common to, many commands, many masses of imperative matter. Thus, amongst other things the catalogue of *collative* and *ablative* events, with respect to *titles* above spoken of, (see No. **9** of this note)[1] will belong in common to all or most of the laws constitutive of the various offences against property. Thus, in mathematical diagrams, one and the same base shall serve for a whole cluster of triangles.

The imperative character essential to law, is apt to be concealed in and by expository matter   **13.** Such expository matter, being of a complexion so different from the imperative, it would be no wonder if the connection of the former with the latter should escape the observation: which, indeed, is perhaps pretty generally the case. And so long as any mass of legislative matter presents itself, which is not itself imperative or the contrary, or of which the connection with matter of one of those two descriptions is not apprehended, so long and so far the truth of the proposition, *That every law is a command or its opposite*, may remain unsuspected, or appear questionable; so long also may

---

[1] In the 1789 edition the parenthesis continues: 'and see the sheet of corrections, last paragraph but one'. The reference is to the paragraph inserted above at the end of n. n 2 on 216–17.

the incompleteness of the greater part of those masses of legislative matter, which wear the complexion of complete laws upon the face of them, also the method to be taken for rendering them really complete, remain undiscovered.

14. A circumstance, that will naturally contribute to increase the difficulty of the discovery, is the great variety of ways in which the imperation of a law may be conveyed—the great variety of forms which the imperative part of a law may indiscriminately assume: some more directly, some less directly expressive of the imperative quality. *Thou shalt not steal. Let no man steal. Whoso stealeth shall be punished so and so. If any man steal, he shall be punished so and so. Stealing is where a man does so and so; the punishment for stealing is so and so. To judges, so and so named, and so and so constituted, belong the cognizance of such and such offences; viz. stealing*—and so on. These are but part of a multitude of forms of words, in any of which the command, by which stealing is prohibited might equally be couched: and it is manifest to what a degree, in some of them, the imperative quality is clouded and concealed from ordinary apprehension. *The concealment is favoured by the multitude of indirect forms in which imperative matter is capable of being couched*

15. After this explanation, a general proposition or two, that may be laid down, may help to afford some little insight into the structure and contents of a complete body of laws.—So many different sorts of *offences* created, so many different laws of the *coercive* kind: so many *exceptions* taken out of the descriptions of those offences, so many laws of the *discoercive* kind. *Number and nature of the laws in a code, how determined*

To class *offences*, as hath been attempted to be done in the preceding chapter, is therefore to class *laws*: to exhibit a complete catalogue of all the offences created by law, including the whole mass of expository matter necessary for fixing and exhibiting the import of the terms contained in the several laws, by which those offences are respectively created, would be to exhibit a complete collection of the laws in force: in a word, a complete body of law; a *pannomion*, if so it might be termed.

16. From the obscurity in which the limits of a *law*, and the distinction betwixt a law of the civil or simply imperative kind and a punitory law, are naturally involved, results the obscurity of the limits betwixt a civil and a penal *code*, betwixt the civil branch of the law and the penal. *General idea of the limits between a civil and a penal code*

The question, *What parts of the total mass of legislative matter belong to the civil branch, and what to the penal?* supposes that divers political states, or at least that some one such state, are to be found, having as well a civil code as a penal code, each of them complete in its kind, and marked out by certain limits. But no *one* such state has ever yet existed.

To put a question to which a true answer can be given, we must substitute to the foregoing question some such one as that which follows:

Suppose two masses of legislative matter to be drawn up at this time of day, the one under the name of a civil code, the other of a penal code, each meant to be complete in its kind—in what general way, is it natural to suppose, that the different sorts of matter, as above distinguished, would be distributed between them?

To this question the following answer seems likely to come as near as any other to the truth.

The *civil* code would not consist of a collection of civil laws, each complete in itself, as well as clear of all penal ones.

Neither would the *penal* code (since we have seen that it *could* not) consist of a collection of punitive laws, each not only complete in itself, but clear of all civil ones. But

Contents of a civil code

17. The civil code would consist chiefly of mere masses of expository matter. The imperative matter, to which those masses of expository matter respectively appertained, would be found—not in that same code—not in the civil code—nor in a pure state, free from all admixture of punitory laws; but in the penal code—in a state of combination—involved, in manner as above explained, in so many correspondent punitory laws.

Contents of a penal code

18. The penal code then would consist principally of punitive laws, involving the imperative matter of the whole number of civil laws: along with which would probably also be found various masses of expository matter, appertaining, not to the civil, but to the punitory laws. The body of penal law, enacted by the Empress-Queen Maria Theresa,[1] agrees pretty well with this account.

In the Code Frederic the imperative character is almost lost in the expository matter

19. The mass of legislative matter published in French as well as German, under the auspices of Frederic II of Prussia, by the name of Code Frederic,[2] but never established with force of law,[a] appears, for example, to be almost wholly composed of masses of expository matter, the relation of which to any imperative matter appears to have been but very imperfectly apprehended.

[a] Mirabeau sur la Monarchie Prussienne, Tom. v. Liv. 8. p. 215.[3]

[1] Maria Theresa (1717–80), Archduchess of Austria, daughter of the Emperor Charles VI, became sovereign of the Hapsburg domains in 1740. The *Theresianische Strafgesetzbuch* was promulgated in 1768.

[2] See above, 23 n. 1.

[3] Gabriel Honoré Victor Riquetti, comte de Mirabeau (1749–91) published *De la monarchie prussienne sous Frédéric le Grand* in 1788.

20. In that enormous mass of confusion and inconsistency, the ancient Roman, or, as it is termed by way of eminence, the *civil* law, the imperative matter, and even all traces of the imperative character, seem at last to have been smothered in the expository. *Esto* had been the language of primeval simplicity: *esto* had been the language of the twelve tables. By the time of Justinian (so thick was the darkness raised by clouds of commentators) the penal law had been crammed into an odd corner of the civil—the whole catalogue of offences, and even of crimes, lay buried under a heap of *obligations*—*will* was hid in *opinion*—and the original *esto* had transformed itself into *videtur*, in the mouths even of the most despotic sovereigns.

21. Among the barbarous nations that grew up out of the ruins of the Roman Empire, Law, emerging from under the mountain of expository rubbish, reassumed for a while the language of command: and then she had simplicity at least, if nothing else, to recommend her.

22. Besides the civil and the penal, every complete body of law must contain a third branch, the *constitutional*.

The constitutional branch is chiefly employed in conferring, on particular classes of persons, *powers*, to be exercised for the good of the whole society, or of considerable parts of it, and prescribing *duties* to the persons invested with those powers.

The powers are principally constituted, in the first instance, by discoercive or permissive laws, operating as exceptions to certain laws of the coercive or imperative kind. Instance: *A tax-gatherer, as such, may, on such and such an occasion, take such and such things, without any other* TITLE.

The duties are created by imperative laws, addressed to the persons on whom the powers are conferred. Instance: *On such and such an occasion, such and such a tax-gatherer shall take such and such things. Such and such a judge shall, in such and such a case, cause persons so and so offending to be hanged.*

The parts which perform the function of indicating who the individuals are, who, in every case, shall be considered as belonging to those classes, have neither a permissive complexion, nor an imperative.

They are so many masses of expository matter, appertaining in common to all laws, into the texture of which, the names of those classes of persons have occasion to be inserted. Instance; imperative matter:—*Let the judge cause whoever, in due course of law, is convicted of stealing, to be hanged.* Nature of the expository matter.—

Who is the person meant by the word *judge*? He who has been *invested* with that office in such a manner: and in respect of whom no *event* has happened, of the number of those, to which the effect is given, of reducing him to the condition of one *divested* of that office.

Thus the matter of one law may be divided among all three codes

23. Thus it is, that one and the same law, one and the same command, will have its matter divided, not only between two great codes, or main branches of the whole body of the laws, the civil and the penal; but amongst three such branches, the civil, the penal, and the constitutional.

Expository matter a great quantity of it exists every where, in no other form than that of common or judiciary law

24. In countries, where a great part of the law exists in no other shape, than that of what in England is called *common* law but might be more expressively termed *judiciary*, there must be a great multitude of laws, the import of which cannot be sufficiently made out for practice, without referring to this common law, for more or less of the expository matter belonging to them. Thus in England the exposition of the word *title*, that basis of the whole fabric of the laws of property, is no where else to be found. And, as uncertainty is the very essence of every particle of law so denominated (for the instant it is clothed in a certain authoritative form of words it changes its nature, and passes over to the other denomination) hence it is that a great part of the laws in being in such countries remain uncertain and incomplete. What are those countries? To this hour, every one on the surface of the globe.

Hence the deplorable state of the science of legislation, considered in respect of its form

25. Had the science of architecture no fixed nomenclature belonging to it—were there no settled names, for distinguishing the different sorts of buildings, nor the different parts of the same building from each other—what would it be? It would be what the science of legislation, considered with respect to its *form*, remains at present.

Were there no architects who could distinguish a dwelling-house from a barn, or a side-wall from a ceiling, what would architects be? They would be what all legislators are at present.

Occasions affording an exemplification of the difficulty as well as importance of this branch of science;— attempts to limit the powers of supreme representative legislatures

26. From this very slight and imperfect sketch, may be collected not an answer to the questions in the text but an intimation, and that but an imperfect one, of the course to be taken for giving such an answer; and, at any rate, some idea of the difficulty, as well as of the necessity, of the task.

If it were thought necessary to recur to experience for proofs of this difficulty, and this necessity, they need not be long wanting.

Take, for instance, so many well meant endeavours on the part of popular bodies, and so many well meant recommendations in ingenious books, to restrain supreme representative assemblies, from making laws in such and such cases, or to such and such an effect. Such laws, to answer the intended purpose, require a perfect mastery in the science of law, considered in respect of its form— in the sort of anatomy spoken of in the preface to this work: but a perfect, or even a moderate insight into that science, would prevent their being couched in those loose and inadequate terms, in which they may be observed so frequently to be conceived; as a perfect acquaintance with the dictates of utility on that head would, in many, if not in most, of those instances, discounsel the attempt. Keep to the letter, and in attempting to prevent the making of bad laws, you will find them prohibiting the making of the most necessary laws, perhaps even of all laws: quit the letter, and they express no more than if each man were to say, *Your laws shall become* ipso facto *void, as often as they contain any thing which is not to my mind.*

Of such unhappy attempts, examples may be met with in the legislation of many nations: but in none more frequently than in that newly-created nation, one of the most enlightened, if not the most enlightened, at this day on the globe.

27. Take for instance, the *Declaration of Rights*, enacted by the state of North-Carolina, in convention, in or about the months of September, 1788, and said to be copied, with a small exception, from one in like manner enacted by the state of Virginia.[b] *Example. American declarations of rights*

The following, to go no farther, is the first and fundamental article.

'That there are certain natural rights, of which men, when they form a social compact, cannot deprive or divest their posterity, among which are the enjoyment of life and liberty, with the means of acquiring, possessing, and protecting property, and pursuing and obtaining happiness and safety.'

Not to dwell on the oversight of confining to posterity the benefit of the rights thus declared, what follows? That—as against those whom the protection, thus meant to be afforded, includes—every law, or other order, *divesting* a man of *the enjoyment of life or liberty,* is void.

Therefore this is the case, amongst others, with every coercive law.

Therefore, as against the persons thus protected, every order, for example, to pay money on the score of taxation, or of debt

---

[b] Recherches sur Les Etats Unis, 8vo. 1788, Vol. i, p. 158.[1]

[1] By Philip Mazzei; translated into French by Louis-Joseph Faure. For Mazzei, who was himself a citizen of Virginia, cf. R. C. Garlick, Jr., *Philip Mazzei, Friend of Jefferson* (Baltimore, 1933).

from individual to individual, or otherwise, is void; for the effect of it, if complied with, is 'to *deprive* and *divest him*', *pro tanto*, of the enjoyment of liberty, viz. the liberty of paying or not paying as he thinks proper: not to mention the species opposed to imprisonment, in the event of such a mode of coercion's being resorted to: likewise, of property, which is itself, a '*means of acquiring, possessing, and protecting property, and of pursuing and obtaining happiness and safety*'.

Therefore also, as against such persons, every order to attack an armed enemy, in time of war, is also void: for, the necessary effect of such an order is, 'to *deprive* some of them of *the enjoyment of life*'.

The above-mentioned consequences may suffice for examples, amongst an endless train of similar ones.c

c The Virginian Declaration of Rights, said, in the French work above quoted, to have been enacted the 1st of June 1776, is not inserted in the publication entitled *The Constitutions of the several independent states of America, etc. Published by order of Congress: Philadelphia printed. Reprinted for Stockdale and Walker, London*, 1782[1]: though that publication contains the form of government enacted in the same convention, between the 6th of May and the 5th of July in the same year.

But in that same publication is contained a *Declaration of Rights*, of the province of *Massachusets*, dated in the years 1779 and 1780,[2] which in its first article is a little similar: also one of the province of *Pennsylvania*, dated between July 15th and September 28th,[3] in which the similarity is rather more considerable.

Moreover, the famous *Declaration of Independence*, published by Congress July 5th,[4] 1776, after a preambular opening, goes on in these words: '*We hold these truths to be self-evident; that all men are created equal: that they are endued* by the creator *with certain unalienable rights:* that *amongst those are life, liberty, and the pursuit of happiness.*'

The Virginian Declaration of Rights is that, it seems, which claims the honour of having served as a model to those of the other Provinces; and in respect of the above leading article, at least, to the above-mentioned general Declaration of Independency. See Recherches, etc. i, 197.

[1] This collection was compiled by a committee of three Congressmen in accordance with a resolution of the Continental Congress passed in December 1780. It was first published in 1781 by Francis Bailey in Market Street, Philadelphia. Bentham quotes from the London reprint of the following year.

[2] Part I of the constitution of Massachusetts, including the Declaration of Rights, was agreed to in a convention begun at Cambridge on 1 September 1779 and continued by adjournment till 2 March 1780.

[3] This declaration was part of the first constitution of Pennsylvania, drawn up between the dates Bentham mentions. The second constitution (2 September 1790) did not incorporate the declaration.

[4] Adopted, of course, on the previous day. For Bentham's earlier strictures on the Declaration cf. his contribution to John Lind's *An answer to the Declaration of The American Congress* (1776): *Correspondence*, in *CW*, i, 341–4 and nn.

Leaning on his elbow, in an attitude of profound and solemn meditation, '*What a multitude of things there are*', (exclaimed the dancing-master Marcel), '*in a minuet?*'—May we now add?—*and in a law.*

Who can help lamenting, that so rational a cause should be rested upon reasons, so much fitter to beget objections, than to remove them?

But with men who are unanimous and hearty about *measures*, nothing so weak but may pass in the character of a *reason*: nor is this the first instance in the world, where the conclusion has supported the premises, instead of the premises the conclusion.

INDEX OF SUBJECTS

Note. The symbol 'vs.' is used below to indicate 'as distinct from' or 'as opposed to' Other abbreviations for frequently occurring phrases are:

p. of u.: principle of utility

pl(s). and pn(s).: pleasure(s) and pain(s)

References to Bentham's notes are given by means of the page and identifying letter (or letter and number). Where a note extends over more than one page and the reference is to a part of it only, the general reference is followed by a specific page number or numbers in brackets, thus: 260r4 (263).

The index provides for Bentham's lengthy and complex division of offences (Ch. XVI) in three ways: (i) The general heading OFFENCES lists (*inter alia*) references to the character and structure of the five classes (private, public, etc.) into which offences are divided. (ii) This is followed by separate headings, arranged alphabetically according to the first principal word after OFFENCES, for the subdivisions of these classes (e.g. OFFENCES AGAINST PERSON, OFFENCES AGAINST PROPERTY). (iii) Common crimes are indexed under their conventional designations (e.g. ASSAULT AND BATTERY, ROBBERY); and references and cross-references are given to their nearest equivalents and classifications in Bentham's scheme.

ABDUCTION: servant stealing 240, 243–4; ward stealing 249, 250; child stealing 252, 254; wife stealing 257 (*included under* OFFENCES AGAINST CONDITION, q.v.)

ABORTION: 260r4 (263) (*included under* OFFENCES, PUBLIC, against population, q.v.)

ACCESSORY: vs. principal offences 220s2; connected by way of causality with mischievous acts 222u2

ACCIDENT: *See* NEGLIGENCE, HEEDLESSNESS AND RASHNESS

ACTIONS AND ACTS:

I. *In general.* 74–83 (Ch. VII); end of 11a; when conformable to p. of u. 12–14; vs. events 21c; consideration of utility the only right ground of 32–3; fecundity and purity as properties of 39; elements in, distinguished 75; and circumstances 79–83; what constitutes a single act 79; whole *action* as including *act* and consequences 84; act as motion of body 85b; produced by intention 89; relationship between intentionality and consequences of 92; materiality of 96; and pl. and pn. 98; secrecy of, and habits 118, 121; terminating in an object of property 211; control of, as immediate principal end of punishment 158a; ethics and 282;

ACTIONS AND ACTS (*cont.*)

difficulties in framing clear idea of a guilty 288–9

II. *Distinguished and described.* positive (commission) vs. negative (omission or forbearance) 75, 97, 122, 165b; negative, absolutely or relatively 76; external vs. internal or mental 76; external, transitive or intransitive, stages of 76–7; of discourse 76; indivisible vs. divisible 78; repetition of, vs. habit 78; continued, vs. repetition 78; transient vs. continued 78; simple vs. complex 78–9; intentional 84–9; heedless 90, 92; advised vs. unadvised 90, 92; rash vs. not rash 92; of the mind either of intellectual faculty or of will 75d (76), 96, 97, 223

III. *Approval and disapproval of.* See PRINCIPLE OF ASCETICISM; PRINCIPLE OF SYMPATHY AND ANTIPATHY; PRINCIPLE OF UTILITY; PRINCIPLE, THEOLOGICAL *See also* CONSCIOUSNESS; CONSEQUENCES AND EFFECTS; INTENTION AND INTENTIONALITY; MISCHIEF AND HARM; MOTIVE; OFFENCES; RIGHT AND WRONG; VOLUNTARY; WILL

ADULTERY: 256–7 (*included under* OFFENCES AGAINST CONDITION, q.v.)

AFFECTIONS: of sensible faculty (sympathy and antipathy) 21c; vs. imagination 21c; social and dissocial 44, 48; and sympathy 58, 60–1; of male vs. of female 64–5; circumstances concerning, and influence on sensibility 72; as fictitious entities 111p

AGE: as a circumstance influencing sensibility 52; periods of, and their characteristics 65; influence through primary circumstances 66; legislative provision for 69; as indicative secondary circumstance 70; infants 71r

AGGREGATES: *See* TOTALS AND SUMS

ALARM: meaning of, and example 144–5; vs. danger 147, 149, 151–2; resulting from behaviour of same agent vs. that of others 147; opposed by force of punishment (reformation vs. example) 147g; intoxication produces none 149; none unless mischief to assignable persons 151—example (non-payment of tax) 151–2; governed by agent's apparent state of mind 152. *See also* DANGER; MISCHIEF AND HARM; PLEASURES AND PAINS

ANIMALS: as sensitive beings 44; as objects of benevolence or of sympathy 58; interests of, improperly neglected 282b

ANTIPATHY AND SYMPATHY: as cause of an action 32–3; and right ground of action 32–3; regulated by p. of u. 32–3; resentment as a modification of 32–3; connexions in the way of, as circumstances influencing sensibility 52, 57–8, 60, 61, 64–8, 70, 72; and human nature 61; antipathy and religious profession 69; and corresponding motives 109–12, 118; persons connected by sympathy 144; antipathy and displeasure as a constant influential motive 155; on account of which ill-will may be excited by an offence 158a; sympathy as a motive binding one to consult the happiness of others 284; pleasures and pains of, *see* PLEASURES AND PAINS, v. *See also* CIRCUMSTANCES INFLUENCING SENSIBILITY; PRINCIPLE OF SYMPATHY AND ANTIPATHY

APPETITE: analysis of, necessary 3; as fictitious entity 111p. *See also* PLEASURES AND PAINS

APPREHENSION: *See* EXPECTATION AND APPREHENSION

APPROBATION AND APPROVAL, DISAPPROBATION AND DISAPPROVAL: personal, as a sufficient standard of conduct 15–16, 21–5, 26d; and principle of asceticism 17–18; when considered self-justificatory 25; to be guided by some external consideration 25; ground for, distinguished from cause or motive of 32–3; conveyed in words used in good or bad sense 101; as a sentiment, *see* SENTIMENT. *See also* PRINCIPLE OF ASCETICISM; PRINCIPLE OF SYMPATHY AND ANTIPATHY; PRINCIPLE OF UTILITY; PRINCIPLE, THEOLOGICAL

ARCHETYPE AND ARCHETYPATION: 78i, 79l

ARSON: *See* CONFLAGRATION; INCENDIARISM

ASCETICISM: etymology and meaning 17a. *See also* PRINCIPLE OF ASCETICISM

ASSASSINATION: of Duke of Buckingham 80–1; of Henry IV of France 82o, 129, 132, 154n; of Coligny 123; as effect of fanaticism 156r

ASSAULT AND BATTERY: simple corporal injuries 223–4 (*included under* OFFENCES AGAINST PERSON, q.v.)

ASSIGNABLE AND UNASSIGNABLE PERSONS: *See* PERSONS

ASSOCIATION (OF OBJECTS OR IDEAS): pls. and pns. depending on 42–3, 45, 49, 191i; principle of 119z; of ideas of punishment and offence as analogous 178, 179

AVARICE: as motive in figurative sense 97, 114–15; badness of, as motive 102; this explained 114–15

AVERSION: punishment and public sentiments of 171o; punishment creates, towards offence 180

BANISHMENT, WRONGFUL: 223–4 (*included under* OFFENCES AGAINST PERSON, q.v.)

BATTERY: *See* ASSAULT AND BATTERY

BEHAVIOUR: *See* ACTIONS AND ACTS

BELIEF: as a sentiment 45; means by which intellectual motives influence the will 99; and understanding 145

BENEFICIARY: meaning 207; terms for, in English law and Roman law 207f2. *See also* OFFENCES AGAINST TRUST

BENEFIT: of punishment 147; simple negative mischief as loss of 148; pro-

BENEFIT (*cont.*)
duce of taxes as 150; contingent 150; outweighing mischief 159–60

BENEVOLENCE: God's infinite, vs. ordinary 17a, 120–1; sensitive beings as objects of 44; as a motive in figurative sense 97; and goodwill 116–7; dictates of utility and enlightened 117; when repugnant to utility 117; and love of reputation 118, 131; and desire of amity 119; and justice 120b2; enlarged and private or confined 123, 128; and compassion 128; as a motive (tutelary) 145, 154n, 167, 284; and physical sanction 145. *See also* GOODWILL; ILLWILL; MALEVOLENCE; PLEASURES AND PAINS

BIAS: of sensibility 51; this vs. bent of inclinations 56; influence of secondary circumstances upon 64; of women, less comfortable to utility 64–5. *See also* ANTIPATHY AND SYMPATHY; CIRCUMSTANCES INFLUENCING SENSIBILITY; MORALS; RELIGION

BIGAMY: *See* POLYGAMY

BLACKMAIL: *See* MENACEMENT

BLASPHEMY OR PROFANENESS: 260r3 (264) (*included under* OFFENCES, PUBLIC, against religion, q.v.)

BODY: bodily imperfections as circumstance influencing sensibility 52, 55, 58, 66, 69, 71r(72), 72; radical frame of, as circumstance influencing sensibility 52, 53–4, 61–2, 63, 67, 72; divisibility of 58; how related to mind 62n; emotions of, as indications of state of mind 63; inferiority of female, in strength and hardiness 64; effects of climate on 67

BREACH OF CONTRACT: 228g3 (*included under* OFFENCES AGAINST PROPERTY, q.v.)

BREACH OR ABUSE OF TRUST: 214, 219, 240, 248 (*included under* OFFENCES AGAINST TRUST, q.v.); of judicial trust 260r4 (260–2) (*included under* OFFENCES, PUBLIC, against justice, q.v.)

BRIBERY: 220, 240, 248–9, 250, 252, 254, 260r4 (*included under* OFFENCES AGAINST TRUST, q.v.)

BURTHEN: connexions in way of 59, 66, 72s

CALAMITY: meaning 36, 194; as punishment issuing from physical sanction

CALAMITY (*cont.*)
36; precaution against 159. *See also* OFFENCES THROUGH CALAMITY

CALCULATIONS: of magistrate and sanctions 37; of pls. and pns. 39–40; use of this 40; conformity of men's practice to this 40–1; of quantum of punishment 165–74 (Ch. XIV); all men calculate 174. *See also* PLEASURES AND PAINS; QUANTITY AND MAGNITUDE; TOTALS AND SUMS

CAUSE: pl. and pn. as 11, 34; or motive of act vs. reason for approbation of act 32–3; final vs. efficient 34; of pl. called good 40; of pl. called profit 40; exciting, determines whether pl. or pn. is simple or complex 42; exciting, any incident producing pl. or pn. 51; action of, produces but does not determine quantity of pl. or pn. 51; relation to intention and motive 51a; circumstances influencing sensibility applying to exciting, enumerated 52, 69–71; mechanical 54; physiological 54; magnitude, propinquity and efficacy of an exciting 56; exciting, with which legislator has to do 70–1; determines materiality of circumstances 80; vs. derivation connexion and influence 80; makes for directly intentional act 86; chain of, and effect concluded by consequences of act 143; of mischief 148; act as, of natural vs. artificial consequences 156; invisible vs. visible, of insanity 161; and relation of person to exterior objects 191–2. *See also* CONSEQUENCES AND EFFECTS

CELIBACY: 260r4 (263) (*included under* OFFENCES, PUBLIC, against population, q.v.)

CERTAINTY: *See* PROBABILITY AND CERTAINTY

CHAIN: material image 81n

CHILD: *See* PARENT

CIRCUMSTANCES INFLUENCING SENSIBILITY: 51–73 (Ch. VI); enumerated 52; primary vs. secondary 72; primary, subdivided, enumerated and discussed 52–64; secondary, subdivided, enumerated and discussed 64–9; on which a man's means and wants depend, enumerated 59; original principles changed and modified by supervening 63; necessity of attending to 69; different articles applicable to 69–70; may apply indiscriminately to whole

CIRCUMSTANCES INFLUENCING SENSI-
BILITY (*cont.*)
classes of persons together 69–70;
degree of application to individuals
may be with little difference or of infinite variety 69–70; cannot be fully
provided for by legislator and judge
69–71; and punishment 71, 169, 176;
lists of, useful to legislator and judge
71; some bestow denominations on
persons they relate to 71r (72). *See also*
PERCEPTION, PLEASURES AND PAINS

CIRCUMSTANCES OF AN ACT: 79–83;
dependence of intention with regard
to consequences upon 75; broad definition of 79; etymology and meaning
79l; materiality of 80, 91; related to
an event in point of causality in one
of four ways 80–2; this illustrated by
example—assassination of Buckingham 80–2; and by images of generation
and of a chain 81n; difficult to dis-
cover 82; enter into essence of an
offence 82, 191g; criminative, exculpative, extenuative, or aggravative
83, 95, 167, 191g; evidentiary 83; not
objects of intention but only of understanding 89; determine goodness or
badness of consequences of an act 89–
90; awareness of, constituting an
advised act 90; time of, present past or
future 90; preventive 92; compensative 92; determining secondary mischief, enumerated 152; if unknown,
tendency of act to produce mischief
is unknown 161–2; occasional, which
may render punishment unprofitable
163–4, 171. *See also* CONSCIOUSNESS

CIVIL AND PENAL: *See* LAW; PENAL AND
CIVIL

CLASSIFICATION: *See* METHOD OF ANAL-
YSIS; OFFENCES, II. Division into five
classes

CLIMATE: as a secondary circumstance
influencing sensibility 52, 67, 69, 72

CODE: *See* LAW; PENAL AND CIVIL

COERCION AND COMPULSION: and voluntariness 84a; rendering act involuntary
and hence punishment inefficacious
162; as an evil of punishment 163; mental 223; positive (compulsion) vs. negative (restraint) 223; wrongful 223–4,
224x2 (*included under* OFFENCES
AGAINST PERSON, private and semi-
public, q.v.); coercive vs. uncoercive or
discoercive laws 302; and obligation 302

COMMAND: manifestation of legislator's
will is a command or prohibition or
their negation 205e2 (206); negation of,
is act uncommanded and negation of
prohibition is permission 205e2 (206);
express or virtual, and punishment
constitute legal obligation 207f2; forms
of imperation 299b2; coercive, vs.
discoercive or permissive 302, 305, 307;
every law is a, or its opposite 304; imperative character of law concealed
304–5, 306–7. *See also* LAW; LOGIC

COMMON OR JUDGE-MADE LAW: a
fictitious composition 8; yet everywhere the main body of legal fabric 8;
rules of succession and p. of u. 21c (22);
mischievousness of 21c (22, 23);
instinct vs. reason in 21c (24); uncertainty of 308. *See also* CUSTOMARY
LAW; JUDGE

COMMON SENSE: dictates of, drowned by
imagination 21c (22, 24); as a subjective standard of right and wrong 26d;
and repugnancy to nature 26d (27–8)

COMMUNITY: a fictitious body 12; interest of 12; and subjective standards of
approval 26d (28–9); and legislator's
end 34, 158; estimating tendency of an
act affecting interests of 39; influence
of government on affections directed
to 68; and mischief of an act 143, 148,
150; powers necessary to, listed 159–
60; displeasure of foreign communities
164; effects of benevolence to offender
sometimes harmful to 167–8; good of,
and offences against 188; public and
semi-public offences as mischief to
188–91; mischief resulting from war
made to impend indiscriminately over,
whole 197. *See also* OFFENCES, III, Class
2, Semi-public; OFFENCES, PUBLIC

COMPENSATION: satisfaction of injured
party as collateral end of punishment
158a; vindictive vs. lucrative 158a
(159), 182; certainty of, making
punishment groundless 160; when not
sufficient punishment 170n; subserviency to, a property of punishment 182;
only offences against individuals admit
of 275–8; when a sufficient ground for
remission of punishment 276

CONDITION IN LIFE: a secondary circumstance influencing sensibility 52,
72; meaning 192–4, 194k; a fictitious
object 193, 194k; trust and property
distinguished from 208–14; of a

CONDITION IN LIFE (*cont.*)
trustee 208g2; possession of trust or 214–15, 214j2, 215m2; how constituted 234–9, 264–9; domestic vs. civil 234, 238–9, 268; domestic, founded on natural relations 234–6, 250, and on purely legal institutions 236–9, 250; contiguous and uncontiguous relations and domestic 257–60; civil, how constituted 264–9; fiduciary 264–5; non-fiduciary 266–9. *See also* GUARDIAN; MASTER; MATRIMONY; OFFENCES AGAINST CONDITION; PARENT; RELATION(S); SERVANT; WARD

CONDUCT: *See* ACTIONS AND ACTS

CONFINEMENT, WRONGFUL: 223–4 (*included under* OFFENCES AGAINST PERSON, private, q.v.)

CONFLAGRATION: 224z2 (225) (*included under* OFFENCES THROUGH CALAMITY, q.v.)

CONSCIOUSNESS: accompanying action 90–5 (Ch. IX); as knowledge of circumstances of act 89, 90–1; and goodness or badness of intention 89; determines whether act is advised, unadvised, or heedless 90–1; connexion with intentionality 92; and mis-supposal 95; upon which consequences of act may depend 95; and circumstances criminative, aggravative and extenuative 95; as a circumstance determining secondary mischief 152–4; unconsciousness making punishment inefficacious 161–162. *See also* INTENTION; KNOWLEDGE

CONSEQUENCES AND EFFECTS: of an act 15, 32; may determine judgment of motive 32–3; are infinite 74; which material 74; determine tendency of act 74; goodness or badness of, dependent on circumstances of act 79, 88–9; intentionality of 84–6, 92–4, 95; of act and goodness or badness of disposition 125–6; of a mischievous act 143–57 (Ch. XIV); as concluding link in chain of causes and effects beginning with act 143; of an act, primary vs. secondary 147; a third order of 152n; how pernicious, of a mischievous act are affected by motives 154; secondary, of a mischievous act 154–6; natural vs. artificial 156–7; punishment as an artificial 157, 186; of a motive vs. intention 167; an act simple or complex in its effects 222. *See also* TENDENCY

CONSPIRACY: an aggravative circumstance 191g

CONSTITUTIONAL LAW: *See* LAW

CONTRACT: engaging in, an investitive event 228g3; a ground of obligation to render services 228g3; matrimonial 254–6

CRIMES: *See* OFFENCES

CRIMINAL LAW: penal law so described under certain circumstances 299. *See also* LAW

CULPA: how used in Roman law in regard to intentionality and consciousness 94–5. *See also* INTENTION AND INTENTIONALITY

CUSTOMARY LAW: vs. statute law 298. *See also* COMMON OR JUDGE-MADE LAW; LAW

DAMAGE: the most material circumstance common to offence and punishment 178

DANGER: purely physical, vs. that depending on detection 137–8; opposition on the spot vs. subsequent detection 138; meaning 144; example 144–5, 194; as chance of pain or of loss of pleasure 144, 148; secondary mischief consists partly of 144; vs. alarm 147, 148, 152; resulting from behaviour of same agent vs. that of others 147; opposed by force of punishment (reformation vs. example) 147g; averting of, as affording security 148; governed by real state of mind 152; physical, and inefficacious punishment 162; felt by lawbreakers 163; when actualised into mischief 194; offences productive of, to persons 194. *See also* ALARM; PLEASURES AND PAINS

DEFAMATION: 226, 289k (*included under* OFFENCES AGAINST REPUTATION, q.v.)

DEFRAUDMENT: *See* FRAUD AND DEFRAUDMENT

DEITY: *See* GOD

DELINQUENCY: danger intentionally created said to originate in mere 194

DEMAND: present casual, as a circumstance upon which wants depend 59

DESERTION, MILITARY: 260r4 (262) (*included under* OFFENCES, PUBLIC, against public force, q.v.)

DESIRE: the universally desirable end of human action 11a; governed in a great degree by habits 59; physical, as

DESIRE (*cont.*)
motive resulting from pls. of the senses
103, 155; gratification of, as profit of
offence 166c. *See also* MOTIVE; PLEA-
SURES AND PAINS, v(c). Pains of
privation

DETAINER: *See* DETINUE AND DE-
TAINER

DETERRENCE: *See* PREVENTION AND
DETERRENCE

DETINUE AND DETAINER: wrongful
detention or detainment 229, 233 (*included under* OFFENCES AGAINST
PROPERTY, q.v.)

DISCOURSE: *See* LANGUAGE

DISEASE: as a circumstance influencing
sensibility 53–4. *See also* CIRCUM-
STANCES INFLUENCING SENSI-
BILITY; PLEASURES AND PAINS

DISPOSITION: in general 125–42 (Ch. XI);
to feel pl. or pn. as *quantum* of sensibility 51; irritability as 54; as a primary circumstance influencing sensibility 72; and acts 75; good or bad
effects according to 125; effects of, on
self vs. on others 125–7; a fictitious
entity 125; mischievous 126; that
which produces habit of doing mischief cannot be good 127d; nature of,
depends both on apparent tendency of
acts and on motive 127; cases of this
dependency enumerated 127–34;
measure of depravity of, depends on
degree of sensibility to various motives
134, 139; as sum of intentions 134;
temptation and depravity of 138–41,
167; rules for measuring depravity of
140–1; tendency or consequence of an
act may depend on 143; as a circumstance determining secondary mischief
of act 152, 156; of mind and influence
of punishment 161; punishment and
inculcation of beneficial 171o; calculation and warmth vs. coolness of 174;
beneficial quality of an act often
depends on 292

DISUTILITY: *See* UTILITY AND DIS-
UTILITY

DOLUS: how used in Roman law in regard to intentionality and consciousness 94. *See also* INTENTION AND
INTENTIONALITY

DRUNKENNESS: 149, 191g, 224z2 (225)
(*included under* OFFENCES AGAINST
PERSON, Self-regarding, q.v.); primary
and secondary mischief of 149; as a

DRUNKENNESS (*cont.*)
condition rendering punishent inefficacious 161; as extenuation 191g;
difficulties of extirpation of, by law 290

DURESS: *See* COERCION AND COMPUL-
SION

DUTY AND OBLIGATION:
I. *In general.* according to ascetics, to
court pain 18; but not to inflict pain
on others 19–20; obligations as acts
enjoined or prohibited 21c; mischief
as basis of duty to abstain 26d (28–9);
sanctions rendering conduct obligatory
34a; pernicious principles about 164;
a fictitious entity 205e2 (207); ethics
and duty to oneself (prudence) vs. to
others (probity and benevolence) 284;
rules of moral 289
II. *Legal.* and powers and rights 205e2,
215, 234; extra-regarding vs. self-
regarding 205e2 (206); self-regarding
have no corresponding rights 205e2
(206); and trust 205–7, 215; constituted
by command and punishment 207f2;
and property 210, 215m2; law operates
only by imposing, when it first intervenes 236–7; power to enforce 237;
absolute and relative 264–5; absolute,
and p. of u. 265; created by imperative
laws 307. *See also* RIGHT(S);
POWER(S); PROPERTY; TRUST

EDUCATION: never kills instinct 21c
(24); as a secondary circumstance influencing sensibility 52, 66, 70, 72; and
hardiness 54–5; erroneous to attribute
all occurrences in a man's life to 62–3;
defined and divided into physical,
intellectual, and moral 66; principal
medium through which government
operates 68; influenced by religion 69;
instruction sometimes renders punishment needless 164; the business of
private, vs. that of private ethics 246;
art of government as art of, public vs.
private 283

EFFECTS: *See* CONSEQUENCES AND
EFFECTS

ELOPEMENT: from master 243–4; from
guardian 248, 249, 250; from parent
252; from husband 257 (*included under*
OFFENCES AGAINST CONDITION, q.v.)

EMBEZZLEMENT: 229–30, 231 (*included
under* OFFENCES AGAINST PROPERTY,
q.v.); why not usually punished as
theft 160e; appropriate punishment
for 180

EMOTIONS: analysis of, needed in principles of morals 3; of the body vs. of the mind 63

EMPLOYMENT: *See* MASTER; SERVANT

ENGLISH LAW: forfeiture of moveables as punishment in 176a; *cestuy que trust* beneficiary in 297f2; wife's *consortium* in 211i2 (212); detinue and detainer in 229h3, 233r3; physical vs. legal possession in 229h3

ENJOYMENT: all pleasures are of, except those of expectation 45f

ENTICEMENT: *See* ABDUCTION

ENVIRONMENT: *See* CIRCUMSTANCES INFLUENCING SENSIBILITY; EXTERNAL OCCURRENCES

ETHICS: defined 282; private, vs. legislation 281, 285–6, 292s; at large vs. private 282; and rules of prudence, probity and beneficence 284; thunders of law vs. whispers of morality 287; private, where punishment is groundless, inefficacious or needless 286–9

EVENTS: as consequences of act 80; related to some circumstance in the way of causation 80–3; previous and posterior 98; collative and ablative 304; investitive and divestitive, *see* INVESTMENT AND DIVESTMENT

EVIDENCE: consequences of act as 74

EVIL: *See* GOOD AND EVIL

EXCUSES: *See* PUNISHMENT, II

EXISTENCE: vs. unreality, distinguished from present vs. past, deficiency of language 99d

EXPECTATION AND APPREHENSION: prospect of pl. (hope) vs. prospect of pn. (fear) 18; of pl. or pn. and sanctions 35–6; pls. of 45; degree of 46; pns. of 48–9; as motive or temptation 49; apprehension as quality of strength of intellectual powers 55; inclination to expect pl. or pn. 56; strength of, as circumstance influencing sensibility 59, 72s; as internal motive 97–8; vs. pn. accompanying 99c; pn. of, as alarm 144–5; of pl. or advantage in every motive 145; evil of apprehension as evil of punishment 163; of profit as motive of offence 166c. *See also* MOTIVE; PLEASURES AND PAINS

EXPOSITORY MATTER: in laws 303–8; conceals imperative character of law 304–5. *See also* LAW; TITLE

EXTENUATION: *See* CIRCUMSTANCES OF AN ACT

EXTERNAL OCCURRENCES: affect the mind 62; affect influence of education 66

EXTORTION: 224x2, 230–2; *included under* OFFENCES AGAINST PROPERTY, q.v.

FALSE IMPRISONMENT: wrongful confinement 223–4 (*included under* OFFENCES AGAINST PERSON, q.v.)

FALSE PRETENCES: obtaining by, *see* FRAUD AND DEFRAUDMENT

FALSE STATEMENTS: *See* FALSEHOOD

FALSEHOOD: as a circumstance of an offence 191g, 221, 279p5, 280q5; meaning and modes of 203–4; when not an offence 205. *See also* FRAUD AND DEFRAUDMENT; OFFENCES BY FALSEHOOD

FANATICISM: religious, opposed by no other motives 156r

FEAR AND HOPE: meaning 18; superstitious fear more powerful than hope 18; the vulgar liable to fear 19; as motive 44; directed by magistrate 68; fear of shame as tutelary motive 145–6; fear of divine displeasure as tutelary motive 146; fear of pain as self-regarding motive 155. *See also* EXPECTATION AND APPREHENSION

FELICITY: fabric of, to be reared by reason and law 11; greatest felicity principle 11a; object of exercise of powers of government 11a; and pl. and pn. 11a; of after-life and religion 69. *See also* HAPPINESS; PRINCIPLE OF UTILITY

FICTIONS AND FICTITIOUS ENTITIES: common law a fictitious composition 8; community as 12; no common genus, hence difficulties of exhaustive arrangement and definition 52c (53), 205e2 (207); circumstances influencing sensibility as 52c (53); habits as 78i, 119z; motives as 97; passions, appetites and affections as 111p; dispositions as 125; condition as 193, 208g2, 212; reputation as 193, 212; religion as 202z; power and right as 205e2 (206, 207); duty and obligation as 205e2 (207); trust as 208g2; incorporeal objects of property as 212, 241; relation as 235v3; jurisprudence as 293

FORBEARANCE: *See* OMISSION AND FORBEARANCE

FORCE: *See* COERCION AND COMPULSION

FORGERY: 203, 204 (*included under* OFFENCES BY FALSEHOOD, q.v.)

FRAUD AND DEFRAUDMENT: 226–7, 230–2, 269, 279p5 (*included under* OFFENCES AGAINST PROPERTY, q.v.); mercantile, punishment of 160e; appropriate punishment for 181

GAMES: pls. associated with 45

GAMING: 232m3, 260r4 (264) (*included under* OFFENCES AGAINST PROPERTY and OFFENCES, PUBLIC, against national interest, qq.v.)

GENERALIZATION: proper division of offences and 273

GLUTTONY: 224z2 (225) (*included under* OFFENCES AGAINST PERSON, self-regarding, q.v.)

GOD: benevolence of, according to ascetics 17a; this and religion generally 120–1; revealed vs. presumptive will of 31; need for ample interpretations of will of 31; pleasure and displeasure of 31g, 48; intervention of, and religious sanction 35; act or judgment of 36c; and powers of nature 37; as sensitive being 44; goodwill or favour of, as source of pl. of piety 44; gratitude excited by comtemplation of 49p (50); desire for favour of, as motive 108–9; fear of displeasure of, as motive 146; a real being 202z; no offences against 202z

GOOD AND EVIL: and utility 12; good or bad tendency of an act 40, 74; pl. called good, pn. evil 40; cause or instrument of pl. or pn. 40; nothing good or evil in itself except pl. or pn. 89; danger of exaggeration of small evils 125a; as consequences of each other 152m; punishment as an evil 158, 168; four branches of such evil 163–4

GOOD FAITH: keeping of a promise 207f2

GOOD NAME: *See* REPUTATION AND GOOD NAME

GOOD-WILL: and pls. of amity 43–4; as source of benefits 44; deprivation of, and pns. of ill-name 47j; as motive 109–11; a social motive 116; coincidence of, with utility 116–17. *See also* PLEASURES AND PAINS

GOVERNMENT: and greatest felicity 11a; end of, and p. of u. 11a, 12–13, 14d, 74; measure of, when conformable to

GOVERNMENT (*cont.*) utility 13, 198t; and principle of asceticism 19; and principle of sympathy and antipathy 21; and theological principle 31; as a secondary circumstance influencing sensibility 52, 67–8, 72; and taxation 150–2; necessity of 186r; mischief produced by influence exerted on operations of 196–200; operations of, can make addition to positive good 198; instruments of, distinguished 199; *the* government and the sovereign 200; engines of, punishment and reward 201; the art of directing actions to greatest happiness 283; as education of non-adults 283. *See also* JUDGE; LEGISLATOR; OFFENCES, PUBLIC

GRIEF: external indications of, fallacious 63; difficulties in measurement of 63p

GUARDIAN: condition of (powers, rights, duties) 238, 240a4, 244; this a private trust 247; offences touching condition of 247–9 (*included under* OFFENCES AGAINST CONDITION, q.v.). *See also* CONDITION IN LIFE; WARD

HABITS: habitual occupations as primary circumstances influencing sensibility 52, 58, 65, 67, 72; bent of inclination as a primary circumstance influencing sensibility 52, 56, 57, 58, 64, 65, 66, 67, 68, 70, 72; inclination to expect pl. from an object 56–7; of expense 59, 66, 72s; govern desires to a great degree 59; habitual recreations and education 66; force of, in religious profession 69; vs. repetition of an act 78; a fictitious entity 78i, 119z; and secrecy 118; influence of, in restraining disreputable acts 118–19; of committing offences 170; pernicious vs. beneficial 171o; of obeying, in a community 188

HAPPINESS: and utility 11a, 12–13; greatest happiness or felicity principle 11a, 282; and God's benevolence 17a; augmentation of, disapproved by principle of asceticism 17; of individuals composing community (=their pleasure and security) should be legislator's sole end and sole standard imposed by him 34, 74, 158; and pls. of imagination 49p; and connexions in the way of sympathy 60; consists of enjoyment of pls. and security from pn. 74; effect of dispositions on 125; of

HAPPINESS (*cont.*)
a person, related in the way of causality to exterior objects 191–2; individual's own knowledge, inclinations and power as productive of 244; each man knows best what is conducive to his 244; of animals, and cruelty 282b (283); and ethics in general 282–4; end of both ethics and art of legislation 285; limits between these two arts in production of 285–93. *See also* FELICITY; PRINCIPLE OF UTILITY; UTILITY AND DISUTILITY

HARDINESS: as a primary circumstance influencing sensibility 52, 54, 64, 66, 67, 70, 72

HARM: *See* MISCHIEF AND HARM

HEALTH: as a primary circumstance influencing sensibility 52, 53, 54, 55, 64, 66, 67, 70, 72. *See also* PLEASURES AND PAINS

HEEDLESSNESS: *See* NEGLIGENCE, HEEDLESSNESS AND RASHNESS

HERESY: 260r4 (264) (*included under* OFFENCES, PUBLIC, against religion, q.v.)

HEROISM: acts of heroic kind rare 154o

HOMICIDE, WRONGFUL: 85b, 224 (*included under* OFFENCES AGAINST PERSON, q.v.); not rendered innocent by motive 154n; punishment of, in English law 176a

HONOUR: sense of 57; extension of, via connexions of sympathy 61

HOPE: *See* FEAR AND HOPE

HUMAN NATURE: and p. of u. 13–14; and consistency 14; and sanctions 35; and sympathy and antipathy 61; and motives 115; men apt to depreciate character of others 129g; every man has his price 166f; all men calculate 174; and prejudice 226. *See also* CIRCUMSTANCES INFLUENCING SENSIBILITY

HUSBAND: *See* MATRIMONY

IDEAS: intellectual, derived from sensible 34a; of pls. and pns. of future life, liquidated and unliquidated 36–7; and quantity and quality of knowledge 55; interesting 55; and strength of intellectual powers 55; perverse association of, exemplified 101–2; all derived from senses 191–2; progress of, marked by state of language 198. *See also* ASSOCIATION

IDLENESS AND INDOLENCE: 232m3, 260r4 (263) (*included under* OFFENCES AGAINST PROPERTY, self-regarding, and OFFENCES, PUBLIC, against national wealth, qq.v.); as a figurative motive 97

ILL-WILL: as motive 111; punishment of offences originating from 181; pls. and pns. of, *see* PLEASURES AND PAINS

IMAGINATION: as fantasy vs. affection of sensible faculty 21c (21–4); dictates of common sense drowned by 21c (22, 24); vs. reason 21c (22); vs. memory 45; pls. and pns. of, *see* PLEASURES AND PAINS; vividness and rapidity of, as quality of strength of intellectual powers 55; and religion and value of goods 69g

IMPERATION, IMPERATIVE: *See* COMMAND

IMPRISONMENT: deprivation of pls. of imagination an evil of punishment by 49p (50); as efficacious punishment with respect to disablement 182; as remissible punishment 184

IMPRUDENCE: *See* PRUDENCE AND IMPRUDENCE

INCENDIARISM: 234s3 (*included under* OFFENCES AGAINST PERSON AND PROPERTY, semi-public, q.v.)

INCEST: 226a3 (*included under* OFFENCES AGAINST REPUTATION, self-regarding, q.v.)

INCLINATION: *See* HABITS

INDECENCY: not public 233 (*included under* OFFENCES AGAINST PERSON AND REPUTATION, self-regarding, q.v.)

INDOLENCE: *See* IDLENESS AND INDOLENCE

INDIVIDUALS: *See* PERSONS

INFANCY: extreme, making punishment inefficacious 161; and necessity for guardianship 244–5. *See also* GUARDIAN; WARD

INJURY, LASCIVIOUS: 232 (*included under* OFFENCES AGAINST PERSON AND REPUTATION, q.v.)

INJURY: *See* MISCHIEF AND HARM

INSANITY: as a primary circumstance influencing sensibility 52, 58, 69, 71r, 72; making punishment inefficacious 161; and necessity for guardianship 244–5

INSECURITY: *See* SECURITY AND INSECURITY

INSOLVENCY: 227; *included under* OFFENCES AGAINST PROPERTY, q.v.

INSTINCT: and p. of u. never killed by education 21c (24)

INSULT: personal vs. corporal 226; may be treated as a distinct genus of offence 227; corporal 232–3 (*included under* OFFENCES AGAINST PERSON AND REPUTATION, q.v.)

INTELLECTUAL POWERS: strength of, as a primary circumstance influencing sensibility 52, 55, 64, 68, 70

INTENTION AND INTENTIONALITY: 84–89 (Ch. VIII); produced by pl. or pn. in character of a motive, and vs., exciting cause of pl. or pn. 51a; regarding *act* itself or its consequences 84; if both whole *action* is intentional 84; and different stages of act 84b, 88; with regard to consequences of act 74–5, 84–5, 92–3, 126–7, 143; as to consequences and rational vs. irrational agency 74–5; as to consequences, depend on state of will as to act and of understanding or perception as to circumstances 75; intentionality distinguished from consciousness 75; *intentional*, when synonymous with *voluntary* 84a, 85b, 153; direct vs. oblique, ultimate vs. mediate, exclusive vs. inexclusive, conjunctive vs. disjunctive vs. indiscriminate, with vs. without preference 86–8; example 87–8, 91–2; proof of 88; good or bad, only by reference to consequences or motives 88–9; circumstances not intention objects of consciousness 89; goodness or badness of, resulting from consequences and so from consciousness 89, 92; how connected with consciousness 92; vs. motive 92–4, 116; when innocent 94; Roman law relating to 94–5; suggested Latin terminology for 95; degree and bias 95; motives as cause of 116, 134; and disposition 126, 134; correspondence between intention and consequences and between intentions at different times 127; as circumstance determining secondary mischief 152–4; and heedlessness 153; unintentionality makes punishment inefficacious 161; and danger and semi-public offences 194. *See also* ACTIONS AND ACTS; CONSCIOUSNESS

INTERESTS: number of, affected 11a; cannot be defined in ordinary way 12c; of the individual 12, 40; of the community, meaning 12; sinister, of government 14d; effect of motives on 116; persons connected by 144; pecuniary, as motive, 154o, 174; of one individual vs. of others 164; offences due to indolence and pecuniary, and appropriate punishment 181; of the public and mischief affecting 196; motive for consulting one's own, adequacy of 284

INTERNATIONAL: a new word 296x. *See also* LAW; SOVEREIGN

INTOXICATION: *See* DRUNKENNESS

INVENTED TERMS (GREEK DERIVED): 260r4 agatho-poieutic (262, 263); antembletic (262); autochirous (263); demosio-tamieutic (263); epistemo-threptic (262); ethno-plutistic (263); eupoedagogic (262); hedonarchic (262); heterochirus (263); moro-comial (262); noso-comial (262); phthano-paranomic (262); phthano-symphoric (262); polemo-tamieutic (262); presbeutic (264); ptocho-comial (262); symbouleutic (264)

INVESTMENT AND DIVESTMENT: wrongful investment, non-investment, and divestment in various offences against trust, property, and condition 216–17, 218, 220–1, 226, 227, 230j3, 233, 234, 239, 240–1, 242, 248–50, 251–3, 257; collation and ablation suggested as better terms for 216n2 (217), 242 (*editorial note*); and title 227, 304; and payment 227e3; and contract 228g3; powers of 260r4 (263); and meaning of word judge 308. *See also* CONDITION; PROPERTY; TRUST; OFFENCES AGAINST CONDITION; OFFENCES AGAINST PROPERTY; OFFENCES AGAINST TRUST

JUDGE: and political sanction 35; magistrate in character of tutor to members of state 68; or executive magistrate makes provision for circumstances which cannot be fully provided for by legislator 69–70; applies punishment to particular persons 70; should have lists of circumstances influencing sensibility 71; disposition of 98, 289; and rules of proportion of punishment 169; functions of, and of police 198;

JUDGE (*cont.*)

judicial trust 260r4 (260–2); meaning of word 308. *See also* COMMON OR JUDGE-MADE LAW; JUSTICE; OFFENCES, PUBLIC, against justice

JURISPRUDENCE: ideas and words expounded in universal 6, 295; local, and the legality of a mandate 123; new tools to cut new road through wilds of 214j2 (215); one branch of, contains the art and science of legislation 293; expository vs. censorial 294; authoritative vs. unauthoritative 294; five principal branches of 294–300; local vs. universal 294–5; internal vs. international 296–7; national vs. local 297; ancient vs. living 297–8; civil vs. penal or criminal 298–300. *See also* LAW; LEGISLATION; LOGIC

JUSTICE: divine and human 110o; an imaginary person 120b2; dictates of, are dictates of utility or benevolence 120b2; offences against 196, 200, 260r4 (260–2) (*included under* OFFENCES, PUBLIC, q.v.); functions of, vs. of police 198

JUSTIFICATIONS: of common law by Coke 21c (22); vs. origin of moral sentiment 26d; for withholding taxes 151; missupposal of 153; consent as, for an act 159; of benefit outweighing mischief 160; of compensation 160

KNOWLEDGE: quantity and quality of, as a primary circumstance influencing sensibility 52, 55, 64–5, 66, 67, 68, 70, 72; of circumstances of act as consciousness 89; defective, making punishment inefficacious 161–2; ignorance admits of a cure 173; perfect, of objects composing a logical whole 187a; useless if too unpalatable 196q; each knows best what is conducive to own happiness 244; offences against promotion of, as offences against positive increase of national felicity 260r4 (262) (*included under* OFFENCES, PUBLIC, q.v.); pls. and pns. of, *see* PLEASURES AND PAINS. *See also* CONSCIOUSNESS; INTENTION AND INTENTIONALITY

LABOUR: inevitable lot of humanity 10; nature of 59; profit of 59; and religion 69q; penal, as reformatory punishment 181; penal, as chronical remissible punishment 184

LANGUAGE: universal jurisprudence concerned with import of words 6, 295; difficulties arising from nature of 19 (act), 53 (fictitious entities), 99d (existence), 102 (names of motives), 187a, 190f, 230i3, 271–2 (offences), 208g2, 214j2 (trust), 210 (property and condition); does not determine acts as positive or negative 76; acts of discourse 76; ambiguity of, unless informed by occasion and purpose 79; ordinary discourse and goodness and badness of intentions 92; and of motives 100–2; shackles of ordinary 102g; need for invented terms 102, 216n2, 230i3, 271–2; the multitude are the manufacturers of 107; as key to a people's moral sentiments 130g; names given before knowledge of objects perfected 187a; need not to depart too far from customary 187a, 190f, 214j2, 271; state of, marks progress of ideas 198t; faculty of discourse 203; need for verbal discussions 214j2; legislator's mastery of arts of 289; strict speech vs. usage 295; all asserts 299b2; expresses state of understanding or of will 299b2; of will unexplored 299b2. *See also* INVENTED TERMS (GREEK-DERIVED)

LARCENY: *See* THEFT OR STEALING

LAW:

I. *Analysis and science.* a complete body of law 6, 299b2, 305; science of, a branch of logic of will 8–9, 299b2; importance of notion of a single complete law 8, 282, 296; and rights powers and obligations 205e2, 234, 236–7; can only prohibit or command 281; a law vs. parts of a law 282, 301; what law is vs. what it ought to be 292s, 293–4; an abstract or collective term, division into branches determined by extent, political quality, time, manner of expression, and concern with punishment 294–300; definition deferred 294v; abstract and concrete senses of, distinguished in European languages 294w; substance and form 295; definition of, belongs to universal jurisprudence 295; international, whether properly so called 297; a logical or ideal whole vs. a statute 301; declaratory, not strictly a law 302; coercive, (a command) vs. uncoercive or discoercive or permissive

LAW (*cont.*)

302, 305, 307; simple imperative and punitory, connection and distinction between 302–7; expository matter in 303–8; imperative character of, concealed 304–5; number of laws how determined 305; state of science of legislation 308–10. *See also* COMMAND; LOGIC

II. *Divisions and classification.* concern or subject of penal 3, 74, 126, 134; of procedure 79j, 282; remuneratory branch of hitherto unnamed 126; penal (or criminal) vs. civil 281; penal civil and constitutional codes or branches of 281a, 305, 307–8; division into branches determined by extent, political quality, time, manner of expression, and concern with punishment 294–300; international 296–7; statutory vs. customary 298

III. *Relation to principle of utility, pleasures and pains.* and p. of u. 11, 158; law or dictate of utility 13; constitutional, and application of p. of u. 14d; mischievousness of English judge-made 21c (22); pls. and pns. a concern of 49. *See also* GOVERNMENT; LEGISLATOR

IV. *Miscellaneous references.* influence of connexions of sympathy on hold of 60i; artificial tutelary motives of its own creation 137; *ex-post-facto* 160; favour to responsible persons 160e; weakness in, as mischief produced by unpopular punishment 183; thunders of, vs. whispers of morality 287; and duty to save others from mischief 293

LAW, MAXIMS OF: governing hereditary succession 21c; produced by imagination opposed to utility 21c (22–4); melody of 21c (23–4); only when opposed to general rules can they obtain separate existence 21c (23); that punishment must rise with strength of temptation 142. *See also* ROMAN LAW

LAW OF NATURE: as standard of right and wrong 26d (27); and utility 26d (27–8); offences against 276h5; imaginary 297z; obscure phantom 298a2. *See also* NATURE AND NATURAL

LEGISLATION: principles of, in general 3; projected works on principles of, in

LEGISLATION (*cont.*)

nine different fields 6; art of, how related to logic of will or science of law 8–9; legislative and executive branches of sovereign power 260r4 (263); limits between private ethics and art of 281–93; and administration included in art of government 283; deplorable state of science of, in respect of form 308. *See also* GOVERNMENT; LAW; LEGISLATOR

LEGISLATOR: sole end of, happiness of community 34, 198; ends and instruments of, pls. and avoidance of pns. 38, 74; vs. judge 70–1; and material consequences 74; character of English M.P. compared with Turkish or Indian official 119; vs. moralist, deals with effect of a man's disposition on others 126–7; must not act in ignorance of other forceful sanctions in society 162j; general object of, and four subordinate objects of punishment 165; and habitual offences 170; must provide full complement of punishment 172; should not introduce unpopular punishment 183; should correct public prejudice against punishments 183–4; and influence of religion 202z; manifestations of his will 205e2 (206); to fix sense of names of offences 230i3; reasons for his giving legal power to those who have physical power 237x3; the natural method adopted in division of offences a perpetual lesson to 274; room for private ethics where none for direct interference by 285–9; direct interference of, must be by punishment 285; how far he should reinforce private ethics 289–93; mastery of language in framing offences 289; defect in ability or integrity of 289k; his knowledge of individual men 290; limitations of sanctions of 290–1

LIBEL: 203a2 (*included under* OFFENCES BY FALSEHOOD, q.v.). *See also* DEFAMATION; OFFENCES AGAINST REPUTATION

LIBERTY: as an incorporeal property 212; a liberty and limitation on power of master 241; meaning of, concern of universal jurisprudence 295. *See also* RIGHT

LOGIC: of the will vs. of the understanding 8–9; science of law the most considerable branch of logic of the will

LOGIC (*cont.*)
8; of the will untouched by Aristotle 299b2; its business to exhibit forms of imperation as expressive of volition 299b2; law as logical vs. physical whole or statute 301

LUST: why motives expressed by the word, always bad 102, 114–15

MAGISTRATE: *See* JUDGE

MALEVOLENCE: objects of 44; pls. of 44; pns. of 48; as extra-regarding 49; as dissocial motive for prosecution of offences 154o; excited by offence 158a; punishment producing dissocial pleasure 179–80. *See also* BENEVOLENCE; ILL-WILL; PLEASURES AND PAINS

MANSLAUGHTER: *See* HOMICIDE, WRONGFUL

MARRIAGE: *See* MATRIMONY

MASTER: condition of, and property 210–13; powers obligations and rights constituting legal relationship of, and servant 238–9; offences touching condition of 239–41 (*included under* OFFENCES AGAINST CONDITION, q.v.); and offences against servant 242–4. *See also* CONDITION IN LIFE; SERVANT

MATRIMONY: as circumstance strengthening hold of law 60–1; condition of husband or wife how constituted 254; powers duties and rights 254–5; offences touching matrimonial condition 255–7 (husband), 257 (wife), 257q4 (improvident, on part of minors) (*included under* OFFENCES AGAINST CONDITION, q.v.); incapacity of contracting 260. *See also* ADULTERY; CONDITION IN LIFE

MAXIMS: *See* LAW, MAXIMS OF

MEASUREMENT: *See* CALCULATION; QUANTITY AND MAGNITUDE; TOTALS AND SUMS; VALUE

MEMORY: pls. of 45; pns. of 48; accuracy and tenacity of, as quality of strength of intellectual powers 55; and pls. and pns. of the mind 191i (192). *See also* PLEASURES AND PAINS

MENACEMENT: wrongful, or insulting 223–4, 226, 232–3 (*included under* OFFENCES AGAINST PERSON, and OFFENCES AGAINST PERSON AND REPUTATION, qq.v.)

MENS REA: *See* COERCION AND COMPULSION; CONSCIOUSNESS; INFANCY; INSANITY; PUNISHMENT, II; VOLUNTARY AND INVOLUNTARY; WILL

METHOD OF ANALYSIS: advantages of natural method in division of offences 5, 272–4; analysis on an exhaustive plan required to demonstrate completeness of catalogue of pls. and pns. 42a; fictitious entities, having no common genus, cannot be subjected to exhaustive arrangement 52c (53); analytic view given to test completeness of catalogue and show similarities and differences of objects included 72; analysis of ways in which circumstances are related to consequences of act possibly of use to natural philosophy 83u; distinctions drawn in minute analysis of intentionality useful in exhaustive analysis of mechanical inventions 85b; division of mischief according to nature cause and object exhaustive 148; other principles of division possible 148h; method of bipartition (dichotomous division) necessary to give perfect knowledge of objects constituting a logical whole 187a; exhaustive method aimed at constitutes originality of this work 196q; deviation from this method of analysis necessary 196q; demonstration that bipartition is exhaustive and difficulties of language 214j2 (215); general idea of classification of offences 270–2; how natural method in division of offences exhibits distinctive characteristics 274–80. *See also* OFFENCES, II, *Division into five classes*

MIND: axioms of mental pathology 3; and pls. of association 45; as arena of sensibility 51; primary circumstances influencing sensibility include firmness of 52, 56, 64, 66, 70, 72; and steadiness of 52, 56, 70, 72; and radical frame of 52, 62, 67, 72; condition of, vs. condition of body 55–8, 66; quantity and quality of knowledge in 55; insanity and lesser imperfections of 58; unlike body, is indivisible 58; influence of external occurrences on texture of 62; how related to body 62n; emotions of body as indications of 63; relative deficiency in women of knowledge and comprehension 65; strength of, and

MIND (*cont.*)
rank, 65; effect of climate on 67; and understanding vs. affections 72; state of, produces material consequences 75d (76); act of, is either of intellectual faculty or of will 96; disposition as what is permanent in frame of 125; real vs. apparent state of 152; firmness vs. irritability of, according to which men calculate 174; pain of, is either sufferance or apprehension 223. *See also* CONSCIOUSNESS; DISPOSITION; INSANITY; INTENTION AND INTENTIONALITY; KNOWLEDGE

MISCHIEF AND HARM: vs. inconvenience 21c (24); of subjective standards 26d; as a basis of duty to abstain 26d; of a practice 29; vs. trivialities 29–31; near and remote, effect on antipathy 31; of an offence, what constitutes 49; to the body 66; circumstances to be considered in estimating 69; of intolerant laws 121; magnitude of, and motive 124; and depravity of disposition 138–41; as aggregate of mischievous consequences 143; primary (to assignable persons) vs. secondary (to multitude of unassignable persons) 143–5, 148–9, 151–5; original vs. derivative 143–4; secondary, includes alarm and danger 144; exhaustively divided according to its nature, its cause, and its object 148; produced either by one action or by the concurrence of several actions 148, 149; simple vs. complex 148, 149; positive vs. negative 148, 149; certain vs. contingent 148, 149, 151; self-regarding vs. extra-regarding 148–9; private vs. semi-public vs. public 148–9; intensity, duration, uncertainty, remoteness, extent and fecundity of 151; intentionality etc. and secondary 152–7; exclusion of, as object of all laws 158; punishment as 158, 183; consent as proof that none is done 159; and cases where punishment should not be inflicted because groundless 159–60; because unprofitable 163–4; because needless 164; prevention of, the object of punishment 165; and expense of punishment 168. *See also* ALARM; CONSEQUENCES AND EFFECTS; DANGER; DISPOSITION; OFFENCES, I. *In general*

MISSUPPOSALS AND MISTAKES: defined 90–1; render act misadvised 90–3; example 91–2; and rashness 92, 153; relevance to estimates of disposition 126; and secondary mischief 153; of justification 153; rendering punishment inefficacious 162; of one's own happiness 289–90

MORAL SENSE: a form taken by principle of sympathy and antipathy 26d

MORALISTS: and principle of asceticism 18; their alternatives for the word pleasure 18–19; concerned with effects of a man's disposition on himself vs. legislator's concern with effects on others 126–7; and shackles of ordinary language 162g. *See also* ETHICS

MORALS: ideas of which analysis is required in principles of 3; moral science 11; phraseology of, and interest of community 12; moral sense 26d; application of principle of sympathy and antipathy to 26d (28); moral sanction 34, 35, 47; primary circumstances influencing sensibility include moral biases 52, 57, 64, 65, 67, 68, 70, 72; and moral sensibility 52, 57, 64, 65, 66, 68, 70, 72; moral sensibility, quantum of 284–5. *See also* SANCTIONS

MOTION: criterion of a positive act 75; and external acts, transitive and intransitive 76–7; acts divisible with regard to 78; three articles to be considered in 85b; and action of objects 191i (192). *See also* ACTIONS AND ACTS

MOTIVE: in general 96–124 (Ch. x)
I. *Analysis, and relation to act, intention, consequences, pleasures and pains, etc.* or cause of an act vs. reasons for approving 32–3; as prospect of pl. or pn. 49, 56i, 100–1, 103–16, 145, 155; intention produced by pl. or pn. as 51a; cause of intention 51a, 89, 116, 134, 143; and consequences or tendencies of acts 75, 98, 100, 122, 143–57; and voluntariness 84a, 97; vs. intention 93–4; speculative 96, 99; meaning of 96, 97, 97b, 100; practical, influencing the will 96–7, 99, 145; internal vs. external 97–8; figurative and unfigurative 97; as determinative of forbearance 97b; refer necessarily to action 98; as previous or posterior event 98; in prospect vs. in *esse* 98; immediate vs. remote 98–9; and understanding 99; pointing out, and giving

MOTIVE (*cont.*)

reasons 99; may act on will through belief 99–100; internal, in *esse* 100; always pl. or pn. 100; creating an imaginary law or dictate 116t; impelling and restraining 122, 165b, 166c, 168; opposing one another 122, 156r

II. *Relation to principle of utility, offences, and punishment.* for following a principle other than that of utility 16; and sanctions 34a, 123; of an offence, temptation 49; coinciding with p. of u. 116–22; materiality of, to mischief and demand for punishment 123–4; and means of combating offences at their source 124; and temptation 138–42, 166c, 167; as circumstance determining or aggravating secondary mischief 152, 154–6; mischief of act and strength, constancy or extensiveness of 155–6; rules of proportion of punishment applicable to all 165b; nature of, determines extent of calculation 174; nature of, upon which depends influence of punishment 180–1

III. *Goodness and badness.* transfer of approbation of act to motive 32–3; none bad in itself 100, 114; import of name of, vs. motive itself 114–15; social, dissocial, and self-regarding 116, 120–3, 127, 141, 154o, 155, 181, 284, 292; good or bad according to goodness or badness of intention arising from 116, 123–4; as a circumstance on which goodness or badness of disposition is liable to depend 127–34; beneficial quality of an act often depends on 292

IV. *Classified and described.* hope and fear as 18; catalogue of, corresponding to pls. and pns. 103–16; catalogue not complete 102h (103); good and bad, classified 115–16; standing vs. occasional 134–5; seducing vs. tutelary or social 134, 145, 146, 166; tutelary 145, 146, 166; of honour 154n; of religion 154n, 156, 162j; self-regarding, strongest 155, 284; of displeasure 155; of pecuniary interest 174; coercive 220, 230–1; to consult happiness of others 284

See also BENEVOLENCE; DISPOSITION; MALEVOLENCE

MURDER: *See* HOMICIDE, WRONGFUL

NAMES: *See* LANGUAGE

NATURAL LAW: *See* LAW OF NATURE

NATURE AND NATURAL: natural classification of offences 5, 272–4; nature and governance of mankind by pl. and pn. 11; unnatural acts, meaning of 26d (27–8); course of nature and physical sanction 35; strength as gift of nature 54–5; nature vs. education and environment in determining sensibility 62–3. *See also* HUMAN NATURE; LAW OF NATURE

NEGLIGENCE, HEEDLESSNESS AND RASHNESS: accident vs. imprudence 36; accident intemperance and negligence causing mischief to the body 66; heedlessness defined 90; ordinary prudence and heedlessness 90; rashness defined 92; unintentionality with heedlessness produces secondary mischief 153; as does missupposal with rashness 153; calamities through negligent acts 225. *See also* MISSUPPOSALS AND MISTAKES; OFFENCES THROUGH CALAMITY; PRUDENCE AND IMPRUDENCE

OBLIGATION: *See* DUTY AND OBLIGATION

OBSCENITY: obscene exhibition or public discourse 224z2 (225) (*included under* OFFENCES OF MERE DELINQUENCY, semi-public, q.v.)

OFFENCES:

I. *In general.* punishment presupposes idea of 4; mischief as a character of 49, 165a, 275–9; profit of 49, 166c, 167, 168k, 169, 170; negative acts or omissions as 75–6; all include acts of some sort 83; circumstances of, criminative, exculpative, extenuative, aggravative, evidentiary 83, 191g; differ in character and effects according to motive 96; temptation to commit 138–9, 158a, 167; motive for prosecution of 154o; prevention of all, as first object of punishment 165, 166, 168; distinction between acts which are, and those which ought to be 187–8; defined as acts prohibited or of which contrary is commanded by law 281; vague or questionable acts not suitable 289; every coercive law creates one 302, 305; exceptions made by discoercive laws 305; number and classi-

OFFENCES (*cont.*)

fication of laws is identical with that of 305. *See also* LAW; MISCHIEF; PUNISHMENT

II. *Division into five classes.* natural method of division 5, 272–4; method of analysis and nomenclature 187a, 190f, 191g, 196q, 271–2; classes 187–91; method applicable to all countries 272; characters of each class 275–80. *See also* METHOD OF ANALYSIS

III. *The five classes.*

1. *Offences against individuals* (private or private extra-regarding offences). defined 188–9; divisions and subdivisions 191–4, 222–70; characteristics of the class 275–6; *divided into* (i) OFFENCES AGAINST PERSON (ii) OFFENCES AGAINST PROPERTY (iii) OFFENCES AGAINST REPUTATION (iv) OFFENCES AGAINST CONDITION (v) OFFENCES AGAINST PERSON AND PROPERTY (vi) OFFENCES AGAINST PERSON AND REPUTATION, qq.v.

2. *Semi-public offences.* defined 189; divisions and subdivisions 194–5, 222, 224z2, 226a3, 232m3, 233o3, 234s3, 257q4; characteristics of the class 276–7; *divided into* OFFENCES THROUGH CALAMITY *and* OFFENCES OF MERE DELINQUENCY, qq.v.; *susceptible also of same further divisions as offences of class 1 into* OFFENCES AGAINST PERSON, PROPERTY, etc., qq.v.

3. *Self-regarding offences,* defined 189, 195; divisions and subdivisions 195–6, 224z2, 226a3, 232m3, 233o3, 257q4; characteristics of the class 277–8; *susceptible of same division as offences of class 1 into* OFFENCES AGAINST PERSON, PROPERTY, etc., qq.v.

4. *Public offences.* defined 189–90; divisions and subdivisions 196, 260r4; characteristics of the class 278–9; *catalogued under eleven divisions, see* OFFENCES, PUBLIC

5. *Multiform* (*or heterogeneous*) *offences.* defined 190–1; irregularity of class 190f; characteristics of the class 279–80; *divided into* OFFENCES BY FALSEHOOD *and* OFFENCES AGAINST TRUST, qq.v.

OFFENCES THROUGH CALAMITY: 194, 224z2

OFFENCES AGAINST CONDITION: private 192–4, 234–60 (domestic), 264–70 (civil); semi-public 257q4; self-regarding 257q4; why separated from offences against trust and against property 208–14. *See also* CONDITION IN LIFE

OFFENCES OF MERE DELINQUENCY: 195, 224z2

OFFENCES BY FALSEHOOD: 190–1; divisions and subdivisions 203–5, 221; relation to offences against trust 221–2. *See also* FALSEHOOD

OFFENCES AGAINST PERSON: private 191, 193–4, 215m2 (216), 222–4; semi-public 224z2 (225), 234s3; self-regarding 224z2 (225). *See also* PERSON

OFFENCES AGAINST PERSON AND PROPERTY: private 191–2, 231, 233–4; semi-public 224z2 (225), 234s3. *See also* PERSON; PROPERTY

OFFENCES AGAINST PERSON AND REPUTATION: private 193–4; 232–3; self-regarding 233o3. *See also* PERSON; REPUTATION

OFFENCES AGAINST PROPERTY: private 191–4, 226–32; semi-public 224z2 (225), 232m3; self-regarding 232m3; why separated from offences against trust and against condition 208–14. *See also* PROPERTY

OFFENCES, PUBLIC: in general, *see* OFFENCES, III, class 4; catalogued under eleven divisions as offences against (1) external security 260r4, (2) justice 260r4, (3) preventive branch of police 260r4 (262), (4) public force 260r4 (262), (5) positive increase of national felicity 260r4 (262), (6) public wealth 260r4 (262–3), (7) population 260r4 (263), (8) national wealth 260r4 (263), (9) sovereignty 260r4 (263–4), (10) religion 260r4 (264), (11) national interest in general 260r4 (264). *See also* GOVERNMENT; PUBLIC, THE; SOVEREIGN

OFFENCES AGAINST REPUTATION: private 193–4, 215m2 (216), 225–6; semi-public 226a3; self-regarding 226a3. *See also* REPUTATION

OFFENCES AGAINST TRUST: 190–1, 205–14; why separated from offences against condition and against property 208–14; divisions and subdivisions 214–21; in offences against property

OFFENCES AGAINST TRUST (*cont.*) 226, 231; in offences against condition 247–8, 264–5. *See also* TRUST

OMISSION AND FORBEARANCE: as negative acts 75; motives and 97, 97b; punishment and reward and 165b. *See also* ACTIONS AND ACTS; WILL

OUGHT: what men ought to do and shall do determined by pl. and pn. 11; only has meaning when interpreted according to p. of u. 13; object which all laws have or ought to have 71, 158; acts which are offences vs. acts which ought to be 187–8; not implied by term beneficiary vs. invented term 'beneficiendary' 207f2; where legislation is not what it ought to be 292s; what law is vs. what it ought to be 293–4. *See also* PRINCIPLE(S)

PAIN(S): *See* PLEASURE(S) AND PAIN(S)

PARENT: as deputy to magistrate 68; condition of (powers, rights, duties) 250–1; offences touching 250–2 (*included under* OFFENCES AGAINST CONDITION, q.v.). *See also* CONDITION IN LIFE

PARTY: *See* PERSON(S)

PASSION: analysis of, needed in principles of morals 3; names of, also names of motives 111; fictitious entities 111p; and calculation 173–4

PENAL AND CIVIL: penal sometimes termed criminal 281, 299, 300; limits between penal branch and civil branch obscure 281; and intricate 299; cannot be settled until known what is a single complete law 299; general idea of the distinction 305–8; civil code comprises mainly expository matter, penal code mainly imperative matter and punitory laws 306; penal and civil code vs. penal and civil laws 306. *See also* LAW

PERCEPTION: pls. and pns. as interesting 42; simple vs. complex 42; original 45; of soul 58; intention depending upon, with regard to circumstances 75; internal, of pl. and pn. as motive 97; and pls. and pns. of the mind 191i (192); and memory 191i (192)

PERJURY: 203; how distinguished from other falsehoods 203–4 (*included under* OFFENCES THROUGH FALSEHOOD, q.v.)

PERMISSION: *See* COMMAND

PERSON: and application of circumstances influencing sensibility 69–70; circumstances bestowing particular denominations on 71r; assignable and unassignable, and identification of mischief as primary or secondary 143–4, 148, 260r4 (261); connected by interest or sympathy 144; no alarm where no assignable, affected 151, 152; assignable by name or description vs. unassignable 188c, 189; assignable or unassignable, and classification of offences as private or semi-public and public 188–9, 194, 196, 275–8; dependence of happiness and security upon own 191; assignable or unassignable, and fiduciary power 238–9. *See also* OFFENCES AGAINST PERSON; OFFENCES AGAINST PERSON AND PROPERTY; OFFENCES AGAINST PERSON AND REPUTATION

PERSONATION: 203; how distinguished from other falsehoods 203–4 (*included under* OFFENCES THROUGH FALSEHOOD, q.v.)

PIRACY: 260r4 (*included under* OFFENCES, PUBLIC, q.v.)

PLEASURES AND PAINS:

I. *In general.* govern mankind 11; as a standard 11; as causes final and efficient 11, 34; and God's benevolence according to ascetics 17a; pl. to be reprobated only if followed by more pn. 18, 21; gross (organical) vs. refined 18–19; pl. as part of happiness 34; pl. as immunity from pn. 34; differ not in kind, only in circumstances of production 36; force of 38; synonyms for 40; cause of pl. as good 40; cause of pl. as profit 40, 166c, 169; as interesting perceptions 42; simple vs. complex, depending on cause 42, 49p; simple, enumerated and explained 42–50 (*see below*, v); analytical view of, why none given 42a; extra-regarding, self-regarding, dissocial 49, 60, 179–80; as temptation 49, 138; and circumstances influencing sensibility 51 ff; names of homogeneous real entities 52c; primary vs. secondary 60; as material consequences of an act 74 80; as the only things good or bad in themselves 89, 100; influence of acts of intellectual faculty on 96; motive nothing more than pl. or pn. 100; different motives determined by vari-

PLEASURES AND PAINS (*cont.*)

ous kinds of 101; catalogue of motives corresponding to that of 103–16 (Ch. x, § iii); death the termination of, with which men are acquainted 112; alarm as secondary mischief or pn. 144; danger as chance of pn. 144; each man the best judge of his pl. 159, 244; real vs. apparent pn. or suffering 180; dependence of, upon own person and upon exterior objects 191; of the mind vs. of the body 191i, 203; future pn. vs. present and past 194; pn. produced by coercion 233; pn. of the mind is either sufferance or apprehension 223. *See also* HAPPINESS; MOTIVE; PRINCIPLE OF ASCETICISM; PRINCIPLE OF UTILITY

II. *Relation to law, legislation, punishment and sanctions.* pl. of malefactors, when a good ground for punishment 18; and legislator 34, 38; sanctions as sources of 34–7; and the law 49; deprivation of pl. and infliction of pn. as punishment 49; pl. as profit of offences 49, 166c, 169; no pl. produced by punishment can be equivalent to the pn. 158a; four evils of punishment as pns. 163; superfluous pn. of punishment 179, 183; pl. not generally equal to pn. in quasi-pecuniary punishment 180. *See also* LEGISLATOR; PUNISHMENT; SANCTIONS

III. *Dimensions of value of.* circumstances or dimensions of value of 38–41; intensity of 38–41; duration of 38–41; certainty or uncertainty of 38–41, 169–70; propinquity or remoteness of 38–41, 169, 170; memoriter verses 38a; fecundity of 39–41; purity of 39–41; extent of 39–41; quantity of, influenced by expectations 56. *See also* CIRCUMSTANCES INFLUENCING SENSIBILITY

IV. *Calculation of totals and sums.* 40, 173–4; used to estimate good and bad tendency of acts 39–41; quantity not uniformly proportioned to cause 51

V. *Distinguished and described.* (a) pls. and pns.: of sense 42, 43, 46–7, 47g, 49p, 53d, 103–4, 113–14, 232; of piety 36, 42, 44, 48, 108–9; of benevolence 42, 44, 48–9, 145e, 163, 109–11; of malevolence 42, 44, 48–9, 111–12; of memory 42, 45, 46; of imagination 42, 45–6, 48; of expectation 42, 45–6,

PLEASURES AND PAINS (*cont.*)

48–9, 144, 223–4; dependent on association 42, 45, 49, 49p. (b) pls.: of wealth 42, 43, 45, 47h, 105; of skill 42–3, 45, 105; of amity 42–4, 48l, 49o, 105, 119; of good-name 42, 44, 57, 61, 105–8; of power 42, 44–5, 48h, 108; of relief 42, 45–6; of novelty or curiosity 47h, 104. (c) pns.: of privation 42, 46, 47g–i, 48k–l, 49, 59, 119, 144; of awkwardness 42, 47; of enmity 42, 47, 48l, 49o; of ill-name 42, 47, 48l, 57, 61

POLICE: etymology, functions and branches of 198–9, 198u; and justice 198, 198u; offences against preventive branch of 196, 200–1, 260r4 (262) (*included under* OFFENCES, PUBLIC, q.v.)

POLYGAMY: 256–7 (*included under* OFFENCES AGAINST CONDITION, q.v.)

POPULATION, OFFENCES AGAINST: 196, 201, 260r4 (263) (*included under* OFFENCES, PUBLIC, q.v.)

POSSESSION: transfer of, as quasi-pecuniary punishment 180; plan for exposition of, and connected notions 205e2; physical vs. legal, in English law 229h3, 230j3; incorporeal object of 241. *See also* POWER(S); RIGHT(S); TRUST; TRUSTEE

POWER(S): effect of magistrate's, on sensibilities 68; those necessary to community are domestic, judicial, military, and supreme 159–60; a valuable object or subject-matter of possession 194k; offences impeding exercise of those beneficial to public 201; of a supreme invisible being 201–2; and rights and trusts 205–7; results of manifestation of legislator's will 205e2 (206); may be over own person, other persons, or things 206; how created and corroborated 206; act of investitive 227e3; included in conditions in life in general 234, 237; physical, as basis for legal, in domestic condition 236x3; in domestic conditions 237–9, 241, 244–5, 247–8, 250–1, 254; rights corroborated by, to enforce obligation 237; party with such rights a superior 237; beneficial 238, 265; fiduciary 238–9, 260r4 (263–4); of superintendent over subordinate 238–9; of principal over superintendent 239; limitation of, constitutes a right (or liberty, privilege, immunity,

POWER(S) (*cont.*)
exemption) 241; physical, as necessary for production of happiness 244; when it is to a man's advantage to be under that of another 244–5; of sovereign should always be fiduciary 260r4 (263); of sovereign may be autocratic or, if not, divided into legislative and executive 260r4 (263–4); investitive and divestitive 260r4 (263–4); executive 260r4 (263–4); public trusts as branches of sovereign 260r4 (264); conferred by constitutional law 307. *See also* CONDITION IN LIFE; GOVERNMENT; OFFENCES, PUBLIC; TRUST

PREVENTION AND DETERRENCE: of mischievous acts as function of punishment 70, 147g, 158a. *See also* PUNISHMENT

PRINCIPLE(S): as extensive and leading reasons 9; etymology and meaning 11b; whether intelligible or mere caprice 15; despotical 16; anarchical 16; wrong, and how proved such 17 ff.; two ways in which those other than that of utility may differ from it 17; as external standard 25; negation of 25; and motives 32–3. *See also* PRINCIPLE OF ASCETICISM; PRINCIPLE OF SYMPATHY AND ANTIPATHY; PRINCIPLE OF UTILITY; PRINCIPLE, THEOLOGICAL

PRINCIPLE OF ASCETICISM: constantly opposed to p. of u. 17; meaning 17–18; conformity of acts to 17–18; as ground for punishment 18; embraced by two classes of men 18; and government 19; origin of, in p. of u. misapplied 21; impossibility of consistent pursuit of 21; and God's pleasure 31g; and dictates of religion 120–1, 131–2; partly accounts for abundance of bad names for motives 130g; and censure of self-regarding offences 278

PRINCIPLE OF SYMPATHY AND ANTIPATHY: sometimes opposed to p. of u., sometimes not 17; meaning 21–5; influence of, in matters of government 21; as principle of caprice 21c; when more appositely called the phantastic principle 21c; as affections of the sensible faculty applied to actions 21c; applied to titles and other investitive events 21c; or imagination exemplified in maxims of law 21c; and punishment 25, 29–30; and politics 25, 28; as

PRINCIPLE OF SYMPATHY AND ANTIPATHY (*cont.*)
negation of principle 25; various systems of morality reducible to 25–6; forms taken by 26d—viz. moral sense (26), common sense (26), understanding (26), rule of right (26–7), fitness of things (27), law of nature (27–8); and despotism 26d (28); mischief of 26d (28); and reprobation of acts as unnatural 26d (27–8); coincidence of, with p. of u. 29; errs by severity 29–31; treats trivial matters as crimes 29–30; errs by lenity 31; and God's pleasure 31g (32); and quantum of punishment 141–2; and censure of offences 275, 277, 278

PRINCIPLE OF UTILITY: recognises governance of pl. and pn. 11; meaning 11–12; and greatest felicity principle 11a, 14d; and systems attempting to question it 11, 13–15; and approval of measures of government 12, 198; meaning of 'ought', 'right', and 'wrong' dependent on 12, 13, 16; direct proof of, impossible and unnecessary 13–16; naturally embraced 13; and human nature 13–14; seldom applied consistently 13–14, 118; criticisms of, all drawn from 14–15; misapplied 15, 19, 21; called a dangerous principle 14d; disproof of, impossible 15; prejudices against, may be countered 15–16; all other principles wrong 17, 32–3; vs. fantasy 21c; and Common Law 21c (22); and such phrases as Law of Reason, Right Reason, etc. 26d (27); whether any other source of moral sentiment 26d (28); whether any other principle can be persisted in or justified 26d (28); and God's pleasure 31g; regulation of antipathy by 33; its own regulator 33; female biases less conformable to 65; goodwill the motive coinciding most with 116–17; dictates of, as enlightened benevolence 117; dictates of, and love of reputation 118–19; dictates of, and religion 119–21, 131; and moral sanction 130; and object of all laws 158; and punishment 158, 165; aversion to punishment grounded on 183; determines what acts ought to be offences 188; and falsehood 205; and distinction of public offences from those against the property of an

PRINCIPLE OF UTILITY (*cont.*) individual 209–10; and absolute duties 265; governs the natural method of analysis 272–4. *See also* GOVERNMENT; LEGISLATOR; UTILITY AND DIS-UTILITY

PRINCIPLE, THEOLOGICAL: meaning 31; not a separate principle since interpreted by reference to other principles 31; dictates of, sometimes coincide with those of other principles 120–1. *See also* GOD; PRINCIPLE OF ASCETICISM; RELIGION

PRIVATE ETHICS: *see* ETHICS

PRIVILEGE: as incorporeal object of possession 241. *See also* RIGHT(S)

PROBABILITY AND CERTAINTY: knowledge of probability and intentions 92; probability of a motive in prospect 99; certain vs. probable consequences 143; chance of pn. as danger 144–5; certain vs. contingent mischief 148, 149, 151; profit of an offence more certain than punishment 169; of punishment, *see* PUNISHMENT; of pls. and pns., *see* PLEASURES AND PAINS

PROCEDURE, LAW OF: *See* LAW

PROFESSION: a non-fiduciary condition 266; constituted by mere permission of legislator 267; religious, *see* RELIGION

PROFIT: of an offence 40, 166c, 169; habitual occupations as pursuit of 58; of labour 59; influence of rank on connexions importing, and sensibility 65–6; and pecuniary circumstances 72s; connexions in the way of, and in the way of sympathy 72s; of delinquency may be greater than punishment 166f; of a punishment 179. *See also* OFFENCES; PLEASURES AND PAINS; PUNISHMENT

PROHIBITION: *see* COMMAND

PROMISE: trust may be created without a 207f2; obliges more effectually, but this is an accidental circumstance 207f2

PROPERTY: value of, and p. of u. 40–1; pecuniary circumstances influencing sensibility 58–60, 68–9; as a thing from which a man derives happiness or security 192, 248; fictitious or incorporeal objects of 192–3, 211–12; these in civil condition 193, 210; in reputation 193, 211; a branch of the system of rights and powers 205e2 (206–7); modifications of 205e2 (206), 265; why offences against trust and

PROPERTY (*cont.*) condition, in different divisions from offences against 208–14, 265–8; always implies a benefit in proprietor 210; created by commands and obligations laid on others 210, 215m2; loose use of phrase ' object of property ' whenever law benefits a man 211–12; liberty as object of 212; line between, and condition depends on existence of common names characterising 213; distribution of 215m2. *See also* CONDITION; OFFENCES AGAINST CONDITION; OFFENCES AGAINST PERSON AND PROPERTY; OFFENCES AGAINST PROPERTY; OFFENCES AGAINST TRUST; TRUST

PROPINQUITY AND REMOTENESS: *see* PLEASURES AND PAINS

PROPORTION: approbation of actions proportioned to their tendency to augment or diminish happiness 11–13; of punishment and disapprobation 21–5; as a feature of sensibility 51; quantity of pl. or pn. not uniformly proportionate to cause 51; ratio of sympathetic sensibility to pls and pns. of sensitive beings 57; of means to wants 58–9; demand for punishment is in proportion to disturbance of society 74; of evil of punishment and evil of offences 163, 165–74; of real to apparent suffering 180; between punishment and offences, *see* PUNISHMENT, III

PROSPECT: *see* EXPECTATION AND APPREHENSION

PRUDENCE AND IMPRUDENCE: suffering due to imprudence as punishment of the physical sanction 36; ordinary prudence and heedlessness 90; prudence manifested by discharge of duties to oneself 287; rules of prudence least need legal enforcement 289–90; mischief of law's interference 291

PUBLIC, THE: meaning 196, 209; interest of, how affected by mischief 196; offences against, *see* OFFENCES, PUBLIC. *See also* COMMUNITY

PUBLIC MISCHIEF: *see* OFFENCES, III, Class 2, semi-public; OFFENCES, PUBLIC

PUBLIC OPINION: as moral or popular sanction 35b; as to punishment 164, 171o, 182–4. *See also* PUNISHMENT, IV; SANCTIONS

PUBLIC ORDER: menacement by tumultuous assemblies 224z2 (225) (*included under* OFFENCES OF MERE DELINQUENCY, q.v.)

PUBLIC SPIRIT: as branch of principle of benevolence 154o; as motive of prosecution 154o

PUNISHMENT:

I. *In general.* presupposes the idea of an offence 4; a constituent of obligation 21c; and sanctions 36, 145–6, 172; only inflicted by production of pn. or deprivation of pl. 49; and religion 69o; constitutes tutelary or restraining motive 145, 165b, 166c; primary vs. secondary consequences of act of, may be of opposite nature 147; outrage motivated by self-regarding motives more severely punished than if motivated by vengeance 155q; as an artificial consequence of offence 157, 186; as a mischief or evil 158, 163 (four branches), 179; and other offences probably committed by an offender 170; as a moral lesson 171; pecuniary most frugal 180; influence of, depends on motive causing offence 180–1; capital 181, 184; profit of, vs. expense of 186; punitory laws may command or simply permit 302

II. *Ends of, grounds and demand for.* grounds for, according to principle of antipathy 25; inappropriate for trivial incidents 29–30; mischievous act as ground for 70; terror of, used to prevent mischievous acts 70; and business of government 74, 201; demand for, proportionate to disturbance of happiness of society 74; demand for, depends on offender's intention 95; and depravity of disposition 141–2; hatred as a ground for 142; operating in the way of reformation vs. in the way of example 147g; gratification of ill-will a collateral end of 158a (159); compensation vindictive and lucrative 158a, 182; example most important end of 158a (159), 179, 185i; none merely for vindictive compensation since pl. produced by, less than pn. 158a (159); ought not to be inflicted where inefficacious 159, 160–2, 166c, 167, 170, 178–9; groundless 159–60, 188, 286; needless 159, 164, 179; unprofitable 159, 163–4, 171, 287; four subordinate objects of 165

PUNISHMENT (*cont.*)

III. *Proportion and quantity.* proportion and measurement of, according to principle of sympathy and antipathy 21–5, 29–30; estimating impression made by 69; circumstances influencing sensibility and quantity of 71; estimates of influence of circumstances on, by legislator and judge 71; plans for such estimates 71; uncertainty and real vs. apparent value of 146; uncertainty of 146, 170, 183; as a mischief or evil 158, 163 (four branches) 179; proportion between, and offences 165–74 (Ch. XIV); rules of this proportion 166–72; quantum or value of 167–8, 170–1, 175, 177, 180, 182, 183; profit of an offence commonly more certain than of punishment 169; summary of circumstances relevant to establishing proportion between punishment and offence 172–3; allowance for other sanctions 172; quality of, to be regulated by quantity 175

IV. *Varieties and properties.* examples of simple afflictive 54; modes of 158a, 175–6, 178, 180, 185; properties to be given to 175–86 (Ch. XV); variability 175, 185; equability 175–6, 185; pecuniary and quasi-pecuniary apt to be inequable 176; commensurability to other punishments 177, 186; characteristicalness or analogy to offence 177–8, 179, 182–3, 186; exemplarity depends on apparent vs. real 178–9; and may be increased by solemnities accompanying 179; frugality 179–90, 183, 186; pecuniary, most frugal 180; subserviency to reformation 180–1, 186; efficacy with respect to disablement 181–2, 186; subserviency to compensation 182, 186; popularity 182–3, 186; remissibility 184–5, 186; remissibility depends on punishment being chronical vs. acute 184

See also CIRCUMSTANCES OF AN ACT; GOVERNMENT; LEGISLATOR

QUANTITY AND MAGNITUDE: quantity of pl. and pn. not uniformly proportioned to causes 51; degree or quantum of sensibility 51, 64; magnitude as value of an exciting cause vs. propinquity 56; of pl. and pn. 56, 57; quantity of pn. 63p, 175; difficulties in measurement of grief 63p; degree of

QUANTITY AND MAGNITUDE (*cont.*) sensibility 65, 68; necessity of attending to circumstances in taking account of quantity of pl. and pn. 69; quantum of satisfaction 69; measurement of depravity of disposition 134; degree of strength of temptation 138–42; force of motive compared to force of friction 141; quantity of danger 149; of kinds of mischief 149; quantum of evil 164; limitations of the term *quantity* vs. *value,* 169; less certainty or proximity of punishment, more punishment required 170; sanctions other than political less quantifiable 172; quality of punishment regulated by quantity 175; quantity of happiness 282. *See also* VALUE

RACE AND RACIAL ORIGIN: as a secondary circumstance influencing sensibility 52, 65–6, 67, 69, 70

RANK: as a secondary circumstance influencing sensibility 65–6; as a nonfiduciary civil condition 266; how constituted 266. *See also* CONDITION IN LIFE

RAPE: 232 (*included under* OFFENCES AGAINST PERSON AND REPUTATION, q.v.)

RASHNESS: *see* NEGLIGENCE, HEEDLESSNESS AND RASHNESS

REASON AND REASONING: and law 11, 215m2; in support of p. of u. 15; vs. imagination 21c; vs. instinct in Common Law 21c (24); rational agency depends on intention 74–5

REASONS AND GROUNDS: and principles 9; political, statement of to accompany proposed body of law 9; for approbation vs. causes and motives of acts 32–3; motives as reasons 32–3; pointing out motives as giving reasons 99; natural division of offences suggests, for law 273; grounds of punishment, *see* PUNISHMENT, II

REBELLION: 260r4 (263) (*included under* OFFENCES, PUBLIC, against sovereignty, q.v.); robbery and 199v; and hostility 199v; dictates of ethics when dictates of legislation not what they ought to be 292s

RECKLESSNESS: *see* NEGLIGENCE, HEEDLESSNES AND RASHNESS

REFORM: *see* PUNISHMENT

RELATION(S): of a person to sensible objects 191–2, 191i; constituting conditions in life in general 234; legal vs. natural 234, 236; a fictitious entity 235v3; meaning of, in general 235v3; named and unnamed 268–9

RELIGION: sanction of, 34–7, 44, 48, 146, 162j; religious sensibility or bias as a primary circumstance influencing sensibility 52, 57, 64, 65, 66, 67, 68, 70, 72; religious profession as a secondary circumstance influencing sensibility 52, 68–9, 70, 72; as a good motive 115; as a social or semi-social motive 116; dictates of, and p. of u. 119–21; variable influence of 119, 156, 162j; as indication of disposition 131, 132–3, 154n; savours of asceticism 132; holy wars and persecutions 132–3; as a tutelary motive 136–7, 146; motive of, may increase mischief of act 156; offences against 196, 201–2, 260r4 (264), 270 (*included under* OFFENCES, PUBLIC, q.v.); as kind of allegorical personage 202; a fictitious entity 202z; legislator concerned only with influence of, on present life 202z; p. of u. and absolute duties 265; may furnish motive to consider happiness of others 284; pls. and pns. of, *see* PLEASURES AND PAINS. *See also* GOD; PRINCIPLE OF ASCETICISM; PRINCIPLE, THEOLOGICAL; SANCTIONS

REPROBATION: *see* APPROBATION AND APPROVAL

REPUTATION AND GOOD NAME: and moral sanction 44, 162j; love of, as a motive 105–8; good and bad senses and various names for love of 106–8; love of, as a good motive 115; as a social or semi-social motive 116; and dictates of utility 118–19; love of, as indication of disposition 129–31, 154n; variable influence of 162j; meaning of 193; a fictitious object 193; love of, as motive binding one to consult happiness of others 285; pls. of, *see* PLEASURES AND PAINS; offences against, *see* OFFENCES AGAINST REPUTATION, OFFENCES AGAINST PERSON AND REPUTATION. *See also* SANCTIONS

RESENTMENT: vs. grief 51

RESPONSIBILITY: vicarious 61; criminal, *see* PUNISHMENT

RESTRAINT: *see* COERCION AND COMPULSION

RETALIATION: as mode of punishment bearing closest analogy to offence 178; admitted only in offences against individuals 275–8

REVENUE, PUBLIC: offences against 260r4 (263) (*included under* OFFENCES, PUBLIC, against public wealth, q.v.)

REWARD: and punishment as business of government 74, 201; the remuneratory a hitherto unnamed branch of law 126; same rules of proportion apply to, as well as to punishment 165b; doubtful matter for legislation 285d

RIGHT AND WRONG: human conduct 11a; action 13; no meaning without reference to utility 13, 16; and principle of sympathy and antipathy 25–31; whether utility actual ground of 28–9; ground of action and sentiment of antipathy 32–3. *See also* PRINCIPLE OF ASCETICISM; PRINCIPLE OF SYMPATHY AND ANTIPATHY; PRINCIPLE OF UTILITY; STANDARD(S)

RIGHT(S): source of titles to 21c; as actions allowed (vs. obligations) 21c, 212–13; investment of 21c, 228g3; and trust 205–7, 215; and powers 205–7; uncorroborated by powers, 205, 237, 239; and property 205e2, 265; as manifestation of legislator's will 205e2 (206); all have correlative duties but self-regarding duties are without correlative rights 205e2 (206); how expounded 205e2 (206, 207); fictitious entities 205e2 (206, 207); right to money vs. right to be paid 227s3; as elements in conditions in life 234, 265; and corroborating powers 237–9; as limitations on master's powers 241; liberties, immunities, etc. 241; rights to rights and to powers over things 265. *See also* CONDITION IN LIFE; PROPERTY; SERVICES; TRUST

ROBBERY: 155q, 168k, 176a, 199v, 224x2, 230, 231, 232–3 (*included under* OFFENCES AGAINST PROPERTY, q.v.); appropriate punishment for 181

ROMAN LAW: *servitus servitutis non datur* 21c (23); intentionality and consciousness in 94, 95g; *infortunium* 94; *dolus* 94–5; *culpa* 94–5; *malo animo* 95g; *fideicommissarius* 207f2; legitimation by subsequent marriage in 251l4 (252); want of method in 273y4; confusion and inconsistency of 307;

ROMAN LAW (*cont.*) concealment of imperative character of law in 307

RULES: operations of both will and understanding delineated by 8; general 21c (23); settled and concerted, and moral sanction 35; of proportion of punishments to offences 165–74 (Ch. XIV); same applicable to rewards 165b; for guidance of legislator vs. judge 169; of moral duty 289; of prudence 289; of probity 292; of beneficence 292; of conduct of sovereigns, international law 296–7

SAINTS: 20. *See also* ASCETICISM; PRINCIPLE OF ASCETICISM

SANCTIONS: four forms of (physical, political or legal, moral or popular, religious) 34; give binding force to law or rule 34; etymology and meaning 34a; and expectation of pls. or pns. 35–7; and punishment 36; reasons for common name 37; as moral forces 37; all four may contribute to same effects 172

I. *Physical*. in general 34–7; the groundwork of the others 37; benevolence is a branch of 45

II. *Political*. dispensed by judge according to will of sovereign 34–7; gives rise to self-regarding motives in an individual 123; and legality of a mandate 123; providing punishment 145; how weakened by past offence 146; unlike other sanctions may be precisely quantified 172

III. *Moral*. or popular 34–7, 57, 61; and public opinion 35b; effect of pls. and pns. of, as indicative of moral sensibility 57; motives corresponding to 105–7; fear of shame is tutelary motive belonging to 145–6; how weakened by past offence 146; and indignation 146; may render punishment inefficacious 162j; adopted by the political 172; and uncontiguous domestic relations 259; pls. and pns. of, *see* PLEASURES AND PAINS, V, pls. of a good name, pns. of an ill name. *See also* GOOD-WILL; ILL-WILL; REPUTATION AND GOOD NAME.

IV. *Religious*. in general 34–7; motives corresponding to 108–9; fear of divine displeasure is tutelary motive belonging to 146; may render punishment inefficacious 162j; pls. and pns.

SANCTIONS (*cont.*)

of, *see* PLEASURES AND PAINS, V, of piety. *See also* GOD; MOTIVE; PRINCIPLE, THEOLOGICAL; RELIGION

SATISFACTION: quantum of, as reparation 69; of an injured party as collateral end of punishment 158a; not sufficient ground for punishment 158a. *See also* COMPENSATION

SECRECY: *See* ACTIONS AND ACTS, I

SECURITY AND INSECURITY: security a part of happiness 34; afforded by the averting of pn. or danger 148; insecurity as negative mischief 148; security dependent upon own person and exterior objects 191; offences against external security 196, 200, 260r4 (*included under* OFFENCES, PUBLIC, q.v.)

SEDITION: favouring deserters 260r4 (262) (*included under* OFFENCES, PUBLIC, against public force, q.v.)

SEDUCTION: 232, 256p4 (*included under* OFFENCES AGAINST PERSON AND REPUTATION, q.v.)

SELF-PRESERVATION: as a motive corresponding to several sorts of pn. 112–13; as a tutelary motive 137, 145, 154o; and danger 137

SELF-REGARDING CONDUCT: self-regarding motives listed 116; and utility 117, 121; self-regarding motive as evidence of disposition 127; self-regarding vs. extra-regarding mischief 148; most powerful and constant motive 155, 284; duties as to, have no correlative rights 205e2 (206); and duty to oneself 284; ethics in part the art of discharging such duty 284; and prudence 284, 289; legislation least needed to support, 284, 290–2. *See also* MOTIVE, IV; OFFENCES, III, Class 3; PRUDENCE AND IMPRUDENCE; UTILITY AND DISUTILITY

SENSES: all ideas are derived from 191i (192). *See also* PLEASURES AND PAINS, V; SENSIBILITY

SENSIBILITY: degree or quantum of, general vs. particular 51; bias or quality of 51, 284; analogy with momentum 52b; and moral physiology 52c; bias of, vs. inclination 56; moral and religious, and bias, 57, 65–6, 68, 72; sympathetic, and bias 57, 65–6, 68, 72; original frame of body and mind 61–3; external appearances of, and

SENSIBILITY (*cont.*)

command over these 63–4; of the female greater in quantity than of male 64; rank and 65; and education 66–7; and government 67–8; to the moral sanction 106m, 129g (130); and disposition and motives 134; circumstances influencing, *see* CIRCUMSTANCES INFLUENCING SENSIBILITY. *See also* DISPOSITION

SENTIMENT(S): p. of u. as 11b; and approbation 11b, 15–16, 25; unfounded 15; and reflection 16; those of the bulk of mankind vs. elevated 19; as standards 25–33; origin vs. justification 26d (28); of antipathy considered as a right ground of action 32–3; belief as 45; of aversion 171o. *See also* ANTIPATHY AND SYMPATHY; BENEVOLENCE; MALEVOLENCE; PLEASURES AND PAINS; PRINCIPLE OF SYMPATHY AND ANTIPATHY; SENSIBILITY

SERVANT: condition of 210–13, 238–40; 241–2; and breach of duty 240; offences touching condition of 241–4 (*included under* OFFENCES AGAINST CONDITION, q.v.). *See also* CONDITION IN LIFE; MASTER

SERVICES: fruit of amity 43–4; good-will as source of 44; fruit of good name 44; fear and hope used to gain 44; happiness or security derived from others through 192; rights and obligations in relation to, constitute a condition 192–3, 265; rights to, of a magistrate 205e2; and property vs. condition 213–14; payment as a sort of 227e3; breach of contract is wrongful withholding of 228, 231; grounds of obligation to render 228g3; negative and positive 228g3; affecting person 228g3; the word, in utmost latitude covers the whole law 228g3; as an object of property 228–9, 231; of forbearance where duty negative 265, 268; legislator's forbearance to prohibit as a, constitutes a profession 266–7. *See also* CONDITION IN LIFE; OFFENCES AGAINST PROPERTY

SEX: as a secondary circumstance influencing sensibility 52, 64–5, 66, 67. 69, 70, 72; influence of climate on *See also* PLEASURES AND PAINS, V

SHAME: *See* REPUTATION AND GOOD-NAME; SANCTION(S), III. *Moral*

SLANDER: *see* DEFAMATION

SLAVERY: 211i2; pure, vs. various modes of servitude 241–2; as treatment of men as animals 282b

SMUGGLING: 260r4 (262) (*included under* OFFENCES, PUBLIC, against national wealth, q.v.)

SOUL: indivisibility of 58; materiality or immateriality of 62n

SOVEREIGN AND SOVEREIGNTY: sovereign should take up pen rather than sword in certain cases 164; offences against 196, 200, 260r4 (263–4) (*included under* OFFENCES, PUBLIC, q.v.); meaning 200; not found in all governments 200x; may be in one person or shared 200; a trust or fiduciary power 260r4 (263); distribution of 260r4 (263–4); and international law 296–7.

STANDARD(S): for creation and distribution of rights, afforded by axioms of mental pathology 3; of right and wrong and p. of u. 11a, 15–16; must be grounded on reflection 16; despotical 16; anarchical 16; appeal to external, how avoided 21–31; for legislator 34; natural arrangement of offences as a 274. *See also* PRINCIPLE OF ASCETICISM; PRINCIPLE OF SYMPATHY AND ANTIPATHY; PRINCIPLE OF UTILITY; RIGHT AND WRONG

STATE, THE: *See* GOVERNMENT; LAW; SOVEREIGN AND SOVEREIGNTY

STATUTE: vs. a single complete law 301. *See also* LAW

STEALING: *See* THEFT OR STEALING

STRENGTH: as a primary circumstance influencing sensibility 52, 53, 54, 64, 67, 70, 72

SUBORNATION: an accessory offence 220s2

SUFFERANCE: *See* PLEASURES AND PAINS

SUICIDE: 224z2 (225), 260r4 (263) (*included under* OFFENCES AGAINST PERSON, self-regarding, and OFFENCES, PUBLIC, against population, qq.v.); punished by forfeiture of moveables 176a

SYMPATHY: *See* ANTIPATHY AND SYMPATHY; PRINCIPLE OF SYMPATHY AND ANTIPATHY

TAX AND TAXATION: non-payment of, an offence 75d (76), 260r4 (262); in

TAX AND TAXATION (*cont.*) what way a mischievous act 149–52 (*included under* OFFENCES, PUBLIC, against public wealth, q.v.)

TEMPTATION: *see* MOTIVE

TENDENCY:

I. *Of action.* actions approved of by p. of u. according to apparent 11–13; and also by principle of asceticism 17–18; procedure for estimating 38–9; good or bad 40; creates demand for punishment 74, 75; mischievous, bad, pernicious 74, 84, 122, 143, 165a; depends on material consequences 74, 143; which in turn depend on act itself, circumstances, intentions, motives, and dispositions 75, 143; to produce pl. or pn. determines materiality 96; apparent, and motive as indications of disposition 125–6; ten cases distinguished 126–34; apparent vs. real 126; secondary mischief dependent on intentionality 152–3; on consciousness 153–4; on motives 154–6; on disposition 156

II. *Of a motive.* 32, 114.

See also ACTIONS AND ACTS; CONSEQUENCES; MISCHIEF AND HARM; MOTIVE

THEFT OR STEALING: 230, 232, 248, 250, 252, 254 (*included under* OFFENCES AGAINST PROPERTY, q.v.)

THREAT: *See* MENACEMENT

TIME: duration and propinquity or remoteness of mischief 31; of pl. or pn. 38–9; influence on value of pl. or pn. 40–1; influence on worth of a sum of money 59; consciousness of circumstances as past present or future 91; and motives 99, 141; proximity an important element in value of punishment 169–70, 173; danger and future mischief 194

TITLE: choice of, to rights on grounds other than utility 21c; exposition of meaning of, connected with that of rights and powers 205e2; explanation of, as part of expository matter of law against theft and laws of property 303–4, 308; such exposition exists only in form of customary law 308

TOTALS AND SUMS: of pls. and pns. of individual 12; of values of pls. and pns. 40; of means and wants 58–9; balance of effects of a motive 114; strength of temptation as a sum of motives 138–9;

TOTALS AND SUMS (*cont.*)
mischief as an aggregate 147; of motives 154o; of positive good 198. *See also* PLEASURES AND PAINS

TREASON: 260r4 (*included under* OFFENCES, PUBLIC, against external security, q.v.)

TRESPASS: wrongful use or occupation 229, 231–2; wrongful disturbance of proprietary rights 232 (*included under* OFFENCES AGAINST PROPERTY, q.v.)

TRUST: meaning 205–7; meaning of trustee and beneficiary or *cestuy que trust* 207–8, 207f2; may be created without a promise 207f2; trust, condition, and property distinguished 208–14; conferred, imposed, etc. 208, 216n2; a fictitious entity 208g2, public 209, 221, 239, 260r4 (263–4); possession of 214j2, 215m2, 216; powers rights and duties annexed to 215; as a burden or benefit 215, 217; investment and divestment of 216n2, 217–18; and p. of u. 217–18; semi-public 221, 239; power coupled with, is fiduciary 238–9; guardianship a private 238, 247; judicial, and other branches of public, described and assigned new Greek-derived names 260r4 (261–4). *See also* OFFENCES AGAINST TRUST; OFFENCES, PUBLIC

UNDERSTANDING: logic of, distinguished from logic of will 8, 299b2 (300); as a subjective standard of right and wrong 26d; strength of, as a circumstance influencing sensibility 72; and disposition 72; state of, in intention 75; acts and consequences objects both of will and of 89; circumstances of acts objects only of 89; and acts of intellectual faculty 96; influence on, vs. influence on will 145, 164, 299b2 (300); informing of, as sometimes rendering punishment needless 164; of things through method of bipartite division of genus or logical whole 187a

UNNATURAL: *See* NATURE AND NATURAL

USURY: treatise on 4; natural classification of offences and 5; should not be an offence unless it coincides with defraudment or extortion 231l3

UTILITY AND DISUTILITY: and happiness or felicity 11a; defect of the term utility 11a; and number of interests 11a; meaning and synonyms 12; and

UTILITY AND DISUTILITY (*cont.*)
natural classification of offences 272–3. *See also* FELICITY; HAPPINESS; PLEASURES AND PAINS; PRINCIPLE OF UTILITY

VALUE: of pls. and pns. 38–41; of an article of property 40–1; of an exciting cause (magnitude vs. propinquity) 56; and time 59; and imagination 69q; of punishment (real vs. apparent) 146; this diminished by uncertainty 146; of mischief of an act vs. of benefit 159; term *quantity* vs. 169. *See also* PLEASURES AND PAINS; QUANTITY AND MAGNITUDE; TOTALS AND SUMS

VIRTUE AND VICE: analysis of, needed in principles of morals 3

VOLITION: *See* WILL

VOLUNTARY AND INVOLUNTARY: ambiguity of 84a, 292; three senses of voluntary 84a; involuntary not opposite term 84a; completely unintentional acts properly termed involuntary 85b, 153; voluntary forbearance 97; no secondary mischief if act involuntary 153; voluntary conduct and political constraint 292

WANTS: effect of pecuniary means on 58–9; circumstances on which they depend 59; means by which religion augments 69q

WARD: condition of (powers, rights, duties) 238, 244; offences touching condition of 249–50 (*included under* OFFENCES AGAINST CONDITION, q.v.)

WEALTH: analytical view of the constituent articles in a man's pecuniary circumstances 72s; love of, as a motive 155; national, vs. public 199–200; offences against national 196, 201, 260r4 (263), 269 (*included under* OFFENCES, PUBLIC, q.v.); offences against public 196, 201, 260r4 (262–3) (*included under* OFFENCES, PUBLIC, q.v.); payment of money 227e3

WIFE: *See* MATRIMONY

WILL: science of law as branch of the logic of 8–9; of God 31; power of, over indications of sensibility 63p; and intention 75; involuntary vs. voluntary acts 84a, 85b, 97, 292; acts vs. circumstances as objects of 89; acts of mind

WILL (*cont.*)

are either of intellectual faculty or of 96; motives acting on 96–7, 99–100, 145; vs. understanding 96, 99, 145, 164, 299b2 (300); acts of, are positive 97b; punishment operates on, in the way of reformation or example 158a; punishment inefficacious where will cannot be deterred 161–2; lack of free, or vicious 151g; influence on, may render punishment needless 164; logic

WILL (*cont.*)

of, or of sentences expressing volition 299b2. *See also* ACTIONS AND ACTS; GOD; INTENTION AND INTENTIONALITY

WOMEN: sensibility of, vs. of men 64–5

WOUNDING: simple corporal injuries and irreparable corporal injuries 223, 224 (*included under* OFFENCES AGAINST PERSON, q.v.)

WRONG: *See* RIGHT AND WRONG

INDEX OF NAMES

Note. This is an index of names of persons and places occurring in the text and notes, the latter (whether Bentham's or the editors') indicated by 'n'. Where a note extends to more than one page and the reference is to a part of it only, the general reference to the initial page of the note is followed in brackets by a specific page reference. Under Bentham's own name only references to his other works are indexed.

ADDISON, Joseph: 116n
AENEAS: 136
AINSWORTH, Robert: 34n
ALEXANDER the Great: 10
ARISTOTLE: 8, 245n, 299n
ASHBURTON, Lord: *See* DUNNING, John
ATIA (mother of Augustus): 259
AUGUSTUS, Roman Emperor: 140 & n, 259n
AUTOLYCUS: 146

BAILEY, Francis: 310n
BARBONE (or BAREBONE): 63n
BEATTIE, Dr. James: 26n (26 & 28)
BECCARIA, Cesare, Marchese de Beccaria-Bonesana: 166n, 298n
BENGAL: 21n (22–3)
BENTHAM, Jeremy
Correspondence: 2n, 14n, 30n, 202n, 281n, 300n
Defence of Usury: 4n
Fragment of Government: 2n, 5n, 14n, 205n, 272n, 292n
Letters to Count Toreno: 167n
Of Laws in General: 1n, 207n, 228n, 237n
Plan of a Penal Code: 1n, 55n, 72n, 74n, 86n, 124n, 160n, 202n
Rationale of Punishment: 158n
Rationale of Reward: 158n
Table of the Springs of Action: 96n
Théorie des Peines et de Récompenses: 158n
Theory of Punishment: 158n
Traités de Législation Civile et Pénale: 124n, 158n, 297n
View of the Hard-Labour Bill: 177n, 184n
BENTHAM, Sir Samuel: 300
BLACKSTONE, Sir William: 297n
BLAESUS: 63n
BRUTUS, Marcus Junius: 21n (24)

BUCKINGHAM, 1st Duke of: *See* VILLIERS, George
BURLAMAQUI, Jean-Jacques: 298n

CAESAR, Lucius Julius: 259
CAESAR, Gaius Julius: 140n, 259 & n
CALCUTTA: 21n (23)
CARMER, Johann von: 21n (22)
CASSIUS, Longinus Gaius: 21n (24)
CATHARINE II, Empress of Russia: 30n, 237n
CHARLES I, King of England: 80–1
CHARLES VI, Emperor of Austria: 306n
CHARLES IX, King of France: 122 & n
CLARKE, Dr. Samuel: 27 & n
COCCEJI, Samuel von: 21n (22)
COKE, Sir Edward: 21n (22–5)
COLBERT, Jean Baptiste: 283n
COLIGNY, Gaspard III de: 122–3 & n
CONSTANTINOPLE: 119
COOPER, Anthony Ashley, 3rd Earl of Shaftesbury: 26n
CRILLON, Louis Balbais de Berton de: 122–3 & n
CROMWELL, Oliver: 63 & n

DAGUESSEAU, Henri François: 296n
DENMARK: 132
DIPPEL: 132n
DUMONT, Etienne: 124n, 158n, 297n

EMPEDOCLES: 79n

FAURE, Louis Joseph: 309n
FELTON, John: 80–1 & n
FICINO, Marsiglio: 146n
FREDERICK II, King of Prussia: 21n (22), 306
FRENCH WEST INDIES: 282n

GANGES: 109
GEORGE II, King of Great Britain: 301

GERMANY: 21n (23–4), 200n
GODWIN, Earl of Wessex: 166n
GONDOMAR, Diego Sarmiento de Acuna, Conde de: 296n
GROTIUS, Hugo: 298n

HARRIS, James: 299n
HARTLEY, David: 119n
HASTINGS, Warren: 21n (23)
HEINECCIUS, Johann Gottlieb: 273n
HELVETIC BODY: 200n
HELVETIUS, Claude Adrien: 102n
'HINT, Peter': (St. James's Chronicle) 177n
HOMER: 94n, 146n
HUME, David: 26n, 30n, 63n, 87n, 166n
HUNTER (publisher): 96n
HUTCHESON (HUTCHINSON), Francis: 26n

IMPEY, Sir Elijah: 21n (23)
INDIA (INDOSTAN): 21n (23), 119
IRELAND: 21n (23)
ISMAIL, Moulay, Emperor of Morocco: 140n

JAMES I, King of England: 30n, 296n
JOSEPH I, King of Portugal: 154n
JULIA, (sister of C. Julius Caesar): 259 & n
JUPITER: 81 & n
JUSTINIAN, Roman Emperor: 307

LEPIDUS, Marcus Aemilius: 140n, 259 & n
LIND, John: 14n, 310n
LOUGHBOROUGH, Lord: See WEDDER-BURN, Alexander
LOUIS (LEWIS) XIV, King of France: 132 & n, 282n, 291, 296n
LYCURGUS: 20 & n

MANDEVILLE, Bernard: 102n
MARCEL (dancing master): 311
MARIA THERESA, Empress-Queen of Austria: 306 & n
MARIUS, Gaius: 140 & n
MARK ANTONY: 140n
MASSACHUSETTS: 310n
MAZZEI, Philip: 309n
MILL, James: 21n (23), 119n
MOHAMMED, Moulay (Muley Mahomet): 140 & n
MONTESQUIEU, Charles Louis de Secondat, Baron de la Brède et de: 168n, 172n, 178, 198n

MORELLET, André: 166n
MOROCCO: 140 & n
MORZILIUS, Sebastian Fox: 146n

NAPOLEON BONAPARTE: 166n
NORTH CAROLINA: 309

OCTAVIUS (OCTAVIAN): See AUGUSTUS
OVID: 301

PANNONIA: 63n
PENNSYLVANIA: 310n
PERITHOUS: 110n
PETTY, William, 2nd Earl of Shelburne (later 1st Marquess of Lansdowne): 281n
PHILIP III, King of Spain: 296n
PLATO: 146n
POMBAL, Marquis de: 154n
PRICE, Richard: 26n (26 & 29)
PRIESTLEY, Joseph: 119n
PRUSSIA: 21n (22, 23)
PTOLEMY: 10
PUFFENDORF, Samuel: 298n

RAVAILLAC, François: 82n, 129 & n, 132, 154n
RALEIGH, Sir Walter: 30n
ROCHEFOUCAULD, François, 6th duc de la: 102n
ROME: 82n, 200n
ROSSLYN, Earl of: see WEDDERBURN, Alexander
RUSSIA: 30n

SEIGNELAY: 283n
SELDEN, John: 296n
SERVIUS: 34n
SHAFTESBURY, 3rd Earl of: See COOPER, Anthony Ashley
SHELBURNE, Lord: See PETTY, William
SMITH, Richard: 158n, 160n, 194n
SOLON: 237n
STREON, Duke: 166n (167)
SULLA (SYLLA), Lucius Cornelius: 140 & n
SWIFT, Jonathan: 30n
SWITZERLAND: See HELVETIC BODY

TACITUS, Publius or Gaius Cornelius 63n
THAMES: 109
THEOCRITUS: 202n
THESEUS: 110n
THUCYDIDES: 146n
TRIBOLET, Franz Ludwig: 202n

TYBURN: 81n
TYRREL, Sir Walter: 87–8 & n, 91–2

UNITED PROVINCES: 200n

VIBULENUS: 63n
VILLIERS, George, 1st Duke of Buckingham: 80–1 & n
VIRGIL: 94n
VIRGINIA: 309 & n, 310n

VOLTAIRE, François Marie Arouet de: 292n
VORSTIUS, Conrad: 30n

WEDDERBURN, Alexander, 1st Baron Loughborough and 1st Earl of Rosslyn 14n
WILKINS, David: 166n
WILLIAM II, King of England: 87–8 & n
WOLLASTON (WOOLASTON), William: 26n (27)